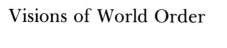

Visions of World Order

Your young men shall see visions, and your old men shall dream dreams.

Isaac Abrabanel,
who died in Venice in 1508

Age doth profit rather in the powers of understanding, than in the virtues of the will and affections.

Francis Bacon, Baron Verulam,
Essay "Of Youth and Age," 1612

Visions of
World Order

Between State Power and Human Justice

JULIUS STONE

The Johns Hopkins University Press
BALTIMORE AND LONDON

The Johns Hopkins University Press, Baltimore, Maryland 21218
The Johns Hopkins Press Ltd., London

The paper in this book is acid-free and meets the guidelines for permanence and durability of the Committee on Production Guidelines for Book Longevity of the Council on Library Resources.

Library of Congress Cataloging in Publication Data
Stone, Julius, 1907–
    Visions of world order.
    Includes index.
    1. International law. 2. Sociological jurisprudence.
3. Justice. 4. International organization. I. Title.
JX3180.S73V57 1984 341'.01 84–5749
ISBN 0–8018–3174–1

To our grandchildren
AURIT, EMILY, ADRIENNE, BENJAMIN,
JANE, ELIZABETH, *and* DAN
*in the hope that their world grows safer
and more peaceful than it now appears*

Contents

Preface

A main purpose of this book is to explore in contemporary context the meaning of international law for the human beings who make up the populations of the states that that law primarily addresses. While much has been written, sometimes by very eminent international lawyers, concerning individuals and international law, these writings usually have had rather a technical legal import. They have been concerned to establish, more or less expansively, areas of international law within which, and the conditions under which, individuals have been recognized as bearers of rights and obligations under it. Outside these areas, it is assumed, states alone are the bearers of these rights and obligations.

The present inquiry, however, has a different and much wider ambit. It is concerned, not with the technical precepts of existing international law, but with two other matters. One concerns the factual substratum out of which that law can be thought to arise, or at least ought to arise, including especially the conditions of life, expectations, and aspirations of the men and women who constitute the populations of the several states. The other matter, closely related, is the degree of relevance of this factual substratum to discussions of international justice as well as of international law. How far, for example, does it make sense to argue about justice between states without penetrating behind the state entities to the claims and aspirations of human beings whom, with more or less authenticity and even sincerity, these entities are said to represent? I am concerned, in other words, not so much with some branch of international law called human rights as with the credentials of international law as a whole to be regarded as an order dedicated to the maximum degree possible to the satisfaction of human demands.

The beginnings of this design arose from an invitation to deliver the Tagore Lectures at the University of Calcutta in 1968, which I was honored to accept. I gave these lectures the tentative title "International Law and International Justice"; and their preparation had begun when a

sudden deterioration of my health (now only a memory) led me regret-
fully to ask to be relieved of this important assignment. The lectures
therefore were never delivered and, indeed, never completed.

Most of the present book is part of more recent work of the late 1970s
and early 1980s. It seeks to come to terms with some trends in the practice
and theory of international law of the last two decades and to understand
their implications for some turbulent contemporary problems. In chapter
1, I have built upon a number of ideas first developed in my Hague
Lectures (published as "Problems Confronting Sociological Enquiries
concerning International Law" in *Hague Recueil* 89 [1956]: 63–180). In
chapter 8, I have reexplored in the present context the ambivalences of
the "equality of states" doctrine, which I first discussed in *Trends and
Patterns*, the opening volume of *The Future of the International Legal Order*,
edited by R. A. Falk and C. E. Black ([Princeton: Princeton University
Press, 1969], chap. 8 [372–463]); excerpts therefrom are here reprinted
by kind permission of Princeton University Press. Chapters 2–7 and 9–12
are newly written. I hope that all these together may contribute to the
movement of thought about the sociology of international law, about
international justice, and above all about the interrelations of these areas
of concern.

I owe a heavy debt of gratitude to my research assistant, Zena Sachs,
LL.B., and to Mrs. Lorna Ledger for their endless, loving patience during
the last eight years, as we proceeded through the many drafts of this work.
My beloved wife Reca has, as with so many previous books, helped its
completion by her interest as well as by her forbearance. I am also
indebted for scholarly facilities and assistance during these years to the
University of New South Wales Law School and its dean, Donald Hard-
ing, and its law librarian, Rob Brian, as well as to the University of
California Hastings College of the Law and its dean, Wayne Woody. I
have also, on one or two matters in chapter 4 and in relation to appendix
12 on the Law of the Sea Treaty, enjoyed the benefit of comments from
Ivan Shearer, my friend and colleague at the University of New South
Wales. I am grateful to him, though of course I alone am responsible for
what finally here appears.

Introduction

INTERNATIONAL LAW AND HUMAN SURVIVAL

In more than fifty years of writing since the publication of my *International Guarantees of Minority Rights* (London: Oxford University Press, 1932), one aspiration had characterized much of my work in international law: to identify from doctrinal writing, treaties, and recorded practice the precepts of international law as they stand "in the books," that is, *as they appear to be in force,* and to examine the degrees and areas of correspondence and divergence between these and "international law in action." I wrote in 1954 that it is impossible to study "international law in action" without relating it both to the supposed interests and conduct of states and (and above all) to those of the men and women of particular times and places. And if this is so, it becomes apparent that the task of assessing the effects on human interests and human conduct of the interposition of state entities between the great aggregations of mankind is an inescapable preliminary (Stone, *Legal Controls of International Conflict* Sydney, London, and New York, [1954], liv).

I explored in 1956, in my Hague Lectures—"Problems Confronting Sociological Enquiries concerning International Law" (*Hague Recueil* 89 [1956]: 63–180)—some of the problems of method and epistemology affecting this preliminary task. In my *Aggression and World Order* (Sydney, London, and Berkeley, 1958), I presented in this context the state of the doctrine and practice as to definition of aggression between states. This was closely followed in December 1960–January 1961 by lectures on international law and the nuclear confrontation delivered on the Australian national radio. These lectures were published under the title *Quest for Survival: The Role of Law and Foreign Policy* in 1962 (Cambridge, Mass.: Harvard University Press) and translated into a number of languages. Some of the somber conclusions that emerged describe with fair accuracy prevailing conditions of international law and international society.

It was then already clear that any early hope of replacing the international balance of nuclear terror by "the rule of law," on the model of successful national societies, was vain. One reason was that states and especially great powers could not find judges in whom they could all trust sufficiently to agree in advance to accept their compulsory jurisdiction in all future disputes. They have also been unable to find such trustworthy executive authorities with effective means of enforcing international law and judicial decisions under it. Behind this lack of trust is the flat refusal of most states, great and small alike, most of the time, to have enforced against them anyone's version of international law except their own. This refusal rests, over and beyond the arrogance of sovereignty, on the inadequacy of the settled content of international law, on the absence of an efficient legislature to make it more adequate, and on the dearth of human leadership at a level of integrity to which Moscow and Washington, not to speak of Peking, Paris, London, Bonn, and the rest, would be willing to entrust their destiny and even survival.

A second reason was that this reality of every state's traditional claim to be the sole judge in its own cause could not be banished even by the awesome realities of threatened nuclear destruction. Even if the stockpiles of nuclear weapons were not of their present "overkill" dimensions on both sides, the *risk* of such destruction could not be removed except by stripping both sides of these weapons, and keeping them stripped. And this latter would imply stripping them also of all other weapons of major violence. The alternative of endowing some Olympian "international" authority with stockpiles of such weapons, clearly superior to either Moscow's and Washington's (and any combination of them), must obviously be ruled out. First, an authority that states would trust to this extent is not to be found; second, it would be impossible ever to be sure that the "international" nuclear endowment was superior enough to prevail without the threat to use it. But that very threat would return us to the risk of nuclear destruction which we are seeking to escape.

Pejoration or name-calling by one side against the other cannot help this situation. Nor is it changed by those who prematurely conjure the risk of destruction into certainty, conclude that any alternative is preferable to this, and forthwith call upon their own state unilaterally to abandon its weapons. Better red than dead! Yet, even if we assumed that such unilateral submission was necessary for survival, we could not be sure that it would be effective for that purpose! The assumption of survival ignores the new and increased dangers in which unilateral nuclear disarmament would itself involve the state concerned. And, for example, in the United Kingdom, it would ignore the fact that unilateral disarmament by one state would not end the nuclear confrontation in which each aligned state—whatever its own armaments—may become embroiled. The wider implications of the unilateral erosion of state power are a major issue to be explored in this volume.

Third, the hope fostered by the Nuremberg trials that individuals, at any rate, can be made amenable to the rule of law and thus deterred from "aggressive warmaking" also proves oversanguine. This is not only because of the difficulties of defining and identifying aggression between states, except in the rare case where a paranoid leader like Hitler lays out in advance the objects of his military adventures. I have shown in my *Conflict through Consensus: United Nations Approaches to Aggression* (Baltimore, 1977) the persistence of these difficulties even after the U.N. General Assembly promulgated its supposed definition in 1974. And events since, such as the hostilities in the Persian Gulf, Afghanistan, Lebanon, and Grenada, confirmed this persistence. But even had these difficulties been overcome, the hope of preventing war by deterring national leaders from "aggression" was, as shown in Discourse 16 in my *Legal Controls*, dim if not desperate. For insofar as we can scarcely expect to try such leaders until after the end of the war, or expect victorious states to allow their own leaders to be tried, only leaders of defeated states would be under deterrent threat. What future national leaders would be deterred from, therefore, was not so much waging a war as losing one. The effect, then, is that once tension in the relations of states moves beyond a certain point, the threat of criminal punishment may actually accelerate resort to war. For leaders of both sides may conclude that they had better act to ensure their side's victory. It sadly accords with this that the number of wars of substantial scale between 1945 and 1980 already exceeded one hundred and thirty, and with a duration (end to end, as it were) of two hundred fifty years during an actual historical span of only thirty-five years.

Fourth, as I also observed in *Quest for Survival*, not only was the use of criminal penalties to deter individuals from initiating wars of aggression thus problematical. It was often almost as difficult for international law to prevent an aggressor state from acquiring legal rights by virtue of its wrongdoing. Thus if, as some advocated, that law were to attempt to deprive an aggressor state that had occupied its victim's territory of the legal rights of a belligerent, the aggressor almost certainly would respond by denying the complementary rights of the inhabitants against himself. The penalty would then fall mainly on the local inhabitants, or other innocent third parties. And so, too, with breaches of war law. These do not, as has sometimes been proposed, result in the suspension of all benefits of the wrongdoing state under war law. For there again the wrongdoing state's response would usually be to spread wider the range of innocent persons injured by violations. The sanctions that international law attempts to use are more limited. As to individual wrongdoing soldiers, their fate on capture is in theory "at the discretion" of the aggrieved belligerent, though in modern practice he may try them for breaches of war law. As against a culprit state, the law accords rights of retaliation and (in due course) of compensation to the victim state. Of course, claims for compensation, like similarly instinctive demands for victorious aggressor states to be stripped of the fruits of victory, pre-suppose that international law can find some way of defeating every aggressor-victor at the moment of his victory. It remains a tragic truth that international law does not have such power nor the means of acquiring it. If we forced it into such a quixotic design against victorious states, we would doom this law to a mothlike existence, fluttering ever helplessly into the destructive flame of state power.

Even in the late 1950s, as I prepared *Quest for Survival*, it was clear that on many matters we were moving in directions that diminished the chances of international peace and cooperation, while these ideals still dominated international fora. Nuclear confrontation steadily escalated, while problems of management became more and more difficult. As we penetrated under land and sea and outwards into space, state activity was thrust into new vacuums of legal control and new arenas of conflict. As even the beneficent effects of science, technology, and medicine spread into decolonized Asia and Africa, the existing global population of 3 billion was projected to rise by 50 million a year, to become 4.25 billion by 1985. New states, as they proliferated year by year, were thought to symbolize a new internationalism rather than resurgence of archaic nationalism and its modern guises of competing blocs and alignments, political, economic, and military.

It is paradoxical, to say the least, that the rather obvious weakening of controls by international law over the behavior of states has been accom-panied by a vast and unprecedented proliferation of treaty law and expansion of the range, mass, and complexity of matters regulated by it. And it is part of the drama of this paradox that this same post–World War II period has seen the flowering of an equally unprecedented literature on the theory of international law and organization. An influential part of this literature, emanating from international lawyers, seeks to establish the theoretical basis for an international law that can serve as an effective law of the international community, conceived as a global community of human beings. This, of course, is a consummation devoutly to be desired; and it is to major works of this tendency that my present title, *Visions of World Order*, refers. My main concern is to assess, as the last decade of this century approaches, the correspondence between these visions and the actualities and prospects of the relations between states and the plight of their human populations.

DIMINISHING EFFECTIVENESS OF MUTUAL ASSURED DESTRUCTION (MAD)

The manuscript of this work went to The Johns Hopkins University Press in July 1983, and as I write this introduction in November 1983 the United States Bureau of Statistics indicates that the annual increase of the globe's population had reached 82 million (as opposed to the above already gloomy projection of 50 millions). Already in 1982 global population had reached 4.721 billion, as compared with the already gloomy projection mentioned above of 4.25 billion for 1985. These totals include an *annual* increase of nearly 16 million in China (now containing 1.006 billion people) and one of 15.5 million in India (now containing 730.5 million people).

On the other hand, many euphoric post-1945 expectations of international law and the United Nations have faded, at this time of writing, into mere banalities if not hypocrisies of speeches at the opening of each year's General Assembly. Even the former scariness of the Mutual Assured Destruction (MAD) way of life in a bipolar world, in which both sides have an excess of nuclear weapon and delivery capacity, seems now to raise a nostalgic sense of security as compared with 1983. We had, after all, "enjoyed" more than three decades in which, despite escalating nuclear stockpiles, these weapons had not been used either by intent or by accident. This suggested the long-term feasibility of rational civilian control at the seats of nuclear power for which perhaps we could not have hoped in 1950.

The prospect in 1984 is that the development of heavy missiles and the increasing number per missile of independently targeted and increasingly accurate warheads were challenging the assumptions that MAD could provide a workable deterrent. Such deterrence rested on the assurance that the victim state of a first strike would sufficiently maintain its own strike force to be able to inflict by way of retaliation unacceptable damage on the cities of the first-strike state. The presupposition of this assurance is that neither side's first-strike capacity can or will be used to destroy the target state's retaliatory nuclear force. Yet, by 1983, the factors mentioned in opening this paragraph had virtually destroyed this presupposition. With it had gone the likelihood that sufficient communications could be maintained, after a "limited" nuclear engagement had been initiated, to preserve civilian control (or indeed any centralized control) over the process of escalation.

Anxieties on this account were no doubt increased by the ever-mounting costs of technological advances in weaponry. American estimates in 1983 placed Soviet defense expenditures at twice those of the

United States, approaching 20 percent of Soviet GNP. (It is admitted that this has to be discounted for dollar costs in the Soviet Union more than half again as high as U.S. costs.) Resources involved in Soviet defense research and development also showed a substantial Soviet lead in manpower commitment. It was the Soviet actual or planned deployment of 300 SS-20 intermediate missiles against Europe that sparked the NATO resolve in 1979 to deploy countervailing Cruise and Pershing II missiles. Both the Soviet and U.S. actual or projected deployments lie behind the massive wave of anti-nuclear demonstrations of 1983 in Europe and the United States. Insofar as these demonstrations are not the outcome of propaganda and manipulation, they are directed against technical developments in weaponry in which both sides may well be entrapped.

It was on 24 October 1983, after a weekend of massive anti-nuclear demonstrations in West Germany, Britain, and other Western countries and no less than 140 rallies in the United States, that the Soviet Union, East Germany, and Czechoslovakia announced the preparation of sites for the deployment of new Soviet missiles, presumably SS-21s or SS-22s and SS-23s. It was also reported that in the week preceding these demonstrations in the West more than 100 leading members of the underground peace and disarmament movements had been rounded up and detained in the Soviet sphere, while others had been warned against public activity. Yet the demonstrations in the West were being hailed as supporting the Soviet case against American deployment of Cruise and Pershing II missiles.

WOULD "SUPERSPEED" DEFENSE HELP?

While demonstrators and government spokesmen wove confused and confusing discourses in terms of "nuclear freeze," "disarmament," "no first strike," and similar prescriptions, new risks came into view to which such prescriptions were simply not responsive. If, in the unfolding technology, strategic arms controls move to "building down" by retiring two or more missiles or warheads for each "new" one deployed, it must be expected that accuracy will increase in new deployments. This could bring a still more rapid undermining of MAD, and a helter-skelter slide towards "launch on warning" (LOW).

The drive to devise vehicles for despatching a shield of defensive laser beams to destroy missiles aimed at the United States, discussed in the text, moved forward, as this introduction was being written, in the work of the Lawrence Livermore National Laboratory of the University of California (See R. Jeffrey Smith, "The Search for a Nuclear Sanctuary," *Science*, 1 July 1983, 3–32; 8 July 1983, 133–38). Tom Mangold, in his BBC talks "Beyond Deterrence" (*Listener*, 15 September 1983, 6–8, 19), has observed that in the new conditions the United States "has just 1800 seconds to defend itself from an initial salvo of, say, 1000 incoming ballistic missiles. It's no use having death rays and space-based lasers unless their entire response can be coordinated and made operationally successful within those 1800 seconds. Missiles identified by satellites on launching would have to be attacked and most destroyed within 250 seconds." Each ICBM that penetrated the shield, probably still throwing many decoy objects, would then have to be identified and destroyed by laser or similar devices, whether still in space or in the atmosphere. "There can be no errors," Mangold observed, "when the equivalent of five million tons of TNT is belting towards Washington at 11,180 km. per hour."

Such developments must bring into awareness additional threats to the hitherto remarkable triumph of rational decision making in nuclear strategy. One is the Pentagon's search, through its Defense Advance Research Projects Agency, headed by Robert Cooper, with an annual budget of $867 million, for computer systems that would replace the *comparatively* leisurely planning and execution of strategies hitherto done by humans. Such systems would yield (in Cooper'saspiration) "super-speed computation at the rate of one billion to one trillion instructions per second, the role of the human Command Authority—consisting of the President and Secretary of Defense—being to turn it on and off." Obviously the lead time before such systems are perfected and put into play will sorely tempt the adversary to a preemptive first strike.

Moreover, even if both sides were able to proceed in tandem, neck and neck, to this supercomputer phase, their end state would be worse than the present, for the interval of minutes for warning before launch would have been reduced to seconds, and human rationality replaced by electronic circuits. With the comparative leisureliness of human decision making, it was apparently possible to detect and defuse seventy-eight false signals of missile attacks in 1979 and sixty-nine in 1980 (L. J. Dumas, "Reacting to Accidental Nuclear War," *International Herald Tribune*, 11 August 1983). Columnist Jack Anderson has alleged other only narrowly aborted erroneous launchings in November 1979 (*Auckland Star*, 12 August 1983).

Another development that, especially as seen by the military, threatens rationality in decision making is the increasing role played by thousands of civilian specialists in keeping high technology functioning in situations short of full nuclear alert. As of August 1983, a Pentagon task force estimated that five thousand such "mission essential" civilians and one thousand "mission critical" civilians were already involved and that these numbers would increase. Whether these civilians could be relied on to continue their tasks in variable conditions of danger, of personal and family anxiety, and of war objectives would become, it was thought, increasingly problematic. This concern would not be allayed, it was thought, by subjecting civilians to the Uniform Code of Military Justice (Dumas, "Reacting to Accidental Nuclear War"). Such concerns were not lessened by the alleged further fact (*International Herald Tribune,* 11 August 1983) that between 1975 and 1977 five thousand persons were removed from duties proximate to nuclear weapons for reasons of alcoholism, drug abuse, or mental illness.

STRATEGIC- AND INTERMEDIATE-RANGE-MISSILE NEGOTIATIONS

Is it then a part of the answer to say with Admiral Noel Gaylor, formerly director of the National Security Agency and deputy director of the Joint Strategic Target Planning Staff, that since there is no sensible military use for any of the nuclear forces—intercontinental, theater, or tactical—the United States should release itself (and by implied invitation the Soviet Union) from the nuclear trap by proceeding to deep cuts in the nuclear arsenal (Gaylor, "Arguments against Nuclear Civil Defense," *International Herald Tribune,* 16 August 1983)? Or to say with others that since deterrence by the MAD strategy of each side's holding the other's main civilian centers hostage against the adversary's first stike has broken down, gigantic civil defense crisis relocation plans should now proceed to maximize survival and the prospects of economic recovery after a nuclear attack?

Would not such measures for civil defense still be seen by the adversary as evidence of preparation for a preemptive first strike? Is such a watershed moment in developing weaponry a promising moment for proposing a comprehensive test ban treaty for a moratorium on testing, in extension of the 1963 limited test ban treaty (Tom Wicker in *International Herald Tribune,* 16 August 1983)?

Can "progress" of this or some other kind, such as control of future deployments in Europe, still be hoped for after the apparently scornful Soviet rejection of proposals in President Reagan's General Assembly address of 26 September 1983? Is there hope of overcoming the long-term, stalemated negotiations (fourth round) on strategic nuclear weapons (START) (stalemated despite U.S. negotiator Rowny's assertion on 5 August 1983, denied by the Soviet side, that there had been "forward movement") and more recent stalemated negotiations in intermediate-range weapons (INF) by bringing into the discussions the reduction or withdrawal of tactical (short-range) nuclear weapons? NATO is said to have 409 such tactical weapons, and the Warsaw Pact 630, stockpiled in Europe, and a NATO ministers' meeting in Montebello, Quebec, on 27 October 1983 decided to withdraw a large number of tactical nuclear warheads in the next five years.

The argument is that reduction of such weapons could produce overdue movement in the more or less static ten-year-old negotiations for "mutual and balanced force reduction in Europe." Insofar as tactical and intermediate-range nuclear weapons have a certain overlap of function, moreover, some think that the linkage could have a fruitful impact on discussions of intermediate-range weapons (Tom Hirschfield in *International Herald Tribune*, 11 August 1983). Indeed, the Soviet–East German–Czechoslovak announcement on 25 October 1983, mentioned above, of the preparation of sites for deployment of new missiles in Europe was in terms of "operational-tactical" missile complexes. (The range of the new Soviet SS-21 is reputedly 100 km; of the SS-22, 1,000 km; and of the SS-23, 400 km.)

Tass's dismissal of President Reagan's apparent concessions of 26 September 1983 as "hypocritical" camouflage of imperialism in effect charges the United States with a disingenuous maneuver to achieve superiority in intermediate-range weapons by denying that 162 French and British missiles are to be taken into account, since they are held by those two countries outside the NATO framework. Even this ostensibly arithmetical argument seems inconclusive. In terms of legal technicalities, Charles R. Gellner, of the Library of Congress, has pointed out that under the NATO treaty, the 64 U.K. submarine-launched nuclear missiles, though assigned to national command in peacetime, are to be under the supreme commander in Europe in time of emergency and targeted in coordination with the U.S. Strategic Air Command (*International Herald Tribune*, 12 August 1983). The United Kingdom's reserved right to withhold its missiles from NATO, it is pointed out, is no more peremptory than that of the United States to withhold its missiles. The French position as to her 80 submarine missiles and 18 land-based missiles is said to be similar. This is not, in Gellner's view, negatived by France's withdrawal from the NATO military organization, that organization having been created some time after the treaty.

The foregoing line of argument, however, concerns the legal technicalities. The Moscow claim, on the other hand, concerns rather the substantial question as to the extent to which these 162 U.K. and French missiles would in fact be available to the NATO military organization to countervail Soviet SS-20 missiles without the deployment of Cruise and Pershing II missiles. On this substantial level the likelihood that France and the United Kingdom would in fact assign their missiles exclusively to their own protection even in wartime and the fact that only a fraction of the 144 submarine-based missiles would be at sea at any one time might favor the U.S.-U.K.-French arithmetic rather than the Soviet. At any rate, despite the altercations then still surrounding the Soviet shooting down of the South Korean passenger liner and its 269 passengers, Washington officials were still canvassing, on 10 September 1983, possible "concessions" in the medium-range-missile negotiations. These were for a level of about 300 missiles on each side, including nuclear weapons on medium-range aircraft. The questions as to which and how many of such aircraft to include, however, have as yet become but another focus of dispute alongside that of the 162 U.K. and French missiles.

LEEWAYS FOR NEGOTIATION?

Even in the fractious aftermath of the Soviet shooting down of the South Korean airliner, including the ban on M. Gromyko's landing at a civilian airport in New York and New Jersey for the opening of the General Assembly, there seemed still to be some flexibilities and some face-saving pretexts available to both sides to soften their positions. First, on the Soviet side is the fact that only a small number of NATO missiles were scheduled for early deployment. After all, despite the play with the word *zero,* there was never any prospect that the United States would deploy *no* Cruise or Pershing II missiles, nor was there any prospect that all SS-20s would be effectively banished from Europe. The NATO ministers' meeting in Montebello, Quebec, at the end of October 1983 stressed that there was room for negotiation on the new missiles until their deployment was completed in 1988.

Second, if, as reported at the end of August 1983, two of the sixteen test flights of the Pershing II exploded, two failed to operate, and one badly missed its target, NATO in any case would require more time to improve its accuracy and reliability. Secretary of the Army James R. Ambrose gave an assurance on 5 August 1983 that Pershing IIs would not be deployed unless that weapon showed 80–90 percent success under combat conditions (*The Australian,* 6–7 August 1983), but there have also been contrary reports (cable from Ian Mather, London, in the *New Zealand Herald,* 12 August 1983).

Third, in October 1983, ambivalence in West Germany towards deployment was highlighted by the reported one million demonstrators in West Germany, despite former Social Democratic Chancellor Schmidt's original initiative and Christian Democratic Chancellor Kohl's present support for the new NATO deployment. Fourth, there is said to be some mixture of feelings among all European NATO members. While they wish to countervail Soviet medium-range SS-20s targeted on Europe, they are also aware that doing so by missiles based in Europe leaves open the possibility of a nuclear war in which the United States itself remains outside the theater.

Perhaps we should maintain the hope that the "walk in the woods" agreement between the U.S. team leader Paul Nitze and his Soviet counterpart, of January 1983, though not endorsed by either Washington or Moscow at that time, still waits in the negotiating background. The mood favoring such an agreement is certainly enhanced by the current attitudes of some elder statesmen of the "cold war" of earlier decades. McGeorge Bundy, George F. Kennan, Robert S. McNamara, and Gerard Smith joined in 1982 in proposing that the United States publicly renounce, for all contingencies, the option of *first use* of nuclear weapons ("Nuclear Weapons and the Atlantic Alliance," *Foreign Affairs* 60, no. 4 [1982]: 753–68). McNamara, after retiring from the presidency of the World Bank in 1983, followed through with an article on "The Military Role of Nuclear Weapons: Perceptions and Misperceptions" (*ibid.*, 62, no. 1 [1983]: 59–80). In it he invoked his experience as U.S. secretary of defense during seven important years to support the thesis that NATO should renounce altogether reliance on the threat to use nuclear weapons, "except only to deter one's opponent from using them" (75).

The main theme of the Bundy-Kennan-McNamara-Smith argument is that while there is no plausible means of abolishing nuclear weapons, the risk of their use can be reduced by the firm adoption by the NATO powers of a policy of "no first use." The authors acknowledge that the very opposite policy—of U.S. willingness to use them first—has underlain every doctrine of deterrence of aggression in Europe since 1945. It was only somewhat more clear when NATO was first formed, before the Soviet Union acquired nuclear weapons, than it later remained. Even the impending deployment of Cruise and Pershing II missiles turns, they think, on the assumed need to maintain deterrence against Soviet aggression by making it clear that nuclear weapons would reach the Soviet Union from Western Europe. These authors, like myself, see the build-up of "enormously excessive nuclear weapons systems on both sides," and the difficulties of preventing nuclear escalation even from mere tactical use, as rendering it ever less feasible "to construct rational plans for any first use" of nuclear weapons by anyone (756).

To renounce such first use, however, implies some solution of the problem of European vulnerability to the assumed Soviet superiority in conventional weapons in Europe. This problem was especially critical for West Germany, as the only major NATO member with a long common frontier with the Soviet sphere and lacking its own nuclear retaliatory (and therefore deterrent) capacity. Substitution of the "no first use" doctrine for overall deterrent doctrines such as MAD would (in these authors' view) involve strategic rethinking in three major respects. First, it would require the political will in the West, as well as the resources, sufficiently to strengthen conventional forces on the central front to give pause to Soviet initiatives by conventional means. Second, clearer allocations of conventional warfare roles among NATO members would become necessary, with a much more important U.S. role in conventional war. Third, the NATO powers would have to make clearer than ever that Soviet nuclear attack would be met by nuclear response.

A firm policy (as distinct from a mere declaration) of no first use "will obviously require time" (761). But the establishment of this policy of keeping nuclear weapons unused as long as others do the same would, in this view, produce the following ameliorations. Future nuclear weapons needs would be limited to survivable and varied second-strike forces, as with those on Polaris submarines. This would allow necessary budgetary shifts to the new conventional weaponry. In particular, it would forestall the struggle for some kind of nuclear advantage in outer space. Further, "adventurism" on either the Soviet or the American side would be reduced. The authors also think that the "no first use" policy would reduce stress between NATO members, for instance, as to the theater projected to receive the impact of nuclear warfare or as to responses to anti-nuclear demonstrators. They even suppose that it might improve Western-Soviet relations.

McNamara's later article adds to the joint article, among other things, certain reflections on the strategic conceptions that have succeeded each other in official American thinking. Coming from one who for seven years was U.S. Secretary of Defense, such reflections are naturally valuable. Soon after the beginnings of NATO, it came to be assumed that its conventional forces would not be adequate to meet those of the Soviet bloc and should serve only as a kind of trip-wire, activating what came to be called after NATO document MC14/2, in 1956, "massive retaliation." This was to be by tactical nuclear weapons, of which by 1956 NATO alone had stockpiled several thousands of warheads of various kinds in Europe. From 1962 onwards the replacement of threat of "massive retaliation" as part of a strategy of "flexible response" was strongly debated and finally adopted in 1967. The central precept of "flexible response"was the strengthening of conventional forces so as to enable NATO to respond at whatever level the aggressor chose to fight. McNamara's point is that both on the NATO and Soviet sides it has been overtaken by events.

First, countervailing tactical nuclear weapons of the Soviet bloc made it most likely that a NATO attempt to use a limited nuclear strike as a deterrent would escalate from the battlefield of Central Europe to most of Europe, East and West. Studies done under McNamara in the Pentagon projected quite unacceptable levels of casualties and damage even from such merely tactical resort. Second, losses of this magnitude would motivate one side or both to use the store of twenty thousand or more warheads in the U.S. and Soviet *strategic* arsenals as a way of avoiding defeat. Third, since each side knows that a first strategic nuclear strike would result in nuclear retaliation inflicting unacceptable loss on the initiator, the NATO threat to use strategic nuclear weapons by way of ultimate response would not be credible to Moscow (nor vice versa). Being thus not credible, it could and would not function as a deterrent—at any rate not from conventional attack. "To the extent that the nuclear threat has deterrent value, it is because it in fact increases the risk of nuclear war." And it is thus only as against nuclear attack that the threat of use of nuclear weapons continues to be credible as a deterrent.

All this proceeds on assumptions one or other of which many will think rather wishful. One is that the West has steadily overestimated the Soviet superiority in conventional weapons in Europe. A second is that the West has underestimated the extent to which any such superiority has already been reduced and can be further countervailed. A third is that the West has also underestimated the degree of Soviet sensitivity to the costs and risks of aggression in Europe even by conventional weapons. A fourth is that Soviet "no first use" statements (themselves only of the last eighteen months and replacing many years of statements from Soviet military sources affirming the belief that a nuclear war *could* be "won") are sincere and reliable. A final (and especially critical) assumption is that in the use by either side of strategic nuclear weapons the accuracy and massive number of warheads launched on the first strike could *not* be such as to disable at the outset so many of the victim's retaliatory weapons and command systems as to make effective retaliation impossible. For insofar as each side deemed this possible, or believed the other side to deem it possible, "no first use" would inevitably give way to "launch on early warning," or, as it is more often termed, "launch under attack."

Other recent literature also seeks to affirm in geopolitical rather than sentimental or nostalgic terms that there have been serious misunderstandings of the threats from the Soviet Union. These have led us, it is claimed, into an unnecessary "nostalgic pursuit of the will-o'-the-wisp of nuclear superiority" (Robert H. Johnson, "Periods of Peril, The Window of Vulnerability and Other Myths," *Foreign Affairs* 61, no. 4 [1983]: 949–70, and literature there collected). Michael Howard reaches conclusions converging with these ("Reassurance and Deterrence," *ibid.*, 61, no. 2 [1982/83]: 309–24). He sees the problem as one of reconciling anew deterrence of Soviet aggression in Europe with reassurance of European countries, objectives that have become increasingly at odds with each other with the actuality or the prospect of nuclear parity. This reconciliation, he thinks, requires reversal of the general NATO tendency to seek to maintain deterrence by intensification of the U.S. nuclear commitment. This intensification, however, has led to the increasing European fear that the threat from nuclear war is greater than the threat from Soviet aggression. What is required, in this view, is basically a turning back from nuclear to conventional deterrence, and from Europe's primary reliance on the United States for defense to its primary self-reliance for its own territorial defense. Nuclear weaponry would, in this view, be relegated to the unlikely contingency of Soviet nuclear attack. It adds little to this recipe to be told that it requires "moral courage, human compassion, . . . a sense of proportion" and that "we should all grow up."

It remains to be seen, of course, whether such arguments or even the Soviet suspension of intermediate-range-missile and START negotiations or the threats of 24 October 1983 to begin to prepare sites to receive still further Soviet missiles will induce the NATO powers to postpone further deployments of the 572 Cruise and Pershing II missiles which began as scheduled in late 1983. They may indeed be led in the opposite direction by recalling that the Soviet suspension of strategic weapons talks after the initial NATO decision in 1979 to deploy Cruise and Pershing II missiles proved to be only temporary.

In fact some questions vital to any compromise whatever had barely begun to be studied, let alone negotiated. These included verification of any regime that may be agreed concerning either strategic (START) or intermediate-range weapons (INF) (*International Herald Tribune*, 28 July 1983). Still other questions about nuclear weapons that have been assumed to be settled add to the perplexities of 1984. At the same time as many are pronouncing nuclear weapons to be totally useless, and as the United States and the Soviet Union are reported to have stockpiles of weapons capable of destroying their enemies many times over, serious scholars are also presenting other startling facts. A study of targeting policy for the London-based International Institute of Strategic Studies done by Desmond Ball and released in August 1983 asserts that the number of U.S. nuclear weapons expected to reach Soviet targets in case of conflict was less than four thousand, while the identified list of targets in the Soviet Union in 1983 was now ten times that number. (This number had risen from twenty-six hundred in 1960 to twenty-five thousand in 1974 and now forty thousand in 1983.) And it is perhaps not entirely a coincidence that the United States Arms Control and Disarmament Agency (ACDA) has been afflicted in the current period by turbulent events surrounding the resignation of director Eugene Rostow and the confirmation of appointee Kenneth L. Adelman.

LAW AND NUCLEAR WEAPONS: THE PARADOX OF MAD

Such a moment is apt for reviewing, as recently C. H. Builder and M. H. Gaubard (*International Law of Armed Conflict . . . Concept of Armed Destruction*, Rand Corporation R-2804-FF [1982]), R. A. Falk and R. J. F. Lifton (*Indefensible Weapons* [1982]), and R. A. Falk ("Towards a Legal Regime for Nuclear Weapons," *McGill Law Journal*, May 1983) have done, the standing of nuclear weapons under international law. These studies expose a dramatic paradox. The Rand study proceeded on the basis of ordinary criteria of the international laws of war, which, for example, forbid attacks on civilians and require that violence be not indiscriminate, but aimed at military objectives. They probably also require that in any harm to civilians incidental to attacks on military objectives, there should be a certain proportionality between the harm and the importance of the military objectives and of "necessity" of incurring such harm in reaching those objectives.

By such criteria, the deterrence principle of Mutual Assured Destruction (MAD), accepted for more than a quarter of a century by both Moscow and Washington, seems to involve the most grossly illegal use of nuclear weapons. And this would be reinforced if other independent restrictions were implied from the notions of "laws of humanity" and "dictates of public conscience" invoked by the Martens clause of the preamble to the Fourth Hague Convention, 1907, for cases not expressly covered by the convention. For MAD requires that most important military objectives, such as missile silos containing nuclear weapons for retaliation against first strikes, shall *not* be attacked and also that cities and civilian populations shall be left exposed to nuclear attack. For it is the joint circumstances of each side's retaliatory weapons being left intact and its cities and civilians being left exposed to them that operate as the effective deterrent to both sides.

The paradox is that while this agreed deterrent strategy of MAD thus involves the acme of illegality, when we try, as did the above Rand report, to describe uses of nuclear weapons more consistent with traditional international law principles, these principles appear to produce a most unstable and dangerous strategic situation. For to obey the legal principles, the opposing states must, if they are to give their missiles any role at all, target them on military objectives, which means as a practical matter on silos and similar deployments and (subsidiarily) on objectives such as conventional forces, communications centers, and munition factories. For unless the enemy's nuclear force is thus neutralized, a belligerent would be vulnerable to its crippling use against him, whatever its own successes against other military targets.

This legal situation would not only motivate but virtually invite each side to consider being first to use nuclear weapons. In fact, as I show both earlier in this introduction and also in chapter 12, the developing technology of the weapons may already, independently of international law, be pushing Washington and Moscow towards this compulsion. The operative factors include not only the growing accuracy of warheads, the use of multiple warheads with independent targeting, the vast overkill capacity of both sides' stockpiles in relation to silos, and the reduced, split-second interval available for deliberation between the possible warning about the launching and any chance of the victim's taking of preemptive or aborting action.

Strategically and realistically, in other words, the best hope of avoiding the use of nuclear weapons is some optimal variant of the flagrantly "illegal" Mutual Assured Destruction (MAD), while the least hope of avoiding such use lies in the rules for such weapons that could plausibly be implied from traditional international law. This latter pseudo-legal regime not only would accelerate nuclear exchange against military objectives but in fact also would fail to protect civilian populations. As Richard Falk and others point out, it would not in fact save cities or civilian populations from nuclear devastation, by reason both of the nature and aftermath of the weapons and of the locations and variety of military targets in relation to cities and populations. And it is in any case most doubtful, as Desmond Ball has pointed out, whether once nuclear weapons had been used, communications could be maintained sufficiently for a central command to set limits to the use of the weapons. Moreover, the nature of this nuclear confrontation deprives the already difficult distinction between "aggressive" and "defensive" use of weapons of much utility in most foreseeable situations.

All this adds up to the fact that arguments about the standing of nuclear weapons under international law *de lege lata* are rather futile, as one might jurisprudentially expect with such a quantum leap in weaponry. Only what the law ought to be—the *de lege ferenda*—is worth discussion at this stage; if, indeed, law of any kind is as a practical matter worth discussing. I would certainly want to agree with Richard Falk in his affirmative answer and his articulation of three policy goals as paramount for basing the law that ought to be. These are: (1) avoiding nuclear war; (2) minimizing crisis instability; and (3) reducing the arms race. These policy goals have to be sought, moreover, in a world that, whether we like it or not, is dominated by territorially based state entities whose leadership feels willing and even bound, Falk correctly observes, to risk virtual self-destruction to avoid military defeat, as well as to feel justified in using military power to secure positions of privilege, power, and wealth in human affairs for itself and its people.

This view agrees, it may be observed, with that expressed in my *Quest for Survival* in 1961, and summarized above, that demands for the abolition of these weapons, however self-gratifying to the demandants, have no action value and that there is simply no way of instilling sufficient confidence in international institutions to allow control over nuclear weapons or decisions about their use to be transferred away from sovereign states. By the same token, legal precepts addressed to governments at this stage may have to be seen as hortatory and educative rather than imperative or prohibitory. Their value is in promoting the ideas that any actual use of nuclear weapons almost necessarily involves crimes against humanity such as traditional war law cannot accommodate and that this use includesa first use of nuclear weapons, even in self-defense, against a prior *nonnuclear* armed attack. In particular, also, despite the paradox discussed above, the central notion of MAD—of the retaliatory uses of nuclear weapons against cities and other primarily civilian targets—should be recognized as grossly at odds with traditional war law. Falk would also wish to condemn all weapons systems, plans, and strategic doctrines and all political leaders and experts knowingly associated with first-strike roles as also guilty of war crimes. But this is stated in terms that are rather too broad, terms that do not take into account, for example, that experts may be "knowingly associated" with "plans," and so on, having first-strike characteristics, merely for the purpose of preparing defensive responses to the contingency of such a first strike by the adversary.

For the rest, having been unable to welcome the Rand study's attempt to subject nuclear weapons literally to traditional war law, for the reasons above explained, Falk sees international law as capable of adding only a general exhortation similar to Article VI of the Nuclear Non-Proliferation Treaty, that states should minimize the role of nuclear weapons through negotiations in good faith. And he thinks that citizens should urge their governments to achieve "law-oriented" foreign policies and to accept the normative consensus of the public that nuclear weapons are not lawful instruments towards those policies, and to do so if need be by nonviolent acts of civil disobedience.

How far all this is from "a legal regime for nuclear weapons," as Richard Falk terms it, is apparent in his readiness to accept "a formal no-first-use pledge, coupled with comprehensive plans for non-nuclear defense of vital interests" as the best sign that law is doing what it can. I would certainly share the view that the realities of present reliance by states on nuclear weapons make it impossible to avoid a degree of incoherence in both "legal" and ethical judgments concerning them. As we have seen, even *de lege ferenda*, a legal regime could not exclude their retaliatory use, at least against a prior nuclear attack. And once that is conceded, we face a choice between trying to limit retaliation to isolated military objectives, threats to which would not deter and, not so limiting it, which would result in gross violations of traditional war law. Even the noncynic may be forgiven for thinking that he awaited the law and was given a preachment!

Chapters 1, 2, and 6 introduce the preliminary issues as to the accessibility to knowledge of the substratal elements of international law, especially at the level of individual human beings. Chapters 3, 4, and 5 present, I hope with understanding and sympathy, three major contemporary visions of world order by leading publicists of the last generation. These chapters display the textures of various threads that run through the problems of erosion of state power (chapter 7), of justice and equality among nations (chapter 8), of justice as a relation between states as opposed to justice as a relation between human beings (chapter 9), and of the proposed "new international economic order" (chapter 10). Chapters 11 and 12 confront a number of politico-ethical issues concerning the concurrence or conflict among rulers, especially in democratic polities, of their responsibilities inwards, towards the members of their own nation, on the one hand, and their responsibilities outwards, towards the leaders and peoples of other nations, on the other. Even in times of economic comfort and stability, this interplay of internal and external responsibilities of rulers can raise serious problems. In times of economic stress and instability, the problems are among the most intractable of all. Yet the more these problems are articulated, at any rate in the industrial democracies, the more chance there will be of fair and stable adjustment between the claims of some at home for better living standards and the claims of foreign aid for providing the merest subsistence to tens of millions who lack even this.

List of Abbreviations

ASAT	Anti-Satellite Technology
Brandt Report	Report of the Independent Commission on International Development Issues appointed by Chairman Willy Brandt on 28 November 1977; reported 17 December 1979 (18 full-time members, with 10 from the Third World)
CIEC	Conference on International Economic Cooperation
GATT	General Agreement on Tariffs and Trade
Hague Recueil	Academie de Droit International, La Haye, *Recueil des Cours*
IMF	International Monetary Fund
INF	International Nuclear Forces (Talks)
LDC	Less Developed Country
LOW	Launch on Warning
MAD	Mutual Assured Destruction
MIRV	Multiple Independently Targeted Reentry Vehicle
MX	Missile Experimental
NIEO	New International Economic Order
ODA	Official Development Assistance
PPSSCC	President's Private Sector Survey on Cost Control
SALT (I or II)	Strategic Arms Limitations Talks
UNCLOS	United Nations Conference on the Law of the Sea
UNCTAD	United Nations Conference on Trade and Development

Visions of World Order

1. The Sociological Substratum
of International Law

The very notion of a sociology of international law assumes the existence of extralegal data knowledge of which is relevant to understanding the role of that law, its stability, change, and breakdown in the course of its development—the existence, in short, of what may compendiously be termed "the sociological substratum of international law."[1] It also assumes that this substratum is cognoscible to a degree permitting scholarly communication concerning it. The former assumption—that there is a sociological substratum of international law—is scarcely open to doubt; to deny it would be to deny altogether both the earthly origin and the operation on earth of international law. Even the most intransigent detractors and the most despairing Cassandras of international law could not go so far.[2] The second assumption—that the sociological substratum is within the realm of human cognition—calls first for a preliminary glance at the kinds of factors that make up this substratum and then for a look at the formation, range, and internal and external relations of those factors.

It is reasonable to assume that the range of these factors bears some correlation with the apparent range of operation of international law itself. Geographically, all parts of the earth, its superjacent air and space, and its subjacent regions may fall, as a result of technological developments, within the control or claims of some state or other. All of these are therefore of potential relevance, though at a particular time some of them may not be actually so. The line between potential and actual relevance will depend mainly on the momentary state of the development of technological power and on the range and intensity of human demands. Within this geographical range, the physical, biological, and psychological realities may all be material. The physical realities of distance, fertility, chemical and mineral distribution, waterways and water supply, and submarine characteristics may decisively influence the contents of international law and their development. The same is true of the biological realities—the life cycles and ecology of the flora and fauna, and of

1

microorganisms, the racial differences among humans, the level of re-production among the various populations, and their varied biological inheritances and conditionings.

On the human side, moreover, these primal elements merge into those of human psychology and culture. The mental and emotional patterns and expectations of individuals and groups, especially, of course, of those constituting the populations of state communities, are important; indeed, as human mastery over mere physical nature expands, they are perhaps the most important determinants of the course of international law. Contemporary psychological trends and crises make impact often at cross-purposes with traditions of culture as institutionalized in laws, customs, and religions, with their attendant received ideals. Some of the gravest obstacles to cognoscibility lie in the intractabilities of this "ideal," that is, eidetic, sphere of "objective mind."

A sociology of international law, then, presupposes the availability for its pursuit of minds competent in technical legal exposition and criticism and in imaginative reflection on legal materials in the light of the findings in other major fields of knowledge, especially the empirical social sciences. It also presupposes the accessibility to study of the mental and emotional patterns of the men and women who are the populations of the states of the world. We shall have to examine closely this question of accessibility.[3]

The difficulties arising from the variety and range of the factors present in the sociological substratum are increased by the absence of a priori or otherwise clear principles of uniformity, hierarchy of levels, or weight or channels of influence among these factors. For example, while the influence of cultural patterns seems ontologically to presuppose a deeper level of psychology, this is not necessarily (or indeed at all) any guide to the relative weight of influence in a particular problem.[4] Indeed, on the practical level, this "ontological" precedence of psychological processes over cultural patterns may have to be reversed altogether. Similar riders have to be added concerning the ontological precedence of biological facts over psychological facts and of physical facts over biological facts. Conceivably, the biological facts of population increase, the physical facts of soil infertility, or the physiobiological fact of population pressure within particular states might directly determine the creation of a rule of international law, granting to states so handicapped privileged rights to exploit the marine and submarine resources of the high seas. But such factors are more likely to operate remotely by stimulating psychological processes that produce aggressive tendencies or clamant demands on other states or on international organizations, which in turn lead to coerced or agreed legal change.[5]

While it is permissible and indeed necessary to detect fruitful correlations from the direct and indirect factors here involved, it is vital to remember that this abstraction has taken place and that beyond a certain point, abstraction for purposes of study becomes vicious over-simplification. A great deal of honest advocacy of "world government" has, by failure to observe this precept, oversimplified its recipe for world peace by excluding from consideration at least certain vital cultural and psychological facts concerning the state of human communication.[6]

The need for constant awareness of the simplifications involved is intensified when we observe that even the directness of the relation between the sociological facts and international law does not make clear their relative importance and that, indeed, all such generalizations are hazardous. For example, the facts of cultural and psychological reality are admittedly more complex and changeful than those of the biological and physical spheres from which they emerge. It might seem reasonable, therefore, to say that the biological and physical facts form a crucial level of the substratum of international relations and law. Yet, in the sense in which they are so crucial, biological and physical realities may have little meaning at all for our inquiries about international law. They merely hold the possible correlations between certain poles of possibility, whereas the really interesting questions require taking a position between these poles. They could tell us something about the possibility of applying inter-national law to our relations with other planets, or to a world in which men have learned to take sufficient food from breathed air, but in themselves they can tell us little about the nascent rules concerning the law of resources of the continental shelves of existing states or the regimes of the deep ocean bed. And this should in no way surprise us, if we remember that since any given biological and physical fact may be associated with many alternative cultural and psychological patterns, the biological and physical facts themselves cannot be decisive as between these alternatives.

Closely connected with the distorting impact on cognition of moral and political value judgments, two other characteristics of modern methodo-logical tendencies present dangers to the growth of sociological knowl-edge concerning international law. They may be described as the mechan-isms of cognitive irradiation and cognitive contamination. These mechanisms are found to operate whenever thought becomes organized as a self-conscious movement or school, usually identified in modern times by the suffix *–ism*. Such a school often takes on the function of conquest or defense, or both, of the field of knowledge to which it relates and in any case almost always becomes insulated to a degree from other contemporary trends. Its adherents see reality through the glass of the school's ideas praising, by a kind of irradiation of the school's intellectual sympathies, whatever seems congenial to its positions or blaming, by a kind of corresponding contamination, whatever seems uncongenial. Cognitive irradiation and contamination are especially dangerous in fields of knowledge—like that under discussion—where exactness and cogency of proof are difficult or impossible to attain. They constitute a major methodological contribution to the disturbance and breakdown of human communication between contemporary scholars concerned with the sociology of international law.

In the international society, as in all human societies, human communication is basic to the common life. It is, at the least, an intermediate source of the greatest potentialities and perils of that life. As such, it must be regarded as a critical part of the subject matter of any sociology of international law. The entire substratum of international law must obviously be affected by the level of human communication inter se between the people who inhabit each of the various states. Unless this factor receives due attention, no body of knowledge concerning this substratum and its relation to international law is conceivable at all. It follows from the geographically worldwide ambit of international law and its substratum that knowledge relevant to an understanding of their relations cannot become accessible without a high degree of efficient human communication not only within but across the frontiers of states. Without this high degree of efficient communication, the results of sociological inquiries would amount only to disparate insights drawn by separate individual and national workers from different and incommensurable parts of the geographical range. Such results would be but a rather haphazard collection of parallel factual data and hypotheses, none checked against the others or against the facts on which the others are based. Moreover, it may be found that the level of human communication across state frontiers does not reach the minimum necessary to support the assumption that international law, as a homocentric law, consists of operative norms as distinct from mere verbal formulations. While in its absolute form this contingency is unlikely, the sociological inquiry cannot ignore the likelihood that it may provide the true explanation for the existing condition of some segments of international law.

The problems of human communication are especially complex as they affect interstate relations. Yet these complexities are only superimposed on the general features of all communication. Human communication in general may be aborted through any of its components. Thus, in terminologic confusions it is aborted by inadequate symbols. In perplexities arising from illogicality, the references are badly organized. In fields of settled knowledge, usually little difficulty arises from the nature of the object to which the communication relates. But even this may cause trouble, for instance, where the communication concerns an object within a field of knowledge insufficiently explored or in its nature merely speculative or intuitive, as with "the reasonableness of man" as an object of natural law thought. And, of course, situations that thus tend to abort communication may arise not merely from vices contained within the symbol, reference, or object itself as it is transmitted but also by reason of deficiencies at the receiving end of the communication. A transmission free of vice on all other counts may nevertheless come to nothing if the recipient lacks a basis of experience, modes of thought, and familiarity with the symbols that lie behind the transmission.

The primordial form of obstruction to communication is, of course, that of separation of the parties in space and time. Communication always involves at least the overleaping of this obstruction, since the individuals concerned are always separated from each other by space and/or time. Modern civilization has placed at man's disposal wondrous means of overcoming these obstructions. It is less often observed, though no less important, that technological advance also produces new kinds of blockages to communication, whether by calculation, as in the jamming of broadcasts in ideological warfare, or merely incidentally, as in the congestion of roads with motor vehicles or the saturation of the air with radio waves. The very means of expeditious physical communication may thus produce its own frustration.

Disturbances of communication on the psychological level are multifarious, and may reduce the physical means of communication to a weak or impotent state. Failure to receive the symbols and to understand the thoughts transmitted may arise independently of any conscious resistance to their reception, from concealed irrationalities on the subliminal level, which may even frustrate the conscious will to receive what is transmitted. Obstacles of this subliminal origin are of intense significance in the relation of international law to its social substratum. They spring not only from various psychopathic tendencies of the individual but also from the conditioning of individuals by sociopolitical pressures of the environment, including the mind-controlling activities of the state apparatus.

In a stable community, communication operates, for the most part, in a medium consisting essentially of a historical culture and way of life. Admittedly, certain basic biological and psychological drives common to all human societies form a common background of communication. But these account for only a small proportion of all acts of communication. Within modern state communities, the bulk of acts of communication presuppose for their efficacy a certain community of concepts, ways of life, social institutions, and other historically given experience; difficulties may arise, however, in attempted communication between different social groupings with diverse educational training and backgrounds.

Disturbances or blockage of communication arising from discrepant idioms, concepts, and ways of life obviously must be especially grave in communication across state frontiers. Language differences constitute a serious obstacle. No language is fully translatable into another, for a language necessarily reflects the experience and the environment of those who use it. Yet these are but minor difficulties as compared with those ensuing directly from conflicting concepts of social life and of the public good, as between modern state communities. If these conflicts go beyond a certain point, lines of human communication may break down completely. And when, as in our own day, each state entity tends to fix, or at any rate to mold, the prevalent concepts of life and of the public good within its borders, the breakdown of communication is accelerated and intensified. A state's techniques of blocking, distorting, and censoring communications directed at its citizens from outside, not to speak of rewriting history, may reduce human communication to a travesty.

Even within national communities, the proliferation and specialization of knowledge, although in a sense it enriches and differentiates thought, and language for transmitting thought, does not necessarily increase human communication. For while more specialized minds are able to press the boundaries of knowledge outwards along lonely paths, that hinders dialogue with ordinary people, who either are lost to the dialogue altogether or entrench themselves incommunicado behind outrun "truths." In any case, human communication about an object is bound to be defective to the extent that human knowledge is defective. But it does not always follow that enlargement of human knowledge concerning an object leads to more effective communication concerning it. Some objects of knowledge, like the law, have been regarded as esoteric for centuries, and members of the legal profession have been feared, hated, ridiculed, scoffed at, and even despised, thus hindering better communication about it. As to objects concerning which in a previous state of knowledge there was apparent common ground of experience and therefore the possibility of communication, the advance of knowledge may destroy what was apparently common ground, substituting esoteric concepts and reasoning. A fundamental unsettling of first principles, such as our age has suffered concerning the nature of matter and energy, may leave those who reach the new level of understanding rather isolated among their bewildered, sullen, and largely unlistening fellows. In such circumstances, the maintenance and, where necessary, reestablishment of sufficient common ground for the resumption of communication is a task as formidable as it is urgent.

It would be hasty to say that contemporary disturbance in the processes of human communication foredooms any early prospect for the establishment of stable international relations based on orderly processes of law. Yet it would also be oversanguine to engage in inquiries about the relation of international law to its social substratum without awareness of the jeopardy into which the state of human communication throws this enterprise of studying international law as a planetary homocentric order.[7]

In certain limited respects, of course, it is true that modern technical advances in physical communications do increase human communication. This is so wherever fulfillment of a state's functions depends on common parallel action by other states, as in the growth of sea and air travel or the control of epidemic diseases. Some areas may also be found within the field of international law—air navigation, for instance—in which the state of human communication is vastly improved by growth in physical communications and presents no serious obstacles to either legal growth or the sociological study of legal growth.

Is it possible to base upon such instances any general optimistic prognosis? Such gains as have been made in the extension of human communication must be given their due weight in the overall picture. First, it must be recognized that extension of worldwide communications is not the same as extension of humanitywide communication. The physical means of communication are in themselves no assurance of the commerce of minds. Second, just as advanced means of communication do not assure human communication, the commerce of trade is not necessarily correlated with the commerce of minds. Economic interdependence, despite many contrary assertions, is not per se an assurance of growth rather than atrophy in human communication.

Third, it must be added that (as already mentioned) the increased tempo, scope, and efficiency of communications may actually impair human communication. A medieval traveler was forced by the slowness and labor of his journey to learn something of the ways of thought and life and values of the inhabitants of foreign parts. A modern traveler may see no more than efficient air terminals and cosmopolitan hotels and may speak only to the air hostess or his foreign agent. In this sense, facilities for physical communication may destroy the occasions for human communication. Fourth, global communications, insofar as they have brought a great variety of civilizations under the aegis of Western concepts, have made possible a degree of human communication between Western and Eastern peoples and, in our own present subject, a vast and rapid extension of the domain of international law. But in the course of this increased communication, Western concepts have been diluted, and it is certain that this diluting stream has to a certain extent flowed backwards also to reduce and confuse communication among Western peoples inter se. Indeed, as concepts move across to alien groups that are also hostile, they may become not only diluted but wholly spurious: their meanings may be reversed and twisted and the emotions associated with them pried away from the original object and attached to objects of a quite different and often opposed kind.[8]

Fifth, nor can the vast potentiality of radio, television, and satellite transmitters for planetwide human communication be taken at face value. Between hostile groups of states and peoples, into which the present world is split, short-wave radio may rather have to be counted among the factors most destructive of human communications. For instance, between the Communist-orientated states and those of the Western groupings, radio may be above all a weapon. The target states defend themselves, not merely by jamming, but by all kinds of measures for "protecting" their populations against all unapproved messages. Soviet transmitters are reported to have begun jamming the Voice of America broadcasts of Pope John Paul's visit to Poland in June 1983 within half an hour of its start. The Madrid Conference on European Security and Cooperation was ostensibly then engaged in strengthening the Helsinki Agreement, which forbids jamming of this kind. Whether this insulation and immunization are achieved by jamming or by other negative measures such as withholding of receiving equipment, condign penalties for listening, or the more dispersed pressures of identifying listeners with "fifth columnists," "traitors," "fellow travelers," "collaborators," or "deviationists"; or by the more positive methods of promoting, through the organs of mass communication, stereotyped attitudes towards the main issues that arise, the net result is to constrict not merely communication by short-wave radio but all human communication by other means, such as books, newspapers, private letters, or direct speech.

The potentiality of planetwide human communication by radio thus ends in a degree of blocking of human communication across state frontiers by every known means. Perhaps what we have here is some fearful analogy to Sartre's pathological individualism, forcing a person to choose between submission to others and suicide, an analogy reflected also, as James Fawcett has well observed, in the modern juxtaposition of interdependence of peoples and their nuclear armaments.[9]

No less tragic in its paradox is the sixth caveat, concerning the effects of the extension of literacy or "fundamental" education. Just like the very planet-ranging power of radio-activated defenses for blocking of all communication, the increased access to the human mind resulting from general literacy has been in part appropriated by the state entity for the creation of stereotyped attitudes among its people towards other states and peoples. The frontier barrier against communication between human beings is thus reinforced as education becomes more universal.[10]

The state itself is, sociologically conceived, a product of a great number of intricate sociopsychological processes in which interindividual communication and inhibitions on it play an important and sometimes decisive role. The state's role, in turn, as a bridge or barrier—or torture rack—for communication across frontiers is closely related to the conditions of communication within its boundaries.[11] This negative function of the state entity—blocking or distorting communication both among its own people and across its frontiers with other peoples—bears most gravely on the data available for sociological study of the substratum of international law, bringing into doubt the very feasibility of relating that law to human claims, aspirations, and expectations. It also, of course, stands in the way of basic reforms obviously necessary for disciplining the conduct of state entities, such as the establishment of a real standing international criminal court or even the proscription and punishment of acts of soliciting, giving, or receiving illicit payments by foreign government officials to influence their official conduct.[12]

Wilhelm Reich described as "the character armour" that part of psychic energy which is organized to protect the personality against influences deemed hostile. Even for individuals, the armor insulates, not only against the threats, but against all other influences until these have been screened.[13] All thoughts communicated are held up or refracted before reaching the consciousness of the recipient. Of course, insofar as all state interference with thought and communication is forbidden, as by classical liberal ideals, the analogy would be wholly rejected. Insofar as such blocking and distorting activities of the state are deemed legitimate for the protection of the state community, or in any case continue even if disapproved, they can be seen as a kind of "character armour" warding off harmful communication, especially across its frontiers.

Such activities, of course, go far beyond physical blocking to the creation of psychological blockages and molds of mental stereotypes that shape all incoming communications and confront all inconsistent ones with impatience, intolerance, incredulity, hatred, or contempt. This officially promoted prejudging of content limits any intellectual and emotional rapport between the human senders and receivers of communications. It constricts the opportunities of men and women to develop a sound sense of political, legal, and cultural realities, as well as to influence each other, and the men and women of other state communities, by an active two-way flow of communication. And insofar as a sociological study of international law as a homocentric law presupposes that this law depends on relations between the human beings who inhabit the several states and not merely between one state apparatus and others, such defective human communication across frontiers must create corresponding difficulties in this field.[14] This raises questions—which will haunt the present work—as to whether this part of the sociology of international law can fruitfully proceed at this time.[15]

2. International Law As Humanity Based

That part of the substratum of international law that is centered on the human inhabitants of the planet—the conditions of their physical life, demands, aspirations, and expectations—must obviously have a certain preeminence. This is not an epistemological truth but only a heuristic implication from the general assumption that must be made by sociological enquiries, namely that international law is a law made by and for human beings—that state entities in some manner and degree represent their human populations—in short, that international law is a homocentric law, to be studied as such. As H. D. Lasswell and M. Kaplan once observed: "'State' and 'government' have reference to special cases of inter-personal relations, and are not the basic concepts from which all others are derived, or in relation to which they must be defined."[1] Insofar as this is so, the testing of this homocentric international law for its effects on human demands, aspirations, and expectations, and for its responsiveness to these, is perhaps the most important task of the sociology of international law. Conceivably this may change. A race of robots might sometime seize power in each of the various states of the world, for whom the sociology of international law might be not homocentric but robot-centric. Happily, this branch of knowledge is still homocentric and can, it is hoped, be kept so.

This basis in humanity has momentous implications, especially in view of the conditions of human communication within and across frontiers. It is as commonplace as it is false to think that because of the growing efficiency of modern communications in the physical sense of rapid transportation and electronic transmission, nations are drawn closer together towards interdependence, international understanding and peace, and even towards a "real" world community and world law. In chapter 1, I exposed the paradox that the marvels of *physical* communications may be accompanied by impairment of *human* communication; it is the latter that is of most central sociological concern.

The operations of state entities are a main source of the impairment of human communication. They thus present a formidable barrier to any basic sociological study of the impact of international law on men and women, and of men and women on international law. This was a main theme of my work in the 1950s. There have been notable and sometimes heroic attempts since then to bypass this intractable problem of the conditioning of human communication by historically given state entities, the power centers that dominate these, and their operations with power. Three of the better known of these modern visions may be identified (they will be examined in later chapters).

1. *An existing "common law of mankind" (Wilfred Jenks)*. In this vision, the contents of international law are seen as determined by the interplay, comparison, synthesis, and manipulation of legal rules, principles, conceptions, and policies found among the various human societies. The tasks of both doctrinal writers and decisionmakers are here given a magistral autonomy in revealing a body of data consisting of legal ideas shared by mankind generally. I shall show that this view simply avoids the central question of the sociology of international law as a legal order that purports to be homocentric.

2. *Policy-oriented decision making within the world power process (M. S. McDougal)*. When the decisionmakers of international law are seen as including officials, not merely of states and international agencies but of an indeterminate number of other actors, the generally assumed decisiveness of the role of state entities is diminished. And if "law" is redefined in correspondingly indeterminate terms as "the process of decision making," that role is also diminished in terms of doctrine. When decisionmakers include voluntary associations dedicated to particular ideals or causes, business or workmen's associations dedicated to the protection of their own interests, transnational business corporations dedicated to making profits and using power to secure and increase such profits, professional and other expert associations dedicated to the furtherance of the particular vocation or intellectual discipline, and even individual human beings, then state entities and international governmental organizations are merely sharing with them a power of decision making that is finally resolvable into a struggle to realize values for human beings. It is perhaps easy to see all this as a description of what international law should be. But McDougal's thesis is that this is what international law is; and his "policy science" seems to aim at validating this view by comprehensive sociological study. International law is (or should be?) a process of realizing these values through the world power process.

Here, as at other critical points in his formidably elaborate apparatus, McDougal tends to try to have it both ways. On the one hand, he asserts that decision processes do not depend on whether a structure is called "governmental." But he immediately adds that "on a wide range of

matters the principal nation states may—and do—continue to perceive
one another as unilaterally making the critical decisions, for which they
accept, and reciprocally enforce, a substantial measure of responsibility."
It is possible that McDougal's framework of inquiry, by insisting on the
concurrent decision-making roles of nonstate actors at substate or nonstate levels, does to an uncertain degree bypass problems of legal preeminence of state entities in the conventional theory of international law.[2] We
shall see, however, that all this does not overcome the problem of factual
preeminence of state entities in controlling human claims, demands, and
expectations of their respective populations. Nor does it remove the
blockage and distortion of relations and communications between human
beings across frontiers which, as I have shown, is the threshold barrier to a
full sociology of international law. Nor, as we shall see, can its listing of
"basic values" to orient decision making really explain (much less justify)
choices between such values, or between versions of each value, or
between preference of a value as realized in the particular case and the
overall working of the legal order, when these conflict.

   3. *World order models revealed by growing planetary consciousness.* If Jenks
is seen as seeking to transcend statehood from above by the power of
intellect to integrate a common law of mankind, Richard Falk's World
Order Models Project might be seen as seeking to bypass state power
centers from below by the surge of heightened human planetary consciousness. Falk's project is a blueprint for transition from the dysfunctional territorial divisions of the planet and its peoples, each controlled by a state apparatus of domination, to a human community in
which planetwide central guidance of critical functions serves the needs
and claims of all. Success in such an enterprise would, indeed, replace pro
tanto the international law based on coordination of sovereign statehoods
by a planetary law (or "world law") based explicitly on planetwide communication between human beings. It would show that the study of
international law in relation to its human substratum—a main part of the
sociology of international law—is possible despite state entities. Such
success would remove the obstacles presented by state entities for conceiv-
ing international law as homocentric. The question is not whether such a
goal is in sight but whether we are yet moving in its direction.

   All three of these movements of thought are seeking a frame of
sociological reference within which they can speak sensibly of a world
legal order that will embrace within its legitimate authority and protection
all the men and women of the planet. The social order to which this legal
order corresponds is to be one of human beings, not merely a coordination of the sovereign states that dominate the present international
legal order. If I may adapt the poetically telling Tönniesian distinction of
Georg Schwarzenberger, they seek a frame for seeing international law as
governing human relations "based on love" ("community," *Gemeinschaft*)

rather than, as at present, reciprocal relations between states "based on fear" ("society," *Gesellschaft*).[3] Allowing for the oversharpness of these as Weberian ideal types, the above theories seek (or rather postulate) a substratum for international law resting on human conviviality and on common objectives and norms, rather than a coordination or coexistence between sovereign state entities born of mutual fear.

The last two of these movements of thought share another apparent assertion: that in the emergent planetary legal order there is ultimately little place for sovereign state entities in the traditional sense. The interstate system is to be progressively superseded by a more fully homocentric world or planetary system. The aspiration is quite explicit in Falk. In McDougal it is ambivalently secreted in the complexity and indeterminacies of the "world power process" and the emotive overtones of systems of "world public order."

So also Richard Falk summarized his 1974 "Yencken hypothesis," in the following terms.[4] There is no way, he thought, to sustain a contractual relationship between the people and the government at the state level without protracted reliance on repressive force so long as the territorial state system persists. Moreover, to achieve a social contract on the state level based on some notion of consensual rule, it will be necessary simultaneously to reach a social contract on a global level. A global social contract presupposes in its turn a successful process of transition to a condition organized around the emergence of nonterritorial central guidance capabilities as well as drastic redistribution of power, wealth, and influence. For this approach, then, two questions become paramount: Can this favorable outcome be brought about? What is the most beneficial way for individuals and groups to work towards this result?

The feasibility of the process envisaged for this displacement is, in my view, a touchstone of sociological credibility. A caveat must be laid at the outset against the belief that because we can form and conceptualize a heart's desire, we must be able to fulfill it. Whether I don my jurisprudential hat or my publicist hat, I see few signs of any tendency for sovereign states and their apparatus of coercion to disappear. Quite the contrary. So that if there are at present the beginnings of a planetary human community governed by planetary law based on the consciousness of its human members, these still remain merely interstitial or even underground phenomena.

Georg Schwarzenberger recently teased us by suggesting that even mere utopian prescriptive speculation about world society and world law is worth attention. He pointed out that under the eighteenth-century French *ancien régime*, "the slogans of the bourgeois revolutionaries of the eighteenth century were Utopian. Yet the social and political revolutions of 1789 made them realities."[5] It is unusual for Schwarzenbeger to indulge in facile analogies between the transformation of a municipal society, where centers of decision making are few, localized, and simultaneously seizable, and the international states system, where a multitude of widely dispersed power centers would have to be seized simultaneously to give the utopia even the beginnings of reality. We should be conscious, I believe, of questions of degree, even in utopia.

3. "The Common Law of Mankind"

Wilfred Jenks's broad thesis in his magnum opus of 1958 was that international law is to be seen as the common law of mankind, that is, of an organized community constituted on the basis of states but discharging its community functions increasingly through a complex of international and regional institutions and conferring rights and obligations on individuals. The repercussions of state policy and action transcend the level of interests of states per se and inter se. The increased complexity and interdependence of the relations of nations and the increasing involvement of individuals in transnational relations pressed, he thought, towards a universal law of mankind, towards humanitywide criteria of right and wrong. Jenks thought that we could move to full development and enjoyment of this world law by a great juristic effort of "multicultural," "multi-legal" working over of the vast output of rules emerging from the activities of states and international organizations. Wilfred Jenks was certainly at pains to anticipate and reject any idea that his work *The Common Law of Mankind* (1958) was merely speculative or wishful.[1] He claimed full awareness of "all the strains and stresses to which international law is exposed" but insisted that the issue was not between optimism and pessimism or between belief and unbelief but the overall strength of the empirical evidence.

An initial problem is that Wilfred Jenks presented his thesis as one calling for action primarily by international lawyers and jurists. He therefore struggled valiantly to avoid letting issues center on current matters involving political and strategic controversies. Yet clearly the empirical evidence relevant to the correctness of his thesis includes the most burning political and strategic controversies between states, which at present block from view the supposed law of mankind. It does not avoid this necessity to try, in Jenks's words, "to look beyond the immediate difficulties . . . and to try to gauge the problems and prospects of international law in a longer perspective, stretching from a generation ago to a generation ahead." On this basis, at any rate, he felt able to discount tensions between Western and Soviet blocs, as well as many discouraging implications of events to 1958, and would no doubt have continued to do so thereafter.

Yet what empirical evidence was there in 1958, or is there now in 1983, that the ideological, economic, and military struggles between Moscow and Washington and the struggles between developed and developing states are not a part of the "longer perspective stretching from a generation ago, to a generation ahead" which Dr. Jenks was seeking? While he noted as alarming the unwillingness of most newer states to make standing submissions to the International Court of Justice, he showed little awareness of the very empirical reasons for this refusal to submit to his "law of mankind."

What Wilfred Jenks saw as evidence lay rather in the vast diversification of international activity and treaty making promoted by international organizations, of which he gave an unrivaled *aperçu*. He argued that these developments amounted to a revolutionary drive to a law of mankind and had so transformed the character and content of international law that it could no longer be presented within the traditional framework. The substance, as it were, of the law of mankind was there; it was for the jurists to revise the structure and scope of international law, so that "form" could catch up with "substance" and the new content could be naturalized and normalized into textbooks of international law.

What do the many activities and instruments thus invoked by Jenks amount to as a birth certificate of a new law of mankind? It must be said, first, that some of the instruments offered to show that the traditional system was bursting at the seams had little operative validity even in terms of ratifications. Second, even ratified conventions may not necessarily be of much operative significance. Only when the subject matter and paper obligations are taken along with any reservations, and with the relevant practice before and after the treaty, can the operative content be evaluated as evidence of an existing law of mankind. States are most unlikely to find that they have been robbed unawares of their sovereign virtue by the disarming blandishments of draftsmen of law-making conventions. The significance of much activity of international organizations depends, finally, as Gunnar Myrdal well observed in his *Realities and Illusion in Regard to International Organizations* (1958), on the extent to which governments can be induced to use the organizations as instruments in seeking their own objectives. Their role *in blueprints* for international action is not an adequate substitute for their role *in action*.

All this affects Jenks's profession of faith that "despite all . . . disappointments and difficulties the rapid development of international organization in the last forty years has already created a situation in which international law can exercise a far more constructive influence in the future than it was ever able to exercise in the past." For it is a long way from detailing "a mood for creative progress" since 1914 to affirming that this "justifies a firm faith in the future." Jenks offered seven supporting lines of empirical evidence. The first was the extent to which he thought that the Covenant of the League, the Pact of Paris, and the Charter of the United Nations had barred the use of violence between states. This, I observe, ignores serious legal issues as to the Charter prohibition, as well as an actual world in which major hostilities were frequent when he wrote, as they have remained since, and in which threats of violence, whether by conventional or nuclear weapons, were and are of unprecedented gravity. Second, Dr. Jenks vouched the common law tradition of systematic, authoritative, judicial exposition and development of the law established by the International Court of Justice and its predecessor. Yet, in 1958, the Twenty-fourth Commission of the Institut de Droit International (including Wilfred Jenks as rapporteur) was observing on the regression in, and the poor hopes for, the compulsory jurisdiction of the International Court. His third and fourth supporting grounds were the growth of international legislative action and the development of new rules of customary law through international organizations, grounds already questioned above. The fifth line of evidence offered for the existence of a common law of mankind was the appearance of U.N. forces to maintain and restore order, in forms such as the unified command in Korea or the emergency force in the Middle East. The sixth was the range of operational economic and social activities of the United Nations and its specialized agencies. The seventh was increased international concern with human rights and fundamental freedoms.[2]

It is extraordinary that in a world where fear and magnitude of violence between states had never been greater, Wilfred Jenks still regarded the main challenge of full recognition of the common law of mankind as addressed to the exponents of international law and to be met on the doctrinal level. He acknowledged problems on even this doctrinal level, however. Although for the classical writers and for writers well into the eighteenth century, international law was part both of a general system of jurisprudence and of a universal moral code, and although, he thought, this idea had survived the assaults of positivism, many Asian and Middle Eastern writers, especially Moslems, take (as did medieval Christendom) a sharply different view. Both Christendom and Islam (he could have added China, of course) assumed that mankind constituted one community, bound by one law and governed by one ruler. The character of such a state was entirely exclusive: by definition, it did not recognize the existence of a second world state. The aim of each of these "world states" was the proselytization of the whole of mankind.[3] For Jenks, the challenge thrown up by "the far-reaching changes in the balance of political, economic, social and cultural forces in the world, which have occurred during the last generation" was to produce a synthesis that would reconcile these, and the consequential contrasting doctrinal positions. He declared that we can "deduce a sufficient consensus of general principles from legal systems so varied as the civil law with its multifarious European, Latin American and other variants, the common law with its variants, Islamic law with its variants, Hindu law, Jewish law, Chinese law, Japanese law, African law in its varied forms, and Soviet law to give us the basic foundation of a universal system of international law."[4]

His wishful basis for this he found in acceptance of a "world-wide perspective," already manifest in the arts, letters, philosophy, and the natural and social sciences generally. A vast "multi-cultural and multi-legal-system" scholarly project was called for to complete the unveiling of the common law of mankind. With this unveiling, the refusal of the new states to bow to the yoke of law, by accepting, for example, the jurisdiction of the International Court, would also disappear.

The thesis thus resolves itself into the following argument: (1) We can no longer assume that traditional international law will be accepted by the world, (2) the West must learn to "think instinctively" in terms of Latin American, Islamic, Hindu, Jewish, Chinese, Japanese, African, Soviet, and other major legal systems and must seek in these systems common elements for a universal legal order, and (3) if this is done, we may reasonably expect the newer countries to "accept" the traditional law as an "essential element" in the universal community life in which they share and to recognize Jenks's nine principles as minimum conditions of membership in the international community.[5] Yet Jenks's own account offers little ground for believing that in terms of non-Western state acceptance, these principles had any hope of becoming practicable. The nine principles may be briefly indicated as follows: (1) sovereignty is subject to law; (2) there is a need for third-party judgment and *audi alteram partem;* (3) self-defense is a limited legal liberty; (4) *pacta sunt servanda;* (5) legally vested rights are to be respected; (6) there should be consultation by a state with other states whose interests are affected by its action; (7) there should be liability for unlawful harm to one's neighbor; (8) there should be respect for human rights; (9) international law is not a set of rigid rules, but "living principles" capable of "resolving" new problems.

Jenks was certainly right to worry about the attitudes of many if not of most new states towards international law. However, the assumption that these attitudes could be removed by juristic exercises in enriching international law with "multi-cultural" and "multi-legal-system" elements is a simple *non sequitur,*[6] for this assumes that the problem is basically one of legal-cultural conflict. And this in turn obscures the reality that the attitudes of the supposedly recalcitrant states may arise from demands for basic changes in the distribution of physical and technological resources sanctified by the existing international legal order. Insofar as this is so, the problem is one of a clash of interests, predominantly—as contemporary events, like the struggle over the oceans and the deep ocean bed, the conflicts following the Arab oil boycott of 1973, and those surrounding "the new international economic order" indicate—of material interests, rather than one of legal cultures. Like the ideological, economic, and military struggle between Moscow and Washington, and intermeshing with it, this view directs us to confrontations between states and peoples whose interests are sanctified by the traditional legal order and states and peoples that (justly or unjustly) demand change. These confrontations, moreover, are between states and alliances of states and are not a matter on which "mankind" in any planetary sense has spoken or is able to speak, except through these states. The sociological reality is still a regime of coordination between states rather than a creative acceptance by men and women of the world of Wilfred Jenks's "common law of mankind."

It might indeed by argued that a common law elaborated by jurists on his proposed "multi-cultural, multi-legal" basis would be still more removed from the concerns of ordinary men and women than is traditional international law. Yet throughout forty years of dedicated thinking about major problems of international law, including a lifetime in the service of the International Labour Organisation, Wilfred Jenks sustained his single-minded vision of its adaptability to the fulfillment of human needs. His exemplarity was a constant challenge—not least because of its optimism—to colleagues for whom the world is more complicated and darker than the steadfastness of his own vision would allow him to admit. This optimism permeates his monographs on many urgent contemporary matters, including his massive volume *The Prospects of International Adjudication* (1964), as well as *The Common Law of Mankind.* This last work received the award of the American Society of International Law for being an outstanding contribution to the field. The society had made a similar award to my own more somber work, *Legal Controls of International Conflict,* a few years before; thus, its open-mindedness towards the future is to be admired. I have always hoped (and still hope) that Wilfred Jenks rather than myself would prove to be "the better bet." Yet in the final analysis, my mind still does not go with my heart's desire.

4. Policy-Oriented World Power Process

For Myres McDougal, as well as for myself, merely ideologically or technically oriented elaborations of international law are jejune and even misleading for the expansion of knowledge; and mere power-political elaborations are evasive of the raison d'être of international law.[1] McDougal's focus on "policy-orientation," on values or goals of human beings such as respect, enlightenment, wealth, well-being, skill, affection, rectitude, and sincerity as pursued in "the world power process," is a natural projection of his view of Western municipal legal orders. It shares with my work of the 1950s the conviction that as soon as we seek to give an account of international law in terms of its sociological substratum, we must study international law not merely in relation to territorial state entities but also, and finally, in relation to the human beings constituting the populations of these entities.

While for myself the above truths are the basis of sociological description or ethical criticism of international law, McDougal's inference from them is more radical. For him the study of the human substratum is part of the process of actualization of international law, not merely of sociological description or ethical criticism of it. In either view, such description and criticism are salutary in widening the horizons of lawyers. But when law is collapsed (or inflated) into such description and criticism, so that intellectual study of world affairs is not distinguishable from the operations of national or international authorities inquiring whether particular conduct is lawful or unlawful, many confusions are liable to follow. These include McDougal's own vacillations as to whether his approach should be described as the sociology of law or something else.[2] They flow basically from the fact that such merger surrenders any identity of law to an all-embracing global environment and the emerging and changing goals sought within it. Just because at points of stress the application of international law may require reference to the environment and goals, international law does not have to be merged indistinguishably into them.[3] The present importance of this matter, however, is that insofar as McDougal's "configurative" jurisprudence of international law includes by its terms the whole range of data for sociological inquiry, it is appropriate to examine it as part of the sociological perspectives of the 1980s.

According to this view, precepts are "law" when they are "expressions of community expectations," and international law is what emerges from a process[4] of decision making in accordance with such expectations. Conformity with such expectations is demanded by the basic value of human dignity and is implicit in the majority principle adopted in some form by Western democracies. As a fervent though not uncritical disciple of McDougal and Lasswell has recently restated this principle:

> . . . if the dignity and worth of individuals are to be equal, then the expectations of each individual must be accorded equal weight in the measurement of authority. An equality of weight, in fact, compels recognition of the import of generally shared expectations among the participants of a community—all of the participants of a community. Patterns of generally shared legal expectations that are shaped by both majority and minority preferences, I would argue, are the most useful and objective (even principled, but certainly not neutral) guides for a decisionmaker to follow if one is concerned about democracy, human dignity, and a process of self-determination that involves participation by each individual member of the community.[5]

Doctrines thus summarized permeate McDougal's writings on municipal constitutional law and jurisprudence,[6] his writings on particular fields of international law,[7] and his Hague lectures on international law, power, and policy.[8]

The hazards of McDougal's transposition from the municipal to the international sphere begin at the point of the relation of "law" to prevailing human expectations. Whether a particular notion or method can be thus transposed is a question that may be answerable after the appropriate sociological inquiries. To assume that they are thus transposable at the outset of such inquiries is to block the inquiries *ab limine* by begging the main question. It is clear, for example, that McDougal, in his 1953 Hague lectures, transferred to the international level a group of concepts originally devised for operation on the municipal level, without adequately checking their aptness for the different conditions on the international level. This is clearly true of the postulated goals, of which a version for the municipal context is found as early as 1943.[9] It is also true, with consequences still more hazardous, of the assumed role of the "decisionmakers" which inspires the whole approach.[10]

In the case of many important international matters, there may be no decisionmakers in the law-making sense in which they are found in municipal societies. In a loose sense, there are, of course, as many separate sets of decisionmakers as there are states; but the "decision" must still wait for consensus in some sense of all these several decisionmakers. (It is only in certain marginal arenas of international governmental organizations that any precise analogy can be found to the law-making decisionmaker of a municipal social and legal order.)[11] It is around the point of transmutation of the multiplicity of national and transnational decisions into international *law* decision making that the more specific problems of a sociology of international law arise. But one effect of McDougal's transposition from the municipal to the international spheres is to push these specific problems almost completely out of view.[12]

   In the sense in which McDougal defines it, on many matters international law probably does not have any general decision-making process yielding effective and authoritative decisions concerning distribution of values. Yet the fact that such a process is lacking on many matters is no reason to redefine international law in a way that makes unanswerable even the more straightforward questions of whether conduct is legal or not.[13] It is shared ground, in short, to assert that international decision making (including law making) ought to assure and elevate human dignity by conforming to human goals, values, or expectations. It is quite another thing, and not shared ground, that a precept offered as a precept of international law is not such until a certain relation of it to the furtherance of human dignity in the present global circumstances has been demonstrated to the satisfaction of indeterminate levels and ranges of decisionmakers. For this last position forecloses (by begging) the very questions of the relation of international law to human claims, aspirations, and expectations, which should be a main field of inquiry for the sociology of international law.

   Moreover, as I have shown in preceding chapters, whenever state entities prevent reliable access to the human beings who people the various states, the extension of knowledge of the relation of the precepts of international law to the wants, aspirations, and expectations of human beings may be barred *ab limine*. Studies in other areas, for example, of the relation of international law to the activities of officials of various kinds and at various levels, remain feasible. McDougal's approach, however, peremptorily and rather strangely ignores the possible existence of this bar to knowledge of the human substratum.[14] For him, the urgencies and intractability of the human situation under existing international law inspire "the formulation and implementation of an international law of human dignity." It is international *law* that he is to discover and proclaim to this end, not mere sociological knowledge concerning it.

   The emergence of this international law involves the projection from Western municipal law onto the world stage of the "goals" of "human dignity and respect," embracing in these "power, respect, enlightenment, wealth, well-being, skill, affection, rectitude and sincerity," the study of "the participants in the world power process," and their techniques of policy formulation and decision making. The principal decisionmakers, filling more or less parallel roles in the "world power process," include international governmental organizations, transnational political parties and pressure groups, private associations, and individual human beings, along with nation states themselves.

Towards an understanding of international law and its sociological substratum, the following points should be made concerning this whole program.

1. To the extent that McDougal does finally concern himself with the sociology of international law, he seems to treat it as a means, not of extending our range of cognition, but rather of equipping decision-makers to operate the "world power process" in furtherance of his postulated common "goals" or "base values."

2. This know-how conceivably could be provided without extending the boundaries of knowledge or the relation of international law, and the goals pursued by its decisionmakers, to the claims, aspirations, and expectations of the world's men and women. It conceivably would be done, for example, by means of the know-how now emerging of the manipulation of human genetic endowment. Indeed, decisionmakers may be able to further the postulated "goals" by manipulating the "world power process" without knowing anything more than is implied in the goals about any human beings other than the other members of the elites who are the actors in the operative "world power process."

3. McDougal's aspiration is to embrace in the total "context" of his "comprehensive" system all the individual human beings who make up the populations of the various states. "The context," he says in his methodological article, "embraces all persons and groups who are in continuing interaction with one another." Further, "the important actors in community process, at all levels [are] individual human beings." These act through local, regional, and national communities or through the global community. These individuals affiliate with not merely nation states but "local territorial communities, international governmental organizations, political parties, pressure groups, tribes, families and private associations of all kinds." He chides colleagues no less than Max Huber, Charles de Visscher, and Percy Corbett for their more "constrictive notion of a community of States" and complains generally that the sociology of international law has not appreciated "the relevance of an anthropological view which comprehends the whole of man's cultural experience."[15]

The assumed heart of this "jurisprudence of international law," within which the sociology of international law is thus embraced but not distinguished, is "the interaction and interdependence of all individuals in the world," including their relations across frontiers. "Interdependence," which embraces communications (physical and human), includes interdependence of "cultures," interdependence of minimum security, and interdependence in pursuit of "every value which human beings covet." His theory, then, he believes, recognizes "the highly personal impact of all this interaction and interdependence upon the lives of individual human beings."

Even as he thus appears to enthrone human beings centrally in the "world power process," he hedges against the need for empirical attention to them by observing that the complexity and range of the world process may "dwarf, if not obliterate, the effectiveness of any one citizen." He then hedges against that hedge by supposing that the greater knowledge that his own inquiries would bring would allow individual participation to be more widely dispersed. As he stipulates the requirements for such participation by individual human beings, it becomes clear that they cannot be really satisfied before McDougal's "jurisprudence" of international law has already borne its fruits. But this means, of course, that the place of individual human beings in the sociology of international law, which is asserted to be fundamental, is pro tanto illusory. And in the end, Professor McDougal confesses that these are but impressionistic remarks about "the individual human beings' increasing role in and responsibility for world affairs." Even here he does not advert to the problems presented to his enterprise by the nationalization of truth and the role of state entities in this, as raised by me in the 1950s and here further discussed.[16]

4. In any serious effort to tie these matters into a sociology of international law, the postulated "*common* goals" must somehow be checked against the actual "goals" of the men and women who make up mankind. In other words, the operations and outcomes of the "world power process" would have to be checked for correspondence to people's actual claims, aspirations, and expectations. McDougal seems to imply this when he observes that "from the *perspective of scientific description* the individual human being is the ultimate actor in all arenas" (emphasis added). But he offers no serious answer to the question of how his comprehensive approach is to conform to this truth. While his strictures on such terms as "national interest" and "international interest" may be salutary, he seems less than candid about the difficulties of his own distinction (or lack of it) between "general community interest" (and related notions) as seen, on the one hand, by the observer and, on the other, by the members of the community. If, as in his text, the ultimate actors are assumed to be individual human beings, should not this assumption entail empirical checking as to what is the "general community interest" as seen by human beings in the actual world? And how does he propose to do this except through the eyes of observers? or indeed at all?[17] In one breath, indeed, McDougal seems to chide the late W. G. Friedmann for his failure to check

"values" against people's empirically found expectations and ambiguously declares international law to be a "process of authoritative decision making, in which the peoples of the world, in organised as well as unorganised interaction, clarify and implement their common interests with respect to all values." The word *peoples* is, indeed, a word for all seasons! In his own discussion of the relation of "authoritative decision" to "social process," there is no consideration of the problem of accessibility to empirical inquiry of the claims, aspirations, and expectations of individual human beings. Yet he also emphatically agrees with Friedmann that "respect for the human being . . . is a foundation of all social and therefore legal relations."[18]

Of course, this practical neglect accompanying theoretical emphasis on the meaning and impact of international law for human beings is often found among publicists. Among recent examples is James Fawcett's *Law and Power in International Relations* (1982). Fawcett sees typical "practitioners" concerned with the formation, execution, or support of policy, and so on, as ministers, diplomats, and their legal advisers. Despite the ambitious title of his book, Fawcett acknowledges that what he is providing is but "a description of how law and power work with and against each other in international relations" (9–10). Even then, he purports to present international law as law of a community of human beings (albeit "in an early stage of evolution"), in nations made up of "hundreds of thousands of crosscutting social roles" and confined by forces including law and power, so that he is suggesting that somehow the relations involved may be reducible in the end to those of individuals. But finally, at any rate, he has the frankness to conclude that only aggregate behavior can be adequately studied and that "structural features chosen to classify national actors are quite gross."

5. McDougal indicates little awareness, or at any rate concern, for the grave difficulties of checking "values" against people's empirically found expectations discussed in the preceding paragraphs and above in chapters 1 and 2. For as soon as this checking for correspondence is taken seriously, this part of the sociological enterprise is, I have shown, stopped short. It is stopped short by the difficulties, in most state communities, of saying how far official "decision making" is a response (and corresponds) to individual citizen attitudes and behavior or how far, on the contrary, these attitudes and behavior are mere responses to conditioning activities by official decisionmakers and are (above all) outcomes of each state entity's domination over its citizens. In the field of international law, as I have suggested above, this difficulty may amount to virtual impossibility.

McDougal himself notes in his Hague lectures[19] his own earlier comments on the "movements towards 'garrison-police' States . . . with increasing militarisation, governmentalisation, centralisation, concentration and regimentation, and in which all values other than power are 'politicised', in such practices as . . . the 'requisitioning of talent and skill', the 'administration of hate' and 'withdrawal of affection', the 'requisitioning of loyalty', the 'dogmatisation and ritualisation' of rectitude, and so on." Yet he does not advert to the obstacles to basic sociological inquiry, and to his own program, that this state of affairs brings with it.[20] For him it merely signals the urgent need for a grand plan for promoting "an international law of human dignity" which must rest on "the plenum of social reality."[21] And it is perhaps characteristic that when McDougal insists on the "relevance of the total world community context," he invokes the classic natural law vision of Francisco Suarez, not empirical studies of twentieth-century men and women.

Our world, however, is not that of the sixteenth century. And we are not entitled after this lapse of time automatically to identify what seems ultimately right, or even what is right as a next step towards ultimate right, with what is feasible at the present stage of history. As Richard Falk has pointed out, the implicit confused identification of the sociology of international law with international law itself, which has the effect of intruding the world context into each particular decision, prevents uniform application and is incongruous with the nature of any but the most "primitive" law.[22] This confusion is not clarified by McDougal's introduction of the notion of "world public order." As Young observes, McDougal swings in his use of this term between meaning (*a*) the processes protected by the patterns of legal decisions, that is, of the "effective" and "authoritative" decisionmakers, and (*b*) the maintenance of international peace. Neither of these is different from the loose usages in general currency. "It is hard to see any uniquely legal element, point of view or methodology embedded in the phenomenon of world order itself, unless the whole notion of world order is simply absorbed into the category of legal analysis by definitional fiat."[23] I would add that fiat alone cannot clarify the relation between international law and world public order. Social systems, especially primitive ones, moreover, may have order without law, even in the decision-making sense. International law may be such a "primitive" social order.

James Fawcett has recently reached a similar collapse of international law into its social, political, and economic matrix, proclaiming international law to be "a product of authority, influence and coercion, national interests and common objectives, and . . . the outcome of all of them together." From a mountain of General Assembly resolutions, for example, he concludes that "the authority of the General Assembly in declaring rules or standards which *can* serve a clear and accepted common *interest* of nation-states, is reasonably high, but is low where there are conflicts of interest between them." We are not told how the "common interest" (singular) of states is related to "national interests," which Professor Fawcett also insists "are for any nation-state *multiple*."[24]

How this can help in determining legal matters is also not clear. But from this and other studies in Fawcett's volume on power frontiers, economic power, human rights, and the like, Fawcett feels able to present the following conclusions. First, legislators and their constituents "may not be much concerned with law." Second, while practitioners such as "ministers, diplomats and their legal advisers"may have to be more or less "legalistic,"this may not necessarily mean genuine appeal to law but may be a mere tactical use of law and (between the two) appeal to law as a public relations measure or as a basis for further negotiations. Third, judges and arbitrators have the somewhat different function of identifying and applying the law or deciding *ex aequo et bono,* though, if anything, jurisdiction of such organs has decreased since 1939, despite a fivefold increase of states since that time. Thus, Fawcett seems finally to conclude, "the authority" of international law is not as rules but as part of processes of cooperation, exchange, and conflict. While states have some common interests in predictability, these do not have a constant pattern. "In sum, law cannot itself create order in international relations but emerges as a fact of life where there are minimum degrees of order, which it may serve to rationalize and extend."[25] This cautious assertion shares some of McDougal's merger of law into sociological speculation, though this is mitigated by its avoidance of either utopian or scientific pretension.

6. In view of such objections, it may seem necessary to explain how, in a number of major works on, for example, the international law of use of force, the law of the sea, interpretation of agreements, human rights, and the law of space, McDougal was apparently able to expound international law in terms of his "process of decisionmaking."[26] The explanation lies, I believe, in the fact that while in his analysis he takes cognizance (more or less) of empirical data concerning the parallel decision making of officials of state entities, international governmental organizations, transnational political parties, pressure groups and private associations of all kinds, and also, ostensibly, individual human beings, the empirical facts marshaled concerning the participation by individual human beings are, to say the least, shadowy. McDougal might say, perhaps, that individual human beings "participate," at any rate passively, insofar as they are the beneficiaries of the values of "power, respect, enlightenment, wealth, well-being, skill, affection, rectitude and sincerity" to which he requires all decisionmakers to give effect in their decisions. Yet these values themselves, much less particular versions of them, are not presented by him as validated by empirical inquiries in the substratum of international law, but seem to be introduced rather *ab extra scientiam.*

That the vision of values controlling the "world power process" is an instrument for guiding decision-making elites rather than extending knowledge is not inconsistent with his translation of important branches of international law into these terms. It is well observed that the main principles of international law, even as traditionally approached, are problematic or indeterminate to an unusual degree. The introduction into them of further indeterminacies from a plurality of unranked levels of decisionmakers additional to states, seeking to realize rather indeterminately stated and frequently conflicting goals or values,[27] may change the language of exposition. What the resulting change in substance may be and whether the appropriateness of such change could be confirmed by empirical evidence are left in doubt by the preexisting uncertainties of outcome in any case affecting principles of international law.

Young has made the stern comment that the concepts, methods, procedures, and so on, of McDougal's approach provide clear "order of march" into any specific legal topics, and "systematic applications of the apparatus to specific topics produce large tomes that tend to display the characteristics of outlines or agendas for additional research, despite their bulk." He adds that sweeping formulations like "world public order" or "human dignity" may make very important and difficult problems of conflicts of goals rather invisible.[28] Certainly, McDougal has proposed the induction into the materials of international law of a rather imprecise range of decisions hitherto neglected. His work may thus promise contributions to the data of the sociology of international law. To what extent new data of this kind will illuminate the outcomes of that law for the human population of the planet, or the impact on that law of the empirically found claims, aspirations, and expectations of that population, is quite problematic.[29]

7. There seems to be little empirical evidence, in the generation after the doctrinal elaboration and application of international law as "policy-oriented decision-making" in "the world power process," of any improvement in performance of various decisionmakers in realizing McDougal's own postulated goals or values.[30] The skeptic could say that in major respects the empirical evidence is in the opposite direction. In the world since the emergence of the United Nations and of the McDougal-Feliciano blueprint for international control of use of force,[31] the cases of major armed hostilities (neither controlled nor even stigmatized as aggression) passed one hundred by 1970 and are now well into the second hundred.[32] Despite massive work by McDougal and his colleagues on the law of the sea,[33] what the Third United Nations Law of the Sea Conference has secured in terms of their postulated goals, after unprecedented series of great sessions, still remains, as 1984 opens, to be seen. It has, however, brought into additional doubt and chaos much law that was long regarded as settled.[34] And the relation of outcomes still hoped for to the "power, respect, enlightenment, wealth, well-being, skill, affection," and so on, of the men and women of the planet rests rather in conjecture.

As to the law of human rights, which McDougal has also announced in a "comprehensive context" of "world public order,"[35] there can have been few generations of the modern era in which human rights have been more constantly, savagely, and ubiquitously violated.

8. Despite the constant pretensions of empirical inquiry, the reality emerges that contrary to first appearances, the "policy-oriented . . . world power process" approach has found no way through the impasse presented by the state's control of human communication across frontiers to the pursuit of empirical knowledge about the relation of international law to the human level of its sociological substratum.[36] It has perforce had to substitute for empirically found claims, aspirations, and expectations of human beings of the world the views of various elite decisionmakers, especially bureaucratic elites of states and international governmental organizations and, presumably also, observers like McDougal himself, as to what these "common" claims, aspirations, and expectations are. The fact that more traditional international lawyers indulge similar misleading pretensions when they identify a state with its people does not excuse McDougal's more ambitious claims.[37]

The complaint has indeed arisen (in the field of municipal constitutional decision making), even among McDougal's adherents, that he seems to substitute the elites' views about people's "common" interests or values for empirical attention to the interests and values actually pressed by people. For example, J. J. Paust has called for attention by the decisionmaker to empirical data evidencing what expectations are shared by the community, rather than reliance on the decision-making elites' "clarification and implementation of the common interest."[38] So far as international law is concerned, where the empirical data as to expectations would involve thousands of millions of people governed by more than 160 state entities, McDougal could offer better reasons than in the municipal field for avoiding empirical inquiries and relying on the decisionmaker's (or his observer's) more or less subjective view of the "common expectations" of the community. For it is impossible to see how, in the presence of the dominant state entities, the decisionmaker could overleap most of these entities, with their jealous control of communications, distribution, and stereotyping, to make even a rough empirical assessment of actual human expectations in the planetary community.[39]

So far as "observers" à la McDougal are concerned, McDougal states quite explicitly that their tasks far transcend empirical observation. The insistent question, he says, must be: "What basic policy goals is [the observer] as a responsible citizen of the larger community of mankind or of various component communities, willing to recommend to other similarly responsible citizens as the primary postulates of world public order?" The "basic public order goals," he says, "must be explicitly postulated" by the observer, and for this reason he is a "participant." As I have shown, he lists the "goals" without claiming any more empirical evidence for them in human expectations than general references to national constitutions, human rights covenants, and self-evidence; at the same time, he denounces those who rely on "transempirical" or "highly ambiguous" derivations of goals. He seems unaware that his own postulations may show both faults. So also he chastises "historicalists" for basing themselves on "shared subjectivities" without checking them (I presume he means empirically checking) by reference to reaction among disparate groups. Yet, even granted "candid postulation" by those who follow him, are they not similarly proceeding (without empirical checking) on "shared subjectivities"? The subjective reality is not concealed by eloquent but abstract invocation of "human dignity" of "all men everywhere," implying a "wide rather than narrow" shaping and sharing of values, including power.[40]

9. Before concluding, I must make reference to a number of semantic and methodological matters elegantly raised by Philip Allott concerning this McDougal school of thought.[41] First, the "urgency of the style and nature of the argument" often leave the reader unwilling either to assent to or formulate a different view. Second, the "controlled intellectual confusion" of the presentation is no different from that of good traditional writing. Third, the McDougal approach is therapeutic in making it apparent that international law is not ready-made for instant application, rather than constructed in course of application. And construction requires attention to the respective claims and contexts of claims of the opponents. Fourth, the *apparent* relativism of this kind of work conceals its absolutism and subjectivism, to the point of "passionate" assertion, behind the constant use of such words as "fair, reasonable, right, incorrect, misleading, unfortunate, important, profound, vital, fundamental, of great significance, most desirable, arbitrary, intense, unnecessary, little justification, recommended, wholly adequate and, above all, ought, should, may." Fifth, this approach offers not merely possible answers but the right answers, apparently on the basis of appealing to readers sharing the values imported by terms like those just listed.

Sixth, acceptance of the assertion, then, depends on whether McDougal's values are shared; and if they are not, it depends on whether he can demonstrate rather than assert the value or the preferability of one or other of the conflicting values. Seventh, if the McDougal value-criterion is taken to be a fervent "international utilitarianism," it would be unfortunate to treat it (as he does) as a criterion *for finding international law* to be used by those applying law in day-to-day conflicts, *inter alia*, because it would lend itself readily to Marxist or power-political interpretations and because it downgrades the relevance of past experience. Finally, if law finding in every case "is laid open to an explicit battle of interests and values, who then is to be master? Or . . . is the finding of the law to become an endless, actual or simulated process of negotiation?"

It will be apparent that all of these points except the third represent criticisms, sometimes rather severe, of main positions of McDougal's "policy science." Indeed, as recently as 1982, Rosalyn Higgins, the most notable British international lawyer to associate herself with those positions, found it necessary to attempt a defense against these criticisms of Philip Allott.[42] Rather more surprising than this are the contents of the paper that Allott presented to the British branch of the International Law Association on 15 May 1982, entitled "Power Sharing in the Law of the Sea," for Allott's own presentation of this subject matter utilitizes many, if not most, of the features of "policy science" thinking on which he had stringently (and cogently) commented a decade before. Allott does not explicitly abandon these earlier criticisms, though he does observe that the "rationalistic naturalism of some modern international law theory [such as McDougal's] may be more of a coherent underlying ideological structure, however dimly perceived by the participants in international society, than is normally supposed."[43]

The 1982 positions were taken incidentally to an account of the Convention of the Law of the Sea opened for signature at the end of 1982. Their professed purpose "is to suggest a particular and unified structure of ideas within which the significance of the Convention may be perceived as a whole," which also bears upon "the significance of its individual provisions," as well as "our general perception of contemporary international law and society." If this undertaking were intended only as a socioeconomic, political, and ideological study of the momentously laborious negotiatory process from which the Convention on the Law of the Sea emerged, it would not be subject to comment in the light either of Allott's own 1971 positions or of my own position. Unfortunately, the paper at a number of points offers approaches to problems, and language for discussing them, that are indistinguishable from those that face arbitrators, judges, or other practitioners who will have to interpret its complex provisions. And indeed Allott is bold enough to suggest at one point that the insight he provides has contributed to the solution of a list of some of the most intractable legal problems of the *fin de siècle,* namely:

the recognition of states and governments
the right of self-defense
the imposition of trade and other sanctions not under Security Council
   authority
the expropriation of foreign property and investments
the transnational protection of industrial property rights
interstate weapons supplies
the determination of matters within the domestic jurisdiction of a state
the military use of outer space
the application of the principle of *jus cogens* to treaties
the determination of so-called international crimes (including aggression)
   otherwise than by decision of the Security Council
the exercise of criminal jurisdiction (including the so-called effects doctrine
   and extradition, political offenses, and political asylum).[44]

All the problems here canvassed become graver when it is recalled, in conclusion, that McDougal's indicia for "authority" of an international decisionmaker are at least indeterminate and possibly circular. He suggests that decisionmakers who have "effective power" supported by threats of "severe deprivations," and so on, manifested by "frequencies" [presumably of application] are "authoritative" but that this does not include "sheer naked power" or "naked power." (And when is nakedness not sheer?) Yet in the same exposition, he ventures to criticize H. L. A. Hart for offering "no means of protection against the error of mistaking pretended authority for power that is both authoritative and controlling."[45] Should this question not finally be directed to his own position?

10. In view of the preceding difficulties, we need mention only briefly the questions concerning aptness for the sociology of international law of the particular elements of what McDougal is always concerned to call the "configurative" approach based on the thinking of the lamented Harold Lasswell. In Young's view, for example, Lasswell's "configurative elements" (participants, perspectives, arenas, values, strategies, outcomes, and effects) and his list of values and sevenfold classification of decision elements, relied on by McDougal, constitute only one of a number of divergent and competingly available social science frameworks. In Young's view, these elements only help McDougal's approach by providing concepts, which are then not used to expand knowledge in social science. These conceptualizations, he adds, have been a mixed blessing, since they have "done more than anything else to alienate lawyers and legal scholars." On these points, especially the last, I feel compelled to agree.[46]

5. Law As Functional Ordering of the Planetary Human Community

Richard Falk's ambitious and dynamic "world order model" for a functional planetary law that would supersede international law begins at points beyond where Jenks and McDougal stopped short. Like Jenks, Falk has no faith in the consensus or cooperation of sovereign state entities as a basis for developing an adequate world law, though as to the reality to be substituted, he is as preoccupied with its homocentricity as Jenks is neglectful of this.[1] Like McDougal, and in part following him, Falk rejects any exclusive role of the state entity in the law-creation process. But unlike McDougal, he sees as the only replacement possible a law based directly on the claims, aspirations, and expectations of the human community, substantially superseding and not merely supplementing the regime of coordinated state sovereignties. Moreover, again unlike McDougal, Falk courageously confronts the fact that a homocentric planetary law must take seriously the expression of the claims, aspirations, and expectations of the human members of the planetary community: the mere attribution of a "common interest" to them by decision-making elites is not enough.

Since, like me, he is aware of the blockage and distortion of human communication by the operations of state entities, Falk recognizes that transformation requires historical transition. A period is required during which the consciousness of peoples within their present state societies can be raised to a level that transcends national arenas and concerns. It must be raised to a level appropriate for basing the law of a single interdependent planetary community in a crisis age of impending scarcity of resources and nuclear perils.[2] This, of course, is an ethical program for evolutionary action towards a planetary law emanating from the claims, aspirations, and expectations of the world's population, rather than in itself a perspective on the sociology of international law.[3]

In his own summation of 1974:

> Put simply, the planet is too crowded, its resource base too constrained, its social structure too hierarchical, and its political structure fragmented and

33

overly responsive to the concerns and interests of dominant groups to allow for an easy transition to a global community where the needs of the species for survival with dignity could be established. As such, the pressures are mounted against mechanisms ill-conceived for such global integration, and the options narrow to various frantic efforts to stave off disintegration, by refusing to heed the formulated aspirations of peoples. Can this holding operation of the state system succeed? Do we as citizens of a given time and place and members of a species want such a strategy to work during our lifetime? Are there alternatives for the future that transform world order without breaking it asunder? . . . New sparks of political consciousness must be struck if we are going to be able to effectuate a world order solution that serves the interests of the human species as a whole. The only viable moral premise for politics in the sociological age is an anthropological one.[4]

He calls for the design of models of legal solutions for transition problems but recognizes that "the need is more for techniques of getting from here to there than of a vision of what it will be like there," involving the study of "processes of social transformation."[5]

This proposed study is a program that presupposes a certain sociological perspective. It presupposes, for example, (1) that international law, as a coordinated system of sovereign states, cannot meet the contemporary demands of peaceable coexistence or even human survival; (2) that the mere extension of the range of decision-making elites à la McDougal cannot remedy this inadequacy; (3) that state entities by their very existence prevent the spontaneous emergence across frontiers of the planetarywide general awareness of people necessary to support institutions performing essential planetary functions. These sociological propositions base Falk's world order model action program, which is directed at maintaining and spreading among national communities the necessary planetary consciousness to overcome the insulating effects of state entity domination over trans-frontier communication. This action program seems to proceed on two further sociological presuppositions: (4) that state entities will not be aware of, or will be tolerant of, or will become so weak that they will submit to the truncation of their power in the transition to a planetary legal order; and (5) that there will be such submission by a sufficient number and range of state entities to allow the new plantetary institutions to begin to function effectively.

This chapter is concerned with sociological perspectives, not with the acceptability of particular utopias. But it is within the scope of sociological inquiries to comment on the assumptions on which action programs proceed. And it must be observed at the outset that if it is accepted that the richer peoples must assist and maintain at any rate a minimal subsistence for all less fortunate members of the human community, Falk is probably correct in believing that this cannot be done except through a functional

law based on planetary consciousness of human beings. No mere coordinated action by sovereign states as at present can fulfill such a task. The
reasons for this need spelling out, for at first sight the contrary is already
the case.[6]

Thus it may be said (and this is more fully discussed below in chapters 9
and 11) that the more developed states, including Communist states, have
already accepted, each for its own municipal society, the entitlement of all
members to a minimum level of subsistence, as well as a duty to help
underdeveloped countries, whether bilaterally or through international
agencies, and by aid or trade to move their peoples towards a minimal
subsistence. Since the same governments conduct the domestic and foreign policies of states, will they not accept the obligations of a "welfare
world" just as they have accepted those of the "welfare state"?

It is tragic that this argument may fall apart, as will later be seen,
because most of the governments concerned are democratic. It may be
precisely the attitudes of their peoples as voters that prevent any easy
extension from the municipal to the planetary sphere. For it is most
unlikely that democratic governments will be maintained in office past the
point when foreign transfers substantially reduce standards of living that
electors have grown to expect or when inflation or other economic
disasters threaten these standards.[7]

Falk's call for bypassing state entities by raising planetary consciousness
so as to transcend national arenas follows well enough from this sociological reality. It would seem in itself to justify the first three presuppositions listed above. While it is perhaps imaginable that all developed states might come to have dictatorial leaders strong enough to
dispose of the national resources at their own discretion and righteous
enough to use such resources to provide subsistence for all members of
the human community, the prospect of such a combination of humanity-
loving irresponsibles appearing concurrently in all the relevant states is
truly minute.

Finally, then, Falk's thesis is that the mere aggregate of present state
sovereignties cannot as such constitute a meaningful human community
in which justice can be dispensed. It recognizes that the existence of these,
with their present prerogatives, also blocks that access to the claims,
aspirations, and expectations of the men and women of the planet which
is needed to base a truly homocentric law and inhibits the growth of a
sense of commonalty among them. Yet Falk would insist that even then we
must try to maintain and extend (and where necessary create) the integrated vision and elaborate its implications, if the obstacles presented by
the existing state basis of organization are to be overcome. And we need to
devise strategies for overcoming them.

The fourth and fifth presuppositions, namely, that the power centers
of a sufficient number of state entities will be tolerant of or too weak to

resist the growth of superseding planetary institutions, are concerned with these strategies. It is no doubt impressive to proclaim the imperative need for men and women to meet the dangers and fulfill the needs that the state system cannot meet by thinking and organizing themselves on a transcending planetary level. Yet the building and integration of planetary functions would not get far without transfer to the new institutions of powers and resources basically controlled by state authorities. It is not easy to see this transfer being willingly made even by "tired" Western governments, let alone by sovereignty-intoxicated Communist and Third World states. The world order model thesis foresees, indeed, a long transition period of discussion, dialogue, "global multilogue," and "consciousness-raising" generally. Yet it remains difficult to see that most of the states that are members of the United Nations would permit even the mere degree of free criticism internally necessary for "raising consciousness" to planetary levels, let alone sufficiently for this to have transnational consequences. The recent story of Communist states and many new states of Asia and Africa, as well as Central and South America, concerning internal dissent is not encouraging. Short of this point, even discussion groups surviving and flourishing within particular states, debating priorities between peace, economic well-being, justice, and ecological quality, on the most admirable humanity-wide level, could scarcely become high-powered agents for planetary change.

Underlying my disagreement on the fourth and fifth of the presuppositions are, therefore, what seem to be certain hopes of Falk that may seem realistic to him but appear utopian to me.[8] One is that men and women generally within national arenas of the developed world can be induced to sacrifice their own cultural and material concerns for the sake of planetary neighbors who are nevertheless, in other senses, especially geographical, quite remote. Another is that the undeveloped nations can be brought in their time of emancipation and national euphoria to similar sacrifices and restraints, for instance, in regard to population growth and pollution. Still another is the hope that the leaders of sovereign states will prefer the long-term interests of the human community, despite all the contingencies to which they seem subject, to what will seem to them to be their own long-term and short-term interests as wielders of present power. And to this end, I fear, Falk also indulges the hope that dialogues, "global multilogues," teach-ins, and the like on the progressive functional integration of peoples will be able to arrest and reverse what I have called elsewhere the tendency to the nationalization of truth.

The sociological issues about which transformations of consciousness at the grass-roots level are feasible are, of course, crucial for the aspiration—the drive—to justice on a worldwide scale. Falk insists that to meet even the modest goals of survival and subsistence, we need to transcend territoriality, that is, territorial allocation of supreme authority to state entities symbolized in the state sovereignty notion central to traditional international law. It seems clear that by this he does not mean complete abolition of territorial sovereign states but, rather, bypassing or progressively superseding them by establishing distinct central guidance systems for areas of human affairs with which states cannot cope. As late as 1968, when he already was speaking of "requisites of order, fairness and restraint" in global society transcending political systems and subsystems of the predominant statehoods, he envisaged that states would, "so long as is foreseeable," possess "predominant power."[9]

Undoubtedly, state sovereignty is a great hurdle to Falk's vision.[10] I have already spoken of this on the side of donor states, and it is vital to see that it is also a great hurdle on the side of beneficiary states. States at present still exercise rather absolute prerogatives over disposal of all valued things, facilities, and skills that lie, by reason of physical location and otherwise, within their domains; over the distribution of such goods among their own people; over any proposed redistribution, which is, after all, a main part of the business of justice in the international field; over support of or opposition to any particular principle or machinery of redistribution. The human benefits from redistribution are also at the discretion of each of the receiving state authorities. At best, they will distribute among their population according to criteria deemed apt for that society; at worst (as already too manifest), arbitrarily or even not at all.[11] Glimpses of outside guidance for distribution of received benefits may be had, no doubt, in operation of agencies like the World Bank, European regional agencies, or U.N. technical assistance programs. They are, however, glimpses only; they afford no promising vistas of abdicating sovereignties.[12]

Even without the present pressures of inflation, unemployment, oil supply, and doomsday forebodings, the roadblocks against movement for a more just planetary redistribution of resources are intimidating. There is the crude but understandable refusal of state entities—even (perhaps especially) in an age of U.N. human-rights euphoria—to allow intrusion of other states and international agencies for protecting their own population from their own power. There is the wide variation of cultures and attendant values that appears to give each state entity, prima facie, better credentials for adjusting conflicting claims of persons among its own citizenry. There is the reality that each state entity claims to be final judge of the scale, pace, and direction of its own material development. There is the related reality, already mentioned, that state entities are the arbiters of the incidence of benefits and burdens of planetary redistributions. To admit this dominating role of state entities may seem a grave renunciation of noble possibilities, though perhaps it is an error to speak of renouncing what is not within our reach. Yet the outcome is still a critical difficulty in assuring minimal rights of personality and substance to all members of the human community.

If we were also to treat some degree of *equality* among all mankind as a present planetary imperative, we would face (if possible) even more impossible duties. The new planetary institution would have to concern itself, for instance, not only with the tempo and methods of emancipation of the Bantus in South Africa: it would have to concern itself with relieving hundreds of millions of Indians from the continuing de facto oppressions of the traditional caste structure of Indian society, with oppressions arising from tribal rivalries in a score of African states; with those arising from ethnic divisions in Malaysia, Singapore, and Indonesia; with the ethnic claims about second-class citizenship in older countries like Canada, Spain, the United States, and the United Kingdom; and with the claims of oppression of the subdued Baltic peoples and other minorities of the Communist World. Most of these states, even those most zealous against South African racial oppressions, would be very intolerant indeed of any such meddling in *their* affairs.

I have agreed, therefore, with Falk's first three sociological assumptions: that the system of coordinated sovereignties is inadequate to meet demands of human coexistence and survival; that a mere extension of the range of international actors cannot change this, nor can individual human beings within the several sovereignties spontaneously organize the performance of the necessary functions. I have, however, had to disagree with the fourth and fifth of his assumptions, which permit him to think that a sufficient number of existing territorial sovereignties, which are so increasingly at variance with the functional logic of the human community, will permit the placement of an alternative system of non-territorial central guidance by transnational groupings of individuals of heightened planetary consciousness.

I continue to disagree on these last two points of the Falk position with the more sadness, since the effect of this seems to be to imprison the human race within some of its most severe present limitations. My reasons have stemmed from our present understanding of the nature of man and the structure of power. I have now to add that the technological and totalitarian tendencies following on some great humanitarian and pacifist impulses of the last century have again confronted mankind in our times with deep currents of cruelty and savagery, in which *homo homini lupus*. This must augur ill for the power of mere rational or functional suasion. With some peoples, what appeared to be deeply moral convictions emerging from millennia of civilization have proved pathetically fragile in crisis. Emancipating nationalisms have fallen too often into the hands of psychopathic manipulators. For most states, in greater or lesser degree, modern techniques of depersonalized mass destruction have moved state policy to new levels of destructive inhumanity.

Even the great virtue of the democratic state—the principle of responsibility of power wielders to citizenry—takes on sinister meaning as it aggravates the splitting and dispersal of moral responsibility for state action, and in this sense dehumanizes critical choice making. Action is attached to abstract entities like self-determination, liberation, self-defense, vital interests, military necessity, or national security, which can rarely be brought to the bar of justice, morals, or compassion. From the abstraction the command moves forward, dispersing as it goes, into the hierarchy of command, often to be almost lost in the complex apparatus of decision making. Even where individuals are active, their convictions tend to be merged (or submerged) under floods of matter which pass, along with lines of propaganda, through the media of mass communication, into the morally vacuous and inscrutable entity known as "public opinion." In nondemocratic states, where government does not proceed on the principle of responsibility, the men and women who sustain themselves in power tend for that very reason to be rather free of moral compunction, in both propaganda and policy. And recent events in Teheran and Libya show that these attributes are shared by traditionalist theocratic as well as secular modernist regimes.

These trends in the organization of earthly powers march with the unprecedented mastery that man has won over natural forces. And this is the very worst conjunction. Formerly, when the physical and biological harms produced by his folly or ineptitude were but modest, people could rely on natural processes to repair it. They can no longer do so. And the population explosion, together with escalating material expectations, increases the temptation for this generation to deplete and pollute resources that rightly should provide for the generation to come. Such developments no doubt are among those that stir the forebodings that move Falk and others to seek to transform international law and the international order it serves. Tragically, however, insofar as these developments reflect on the present moral condition of humanity and not merely on the defaults of state entities, they may raise doubt rather than hope for the enterprise of raising men and women to the planetary consciousness by which Falk hopes somehow to overleap statal centers of power.

Just as I cannot share a hope, such as that of Wilfred Jenks, that ingenuity of juristic reconstructions can dissolve the major conflicts of power-backed interests between states and peoples, so I also finally have to doubt that we can, by heightening planetary consciousness of people, destroy or even tame the imperatives and asperities of the power of state entities. Nor do I see how we can, without the help of the power centers of state entities, control or even guide the power of the multinational corporations, or for that matter of such cartels as OPEC.[13] In sum, if it is impossible to achieve solutions for the gravest problems through traditional international law centered on a coordination of state sovereignties, it also seems impossible to achieve them through a brave campaign for raising the planetary consciousness of all peoples to a point that will transcend state sovereignties.

I have indicated agreement with Falk as to the dysfunctionality of the territorial state system for the most urgent needs of the human community and have differed only on the feasibility of displacing it. I must add, finally, that we also need at this stage to take what comfort we can from this situation. For while state sovereignty should indeed be seen with all its faults, we must still remember that it *can* serve functions that are not *merely* a rationalization of human greed, folly, or madness. It still corresponds, in measures varying from state to state, to certain basic human interests and values, originating in the fact that cultural inheritance is itself usually territorial. And cultural inheritance is a complex of functional values on which men and women, rightly or wrongly, continue to insist today, sometimes at the cost of their own lives. Such functions include the celebration of common experience, the enjoyment of known and understood relations with other group members, and the resolve to express these and perpetuate their expression in successive generations in all aspects of the group's life. No doubt, Falk's nonterritorial central guidance system, adequate to meet the needs of the human community, if it could be achieved, could leave these functional values intact. Short of that, the present United Nations and its specialized agencies could provide no substitute for them, even if these bodies were not already in danger of becoming mere cat's-paws of particular states and alliances of states in power-political struggles and political warfare.

6. International Law and the
Limits of Knowledge

It must be clear, from what has gone before, that I regard the systematic development of sociological inquiries concerning international law as indispensable for the progressive development of international law *de lege ferenda* and also for the clarification of its present content, *de lege lata*. Insofar as the human future is deemed to depend on the role of international law, such inquiries also have importance for that future. I have been concerned, however, to warn against exaggerated expectations from such sociological inquiries and to point out the limits of their potential contribution to our most urgent present problems.

Cardinal among these limits are the obstacles to full-depth inquiries presented by the parlous state of human communication across state frontiers and the related operations of the state entity in inhibiting, molding, and distorting the formation and articulation of human claims, aspirations, and expectations, as well as the transmission and reception of communications. Insofar as a body of knowledge concerning the sociological foundations of international law would have to describe, *inter alia,* the relation between the rights and duties of each state and the human claims, aspirations, and expectations with which a homocentric international law should finally be concerned, these obstacles are obviously grave. To the extent that those human attitudes within states are mere creatures of the inhibiting, molding, and distorting operations of the state machinery, it becomes a circular and naive (if not hypocritical) enterprise to assume that states in these respects represent the claims, aspirations, and expectations of their human population. If state decisionmakers are themselves the creators of the human claims, aspirations, and expectations involved, *cadit quaestio.*

That, of course, is an extreme totalitarian case. The other extreme would be the type of state community in which the attitudes of the state entity exactly represented those of its human members. Neither extreme is found in actual states. What we actually have are various degrees of reciprocating determination between state policies and the underlying human claims and attitudes. That degree will vary from state to state, and from issue to issue, and may present extraordinary complexities within a single state, for example, in the competing roles of the chief executive and Congress in the United States, in the efforts of both to secure the support of "public opinion," and in the final responsiveness of both to the opinion that is finally most articulate and that has the resources or "channels" to make its articulation heard. The ascertainment of that degree in each state at each relevant moment and on each relevant issue is important to any fundamental study of international politics, and necessary for a full sociology of international law as here conceived.

Insofar, moreover, as international law proceeds finally on a long-term consensus (and therefore compromise) between the policies of many states (not to mention other actors), its content at any particular moment would not correspond to the claims, aspirations, and expectations of the respective bodies of citizens even if the policies of each state had initially corresponded perfectly with the claims, aspirations, and expectations of its citizens. Unless it were to renounce the effort to understand the relations of this law to the lives of individual human beings, a sociology of international law would have to inquire into the component elements of this double compromise: between the state apparatus and its human constituents internally and between states inter se internationally. Such an inquiry, even without the blocking, distorting, and stereotyping activities of state entities, would be rather intractable. In the presence of those activities such an inquiry is virtually senseless.

A sociology of international law cannot itself liquidate the state activities affecting the human communication across frontiers that this aspect of its development presupposes. No doubt, we cleave desperately to the hope that the state entity as an insulating and distorting agent in the channels of human communication will stop short of bringing total collapse of communication across frontiers and total inaccessibility of human minds to objective inquiries. Yet, paradoxically, we also assume that state entities will continue, to a degree, their separate ways. There is also a consequential paradox. So far as the factor of communication is concerned, the best condition for the growth of a body of sociological knowledge concerning international law would be either global political anarchy, where there is no *étatisme* of any sort, or a world state. Yet, of course, in either of these two cases, international law as we know it would disappear, and together with it the need for the instant kind of sociological inquiries.[1]

It would seem to follow that a sociology of international law must, for the time being, renounce any tasks involving the explanation of the contents, or of the phases of stability, change, and breakdown, of international law in terms of the claims, aspirations, and expectations of the human beings generally who make up the various state communities.[2]

Yet, of course, many of the sorties into the sociology of international law after Charles de Visscher's *Théories et réalités* in 1953 and my own *Legal Controls of International Conflict* in 1954 have aimed precisely at this most intractable area of the relation of international law to the claims, aspirations, and expectations of men and women. In the present view, sorties into such areas cannot win new sociological ground. They can produce utopian visions, for instance, of the heightened consciousness of human beings overleaping state sovereignties and somehow subordinating them to a planetary common law. This may be a modern form, though a sophisticated and interesting one, of the old fashioned *civitas maxima*. It remains subject, after two world wars and two world organizations, to M. Huber's view of 1910: "An organisation of an imperative nature (*herrschaftlicher Natur*) embracing all States is a political impossibility."[3]

Or such sorties can produce *Programschriften* in which rather indeterminately symbolized goals or values like power, wealth, knowledge, skill, and so on, as listed by the theorist, are attributed to men and women generally and presented to decisionmakers as criteria. No doubt, all these goals and values abstractly symbolized seem desirable to most men and women and in that sense conform to their expectations. But this very fact—like Aquinas's endorsement of "the good" or the preacher's condemnation of "sin"—means that such formulations offer little new knowledge or even directive force. It is the conflict between these values inter se, and between different men and women even as to what may follow from a single value in an actual situation, not to speak of the conflict between realizing the goal in a concrete situation and pursuing it as an overall objective,[4] that characterizes the problems of international law as we seek to move from black-letter law in the books to a living law of the human community in action. To pretend that a display of goals or values will somehow guide decisions that turn on conflict between and within them gives only an illusion of guidance. The critical questions are left, then, to the arbitrament of a miscellany of decisionmakers or to "the observer" who assumes the role of guiding them. And this should not be concealed by invocation of "common" or "shared" "values," "interests," or "expectations."

We have thus perforce to detach ourselves from great visions of a "common law" or "planetary law of mankind" or "policy-oriented world power process" to less exciting tasks that may lie to hand. Reallocations of some energy and talent from the visions to the available tasks, from the messianic to the foreseeable future, from generalized *Programschriften* to particularization of next steps, seem accordingly to be essential. They are dictated at present, above all, by our inability to overcome the difficulties of access to individual human minds required by a full sociology of international law, access at present blocked for the most part by the activities of most state entities.

If, as is here assumed, a sociology of international law must consist at least of the extension of knowledge outward from international law to the extralegal or substratal factors that influence its contents and growth, then its initial data must include the history and contents of international law as presently known. It must move outward from these data to whatever can be known of the factuality, normativity, and positivity of international law. That is to say, we are concerned, first, with the conditions of space and time in which a rule is found and its relations with other spatiotemporal phenomena. The second, normative aspect refers to the meaning and impact of this law as a product of mind and as an expression of values, as an eidetic and axiotic entity. The third, the positive aspect, refers us to the concrete manifestations of these values under these conditions and in these relations, to its existence and operation as a value-related fact, as a complex fact that is also normative, and as a normative entity that is also a fact. These diverse aspects, of course, are mutually entangled. Yet it is important, as far as possible, to examine each separately.

Even if we take the present pessimistic view of the obstacles to full sociological inquiry caused by the inaccessibility of the substratum of this law consisting of individual human claims, aspirations, and expectations, many tasks still remain possible and useful. Even if only because of a continuing faith in man's intellectual powers based on achievements in other fields, the feasible tasks should not be neglected. In view of the great issues at stake, we are entitled to persist in the hope that human powers and insights will rise to a point that will enhance the human community's prospects, despite the compartmentalized world of state societies.

Even if we leave aside that basic part of the substratum thus affected by inaccessibility, there are vast opportunities for extending our understanding of the content, operation, stability, change, and breakdown of international law in its social, political, economic, technological, and psychological contexts.[5] For even when we leave out its relations to the generality of individual men and women of the planet, decisionmakers of international law at all levels are also human, and their choices and actions are contextually molded and constrained. This is a central truth of McDougal's "policy-oriented" "world power process" notion, which is, however, rather concealed by the more ambitious overtones of that description.

Worthwhile inquiries concerning such choices and actions of decisionmakers would include the following. As to law-observing behavior of states, for example, empirical evidence could be sought as to the kind of circumstances in which states observe a rule of international law when this is seriously prejudicial to their immediate interests. How far is observance the outcome of the *kind* or the *importance* of the observers' own future long-term benefits from the same rule, or of fear of superior power, or of the pressure of particular lobbies (including so-called public opinion), or of conviction that the law is binding, or a face-saving cover for a change of policy?

The answers to these questions would often also illuminate law-violating behavior; the answers to other questions, however, also would be fruitful. In what proportion and kinds of cases have states failed to cover nonobservance with attempts at legal justification or challenges to the aptness or justice of the broken rule? And where nonobservance of a rule cannot be tied to rational pursuit of the violator's interests, to what can it be tied? What evidence is there of the role of psychopathologic tendencies in leaders? Empirical data thus gathered as to the behavior of state officials could base a wide-ranging identification of segments of international law that from time to time undergo or are threatened with change or breakdown because of deviant behavior on the part of state officials. They could also suggest diagnoses and remedial measures.

Such sociological inquiries would also help delimit and expose, within the mass of precepts offered by the jurisprudence of tribunals, by doctrinal writings, and even by the body of treaty law, the gaps, concealed contradictions, escapes and evasions, ambiguities, and other categories of illusory reference in official or doctrinal formulations. The law could be tested for correspondence not only with historical origin (a quite traditional inquiry) but also with the contexts of the present day. Among the points of stress in the law thus exposed, priorities could then be allotted for deeper and wider study *de lege ferenda*. Criteria for allocation of such priorities designed to make optimal use of available intellectual resources could be considered. One such criterion would seek areas the investigation of which would cast light on problems in other areas. Another might be to seek areas where the more or less uncoordinated actions of a multiplicity of state authorities mature into law-infringing behavior and where better coordination of these actions would decrease this likelihood.

Studies in the operation of specialized international agencies and the related behavior of state authorities have perhaps been among the most active since 1945. They are important not merely to the functions of the agencies but for our understanding of the limits of state officialdom's adjustment of national to international policies and of states' short-term interests to their long-term interests. McDougal is surely right to stress the need for a more balanced knowledge of the relative roles of decisionmakers from states' international governmental agencies, transnational corporations, and various voluntary associations, even if one cannot follow him in a too facile assimilation of the YMCA and the Universal Postal Union to the traditional state decisionmaker in the "world power process."[6]

These feasible tasks for a sociology of international law lie at hand, and such a program will no doubt be widely extended as work proceeds.[7] Even then, many may see it as too slight and modest in face of the challenges of the times. They may be impressed not only by the remarkable achievements of natural science but also by the perils of world destruction. The sociological study of international law is undoubtedly relevant to survival, but its concerns are really much wider than those of survival; and those other concerns are worthwhile even if they cannot directly contribute to the tasks of survival.

There are, indeed, dangers in being too moved by the apparent close relevance of international law to human survival. When the practical problems of natural science have been found often to yield only after a remote approach far from the level of present urgencies, it would be sanguine to make contemporary international urgencies an exclusive measure of interest for sociological study of international law. As A. N. Whitehead observed concerning the corresponding problem in natural science, "Success in practice depends on theorists, who, led by other motives of exploration, have been there before and by some good chance have hit upon the relevant ideas."[8] Certain features of international law and relations underscore Whitehead's truth for this field. Any generation of people tends to view its problems in terms of individuals of that generation's life span. And this tendency is very strong in international studies, where the forces under examination may on some hypotheses cut short that life span. The resulting pressure on the inquirer to approach his problems in a time dimension adjusted to his own expectation of life, rather than to the ongoing stream of knowledge, is perhaps responsible for some of the oversimplifications, the wishfulness, the haste, the naïveté and the cynicism that, each in its own way, threaten the objectivity of these studies.[9] These dangers can, I believe, be reduced to proportions that are not fatal to the advancement of knowledge, provided the inquirer brings them into full consciousness. To the extent that they can be thus controlled, real guidance may emerge from the compulsions of contemporary international problems, operating on the more general problem consciousness created by attention to the peripheral areas of change and breakdown of international law.

Yet, as will have become clear from my critiques of the ambitious visions of Wilfred Jenks, Myres McDougal, and Richard Falk, even the optimal cultivation of the fields accessible for the sociology of international law will not assure the removal of the most dire threats to physical survival, nor even assure us of movement towards a just planetwide human community and a law that corresponds closely to the claims, aspirations, and expectations of its men and women. This dispiriting reflection, however, bears only on the prospects of the success of the particular reformative enterprise proposed by each of these theorists. It is a different matter whether and how far each vision (or rather its sociological presuppositions) helps us towards understanding the apparent disorder and even crisis of traditional law. We may be unpersuaded by the purposive vision and yet greatly enlightened by the sociological descriptions that base the presuppositions.

In these terms, Wilfred Jenks's manifesto for a great multicultural multilegal juristic reconstruction of international law appears to be least fruitful for the sociology of international law. Its attempted resolution of international conflict into a cultural conflict of ideas and conceptions, especially legal ideas and conceptions, neglects the most critical layers of the social substratum of international law. The cultural conflict of ideas and conceptions is, of course, a real layer within this substratum, which perhaps both McDougal and Falk may have underpresented. Yet they are clearly correct in giving major attention to the elements of human claims, aspirations, and expectations, the goals and values that emerge from these, the planetary resources available for realizing them, and the distribution of authority to allocate these resources among competing claims.

Falk's expanding planetary consciousness of ever-widening groups of men and women envisions international law as a redeemed legal order finally adapted to its homocentric tasks. His view of outcomes is euphoric and optimistic, since these are held within men's purposeful visions. So, in the outcomes of McDougal's process of decision making, at all its many levels, world public order based on the asserted values is ever working itself pure.

Skeptical as I am of these wished-for outcomes, I acknowledge that when the wishful and utopian elements in these two bodies of ideas are stripped away, they may still hold truths of some value for the sociology of international law. The Canadian writers R. St. J. Macdonald, G. L. Morris, and D. M. Johnston, have presented, perhaps without intending to do so, an account of the invaluable sociological residues that remain from these positions in their seminal paper "International Law and Society in the Year 2000."[10] This impressionistic projection of outcomes of present movements in the substratum of international law envisages by the year 2000 the partial ascendancy of planetary consciousness among the men and women of the world arising from transnational contacts of radical movements in the national arenas more or less institutionalized in a "peoples' assembly." This has a clear kinship to Falk's heightened awareness expanding across frontiers, giving reality to functional planetary consciousness. The Canadian projection, however, like that of McDougal and his followers, also envisions that the multiplicity of decisionmakers will continue to include state and regional entities as major actors of territorially delimited competence.[11] Yet, as I shall show immediately, it sees the outcomes of these and related developments as not (or not yet) held within men's purposeful visions, but rather to be accepted *faute de mieux* with all their massive accompanying disorders and frustrations.

The vision presented, indeed, is not of a legal order sought for, but of a chronic legal disorder that somehow keeps working and cannot be escaped, in view of the conflict of power centers and of values sought. Sophisticated subsystems of intergovernmental agencies manned by specialists; state and transnational bureaucracies; and multinational corporation bureaucracies are often in mutual conflict[12] but also—all three—harassed by "coalitions" of anti-statist, anti-bureaucratic, anti-technological, environmental-protecting, and other single-issue "activist" groups supported by "anti-capitalist" and "anti-imperialist" movements, especially in developing countries. These coalitions will in turn evolve untidily into transnational "inter-populist" movements that may be institutionalized into a peoples' assembly of the world, consisting of "peoples' delegates" from most areas.[13] This "peoples' assembly" will de facto both monitor the activities of and bring pressure on the formal international actors, such as the political leadership and bureaucracy of each state entity, the international governmental agencies, the U.N. General Assembly, and the bureaucracies of these. The tangle of relations at these various points and levels will proceed in chronic "unresolved" conflicts superimposed on and aggravating and complicating more traditional conflicts between state and international officialdoms. Indeed, by the year 2000, this Canadian prognosis sees a world in which "traditionalists" will still pessimistically bemoan an international law chronically in "parametric stress," while "radicals" will wishfully proclaim that this stress must herald such a transformation of international law as will ensure that it no longer obstructs a "rational and humane response to the ordeal of the human condition."[14]

The common basis of this neo-Falkian prognosis has recently been more systematically (and certainly more wishfully) stated in Falk's *Normative Initiatives and Demilitarisation* (1982) in terms of the "positive and negative feedback relations" between the First System (of states and their operations), the Second System (of the state-based United Nations and the specialized agencies), and the Third System ("the system of power represented by people acting individually or collectively through social movements voluntary institutions, associations, churches, labour unions," or, briefly, populist movements) (see 5–11, esp. 5–8, 11). Well-informed and open minds may obviously differ as to particular aspects of such projections. The main lines and parameters, however, do provide sadly illuminating insights from the factors operating to support, undermine, and transform the structure and functions of existing international law.

7. Human Values and Disparate
Erosion of State Power

There are still two major questions to raise concerning the relation to the sociology of international law of even a nonprogrammatic, nonutopian transformation of international law. I assume still that international law is to be seen as law made *by* humans *for* humans, that is, as homocentric. I have already shown that neither McDougal nor Falk has made clear how, despite the blocking, distorting, and stereotyping activities of state entities, they proposed to give observers access to the empirical data of claims, aspirations, and expectations of human beings across national frontiers. Without such access, these essential empirical data would be lacking not only for international decisionmakers but also for sociological observers of this core part of the substratum of law. In fact, the very possibility of the formulation of effective transnational popular movements would be forestalled by the barriers at the frontiers. The Canadian projection, therefore, of the growth of interpopulism and of "peoples' organisations" in a "universal peoples' assembly," while state entities maintain their territorial competences, is similarly lacking in empirically grounded explanation as to how this will come about. The explanation, of course, might lie in the expectation that the interpopulism that crosses the frontiers is not grass-roots opinion but the opinion of small, well-organized cells of dissenters protected from the opinion-controlling activities of state entities by either ideology or an unusual level of intellectual vision and integrity, as well as prudence. This would be a very unrepresentative layer of the human substratum.[1]

An even graver question arises as to the Canadian projection's failure to grasp the full significance of the fact—which they do indeed note—that the Western developed states are, comparatively speaking, "open societies," while Third World states, as well as Communist states, generally are not. The present chapter will be devoted mostly to this significance.

It may be argued at this point that the difficulties first raised by me in the 1950s concerning the accessibility to investigation of the human part of the substratum of international law have already been bypassed by history. At the beginning of the 1960s, the view was rather widely expressed that in the modern state, "whether Communist or capitalist, freedom is something exercised within limits imposed by the state, and these limits are such that there cannot be any fundamental disagreement with the broad ideologies of those that govern.[2]

Against these prospects the American experience of the sixties with the Vietnam War, and all its surrounding tragedies and recriminations, offers a ray of hope. Here was a situation in which the U.S. defense establishment, firmly led by the President and supported by congressional resolution, had committed the nation to the use of force to resist (according to the official version) aggression from North Vietnam. The loss of tens of thousands of American lives in battle might have been expected, in such a cold-war arena, to restrain dissentients at home challenging a course to which the state authorities had thus committed the nation. Yet there was a steady build-up of dissent, which certainly contributed to the deescalation and ending of the war. This power of dissent can only be partly explained by the constitutional protection given by the Warren Supreme Court to free speech. During the earlier McCarthy period, after all, opinion was most effectively dragooned by pressures that hemmed in the individual *within* the area of constitutionally guaranteed freedom—for instance, by pressures of ridicule and hatred through the mass media or by blackmailing and intimidatory pressures in the employment relation.

There was thus a dramatic reversal, in an area of "vital" defense policy of a nuclear giant, of the tendency of citizen opinion to become enslaved to the official version of truth and justice.[3] The enduring capacity of the human mind to say its say as to the human future, a capacity that bears vitally on the international future, manifested itself. This suggested that even if the critical decisions of nuclear war or peace must remain "monarchical," the disposing "monarch," especially in a democracy, must give attention to the citizenry as well as the experts. But not all the indications, of course, are positive. In nuclear confrontation this sensitivity may, even if present on both sides, harass and impede rationality of decision or impair the firmness of implementation or the clarity of signals to the adversary. If present only on one side, it raises other great problems.

Even with these risks, the survival of dissenting opinion, asserting itself against nationalized truth and justice, was a major amelioration of the apparent inaccessibility of human attitudes to sociological inquiries. Yet despite the early vacillations accompanying the ritual and bombast of the de-Stalinization campaign, official Soviet "stop-go" signs on the license to criticize have not up to the present finally qualified the monolithic policy stances of Moscow or the role of the state in holding citizens' opinions within the matrices thus set. And the two Chinese springs when the flowers of opinion were bidden to bloom have not become a part of the climate of the People's Republic of China.

The human situation, along with the sociology of international law, would indeed be transformed if we were in the presence of a general retreat of the control by all statal power centers over the content and movement of individual human claims, aspirations, and expectations, especially across state frontiers. The questions must thus be faced front-ally, in 1984, as to exactly how far and where this is the case and what outcomes of the apparent weakening of state domination over individual lives and attitudes (where it has occurred) can be expected in the light of the answers.

For this purpose it is important to observe that what may be called "the Vietnam phenomenon"—the capacity of individuals to check state power by marshaling opinion in defiance of state-sponsored versions of truth and justice—is no isolated phenomenon of the postwar period. Indeed, in a real sense, U.S. history since World War II has been a series of major detractions from the power and prestige of the state entity. On the international plane, indeed, Franklin Delano Roosevelt may have set the tone of the whole period in the West when he made anticolonialism a centerpiece of American policy. This heralded the decolonization move-ment, which American policy continued to press sternly and with trau-matic effects on the strategic positions of Western states. It had, however, little effect on Soviet spheres of domination; on the contrary, it rather gave corresponding reinforcement to Soviet strategic strength.

Internally the great extension of civil liberties under the aegis of the Warren Supreme Court encroached on many traditional capacities of the state to act internally, notably in the field of free opinion and free speech. *Brown* v. *Board of Education* and its ramifications set a course that has already gone far to limit the freedom of the state and its instrumentalities to use functional criteria of merit as opposed to racial-historical criteria based on presumed disadvantage resulting from past state action. Indi-vidual claims to privacy, especially against official intrusions, received vindication and extension. And this, in due course, was to extend amid the scandals and follies of Watergate into hamstringing the intelligence services of the United States. Almost in unison with the increased protec-tion of individual privacy, the movement for reducing secrecy in govern-ment processes matured into the freedom-of-information legislation of the 1970s. The constitutional struggle between the chief executive and the Congress over the control of the treaty-making and war-making powers has had a similar tendency. Whatever the constitutional outcome, the international effects of these trends necessarily inhibited and con-fused the conduct of an effective foreign policy. And the executive power, in all its aspects, received debilitating and humiliating damage during the Watergate affair, which has continued to manifest itself in both domestic and foreign policy throughout the later American administrations. This progressive slicing away of statal authority has proceeded no less in areas that at first sight have less immediate bearing on politics. One tendency of Ralph Nader's consumerist movement, ancillary to its main targeting on the great corporations, was to tar state regulatory authority with the same brush. And a similar parallelism of anti-capitalist and anti-statist tendencies also emerged from the conservationist and environmental movements, accelerated by the historic report of the Club of Rome. The women's liberation movement and the campaign for the equal rights amendment presented the traditional governmental process of the most open society in the world as a product of an age-old male chauvinist oppression. And successive waves of other "liberations" of the 1960s and 1970s—whether of homosexuals, children, the aged, or the handicapped—have imported a similar chronic chiding of the performance of statal authorities.

Underlying most of these discrete developments, and in a sense a condition of their maturation, are three institutional devices of the U.S. legal order, a combination unprecedented even in the common law tradition. One is judicial review of governmental, including congressional, action in the light more or less clear of the written Constitution. A second, is the inclusion in this Constitution of a bill of rights of which the many indeterminacies invite—indeed necessitate—large-scale judicial creativeness. A third is the unrivaled freedom of expression enjoyed by the press and the media within the expanse of "breathing space" afforded by interpretation of the first amendment of the Constitution. The potency and range in fact of this freedom has, of course, vastly expanded under the regime of freedom of information, and with the technical development of the electronic media. The capacity in particular of the television screen, so critical in the Vietnam years, to legitimate by familiarity postures of alienation from the established order (especially the statal order) is of overall capital importance in eroding the authority of all aspects of that order. The very phenomena of alienation that Emile Durkheim saw as ending inevitably in either the madness or the suicide of the alienated came to represent sensational (and therefore eminently screenable) events. The very screening may often turn each latest alienation into still another anti-establishment movement. In this scenario of the sixties, it was the established order, including the statal order, that seemed to retreat, while the alienated often turned to popular movements.

If these various trends towards an open society were common to the principal states participating in the international legal order, sociological inquiries concerning its human substratum would indeed be opened up. All of the men and women of the several states would be able to express, exchange, and clarify, by mutual dialogue (or "global multilogue" in Richard Falk's terminology) within and across frontiers, the goals they hold. The blockage to such inquiries described in chapters 1 and 2 would no longer exist. It is, however, as already observed, also a part of sociological inquiries to ask whether the pattern is common, and if it is not common, to ask by how many and which state entities it is not shared and what the effect is of the resulting unevenness or disparities among states.

Enlightened Americans and other liberal observers, including myself, applauded the constitutional and other developments in the United States sketched above, which have extended the spheres of individual human dignity and autonomy and hemmed in correspondingly the power of the United States and the several states. And they should and will continue to do so, on ethical principle, regardless of the fact that other states such as the Soviet Union, China, Saudi Arabia, or the states of the Third World generally have undergone few parallel developments. No less clearly, however, the fact that the Soviet Union and the Communist states aligned with her, as well as the People's Republic of China and most of the vast number of states of the Third and Fourth worlds, maintain more or less unchecked state control over the attitudes and expectations of human beings within their territorial domains cannot be ignored by the sociology of international law. It is, indeed, of intense relevance. For it means that despite the American and other Western democratic exceptions, the inaccessibility to full sociological inquiries at the human level of the substratum of international law remains a blocking reality so far as the vast majority of human members, as well as states of the world community, are concerned. My opening assessment of the condition of human communication is thus still correctly in place.

We must still no doubt applaud the outcomes as a movement in the realization of values of dignity and respect for the human beings populating the United States and other Western countries. It is tempting also to state this (using McDougal's terms) as a stage in the realization of the goals of human dignity and respect through the "world power process." We may then even draw the inference that this erosion of statal authority and growth of human autonomy enhance prospects of international accommodation. If, however, we made such a further euphoric appraisal, we would be indulging a basic fallacy of thought. For this step involves the drawing of conclusions from an unjustified transposition of ideas (here certain goal symbols) from a few selective municipal contexts into the "world," or "global," context. For according to the empirical evidence, sadly growing rather than fading as we move into the 1980s, the vast majority of the men and women of the world, governed by the vast majority of states, have scarcely begun to vindicate as against *their* governments any comparable sphere of dignity and autonomy. This means that such basic "goals" have no substantial bearing on decision making by the officials of those states and correspondingly little on the "world power process."

If we avert our eyes from these empirically found disparities between human communities and the various state entities that control them, the effect is to distort and even falsify the description of the human substratum of international law that is being sought. Moreover, the consequences are much graver than love's labor lost. They include, as will be seen, the danger that McDougal's observers, or "decisionmakers," will "recommend" choices of which the longer-term effects may be to destroy human dignity and respect (and what is implied in these) in state societies where they already exist, while not enhancing them among most of mankind, which populates the vast majority of state entities where they are still wholly or substantially unrealized.

The hard fact is that very major groupings of the world's states and their decisionmakers adamantly resist the retraction of state power before claims of human dignity both against their own peoples and against other state and nonstate decisionmakers. Free expression and communication of their citizens with each other, and even more with those of other states, and above all any freedom of dissent and criticism of state authority are still the exception. So far are decisionmakers of these states from being guided or even restrained by values such as human dignity that arbitrary edicts, arrests and imprisonments, torture, exile, spurious commitments to lunatic asylums, or "reeducation" are routinely used to repress them. Most of these states—including the Soviet Union and the People's Republic of China—exalt national sovereignty and the absolute power of the state, especially over its own population, above all other doctrines of traditional international law.[4]

It is ironic, in this context, that even those sympathetic to McDougal's positions think that the importance he gave to decisionmakers in national arenas tended (in Falk's terms) to "vindicate" Western decisionmakers and condemn Soviet decisionmakers on particular issues.[5] But this should not affect the deeper issue here raised concerning debilitating tendencies of state power in the West, even if all of McDougal's own particular recommendations conscientiously grounded in his system were found to be "anti-Communist." As Falk also observes, the very "openness" of the "process" that McDougal claims to be law accentuates "the potentiality for plausible manipulation of legal rights and duties by powerful, anarchistic, or desperate states. . . . The McDougalian image is at once too complex and too vague to provide guidance either to national actors or to global institutions."[6]

Even this, however, does not fully reach the gravity of threat that here concerns us. Falk approached nearer when he observed that "if there is an important law-breaker in international affairs, then compliance (with international law) is a way of encouraging unscrupulous behaviour."

Conversely, compliance by a state with international law is only a stabilizing factor "if there is a minimum of mutuality."[7] I would add to this that
"mutuality" would have to include not merely comparable levels of
restraint through guidance by common norms but also comparable capacities to resume freedom of action in case of default of the adversary. And
this, in the present context, is the critical point about the tendencies in the
United States and other Western countries of erosion of state power.

It remains a reality that must be faced, especially by people of liberal
and even radical outlook, that while we applaud the erosion of state power
in the United States and other Western states for the sake of further
realization of the human values of autonomy, dignity, and respect, this
applause cannot rest unqualified as to the international outcomes. It
requires no paranoia to see that so long as the Soviet Union, for example,
maintains its state power impermeable to claims of human dignity and
autonomy, and the freedom of expression and criticism implied in these,
the erosion of state power in Western states, as these claims are there
increasingly assured, represents vital strategic advantages for the Soviet
Union in confrontations with those states.[8]

In this context, we cannot turn off sociological inquiries merely because we are devoted to civil liberties, liberation movements, or even the
full gamut of McDougal's postulated goals. For us to do so may even
ensnare us in Soviet political warfare. The secret of success of the powerful campaign for "peace and disarmament" in the fifties and sixties (of
which we are perhaps witnessing a revival in the eighties) lay in the
attraction of these symbols for liberal minds.

The massive build-up of Soviet nuclear and conventional armaments
proceeded in parallel with the 1950s campaign, as it has in the seventies
and into the eighties. The dangers of self-deception by liberal minds in
the West are now far greater, however. In the fifties it was possible for
such minds to accept the symbol of "peace and disarmament," even if it
did apparently support Soviet political warfare, in terms of the claim of
the Soviet Union for time in which to reduce its vulnerability to U.S.
nuclear weaponry. At present, however, it is above all Europe directly and
the United States indirectly that are militarily vulnerable. Even if we
assume, contrary to Pentagon assessments but as President Brezhnev
asserted, that the Soviet Union neither had nor seeks nuclear superiority
and that "the Soviet Union since signing the SALT-II Treaty in 1979 has
done nothing in the sector of strategic armament that could lead to a
change of the approximate parity agreed upon," the Western powers are
still triply exposed.

First, Western powers remain deeply vulnerable, despite the build-up
of reserves, to interruption of their oil supply, whether deliberate or (as in
the Iran-Iraq War) incidental. This vulnerability increases as the Soviet
Union moves (for example, in Afghanistan) nearer to the channels of

supply. Second, Western Europe is vulnerable to Soviet conventional military superiority in any situation in which the Soviet Union can be sure that nuclear weaponry will not be used. Third, the Western powers are subject to serious moral, diplomatic, and strategic vulnerabilities by dint of the alignment (even when it is called "nonalignment") of Third World states, even if this springs from the largely historical accident that Western states, rather than Imperial Russia, were formerly the successful colonizers.

So that even if the political warfare advantages sought by Soviet play with the "peace and disarmament" symbols in the fifties are condoned or even approved as a defensive Soviet measure, morally justifiable as such, the position is now very different. Soviet strategies, to which otherwise admirable anti-state tendencies in the West now contribute strength in the eighties, are from a basically offensive posture, even if we call this "competition."

The values associated with recent anti-state movements in the West are, as already observed, very precious to liberal minds in their struggle for justice within their national communities. For them to face as a reality the actual international effects of subjecting state powers to human values places them in a true moral dilemma. For the progressive vindication of human values against their own states may make more likely the long-term subjection of peoples of the Western democracies to state power. And this subjection would be to a state or states whose power has maintained itself impermeable to the erosions that (as later generations may come to relate) were "once upon a time" realized in "open" Western societies.[9]

All this is an important part of the setting within which currently resumed Western-Soviet talks on strategic nuclear weapons have to be interpreted. As 1981 drew to its close, diverse explanations could be offered for the build-up of demonstrations demanding unilateral nuclear disarmament targeted at the governments of Belgium, Britain, France, Greece, Italy, Norway, Spain, Sweden, and West Germany leading up to the resumption of U.S.-Soviet SALT talks in November 1981. The kinds of symbols used in the fifties were still operative. They were undoubtedly given much reinforcement, if not inspiration, by a number of strangely inept and uncoordinated foreign policy and defense statements by spokesmen of the incoming U.S. administration in the second half of 1981. No doubt, too, there had long been controversy in some NATO countries, for example, Holland and Belgium, about the projected basing of the new American Pershing II and Cruise missiles. Yet it also has to be noted that the demonstrations on this wide front were preceded by a meeting of sixty-seven organs of the Communist press in Moscow on 6–8 July 1981 which presumably concerned itself with Soviet policy guidelines.

A World Peace Council thereafter met in East Germany on 3–4 October 1981, at about the same time as the International Federation of Democratic Women in Prague, a congress of the European Peace Force in Kosice, Yugoslavia, and a special congress on "the struggle for peace" of the World Federation of Trade Unions met in Bucharest. In these various manifestations, as in the espousal of unilateral disarmament by the British Labour Party and the call of Catholic bishops in the United States for nuclear disarmament, much attention was given to the dangers from the *projected* Western armaments build-up and comparatively little to *actual* Soviet deployments, such as that of 175 medium-range SS-20 missiles and projected Soviet deployment of 100–150 further SS-20s.

Even if the Soviet Union's negotiating positions are stated in an appealingly reasonable way (as President Brezhnev sought to present them in a long interview with *Der Spiegel* in November 1981, immediately before his visit to Bonn) and even if they are accepted at face value, her strategic advantages as a military state relatively immune by its authoritarian structure from freedom of expression and criticism remain formidable to the present day.

Following shortly on the *Der Spiegel* interview of November 1981 and twelve days before the strategic arms talks at Geneva resumed on 30 November 1981, President Reagan addressed a letter to President Brezhnev containing a four-point proposal, elaborated in a speech on 19 November 1981 to the National Press Club in Washington. First, it offered to cancel deployment of the 572 modern Cruise and Pershing II missiles in Europe if the Soviet Union dismantled its own 175 SS-20, 340 SS-4, and 40 SS-5 medium-range missiles already in place capable of striking Western Europe. These existing Soviet units were reckoned as 1,100, including 525 mounted on 175 SS-20 missiles, 340 SS-4 missiles, and 40 SS-5 missiles, with a further placement of 100–150 SS-20s, mounting 300 to 450 warheads projected. This "zero option" sought to eliminate medium-range missiles from the European arena. Second, it offered new negotiations aimed to reduce U.S. and Soviet strategic arms and forces (START, or Strategic Arms Reduction Talks). Third, it expressed readiness to accept equality at lower levels of conventional forces of NATO and the Warsaw Pact. Fourth, it renewed proposals for a conference aimed to reduce the risks of surprise attack or miscalculation by either side.

The careless reader might see in all this a promise of consensus, but it is to be noted first that President Brezhnev's offer was to limit Soviet medium-range missiles to equal the number deployed by the United Kingdom and France, provided no U.S. Pershing II or Cruise missiles were deployed. Its effect would have been for no further SS-20 missiles to be deployed, not the dismantling of her missiles already deployed. The arithmetic, moreover, by which Brezhnev concluded that there was already parity of medium-range nuclear weapons was at odds with that of President Reagan and West German Chancellor Schmidt. Brezhnev saw the present Western total as already 986 units, as against 975 Soviet units, even before the projected deployment of the above further 572 Western units in 1983–84. The main sources of the startling discrepancy are the inclusion in Soviet calculations of aircraft-borne nuclear units from the United Kingdom or France and from Western nuclear-armed submarines. The actual present ratio is more likely to approximate that estimated by the International Institute of Strategic Studies in London, namely that as of mid-1981 the number of Soviet nuclear units in place was three times greater than the number of Western units in place. Brezhnev's offer, moreover, did not refer to reduction of conventional forces. This is a critical point, since the introduction of nuclear weapons in Europe was initially designed to neutralize a widely recognized superiority of Warsaw Pact conventional forces.

The "escalation dominance" devised by the West in face of this conventional-weapon Soviet superiority in the European arena came mainly from the strategic umbrella of American superiority in ICBMs targeted on the Soviet Union in the deterrent pattern of Mutual Assured Destruction (MAD) and partly from the then superiority of aircraft-borne nuclear weapons located in Europe. This escalation dominance came under challenge (if, indeed, it was not quite reversed) in the 1970s, as the Soviet Union deployed against Europe an array of accurate intermediate-range ballistic missiles (IRBMs) of the SS-4, SS-5, and SS-20 types, the SS-20 being both mobile and triple-warheaded. While in theory deterrence of Soviet offensive action against Europe would still be provided by U.S. ICBMs targeted on the Soviet Union, this implied an excessively rigid and automatic escalation to full-scale nuclear war. It was to meet this situation that the NATO Special Group in 1979 recommended the course that has now matured into planned placement of 572 Pershing II and Cruise missiles in Europe by 1984. This plan was initially as much in response to NATO members' fears of Soviet nuclear missiles as it later became a cause of anti-nuclear demonstrations in NATO countries. The abandonment of these Western plans without the dismantling of the more than one thousand Soviet SS-4, SS-5, and SS-20 missile warheads would leave these not only as a potent deterrent to any Western offensive but also as an additional shield protecting the already superior conventional forces of the Warsaw Pact.

The neoconservative prophets of "the present danger" of the early Reagan administration[10] saw this position as disastrous to the West and all that the West stands for even if no shot of any sort—conventional or otherwise—was ever fired. They saw the failure of the Vietnam effort at containment, and the related failure of confidence in American power, leading to the much hailed Kissinger-Nixon shift to a policy of détente, as one source of this danger. The vulnerability of Western Europe to an alleged eleven hundred accurate Soviet nuclear warheads in place, joined to the superiority of Warsaw Pact conventional forces, produced, they said, nuclear blackmail, leading to a preemptive submission by the European members of NATO to Soviet political, economic, and strategic demands. Indeed, they saw this process, already begun with the massive demonstrations in NATO countries, in effect demanding unilateral Western nuclear disarmament or even a nuclear-free zone in Europe. As of November 1981, reportedly one third of all West Germans were ready to accept neutralization in return for unification with East Germany. According to this view, indeed, the United Kingdom itself was also threatened with "Finlandization." A degree of freedom for the states concerned would continue, but only within limits laid down explicitly or implicitly by the Soviet Union, especially in foreign affairs. All would become inescapably subordinated by superior Soviet military power, even without that power being put directly into use against them. Even if this subordination was less severe than that of Byelorussia and the Ukraine or even the Soviet satellites in Europe, it was, the monitors of "the present danger" urged, unacceptable.

Those who regard "the present danger" as exaggerated or even paranoid press a variety of arguments. They urge that there is no reason to identify equality of military power with symmetry of weapons in a particular arena. They point out that ICBMs from the United States, as well as the Soviet Union, in any case already cover Europe, so that additional cover by Soviet medium-range missiles does not basically change the balance. Nor by the same token, they argue, is the West's matching of these Soviet medium-range missiles necessary to redress the balance. They point out, per contra, that since Western medium-range missiles such as the Pershing II fired from Germany could reach targets in the Soviet Union, as well as in Europe, and could do so in less than five minutes, this would dangerously reduce the warning time and therefore enhance the risk of triggering full-scale nuclear war by miscalculation.

Moreover, it is said that "present danger" theorists are proceeding on the basis of a dangerous misunderstanding of the doctrine of "containment" of the Soviet Union. Such theorists place much reliance on the exposition of this doctrine by George F. Kennan in the famous article "The Sources of Soviet Conduct," signed "X" in *Foreign Affairs* in July 1947, calling for "firm and vigilant containment" of Russian expansive tendencies. Soviet "pressure against free institutions," Kennan wrote, can be contained by "the adroit and vigilant application of counterforce" at appropriate points; it "cannot be charmed or talked out of existence." The critics say that the "present danger" theorists give this a doggedly military meaning that ignores the more flexible political meaning that Kennan himself attaches to it. It could be added that in his more recent pronouncements, in 1981, Kennan denied that the Soviet Union had attained nuclear superiority. He has also taken the view that limitation of nuclear weapons is not feasible and that there is no solution to the nuclear crisis except the abandonment of nuclear weapons by both sides. (I have to confess that I am unable to conceive how abolition can be feasible if limitation is not.)

The most impressive case made against the use of medium-range missiles in Europe would seem to regard the Soviet introduction of these weapons and the Western use of them by way of response as equally vain and dangerous. Desmond Ball's *Can Nuclear War Be Controlled?* (1981) has as its central theme the impossibility of restraining the use of nuclear weapons to tactical purposes. The hope behind the introduction is that medium-range nuclear missiles can, by close command and control throughout the conflict, be used as a tactical weapon without involving full-scale nuclear war. But it is precisely each side's command and control system, he insists, that is most vulnerable to the latest generations of accurate nuclear missiles. Whatever the prewar hopes or intents, the command and control systems of each side are "inherently large fixed and soft targets" and would not long survive intact during supposedly limited exchanges. While, for example, it would take thousands of Soviet warheads to neutralize U.S. bomber, missile, and submarine placements, it would take only fifty to one hundred warheads to disable or destroy the U.S. command and communications systems. The temptation to the Soviet Union would be irresistible.

Moreover, the "hot line" device for maintaining communications is designed only for the onset of hostilities. The hot line operates via two satellites—Intelsat IV and Molinya II. Ball thinks that "the four ground stations and Molinya II are particularly vulnerable," so that once restraint in initiation is abandoned, "the availability of the hot line could not be relied upon." The resulting fog over communication between the antagonists would block each side's perceptions of the other's intentions and make it "most difficult to terminate a nuclear exchange through mutual agreement . . . at some point short of . . . urban-industrial attacks." Ball estimates that the imagined tactical nuclear warfare in Europe would involve, assuming that some restraint was achieved, twenty million casualties, and if restraint broke down, at least one hundred million. This conclusion is intimidating enough, even we cannot follow to his further assertion that even if the parties using tactical nuclear weapons in Europe did not deliberately destroy each other's command and control systems, the idea of "controlled nuclear war is a chimera." (I will consider related fears as to "controlled" strategic use of nuclear weapons in chapter 12.) And this final doubt is especially piquant in view of Ball's expressed conviction that American and Soviet war planners know that at its most controlled, nuclear war would be "suicide on the installment plan."

Historically, the deployment of medium-range missiles has been concerned with the tactical use of nuclear weapons and involves different and later questions from those associated with strategic weapons, delivery of ICBMs, defense against them, the SALT I and SALT II negotiations, and now with the START negotiations. As of 1982, however, the Washington-Moscow confrontations on the one hand as to strategic weapons at meetings in Geneva and on the other hand as to medium-range missiles, on which talks had recently begun, were running along strangely parallel lines.

On 7 December 1982, Soviet Defense Minister Ustinov was claiming that there was in fact a near parity in strategic weapons at present and that the U.S. plan to deploy one hundred MX missiles with ten warheads each would wreck the strategic balance and violate SALT I and SALT II. (President Reagan had reduced the previous administration's two hundred MX missiles to one hundred.) The Soviet Union would respond to this proposed deployment with a similar number of ICBMs of similar class. This was the first Soviet threat since 1950 to deploy a new weapons system, and there were suggestions that production of such a weapon was already in train within the leeway of SALT II. Assuming that no MX missiles were deployed, the Soviet Union offered in December 1982 a reduction of 25 percent in existing missile stocks. Since President Reagan's initial proposal for START in June 1982 had been for both sides to reduce their respective seventy-five hundred nuclear warheads by twenty-five hundred warheads each, the main bone of contention was as to the Soviet demand that the United States should not proceed with production and deployment of the MX, Pershing II, and Cruise missiles. The NATO view, of course, was that such a mere "freeze" would maintain the gross Soviet superiority in throwing power, warheads, and accuracy.

The MX project, of course, faced difficulties at home in addition to Soviet objection. The difficulties of deploying the missile in conditions that would assure its survivability as a retaliatory weapon have already been referred to, mobile underground silo and "dense pack" disposition having both been successively proposed and rejected. Only early in 1983, after many vicissitudes, was the MX project, described (somewhat archaically by this time) as "the proposed land-based mainstay of America's nuclear deterrent for the rest of the decade," given authorization by the House of Representatives Appropriations Committee, on an amendment to cut one billion dollars from production costs being defeated (even then, only by a close vote of 26–26). It was approved by the House and Senate in November 1983.

In May 1983, the President's Commission on Strategic Forces recommended development of a smaller, single-warhead missile, presumably with a view to assuring mobility and perhaps a shift of arms-reduction discussions to counting warheads rather than missiles. On 22 June 1983, recently confirmed Director of the U.S. Arms Control Agency Kenneth Adelmann said that the deployment of 100 MX missiles would proceed unless the Soviet Union agreed to give up the great majority of its 818 "medium and heavy land-based strategic missiles." Congress had approved the MX budget several weeks before, and the MX missile had had its first successful flight test the previous week. In earlier negotiations, the United States had demanded that Moscow reduce its total of SS-17, SS-19, and SS-18 ICBMs from 818 to 210. Reports of 26 June 1983 suggested two possible signs of Soviet flexibility, affecting its earlier demands for the banning of the United States' projected 580 *long-range* Cruise missiles as well as *new* submarine-launched ballistic missiles. Meetings between U.S. START negotiator Edward Rowny, Secretary of State Shultz, and Ambassador Anatole Dobrynin at about this time suggested some movement in the START negotiations.

It is unfortunate that just as with strategic weapons, the United States left itself deficient in tactical nuclear weapons as the decade began, so that in terms of both, the United States and NATO assumed the appearance of wantonly escalating the level and quantities of nuclear weapon technology. In 1982, as the date for projected deployment of 108 Pershing II missiles in West Germany and 464 Cruise missiles in the United Kingdom, Italy, Belgium, and the Netherlands in December 1983 came into view, President Reagan presented what was termed his "zero option." In return for Soviet dismantling of 600 missiles, including 250 SS-20s, the West would refrain from deploying the above 572 medium-range missiles. On 21 December 1982, on the sixtieth anniversary of the Soviet Union, President Andropov called this offer a mockery. He counteroffered to reduce the projected 300 SS-20s to 160, approximately the same number of missiles already deployed on land and sea by the United Kingdom and France. (The United Kingdom had 64 Polaris missiles in submarines, and France had 97 land- and sea-based missiles.) The Soviet Union was still pressing this offer in mid-1983. And this offer was still being resisted because part of the quid pro quo was the abandonment of Pershing II and Cruise missiles, with the result that the 161 older U.K. and French missiles with single warheads would then face 160 highly accurate and modern triple-warhead SS-20s; because the removed SS-20s, for example, east of the Urals, could be moved back to the European theater later; and, further, because the U.K. and French missiles in question were independently controlled by those two countries and not by NATO.

West German Chancellor Kohl was still making this last argument to Moscow on his visit there on 7 July 1983, when there was some sign of apparent willingness on the part of both sides to negotiate on the basis of parity in warheads rather than missiles, perhaps in some combination with numbers of missiles and planes, and the scrapping of MIRVs.

The present concern, however, is not with details of such strategic or tactical calculations but only with the bearing of responsible government, and the related values of free opinion and free speech, on the range of foreign policy and defense options available to the two sides. It may perhaps be added, however, that even if we could be sanguine enough to expect an optimal Soviet response to President Reagan's proposals on medium-range weapons, the strategic outlook for the NATO powers would still be dangerous. For the balance would be thrust back onto conventional weapons and delivery systems based on aircraft in which Soviet capacities, for instance with the backfire bomber, are far superior to NATO's, except as to the F-111 bomber. A more likely outcome would be the failure or rather indefinite protraction of the current negotiations and a Soviet political strategy similar to that pursued in the 1950s. The Soviets would then maintain or even enhance their own military potential while manipulating peace movements in Europe so as to limit or to erode NATO military capacities. The efficacy of this political strategy rests precisely on the degree to which the values of human dignity and free expression in the United States and the Western countries are protected against state power, thus limiting state policy, while the Soviet Union itself is not so limited. This would be so even if a majority of the voters in each Western state supported their government's decision. Obviously, even comparatively small minority groups may create grave obstacles to the projected deployment of 48 Cruise missiles in Belgium, 48 Cruise missiles in the Netherlands, 96 Cruise missiles in West Germany, 112 Cruise missiles in Italy, and 106 Cruise missiles in the United Kingdom.

Demonstrations in the West calling for peace, disarmament, and a nuclear freeze have continued to receive strong support from the Eastern bloc; and a major peace conference was staged in Prague on 26 June 1983. The participants in such demonstrations are predominantly persons protesting against nuclear armaments in NATO countries. When such demonstrators have been given access to Soviet bloc countries, activists for peace and disarmament indigenous to these countries have rarely been allowed to join in and have been threatened with exile from Moscow or, in the case of students, expulsion from their university. Indeed, it was reported that the representatives of the Greens from West Germany attending the 1983 conference in Prague were so outraged by police harassment preventing them from talking to Czech Charter dissidents that they left Prague in protest. And though it was reported that small East German anti-nuclear groups were meeting in East Berlin in the middle of 1983, the reports indicated that their members were being required by the East German authorities to sign applications to emigrate which, unless they desisted, were used to force them to emigrate. Nor were there any signs of receptiveness at the Moscow Pact meeting of June

1983 towards Rumanian Prime Minister Ceausescu's independent-minded questioning of the expressed Soviet intention to match any new weapons deployed by the West. (Nicholas Ceausescu had been a critic of the Soviet invasions of Czechoslovakia in 1968 and Afghanistan in 1979 and indeed recently had given support to President Reagan's call for a "zero option" on medium-range missiles in Europe, shortly to be mentioned.)

Clearly, leaders on both sides are aware of the importance of the unilateralism issue. The Soviet prime minister observed in Helsinki on 9 December 1982, as demonstrations in the West mounted, that the Soviet Union did not seek unilateral disarmament by any country, and "nobody should demand that from us." On the other hand, President Reagan asserted on 22 December 1981, at a time when peace demonstrations were already mounting in Denmark, Switzerland, Italy, and West Germany, that these activities were "bought and paid for by the Soviet Union." Similar allegations were made by NATO Secretary-General Luns to the North Atlantic Parliamentary Assembly. While this assertion did not prove its own truth, it also was not necessarily untrue. And by the tests of cui bono and the intolerance by the Soviet side of peace movements among its own people or among the peoples of the Soviet bloc states and of criticisms of its own armament stance, the assertion seems substantially true.

One-sided pressure of the peace and disarmament movement against Washington continued in one sense to gain strength in 1982–83. The Democratic party platform endorsed in July 1982 by the annual party conference in Philadelphia contained a commitment to freeze not only the deployment of new nuclear weapons but also the development of nuclear weapons technology. In the United Kingdom, Greenham Common demonstrations against the projected deployment of Pershing II and Cruise missiles continued and indeed became continuous. They had the support at the end of December 1982 of public exchanges between the Thatcher government and Archbishop Dr. Robert Runcie of Canterbury, Bishop John Bickersteth of Bath and Wells, and Bishop John Hapgood of Durham.

Meanwhile, a 150-page statement by U.S. Catholic bishops was finally revised and adopted at the national conference in Chicago by a vote of 238–9 on 3 May 1983. It advocated the "curbing" of the testing, production, and deployment of new nuclear weapons systems if a verifiable agreement could be reached with the Soviet Union. This was regarded by the administration as an improvement of an earlier draft which spoke of a "halt" in such activities. While the conference also showed alarm concerning the Soviet military build-up, it took other positions bearing on U.S. nuclear arms policy. It opposed reservations on this point. It urged public resistance to ideas of a "protracted" or "winnable" nuclear war, which had been mooted on both sides. It accorded a grudging "strictly conditioned moral acceptance" of threat of nuclear response to nuclear first strike, presumably on traditional "just war" analogies, but was also concerned to "resist" (though not to "oppose") new first-strike weapons.

Even the Democrat-controlled House of Representatives adopted a so-called freeze resolution on 4 May 1983. By July 1983, however, it was no longer likely that the anti-nuclear campaign could block Pershing II and Cruise deployments, despite possible local problems in the United Kingdom, Italy, and West Germany in the wake of the bishops' statement. Moreover, deep ambiguities affect the strength of both positions, which are conditioned on mutuality and verifiability of the "freeze," and the House's position on its "immediacy" also, and on it being followed within an agreed period of time by reductions in nuclear weapons. Prospective Democratic presidential candidate Walter Mondale was reported on 15 July 1983 to have denied that the "freeze" resolution called for any "unilateral" action; it called rather for "a mutual verifiable arrangement." Moreover, "mutual" meant contribution to each side's security, and "verifiable" meant "enforceability" with due monitoring.[11] Pope John Paul II's advocacy was similarly for nuclear arms reduction "carried out simultaneously by all the parties by means of explicit agreements and with the commitment of accepting effective controls." And when are "new" weapons not merely replacements of worn-out weapons? With these ambiguities, these manifestations were still substantial, but they were probably neutralized by Washington's retreat from confrontation with Europe over the pipeline issue and by the electoral consolidation of the rightist governments of Chancellor Kohl in West Germany, the Thatcher government in the United Kingdom, and the quietus of Williamsburg. Certainly, apart from misleading overtones of the word *freeze*, the Democratic position in the House was rather indistinguishable from the demands of those three governments for a balanced restraining of the escalation of nuclear weaponry.

There had certainly been a threat of grave dissensions within NATO and dissensions in Europe generally concerning deployment of Pershing II and Cruise missiles. This led, indeed, at one point to a vote in a subcommittee of the House Armed Services Committee to reduce U.S. troops in Europe from 355,000 to 331,000 and to charges that there were many Neville Chamberlains in Europe. This position certainly changed after the return of the Kohl government in West Germany late in 1982. And it is important to recall that by the end of 1982, French President Mitterand and former West German Chancellor Schmidt, both heading socialist governments, as well as socialist Prime Minister Papandreou of Greece, had in fact committed themselves to deployment of the new weapons.

The disparity between Western and other states regarding retraction of state power before human values, moreover, has no less important consequences regarding the "new" "decolonized" states, now constituting almost two-thirds of the membership of the United Nations. Here the effects of the disparity are less dramatic and more diffuse, yet still significant.

Confronted by the above dilemma, as a present outcome of a vision in which human dignity and autonomy have been freed from domination by state power and of the dangers of nuclear war, some liberal thought may well prefer to grasp that horn of the dilemma which risks world dominance by totalitarian state power. For such thought a further question arises: whether the three decades of decolonization now experienced offer serious hope that the peoples of the new Asian and African states (who, together with those of the Soviet Union, the People's Republic of China, and other Communist states, constitute most of the human community) have any foreseeable prospect of eroding, limiting, or otherwise escaping the domination of the state entities under which they live.

It must be clear that for some considerable time ahead the chance is slight indeed. Amid the fashionable internationalism of many Western thinkers and the clamor outside the West for new legal and economic orders, and the like, to right the wrongs of the old world, one central part of the old international law stands pat. Indeed, it now appears to have even greater sanctity for Third World states, as well as for the Soviet Union and China, than it formerly had for the nineteenth-century Eurocentric comity of states. It is the doctrine of sovereignty.[12] Non-Western states affirm and extol it with a passion no less than that with which they require the subjection of the sovereignties of Western states to their demands for redistribution of resources and technology[13] and of human and national liberation for the beneficiaries they select from time to time.[14] So that even if Western idealism, in its zeal to vindicate and protect the values of individual human life by restraining state power, were ready to accept as a price the likely subjection of their own states and peoples to Soviet state power, they would still not have redeemed the vast bulk of mankind from the yoke of state power. Under (and, where need be, with the license of) Soviet global power, the peoples of the Third and Fourth worlds would still await redemption from the yoke and from the functional disorder of the territorial state system.[15]

I have to recall at this point that one purpose of the present discussion was merely to examine whether developments since the 1950s—and in particular the Vietnam and Watergate experiences—have bypassed my thesis as to the lack of access of sociologists of international law to knowledge of the individual human layer of the substratum of that law. My answer has been in the negative, and that this implies that time and energy of those concerned with the sociology of international law should be devoted rather to other tasks, some of which were considered in chapter 6.

Unavoidably, that preceding examination has involved an assessment of the possibilities of transforming international law into a system that does not leave human beings subject to the arbitrary power of territorial state entities. In this assessment it has not been my intention to prepare the obsequies for international law. If I have seemed cautious about visions of more "comprehensive," more "policy-oriented," more human value–based,more planetary community–based international law, my reservations have been as to the visions, not as to international law itself.

It is in times of dire trouble, of conflict and disorder, that men dream most vividly and urgently of what might have been and what could still be—if only this or that! It is part of the task of the sociology of international law to assess the plausibility of "this or that" in terms of what is known of the factual substratum of international law, and what can be implied therefrom. My reservations after making this assessment do not signal any despair about traditional international law; if anything, they signal rather that we cannot for the foreseeable future escape from a law of basically this structure, that is, a law of coordination of territorially based power centers.

Yet I have also agreed that in a number of respects this traditional law is now increasingly dysfunctional in relation to the needs and transnational interdependencies of the world community. Does this imply, in view of chronic conflicts between states, in particular between the Western states and the Soviet Union and between the Soviet Union and the People's Republic of China, that I have little hope concerning the survival of either international law or mankind itself?

This is not my conclusion. What I think we cannot achieve is a Houdinilike escape from the situation in which we are. Whether we can escape is not a matter of our wish or even our dire *need* to escape. Necessity is the mother of invention, not of miracles. What this means, by way of precept for action, is not that the world is coming to an end but that we must continue to cope with the world more or less as it is. This, after all, has been the human condition of each generation since the beginning of international law, whether we fix this in the remote worlds of ancient China, Mesopotamia, the Greek city-states, or the Roman Empire or in the comparatively recent Europe of Vitoria, Suarez, or Grotius. No doubt we are now more conscious of the global dimensions of our problems, of their nearly unbearable complexities and interdependencies, and of the constancy and magnitude of the dangers of physical destruction. All of these make it harder, and ourselves less willing, to cope. And one thing at least is clear; "coping" imports a willingness to carry on from where we are, even if we cannot be assured of survival. It is tempting to say that since human survival is necessary, it must be possible to redesign an international law that assures that survival. But it is simply not the case that whatever is necessary to ensure human survival must also be possible. The alternatives must stand on their own feet, as possible in the actualities of the world and within the limits of invention imposed by those actualities. Visions that ignore these actualities may contribute sublimely to the human spirit and the literature that documents it. They may contribute comfort or serenity or inspiration to the visionaries or those who feel their inspiration. They cannot escape those actualities and those limits.

I myself take, indeed, some comfort in the facts of the last thirty years. This era began with an even greater magnitude and immediacy of physical threat from nuclear confrontation than at present. Those who, after Hiroshima, proclaimed that the new weapons had made war obsolete were indeed proclaiming that what was necessary must happen. They assumed that if it was necessary, it must be possible. Of course, this did not make it possible, and humanity has still had to cope with well over one hundred major outbreaks of hostilities since then—and has had to weep for the victims and succor them as it could. We can perhaps now see that those who proclaimed the obsolescence of war could only have been proved right by a method most of them would have abhorred, namely, if the United States had shown itself morally (or immorally, or amorally) willing to use its early lead in nuclear weapons to impose an immediate nuclear-policed world imperium.

When this did not happen, and the Soviet Union's stockpile of weapons and means of delivery grew, it became clear that the effect of the new weapons on the use of violence between states was to be different and more complex. The threat of these weapons pressed in two directions. It increased the demand for cold rationality of decision in matters of war and peace. It also pressed back towards more conventional means of persuasion and coercion in support of state policies, such as alliances, bases, mobility of forces, and flexibility of techniques, within an arena held by the nuclear stalemate. To hold in that arena more clearly, the hot line was invented to minimize the marginal chances of error, accident, and intermeddling deceptions of third parties, and thus aid steady rationality. The hot line fulfills its benevolent role by the unilateral reciprocated grace of each side, a kind of accommodation itself worth some attention and worth further elaboration in the 1980s.

What the hot line betokens is, not any abandonment of the use of force by the states concerned, but their recognition that *nuclear* weapons cannot sensibly be used to solve the *first-level* conflicts of interests (economic, political, territorial, or other) out of which past wars have usually arisen. Nuclear weapons tend to be limited thus, on thoroughly rational grounds, to second-level strategic conflicts, with the function of deterring the opponent from attempting a destructive strike by the probability of at least equivalent disaster to himself. Short of this, conventional types of force continue as instruments of policy in a nuclear-stalemated world.

A second ground for hope of escape from a mere precarious balance of nuclear terror is the tendency for control of final decision as to the use of the new weapons to be vested in one or a few hands and, in the actual situation in both Moscow and Washington, in civilian hands. This "monarchical" tendency of the weapons arises from the immediate dependence of national survival on such decisions. The raison d'être of such weapons is not to use them against the enemy but to deter the enemy from their use. The dependence of deterrence on rational persuasion of the opponent as to the state's intention and capability of using the weapons indicates this kind of vocation. So does the shortness of the interval within which questions of preemptive or retaliatory action may need to be decided. In face of such exigencies, our age may well be thought to have been constructively inventive to a high degree, for instance, as to the preliminary servicing of decisionmakers with expertise, as to efficiency and control of the means of transmitting orders or of activating the relevant systems, side by side with the hot line facility. Whether deterrent effectiveness can survive recent development in the accuracy of first-strike nuclear weapons is a matter to which I shall return in chapter 12.

This fact of personal responsibility of identified individuals for critical nuclear decisions has to be assessed in the light of the level of rationality in decision making imposed on each state by its resolve to survive. On the surface, individuality of decision making seems counterdemocratic in trend, as the metaphor "monarchical" itself implies. And insofar as democratic principle imports a search for maximum consensus based on compromise, *which may be far short of rational* in relation to the policy objectives, nuclear-critical decisions could not in any case be left directly to democratic processes. *Salus populi suprema lex* thus holds a deep paradox for the survival of the powerful U.S. democracy. And, as I have already shown, the paradox is deepened by the strategic disadvantage resulting from recent erosions of state power in title of human values in that great country, not matched by similar erosions in the state power of its adversaries.

Even recognizing these negative aspects, however, the degree of success attained in institutionalizing the process of decision making on these matters in both Washington and Moscow is a gain that no one could confidently have prophesied in 1945 or even in 1950.

Somehow, then, in the last three decades the United States has resisted the temptation to use its nuclear lead for founding a world imperium. For this period, both the United States and the Soviet Union have somehow kept the risks of war between them within an area of rational calculation, which leaves hope for more decades in which nuclear weapons may remain unused. Second, somehow, weapons whose very nature compels "monarchical" control have been kept, finally, within civilian rather than military hands. Third, over a notable range of the countries in conflict, seemingly inexorable trends towards nationalization of truth and justice have been checked and even modified, allowing some hope that the massive populations of the Communist and Third World states will someday also become able to manifest the human capacity and will to criticize and dissent more effectively from official government versions and stances. Fourth, this liberation of human judgment from imposed national versions, insofar as it attains a degree of symmetry, is likely to enhance the possibilities of dialogue and mobility between members of opposed camps. Fifth, the unpromising tactics of the cold war have shown signs (though at present wavering) of leading through the dynamics of interbloc competition in the field of aid to states of the Third World to at least a formative duty (to be examined in chapter 8) of helpfulness of economically stronger to economically weaker states. It is a pleasing irony of the North-South world economic alignment that it cuts across some of the main lines of international antagonism. Sixth, these three decades have witnessed the remarkable speed, comprehensiveness, and comparative peacefulness of the vastly complex process of decolonization and the related more or less humanitywide consensus concerning those aspects of justice, equality, and liberty that were violated by the practice of colonial subjection and exploitation. (The ideas in play will be examined in chapters 8 and 9.) Seventh, but again with some faltering, in the economically troubled times of the seventies and eighties, there has been the acceptance, contrary to the economic autarchic tendencies between the two wars, of the broad principles of progressive expansion of the world economy, based on nondiscrimination, and indeed a degree of benign reverse discrimination. The blueprints for a "new international economic order" have at least a place in the bulky dossiers concerning the world economic recession. There has been in this connection, too, a valuable expansion of the work of the Economic and Social Council and its commissions and of the World Bank and the International Monetary Fund and other specialized agencies concerned with international economic, social, and humanitarian functions, marred from time to time, it is true, by the manipulation of these organs to serve extraneous political warfare purposes of particular states.

In the early 1950s, we had little apparent basis for expecting such elements of hopefulness as have in fact emerged. They testify at least to the capacities of human beings to adapt themselves to unprecedented situations of great difficulty and complexity. They forbid us to despair of the human future, just as the realities of the situation that have been examined forbid us to take that future for granted. Between these commandments, the task is to cope as best we can.

8. Justice and Equality among Nations

The continuing struggle to realize the prophetic vision of the brotherhood of man in the face of so many past failures may be among the more glorious and eternal marks of the human condition, as it is certainly central in the perplexities of the wise and informed in each generation. The main intellectual source of these perplexities resides in our inability to fix any hard core of irreducible meaning for the concept of justice that is *intellectually* convincing (as distinct from more or less plausible to some or others of us). As a result, such meaning as is confidently offered by some seems always no less unacceptable to others, even among the most objective of thinkers within a single municipal society. We can often, it is true, move *towards* a transcending consensus by increasing the abstractness of our theoretical models and statements. But this invariably increases the difficulty we in any case have of emerging from our theorizings near enough to the facts to make any decisive contribution to concrete problems.

In 1946 I was indeed able to feel that there was an identifiable hard core of the notion of justice within most Western societies. This was that society would be so organized that men's felt wants could be freely expressed; that law, in order to be just, must at least protect that expression and provide it with the channels through which it could compete effectively for (though not necessarily attain) the support of politically organized society.[1] Even this kind of "absolute," open-ended as it is in a material sense, cannot really be offered as valid for *all* municipal societies, for it presupposes a mobility and articulateness of demand found chiefly in Western democratic societies which has been less prominent in many civilizations. Furthermore, its meaning for a postulated international community is problematic until we have found some basis for translating the demands made by states into demands that would be made by the human beings who constitute their populations, since these would be in the absence of modifying, suppressive, or distorting influence of state entities. (The question of whether such a relation can be found still stands starkly in the path.)

71

The clamor for human betterment, and for the use of law as an instrument towards this, is ever-recurrent in human history. That some notion like justice has been steadily associated with this clamor, playing a charismatic role in the major movements of human though and action throughout the ages, is also a historical fact of immense importance. Appeals to justice as a means of moving men to the action that marshals power, as well as overthrows it, are associated with some of the most sublime and traumatic experiences of the family of men. It is also doubtful whether any society with a stable differentiated legal order could be named where there was not some awareness among its exponents and appliers of the relation of law to ethically approvable social arrangements, that is, to justice in a broad sense. All this tempts us to the attractive view that whatever its final definition or criteria, the notion of justice somehow gives meaning to the tasks of men who work with the law, as the idea of beauty is thought to give meaning to the work of the artist. It is all the more impressive, in view of this and of the age-old emotional and intellectual alignments already investing the notion of justice on all sides, that men's yearnings towards it have shown themselves to be irrepressible. In every generation, too, are to be found men, and often a substantial proportion of all men, who envision justice as raising issues not to be avoided; issues of more than a merely subjective nature; issues involved in present actualities; issues, finally, always fit for pondering and provisional judgment, even when not for dogmatic conclusions.[2]

We do not need to deceive ourselves concerning the indecisiveness thus far of the search for the ultimate criteria of justice in order to insist that it ought to go on. For there is good reason why the normative tasks of ethical and political philosophy, and the philosophy of justice that is an integral part of them, can never be finished as long as human society itself persists. Every substantial change in man and his environment calls for re-examination of existing values in their application to new situations. This call is more than ever insistent in a world of state societies growing increasingly industrialized and mobile, powered now by an unprecedented technological explosion. What has been said of the continued importance of the critique of law by justice in the municipal sphere seems still more compelling in relation to the future of international law.

With many municipal legal orders, at any rate, substantive and procedural norms, accepted legal ideas and legal techniques, and related institutions are sufficiently launched, sufficiently elaborated, and sufficiently dynamic to maintain overall direction for a substantial time even if attention to theory ceased. In the international legal order, more than three centuries of technical elaboration have not produced any assurance that its launching was a take-off rather than a series of forced landings or crashes. It is an order in which crisis is, as it were, normal; and crisis is the greatest catalyst of reexamination of goals and methods and of the adequacy of the status quo. At the present stage of the international legal order, in which the number of participant states has more than doubled and the range of cultures and of levels of their political, social, demographic, and economic capacity has become frighteningly diverse, even settled areas of the law are increasingly challenged and subjected to the questionings of justice. And these questionings extend beyond particular segments of the law to its very foundations, including the identity of its main participants and beneficiaries—states or human beings?

Even apart from the historical sources of the equality of nations doctrine in natural law theory, no study of international justice could prudently neglect it. For from its tangled exegesis emerged one way or another the main justice issues, for instance, concerning self-determination and self-preservation in modern conditions, economic justice between nations, and the entire role of state entities in the doing of international justice, which still affect the relations of states. These issues, and sometimes their outcome also, were secreted as a kind of by-product of endless struggles to give meaning to the doctrine of equality of nations as an axiom of international law, in a world in which to an untutored mind it appeared to be plainly and simply false.

Underlying the applications of the equality doctrine in the relations of states are the treacherous ambiguities and self-contradictions concealed by the equality notion itself, even as applied to individual human beings. This notion is central to great struggles proceeding within municipal societies today, where it has become a kind of guiding star for the intellectually perplexed and a *tabula in naufragio* for the societies threatened by social and political storms. For, logically, the notion beckons as a means of escaping from mobile and conflicting imponderables into a realm of quantitative, logical, or even mathematical demonstration. And this guides us back (or on) to the one kind of faith that commands a degree of general acceptance even today, the faith in mathematics and exact science. Partially because of its kinship to mathematics, equality seems to have a definite meaning in a sense in which notions of justice or even fairness do not. Moreover, on the side of history, equality as a battle cry is associated in some form or other with many of the landmark struggles of peoples of the Western world towards the attainment of a more just society.

Before we assume from this that the equality notion is an adequate criterion of justice, we should bring to mind its built-in ambiguities. It may refer, first, to the threshold question whether all human beings found within the society are regarded as members of it, among whom justice is to be done, or whether some of such human beings (as with slaves or serfs or outlaws) have no entitlements in the doing of justice. It may refer, second, to the demand that all members of a justice constituency come under the same uniform rules. And in that second reference it ignores the plain injustice to any human beings who might still be *excluded* from the constituency. It also ignores the fact that although all may be subject to uniform rules, those rules may be *unjust* to all of them, as when all are equally subjected to tyrannical oppression. And it further ignores the fact that a uniform rule superimposed on preexisting relevant differences between the factual situations of members may also be grossly unjust, as when, to adapt Anatole France's aphorism, the rich equally with the poor are permitted (or forbidden) to sleep under the bridges of the Seine. Third, equality may alternatively refer to a requirement that rules differentiate among individuals according to the diversity of their situations *so as to produce a greater degree of equality among them after each rule has been applied.* Equality under this third reference may involve, not application of a uniform rule, but the very opposite. The graduation of income tax rates is a simple and pervasive example. Equality in this sense of greater resultant equality is achievable only insofar as the applicable rules of law *do discriminate* in favor of those actually initially disadvantaged.

There are thus at least two reasons why equality fails as an *adequate* guide to just decision. First, insofar as we cannot interpret the notion to mean exclusively that in all matters a uniform rule must be applied to all persons regardless of relevant similarities or differences in their circumstances, we are compelled, as soon as we try to use it, to resort to some value other than inequality before we can come to judgment. We always have to ask whether there are similarities and differences between this case and the cases to which the uniform rule applies that afford a sufficiently relevant reason for treating this case in the same way or differently. This judgment of relevance in turn can be made only by reference to some goal or policy or value (*other than equality*) that justifies applying a different rule in this case. The heart of the judgment of justice is the relevance of the factual differences among justice claimants to other goals than equality also approved by law. Second, equality may mean not only uniformity of rule but, *inter alia,* equality of factual outcome after applying *discriminating* rules. And nothing in the notion of equality itself tells us when each of these rather contradictory meanings is the appropriate one to use.

The rather specific history of international law, and the rather specific role of the doctrine of the equality of nations in it, in any case suggests that the political and sociological role of the doctrine may be of major importance. The existing literature tends to be analytical or historical;[3] and in the absence of definitive work on its political and sociological role, we can here at least attempt to sketch what may be involved. Certainly, no inquiry about international justice can ignore the tangled story of the doctrine of equality of states.

The equivocations that affect the doctrine of equality of states are even more numerous and interesting than those affecting the doctrine of equality in municipal law,[4] and perhaps still more fruitful. For the present purposes, we can distinguish a clustering of no less than four equivocations, each comprising pairs of ideas, and between these pairs (and within each of them) the use of the doctrine may swing in meaning, with striking differences of effect. There is, first, the swing between equality before the law of all *legal* persons (that is, persons recognized by law, and thus not embracing slaves in municipal law or "dependent" nations in international law) and the equality of all *natural* persons (that is, human beings in municipal law and nations, whether dependent or independent, in international law). There is, second, even for the class of legal persons supposedly equal before the law, the equivocation between equal entitlement to *such rights as the law confers on them* and equal entitlement in a substantive sense to *equal rights*. (This equivocation is also expressible as a contrast between equality before the law and factual and political inequality.) Third (as a special international law variation of this last, and thus worthy of separate attention) is the equivocation between the equality of states as an aspect of state sovereignty, the reasoning being that entities each of which is deemed to be "supreme" but all of which coexist in one world must by this very fact be equal,[5] and equality of rights in a substantive sense. It is mainly the complex relations surrounding the notion of sovereignty that have required separate treatment of this third equivocation. Fourth, the doctrine of equality of nations, *if sought to be used as a basic principle of justice* (as distinct from its manifestations or negations in existing law), draws in the perplexities of determining whether the claimants and beneficiaries of international justice consist of states or of the human beings who in their respective politically organized societies constitute these states.

The first equivocation swings, as we have seen, between equality of states and equality of certain natural persons or aggregates of such (such as nations). When the reference is to equality between states, that is, aggregates of men endowed with territory and international legal personality, this is immediately of great negative importance to justice. For it excludes from legal entitlement all entities not yet so endowed. Insofar as protection by law is necessary for justice, this negative aspect imports a dispersed denial of justice to these other men or aggregates of men. When those excluded clamor for justice, the clamor tends to be for admission under the equality principle to the class of international legal persons. And it is in this connection that the present equivocation shows its fertile, creative side. It was easier, for example, for Francisco de Vitoria to plead for justice to the indigenous South American peoples by asserting that all "nations" *were* equally within the protection of international law under some principle like the equality of nations than to argue that *in justice they ought to be brought within this protection*. In modern times, the "right" of self-determination and the "principle" of anticolonialism play similar roles, hovering between an assertion of law and a demand for justice. My lamented friend and colleague C. H. Alexandrowicz, in his doctrine of "reversion to sovereignty," offered a similarly hovering principle simultaneously asserting that peoples whose independence was submerged under colonial rule even centuries ago do not *(or ought not to have to)* enter the international community as new states when the domination now ends in the twentieth century. They are rather *re*entering as independent states that have "reverted to sovereignty," bearing with them all the entitlements of their longstanding independent existence.[6]

This second reference of the present equivocation, which operates as a demand for justice upon law, may also (and perhaps best) be understood as a reaction to the negative implications of the first reference. Insofar as its demands succeed, the successful claimants become entitled as beneficiaries of the principle of equality of states under the first reference. They become legal persons whose battles for justice may now be fought with the weapons of international law. But, of course, other less successful entities still clamoring for justice remain excluded. Ordinarily, as with admission to other privileges, the *nouveau venu* will take his place alongside the old members in resisting the clamor of later aspirants to admission. But sometimes, as with most of today's emancipated colonial peoples, the successful new entrants become a kind of bloc lobbying for peoples still excluded, motivated both by principle and by the self-regarding aim of enhancing the voting power of like-minded states.

Once we see the creative virtue of the second reference of the equivocation under discussion, we are struck by another paradox emerging from the chaos of debate. If we are inclined to regard international law as now entering a new phase, extending to twice the number of former states, we can interpret the consequences in terms of the equality principle thus. The increase in number of claimants and beneficiaries (states) proceeds from clamor of formerly excluded peoples in title of the equality-before-the-law principle. Equality is, as it were, a progenitor of the increased number of states. But these later admitted states are mostly, in the nature of the situation, less strong, less well-endowed, and less organizationally skilled than the older states. This means that, *by their admission,* the range of de facto inequalities between states (that is, of inequalities in the material or political sense) tends to be increased. Equality, in this reference, has helped to transform a "world" order arrested at some line such as "Christendom" or "the civilized world" into one with a fuller horizon. Yet this very transformation, by swelling the number of state entities with newly admitted states from among weaker and less privileged peoples, also deeply aggravated (and continues in 1984 to aggravate) the central problems of reducing material inequalities between states to acceptable levels.

This accentuation of *material inequalities* between states *equal before the law* is only the most troublesome of the problem children of the creative second limb of this first equivocation. Another arises when insistence on the entitlement of all nations to equality before international law (in the sense of full legal personality or participation) *is pushed to extremes.* This produces an extension of the principle of self-determination of nations to a point that cannot be objectively delimited.[7] The guidance to justice from that principle, at best always open to political abuse, then tends to disappear altogether. To make present *dependence,* whether in title of the equality principle or otherwise, a sufficient ground for insisting on immediate *independence,* regardless of the will or ability of the particular people to be thrown on its own resources, puts the principle of equality in critical tension with the idea of justice.[8] The self-determination principle, thus inspired by an extreme version of the equality of *nations* principle, turns the grant of statehood into an imposition rather than an emancipation.[9]

The second problem child of the equality principle brings forth its own, a problem *grand*child. For indeterminacy of application, having thus opened the way for extraneous and extraneously motivated pressures to force a spurious legal independence that cannot in fact be sustained, also opens the way to arbitrary subjection of some peoples' right of self-determination to that of others. Such manipulations are foci of self-interested concerns of the older states, so that all examples that we might offer of this, such as the tribal struggles in the Congo or Nigeria or the Rhodesia problem, will be interpreted differently from different standpoints. We are content to rest on the general point, which is obviously of particular importance in the ethnic conditions of Africa, as related to the often artificial post-colonial boundaries. Obviously, however, as but a thought on Malaya or Indonesia would show, it is not irrelevant to Asia either.

We might summarize the tendencies of this first equivocation of the equality principle under actual world conditions as follows. It tends to fulfill a basic precondition of the doing of international justice by opening up the traditional legal order to hitherto excluded claimants and beneficiaries of international justice. Implied in this, it tends to promote acceptance internationally of what we have seen may be one absolute precept of justice, namely, the maintenance of conditions in which all men may form and formulate their own interests and press these for legal support.[10] Yet, on the other hand, the limits of this opening up are so indeterminate as still to leave quite unclear the ambit of the justice constituency within which these demands are to be adjusted, a problem to which I shall have to return.[11]

The second equivocation—that between equal standing of all states to enjoy such rights as international law confers upon them and equality in the quantum of rights conferred actually on them—also turns on formal and creative references within it, interacting fruitfully on international justice. No doubt those who take doctrines at their face value as data for mere logical testing of their literal ambit easily conclude, though often with despair or cynicism, that the obvious factual inequalities between entitlements of states under international law challenge both these quantitative references.

Yet, in history (as distinct from logical analysis), neither version of this second equivocation can be lightly dismissed.[12] The equal quantum of rights reference, for example, despite its obvious variance for existing law, still operates *as a demand of justice for change in the law*. It exerted pressure, surely quite strong during the last century, for abolition of regimes, of capitulations, and of extraterritoriality such as long characterized Western-Asian relations.[13] One effect, certainly, of the factually erroneous assertion of equality in quantum of rights was that such equalities of status were challenged continually to justify themselves and often failed to do so. Even as positivist exposure of the error was reaching its zenith and as Africa was undergoing colonialist partition, the challenge against such inequalities gained power. So that when, after two world wars, scores of non-European peoples have been accorded statehood, it has not been seriously suggested that inequalities of the type of the old capitulations should be imposed as a condition of this.

This justice demand operating through the equal quantum of rights reference in the present equivocation seems at first sight to merit unqualified applause. Yet, of course, as I will show in later chapters, it may cut radically across the demands for justice through equality between individuals. And, as I must now also observe, it may come into conflict with some forward-looking movements in the international legal order. Since serious efforts towards international organization began in the late nineteenth century, small state insistence on equality has proved a constant obstacle, and often an absolute roadblock, as when it helped to defeat establishment of a court of arbitral justice and an international prize court in 1907.[14] In the flowering of international legal organization in the sixty years that followed, the clash with this justice demand continues to have its dramatic episodes, whether in U.N. voting and representation rules or in the allocation of budgetary burdens and benefits of this or other organizations. In such a context, of course, criticism of this reference of the equality doctrine is functional as well as analytical. In the demand for an equal quantum of legal rights within the new institutions, the doctrine flies in the face of actual economic, military, and political inequalities which, if these institutions were to prove viable, their constitution and operation had necessarily to take into account.[15]

A third equivocation closely parallels the second, except that the formal reference within the third bases the equality of states before the law on the sovereignty of each state, in all its tangle of doctrinal perplexities. Historically, indeed, both of these concepts have been deeply and independently involved in the emergence of the present decentralized international legal order from the medieval unities of the Holy Roman Empire and the Holy See. The ideas of equality and sovereignty were invoked in increasingly articulate form to free the temporal authority from the spiritual in the struggle between emperor and pope and, overlapping in time with this, to make the emergent "national" monarchical states independent of both emperor and pope and also of each other, yielding finally, with the fall of the empire, the system of sovereign states familiar to us.[16] The consolidation of the equality principle, in any case, was certainly a central feature of the order of monarchical states that emerged in the fifteenth and sixteenth centuries. As against the fading claims of Holy Roman Emperor and the pope, each monarch, identified with his state, asserted the freedom and independence that Jean Bodin classically expounded as "sovereignty." Within an international community of sovereigns, equality presented itself as a corollary of sovereignty.

In Emerich de Vattel's eighteenth-century formulations, which served, as we shall see shortly, as a kind of bridge between the natural law and positivist bases of international law, the relation of the equality and sovereignty ("freedom" and "independence") doctrines is worked out. The doctrine of sovereignty, with equality as a corollary, became at his hands the very basis of international law, to the point, indeed, of serious emasculation of the key ideas of an international community and of a *binding* legal order. His classic statement is still worthy of quotation:

> A dwarf is as much a man as a giant is; a small Republic is no less a sovereign State than the most powerful Kingdom.
>
> From this equality it necessarily follows that what is lawful or unlawful for one Nation is equally lawful or unlawful for every other Nation.
>
> A Nation is therefore free to act as it pleases, so far as the Nation is under merely *internal* obligations without any *perfect external* obligation. If it abuse its liberty it acts wrongfully; but other Nations can not complain, since they have no right to dictate to it.
>
> Since Nations are free, independent, and equal, and since each has the right to decide in its conscience what it must do to fulfil its duties, the effect of this is to produce, before the world at least, a perfect equality of rights among nations in the conduct of their affairs and in the pursuit of their policies. The intrinsic justice of their conduct is another matter which it is not for others to pass upon finally; so that what one may do another may do, and they must be regarded in the society of mankind as having equal rights.
>
> When differences arise each Nation in fact claims to have justice on its side, and neither of the interested parties nor other Nations may decide the question. The one who is actually in the wrong sins against its conscience; but as it may possibly be in the right, it cannot be accused of violating the laws of the society of Nations.
>
> It must happen, then, on many occasions that Nations put up with certain things although in themselves unjust and worthy of condemnation,

because they cannot oppose them by force without transgressing the liberty of individual Nations and thus destroying the foundations of their natural society. And since they are bound to advance that society, we rightly presume that they have agreed to the principle just established.[17]

The equality principle, as well as all the accompanying mysteries as to the consequential nature of the binding force of international law, will be found embedded in these lines. Natural law sanctifies the equal "fundamental rights" of all states; and the content given to these equal rights then makes the force of any "governing" law problematic.

It is obvious from Vattel's further elaborations that he was not insensitive to the sea change that his position brought to the natural law foundations inherited from earlier writers and that he purported still to accept as the foundation of international law. He sought to escape the central difficulty, which has been well described in terms of "internal dialectic of sovereignty,"[18] by his well-known distinction between *droit nécessaire* and *droit voluntaire*. The *droits parfaits*, emanating from the *droit nécessaire*, are for Vattel those rights of which no state can be deprived because they are indispensable to the very existence of a state and for that reason give rise to "perfect external obligations" of other states. These contrast with his *droits imparfaits*, which arise out of benevolent or humane considerations (*offices d'humanité*) but cannot be enforced against states with regard to whom they are asserted, since to allow this would violate the principle of equality, destroying in this sense the foundations of "the natural society" of states.[19]

Vattel also elaborated the notion of *offices d'humanité*, governed by what he regarded as the "bold" principle that "each State owes to every other State all that it owes to itself, as far as the other is in need of its help and such help can be given without the State neglecting its duties towards itself." This, he thought, sprang from an "eternal and immutable law of nature," supported by various humanitarian and utilitarian considerations. Even as he asserted such duties of humanity, Vattel was clearly aware of the tensions that they created in his general position. He hastened to assure those who might regard such duties as repugnant to "wise statesmanship" that "Sovereign States . . . are much more self-sufficient than individual men, and mutual assistance is not so necessary among them, nor its practice so frequent." In any case, he added, a state's duties to itself, especially as to its security, require it to be much more careful than an individual in helping others.[20]

We have referred to the changed meaning of *nature* and *natural law* as Vattel used these to base his position. And it is necessary to understand this change in order to see his exact standpoint on equality, which is our present focus. For most of his predecessors, from Aristotle onward, the *nature* of man was his *ideal* nature, what he is in the fullest development of the faculties special to him; and these were seen by the classical writers as his rationality and sociality and sometimes his dependence on others. For Vattel, however, *nature* meant what it meant to Hobbes: the "actual" rather than the "ideal" nature of the creature. For him, as for Hobbes, what was primary was not the *restraint* of natural law but the *license* of the state of nature—of men in their presocial isolation, each self-dependent for survival and as yet uninhibited by the bonds of sociality.

Precisely because natural law comprises these principles applicable to men in their presocial isolation, it is, in this view, apt for governing the relations of independent states. The condition of such states, recognizing no binding human law over them and no human superior, is precisely that of isolated men before civil society and its law arise. Only this kind of "natural" law can claim to control such civil anarchy. The precepts of the Vattelian natural law, therefore, on which his international law is based, must be derived from contemplation of such independent beings, from their "naturally" sanctioned claims, from the "rights" inherent in independence. The precepts must assure those rights of all states in a manner that allows them to coexist. On its theoretical side, Vattel's whole system is an analysis of the precepts that he believed followed from these "fundamental rights" of states, illustrated richly by state practice.

This position, which bridges the naturalist and positivist strains of this body of thought, shows its deeper implications in connection with the fundamental right of self-preservation. According to Vattel, each state not only had such a right, in pursuance of which any other rules of international law could be overriden if necessary, but was also its own final judge as to whether a situation for the exercise of this right had arisen and what action was necessary to implement it. On such a basis, the binding force of all rules became subject, finally, to each state's discretion. The manner in which this *détournement* of natural law pointed towards the "conventional" or "consent" or "positivist" theories of international law, which became dominant in the nineteenth century, is clear in the present perspective.

One sign of this, indeed, was immediately apparent in the virtual fading out of the Grotian theory of "the just war." In war situations, each belligerent's self-preservation is usually invoked: insofar as each is the final judge of what its self-preservation requires, each can in the external world (however it be *in foro conscientiae*) maintain its cause as just, without possibility of legal challenge. To that extent, the distinction between just and unjust as applied to the causes of war became still more indecisive, and with it any basis on which third states might or should discriminate between the belligerents. Here is a central foundation on which Vattel built the modern (though already rather battered) law of neutrality.[21]

Vattel's stress on the *offices d'humanité* was in this perspective part of an effort to stop short of the full implications of his own new positions. It was an effort in particular to show that the related ideas of sovereignty and equality do not exclude duties arising from sociality and interdependence. No doubt this outcome of "the dialectic of sovereignty" is transparently wavering. Yet it is a part of Vattel's position (not to speak of those of later full-fledged positivisim) that is intensely relevant to inquiries concerning international justice. It may be somewhat fanciful to see Vattel's struggle to have each state sovereign and equal to every other state but nevertheless subject to unenforceable duties of helpfulness to its fellows as a forerunner of our own problems. Yet *we* ourselves are still struggling to delimit the duty of aid to developing nations. And our own invocations of some such inchoate duty, but one stopping short of legal obligation, are similar to those of the notion of "conscience" that Vattel's *offices d'humanité* invoked to sway the sovereign monarch.[22]

The difficulties of transcending Vattel's position in the present age have been increased, paradoxically enough, by the very self-assertion of newly emancipated states. The newer states have successfully insisted (admittedly in order to secure their own exclusive power within their own domain, but still in general terms) on recognition of each state's sovereign rights over its own resources.[23] The jealousy with which the new nations prize sovereignty and equality for themselves (*and therefore perforce have to concede it to other states*) makes it difficult to predicate any general *legal* duty of affording aid to them in terms of a limitation on the sovereignty of donor states over *their* resources. It is in these circumstances that the ex-colonial states and their spokesmen have had to elaborate the thesis (to be examined) that would rest the demand for aid to developing states on a duty of compensation and restitution springing from exploitations of the colonial era.[24] No question exceeds in importance that of determining whether we can find a convincing basis, here or elsewhere, for the duty of richer states to give such aid in terms of acceptable and feasible precepts of justice. Only thus can we escape both the wavering indeterminacy of the *offices d'humanité* notion and the impracticality (as well, in any case, as the inadequacy) of the notion of restitution for past wrongs.

The "dialectic of sovereignty" has continued to engage able minds into our own times. Whatever the esoteric construct invoked, be it autolimitation of sovereignty, *Gemeinwille* or *Vereinbarung* of state wills, basic norms of *pacta sunt servanda,* or custom, these efforts assume at least this consensus: that sovereignty (including the related equality doctrine) can be a useful concept only within an assumedly binding international legal order, if it be redefined in some less absolute form than Vattel—as well as Bodin before him and Hegel after him—gave to it.[25] But even to this day this rather obvious truth is constantly obscured by the no less obvious weakness of international law enforcement that allows sovereign states to act often with as much impunity as if their sovereignty were absolute and unlimited, so that scholars have to continue into our own generation to write notable books to demonstrate that state "sovereignty" must be subject to law.[26]

It was this involvement of the equality principle with the central mystery of the theory of sovereignty and the international legal order that required me to separate this present third equivocation from the related equivocation I now proceed to bring to summation. Its first meaning lies (as I have already shown) in the formal legal concept of the equality of all states qua sovereigns. At the height of nineteenth-century positivist writing, this led to a kind of discrediting of the equality principle altogether. J. Westlake in 1904 felt that equality was "merely independence under a different name"; T. J. Lawrence that it was merely a historically given doctrine for which "there is no moral or jural necessity"; Funck-Brentano and Sorel that it was merely an ineffective ideal and that the reality lay rather in the political inequality.[27] E. D. Dickinson, in the first systematic treatise on equality of states, declared after a history survey that the doctrine was "a creation of publicists" and was meaningful only in relation to status before international law and that even there it was often affected by internal and external legal limitations on the "capacity for equal rights" of states.[28] P. J. Baker, in 1923, saw the equality principle as a "positive political danger," rejecting even L. Oppenheim's modest precepts of equality and following Westlake (and with him Sir F. Pollock) rather unquestioningly.[29] Even natural lawyers of this period foreshadowed these conclusions. James Lorimer, for example, declared in 1872 that "all States are equally entitled to be recognized as States" but that this did not mean that they were *equal* States, "because they are not equal States." E. C. Stowell, in 1931, climaxed this emasculation of the creative power of this equivocation. Recalling the Russian proverb that "paper endures all," he asserted that despite its historic pretensions, the oft-proclaimed doctrine of equality of states "exists only between States of same rank in respect to the exercise of power."[30]

Here again, therefore, one reference in the equivocation is finally resolved into a mere formal (many would say empty) truth. It is in this sense that if we postulate that a state as such is absolutely sovereign, then each state must be as absolutely sovereign as any other and therefore in this respect equal to every other. And the other reference—to factual inequalities bearing on legal entitlements—is not to a formal truth but to an ethical and empirical one. Vattel himself, even as he gave us the *locus classicus* of the first meaning, also imported the second by the side of it. For he placed there, as I have shown, the *offices d'humanité*, or duties arising from the special needs of other states. These were in effect directives of justice arising from the actual inequalities between states, the evidence of which formal sovereign equality merely concealed.

These directives, though ignored for the most part when the number and relations of states are fairly stable, as in nineteenth-century Europe, tend to come alive in times of rapid change. They share the creative potentiality that we have seen also arise in the first and second equivocations. In the first, the justice demand was for admission of nations as natural aggregates of men to international legal personality and thus legal entitlement in general. In the second, the demand was for removal of prejudicial legal discrimination against some nations after they became international legal persons. In the present, the third equivocation, the justice demand is again focused on the needs of peoples already admitted to statehood, but it is a demand for positive assistance from other states in meeting the burdens of de facto inequality.

A fourth and final equivocation that the equality of states notion shelters is even more intensely relevant to justice among nations. The name *ius gentium* already had a rich and fruitful history when the founding thinkers adopted it to describe the law that Bentham later renamed "international law." When the classical international lawyers used *ius gentium,* its meaning had of course quietly slipped from its original meaning for the Roman praetor of a "law common to men of all nations" to that of a "law governing the relations between nations." Yet this was neither a quick nor a sharp transition, for the *ius gentium* of the Roman praetor was itself related to and sometimes quite indistinguishable in function from the no less active natural law, and it was upon a derivative of this same natural law that the classical writers built the foundations of modern international law. Thus, as I have shown, early international law doctrines reflected by their starting points the rational and social nature of each human being, and by their reference to the conscience of the monarchical personification of the state, they reflected many principles of the law and justice of municipal societies.

Here, then, were another two (perhaps even three) references between which the meaning of the principle of equality of states or nations also wavered somewhat. One reference is, of course, to equality between *state entities;* the other is to equality between all *the men and women who constitute the populations of such entities,* that is, among all mankind. (I recall for completeness that the third possible reference, to nations as aggregates of human beings, has already been canvassed as part of our first detected equivocation.) The swing of the reference in this fourth equivocation exclusively to state entities has dominated international law at least since Vattel. But in the two centuries since Vattel, and even before his time, another reference has also been to equality among all mankind and to some kind of social ordering or community constituted by mankind. We still find ourselves confronted by a choice between competing references, rather like those in the essential task of delimiting the constituency in which international justice is to be done.[31]

The weapons on both sides of the struggle to throw off the embracing unities of the medieval empire and church included the rich and complex body of theological learning. In particular, the learning as to the *Ecclesia*—the mystical body of the church—with its varied range of meanings, provided what some have thought to be the first concept of a community in the West. Clearly the *Ecclesia*, conceived as a *societas christiana*, must have referred to the condition of individual human beings to whom souls, salvation, and damnation could be attributed.[32] When in the later Middle Ages the notion of *Ecclesia* was transmuted into a *societas humana*, this might have reinforced the reference to human beings. Yet in the concreteness of history, this transmutation served, by its recognition of human concerns lying beyond the pale of Christianity, to aid the emergence of purely secular political power, and its withdrawal, though *in the form of our modern state entities rather than world community of individual human beings,* from overlordship of both church and Holy Roman Empire.[33] In the outcome of this particular struggle, paradoxically, the notion of a community of mankind that emerged did so not literally in terms of human beings but in terms of states deemed somehow to represent the human beings.

Vitoria's work has been thought outstanding because of his unusually early and clear articulation of the reference to the constituency of mankind, in which there was equality of entitlement among all peoples, Christian and non-Christian alike. With great courage and progressiveness, he used his humanitywide ideal to champion the cause of the Indians of South America.[34] The ideal itself, more or less explicitly and still on the basis of divine prescription, is also espoused by Suarez and Gentile. (Its relation to the "law of the sons of Noah," affirmed by the rabbinic interpreters of the Old Testament, may well be worth inquiry.) The transition to affirmation of the same variant of the equality principle is clear enough in Grotius, who affirms a *unitas generis humani* grounded on man's specific attributes of natural reason and his *appetitus societatis*. It is critical to note this specific grounding, for under the very different "state of nature" of the Hobbesian type, yielding the presocial *bellum omnium contra omnes*, equality would still prevail, and yet the mutuality of duties based on reason and sociality would be founded on the merely self-regarding struggle of each for self-preservation.

It seems better in an inquiry like the present one, focused on justice within an assumed future international legal order, to regard this last variant of the equality principle as really *negativing* the idea of a community. (Better, that is, provided that the facts of human life will permit this choice.) And the same is to be said of Vattel's main positions, except so far as we have seen these to be qualified by his notion of *offices d'humanité.* For continuity with the Grotian affirmation we have to turn to Samuel Pufendorf's adjustment of it with the Hobbesian kind of thought. The *socialitas* of the Grotian tradition is tempered by Pufendorf into a sense of men's inability to stand alone, their *imbecilitas*, which drives them in the "state of nature" to the kind of cooperation that had matured into the formation of states. *As between states,* however, this maturation had not taken place, nor did Pufendorf think it shortly would or necessarily should. He thought that states remained capable of achieving the "purposes of legal security," in a "state of nature" governed by the principle of natural equality, all of them insisting on the maxim *superiorem non recognoscere.* On this basis, Pufendorf added, states were still capable of meeting among themselves "when necessary" for cooperation and mutual aid. An interdependence manifesting itself only in such *ad hoc* meetings is obviously rather marginal to the idea of a community of mankind in a world of sovereign states.

A full vanishing point, found later in the same tradition, is at the opposite extreme. Wolff, in his engagement with the dialectic of sovereignty a century after the Grotian consolidation of the young law of nations, saw no other way of apprehending the binding force of its rules on equal states than to assume that this law was the law of the *civitas maxima,* a notional world polity transcending all particular states. In terms of a community of mankind organized in a world of sovereign and equal states, this concept is obviously an evasion of the problems. For in it the aspirations for a community of mankind and of a law that can bind equal sovereign states have been swallowed up in the postulated world polity.[35]

It is not surprising, therefore, that though Vattel was much influenced by Wolff in other aspects, he did not follow him in this desperate bid to end the troublesome dialectic of sovereignty. He reverted rather, as we have seen, to the fruitful equivocations between sovereignty and equality of states on the one hand and to the duties of humanity on the other. His unrivaled influence on the practice of international law in the two centuries since he wrote no doubt reflects predominantly the equality-sovereignty reference in this equivocation. Yet he also affords, along with Grotius, the most influential model for those later writers who were determined somehow to hold on also to the notion of a community of mankind whose welfare should be the concern of all sovereign states.

This model, of course, became even harder to follow as full secularization of the body of law whittled away ancillary support (which Grotius had claimed) from a divinely supported natural law. Yet in certain respects the tensions between the competing references within this fourth equivocation have eased in the present century. No doubt there is much rhetoric in the U.N. Charter's preambulatory invocation of "the *Peoples* of the United Nations," of faith in "fundamental human rights," "the dignity of man," the "equal rights of men and women" (paired, despite the latent contradiction, with those of "nations large and small"), social progress and better standards of life, and the resolve "to employ international machinery for the promotion of the economic and social advancement of all peoples." Yet even within the modest limits of the operative provisions of the Charter, for instance for the Social and Economic and Trusteeship councils, and of developments like the technical assistance program, the work of specialized agencies like the International Labour Organization, the World Health Organization, UNESCO, and ambitious blueprints for an international seabed authority, a "new international economic order," and the rest, the institutionalization of functions concerned with the welfare of mankind on a world scale has made some progress. The fact that such functions are vested in (or envisaged for) entities other than sovereign states eases the strain of their coexistence with the more inward-looking residues of the doctrines of state sovereignty and equality.[36]

This easing, of course, is not really a solution of either the basic theoretical or the practical perplexities involved. It does not, for example, much ease the practical perplexities of stating in acceptable and feasible form the critical precepts for redistributing world resources so as to produce a minimal standard of social and economic justice for men and women throughout the world. Even success in fuller integration of sovereignties in structures like the European Coal and Steel and Economic communities gives only limited promise for the wider reaches of mankind, which lack the proximities, homogeneities, and symbiotic relations that largely explain the degree of regional success. So that I have been and still remain rather skeptical of theses suggesting that somehow a community of mankind with its common law is already in course of establishment (if not, indeed, already established) in replacement of the traditional state system.[37]

Skepticism, in its turn, should not lead us to disdain the role that even integrative structures limited to given regions can play in promoting material and social welfare by increased efficiency of the integrating states as a result of pooling and sharing skills and resources and of greater incentives to better management of men, money, and resources. Nor should we disdain their role in widening the concerns of each nation to embrace the security, welfare, and progress of other nations within the region and even in the wider international community. All this might press the world of states towards a fuller community of all mankind, but it might also only end in the maturation of wider and more powerful units of international rivalry and conflict.

I will later suggest, for the economic sphere, that we are probably at most in a tentative and intermediate stage somewhere before the emergence of a community of mankind. In the final outcome, not a little may yet turn on what sense man can make, in *both* head and heart, of the problems of international justice. Meanwhile, we remain, into our own days, confronted by the actuality of each state as the predominant decisionmaker on all the vital matters concerning the use of its power and resources and concerning the distribution among its own people of burdens and benefits that arise from these decisions. In this respect, the idea of sovereign equality of states, embedded in the traditional law, still awaits the wisdom and the will needed to adapt it to the high purposes of assuring a minimal freedom and subsistence to all men and women.[38]

To identify all the several aspects of the equality principle that bear upon the relations of states—namely, equality of "sharing" (related to freedom of decision) and equality of honor, estimation, and privilege, and the like—does not in itself provide either this will or this wisdom.[39] Neither absolute denial nor absolute affirmation of the equality principle nor elaborate distinctions between the values in respect of which equality can be claimed illuminate much the more difficult contemporary problems of international justice.[40] As with the list of "values" that is so central a feature of McDougal's policy-oriented legal science, national and international, the real difficulties begin after the values have been listed and named, either in general or for the particular conflict. It is after that, usually, that the crucial choices have to be made about which of them is to be sacrificed, and how far. For, except in the simplest cases, not all of them can be equally secured.[41] It is indeed possible that at certain points there is a direct conflict, so far as concerns their import for the realization of accepted values, between the appeals to "justice" and to "equality," respectively. Robert Tucker has drawn attention, for example, to the plausible hypothesis that one of the consequences of replacement of the *bellum justum* doctrine by the principle of equality between combatant nations during time of war was the emergence of commonly accepted restraints on the conduct of warfare, leading to a degree of humanization.[42]

Finally, the denunciation of the principle of equality as a myth obviously at odds with actual state ascendencies and dependencies.[43] which marks the bitterest core of the debate as to equality, can only be fully understood by moving outside that debate itself. For in terms of that debate, as we have seen, the rich cluster of equivocations that the equality formula covers forbids any simple aye or no to the cry of "myth," or to other similar skeptical positions. In terms, for example, of the doctrine's reference to mere equality before the law, that is, to the title of all states to assert before international law such benefits as that law confers, the cry of "myth" cannot literally stand. The deeper meaning of the cry lies in the fact (which the emotive overtones of the equality slogan tend to conceal) that not merely the legal status of particular states but their very existence and whole subsequent life are usually the product of inequalities of power rather than of impartial principles of justice symbolized in the equality notion. This deeper meaning is important not merely for historians and cynics; it is also important in the search for *precepts* of international justice. For it reminds us that we may be compelled, even today and in the future, to recognize the existence of limit situations in which, by the very nature of those situations, justice cannot be effectively achieved through law.

9. States, Human Beings, and International Justice

Ｉf, as many believe, justice is to be sought through mediation of the *meum* and *tuum* of the conflicting claims of the human beings found within the territorial domain and legislative competence of the relevant justice constituency, no less than four critical corollaries are implied for any society, be it municipal or international. First, this constituency must be so organized that all its members can express their felt needs or demands. Second, it is by this process, which directs attention to the sociocultural situation of men and women, that material precepts of justice relevant to present actuality are sought. Third, implied in this, the tasks that face us are most centrally tasks of adjustments of conflicting demands, involving sacrifice of some. Finally, the claimants of justice whose demands set the stage for its drama, as well as its beneficiaries, must be human beings.

When we observe the efforts to achieve a just distribution among members in a particular justice constituency, its achievements as they become stabilized in time may be thought of as historically won enclaves of justice. Within these achievements are precepts that for the people of that constituency are recognized as worthy of acceptance and may even come to *appear* as self-evident and even quasi-absolute.

This enclave metaphor is useful to encourage certain orientations of mood and concern in those who address themselves to problems of justice. It directs us, for example, to the historical struggle of members of humanity, individually and in their societies, to achieve the gains that they now hold, as well as to the forces that threaten what is held or support its defense and to the emotional and intellectual commitments entailed.[1]

The general problems to which these notions of the justice constituency and enclave of justice address themselves become more intense in degree as we approach the questions of justice *between nations*. We can no doubt envision, in Isaiah's metaphor, a world in which swords will be beaten into ploughshares and nation will not lift up sword against nation. We can even accept that in a world of justice for all humanity all nations will have

89

acknowledged some ultimate principle of embracing goodness and the brotherhood among all people that this implies. We should also recognize how important it is that men everywhere, especially in their rather graceless condition, should have such visions kept clear and meaningful by the devotion of some men in each generation.[2]

After we have accepted all this, however, we will encounter grave difficulties for clarity of thought about justice between nations. Among the gravest are those caused by the intrusion into the data with which the criteria of justice must operate of the territorially based political organizations that we call states, each interposing itself between human beings of different nations. If states consisted of mere conduit pipes or channels of communication or distribution of benefits and burdens between all mankind, the difficulties would be serious enough. But the elements of the justice-evaluating process would not be critically different from those with which we have long wrestled, not without success, in the municipal sphere. But, of course, the role of the state cannot as yet be so limited, nor is there any prospect of its becoming so in the foreseeable future.[3]

Despite the phenomenal growth and efficiency of worldwide communications, and other contacts between nations in the *physical* sense, already seen in chapter 1, our age is dominated by tendencies towards direct or indirect control by the state of all socially important means of communication. This control brings with it, despite our best efforts to resist, a tendency to what I have elsewhere called "the nationalisation of truth and justice."[4] Within the rather insulated chambers of each state, the free exercise of the intellectual and moral faculties of men tends to yield place to acceptance of official versions. In matters of international concern, we face, in Richard Falk's words, even a certain "nationalisation of scholarship," as well as its shadow opposites in adversary societies. In realms of the intellect and the spirit, this reinforces rather than weakens the supernatural accouterments of the state. The dominance of "nationalized" values insulates men of each state from those of others; it also deprives them of effective criteria for criticizing their own government and hinders the spread of opinions across unfriendly frontiers. Each state becomes increasingly not only the powerful guardian of its human members as regards their material welfare and security and the fulfillment of their major aspirations; it becomes also a barrier, a rack of torture for their values and sense of justice and a blockage against the transmission of these to their fellow men in other states. The negative effects of these tendencies are further aggravated by the depersonalizing and stereotyping effects of technological progress. Modern weapons not only multiply destructive capabilities but also depersonalize the destructive process by interposing time and distance, and mechanical contrivances, between the actors and the responsibility for horrors perpetrated on the victims; and the decisive weapons become increasingly the monopoly of governments.[5]

We are at best, then, in a kind of purgatory in which, despite the rapid growth of economic and physical interdependencies, the functions and organs, and even the knowledge and techniques, required for common counseling, decision making, and action to implement decisions cannot yet be said to be in sight. The truth is the same whether we state it in terms of world community or in our own terms of a human justice constituency.[6] We must agree, no doubt, that the common concern of nations to eliminate economic misery and destitution already exists independently of state frontiers and ideological alignments and despite deep disagreements about other aspects of international justice. I observed in 1946, in the context of Western municipal legal orders, that the assurance of minimal material standards of individual life was there already a substantially agreed end.[7] No doubt other factors, including bidding for diplomatic support, have helped to promote the remarkable growth of aid from more developed nations to less developed nations. But one factor, certainly, is the extension of the principle of municipal justice, that human dignity implies entitlement to a basic life subsistence and that to this extent at least all members of a society are their brothers' keepers. There is much that can be said about international justice even on so modest a foundation, and I shall return to this point in the concluding section. Yet, in the relevant operations of international aid, it is still each state that speaks with a conclusive voice for the human beings within it.

The following matters, as already briefly mentioned in chapter 5, remain within the prerogative of each state's determinations; and they are obviously crucial for any concept of humanitywide justice.

1. The disposition vis-à-vis other states and peoples of "goods" (in the widest sense, embracing all valued things, facilities, and skills) that lie, by reason of physical location and otherwise, within the state's control according to the existing international legal order.

2. The distribution of such goods among the human beings who constitute its people.

3. The assessment and assertion of the demands of its people against goods similarly controlled by other state entities, the distribution of which among mankind generally is a main part of the business of justice in the international field.

4. Decisions whether to place such power and resources as it controls at the service of the directives of humanitywide justice.

5. Decisions whether to place such power and resources as it controls in opposition to the directives of humanitywide justice.

6. Decisions to withhold such power and resources from participation in efforts to achieve humanitywide justice.

These prerogatives of each state entity result in certain special difficulties, also already referred to, of fixing what we have called the "constituency" relevant to *international* justice. Allocations among all mankind on the basis of one man to one entitlement will not work within this state-dominated frame. Those who have to make the international judgments of justice (be these national or international agencies) must make the allocation to each state authority, which will then distribute among its human members at best according to criteria that it claims to be apt for its own municipal justice constituency, at worst arbitrarily or even not at all. No doubt we already have glimpses, in the operations of such agencies as the World Bank, European regional agencies, or U.N. technical assistance, of devices for guiding or controlling the international redistribution of goods through to their allocation among human beings within the municipal societies concerned. They are, however, glimpses only. Moreover, the regional European experience, because of the highly developed reciprocity there present, is of limited persuasiveness for world purposes. For one thing, the high level of reciprocity among European regional participants is not typical of the reciprocity between Western, African, and Asian nations. Nor have the Europeans had to overcome vast gaps in human cultures or the heavy burdens of past one-way exploitations— resentment on the part of the exploited, guilt on the part of the exploiters.

The vision of a humanitywide justice is also marred by the difficulty that, apart from all persons' basic presupposed rights (involved in human dignity) to form and express their own interests, the justice that appears to be within human reach is somehow conditioned by the environment and experience in time of the particular justice constituency. The judgment of justice also depends on the facts knowable and known at the point in time and space at which the decisionmaker stands; and it is to accommodate such elements of experience and knowledge that the notion of enclaves of justice gained, held, extended, or lost by men in particular societies is so useful. Obviously, when we try to use such notions on a humanitywide basis, matters become very complicated by dint of the great number of peoples involved and the vast gulfs dividing their respective environments, cultures, and experiences. Directives of justice that seem to be thoroughly warranted in the enclaves held by some peoples have little warrant and much incongruity for other peoples.[8] The legislator who may glean helpful directives for the internal life of each people may still have little or no guidance for a society supposedly embracing many or all peoples.

There is, of course, no sharp line between the difficulties of intrastate and humanitywide tasks of doing justice. Municipal societies, like the present South African polity (not to speak of numerous former ones, including those of ancient Greece), have presented acutely many of the difficulties affecting the humanitywide tasks. These include sharp diversity of cultural patterns and experience with justice within a single society and dualism or pluralism of ethical norms (and of entitlements under these) all deliberately maintained by state authority. But the challenge to the legitimacy of such a state of affairs, both by leaders of the oppressed segments and by other states and peoples, and the bitter controversies that surround it indicate that it is now marginal, at any rate in Western *municipal societies.* While all societies, and not least the developing ones, show wide and varying defaults of justice by any standard, the view that such gross defaults within a municipal society can be *ethically* justified is now exceptional in the West. So that we might even hope that here, at least, is an enclave of justice that virtually all modern nations have now reconnoitered and either captured or resolved to capture. Yet, this is to speak only of what is professed by each municipal legislator *towards his own people.* The international legislator who will secure even such marginal entitlements of human beings *as against their own* recalcitrant *government* is still in the future. In this very case, the power and policies by which the South African government insulates white South Africans from sharing in the general moral growth of mankind symbolizes a central difficulty of framing a conception of justice on a humanitywide scale that does not remain mostly speculative.

Can we escape such problems, then, by treating the international justice constituency as consisting of state entities themselves, leaving *outside* the ambit of *international* justice the relation of each to the human being who compose it? This, indeed, is the common assumption of diplomatic and political discourse, which regularly personifies state entities, attributes demands and rights and duties to these, and appears to make judgments of justice on this basis. This facile (and in my view unacceptable) solution is found also in less relaxed discourse. The municipal analogue of it has been a main target of my criticisms of the sociological theory of interests and its related theory of justice, and it is deeply relevant at this juncture in the argument.[9]

This part of Roscoe Pound's theory of interests has endangered clarity of thought about justice in municipal legal orders, especially when we speak of "interests" of a state in its own "personality" or "substance" or of the state as *"parens patriae."* To speak thus, I have pointed out, is to take technical legal devices at their face value as judgments of justice, begging the question of what justice *requires of law as to the human demands involved.* As to the "juristic personality" of a state, is not this, like that of a corporation, but a legal device to secure various interests of human beings protected by its political organization? As to the state's supposed "interests of substance," are not the immunities of the state and its preferential position as a creditor vis-à-vis the citizen—insofar as they are well based at all—only legal devices for securing the social interest in the security and efficiency of political institutions? No doubt, as to the state as *"parens patriae,"* we find legal apparatus of widely varying form and structure by which special attention is given to certain human demands, for instance, care of dependents, defectives, or national resources or supervision of charities or other corporations. Such apparatus ranges from formidable statutory corporations and commissions to informal administrative advisory committees or heads of judicial jurisdiction, like that over lunatics or minors.

It is especially tempting, when some powerful state organ is involved, to think of it as having interests or making demands for itself or for the state and to call these public interests. Yet in principle there is no difference between this and slighter or more ephemeral legal devices or apparatus. The mere fact that pieces of legal apparatus used to secure particular kinds of human demands are relatively powerful and sophisticated cannot turn these pieces of apparatus into human beings, or their rights and powers into human demands, relevant to justice determinations. This being the case regarding the notions of public interests or interests of the state in relation to justice in municipal law, the same *may* have to be said of such notions in relation to justice in the international sphere. These nations may there, too, mislead us into taking for granted that claims made by the states of the world are an adequate basis for making a just distribution among the human beings that constitute their populations.

Roscoe Pound, indeed, introduced this perilous lapse of thought into international law itself, though international law was not his main concern. With a surprising inadvertence to the difference between a state entity as arbiter of justice among its own human members and a state entity as one of the members of an international community among whom justice is to be done, Pound also offered the supposed "absolute," "fundamental," or "natural" "rights" of states under international law, for instance, of self-preservation, independence, equality, and dignity and of exclusive territorial jurisdiction and *imperium* as examples of "public interests." Are these to be regarded as relevant to international justice? The question is tangled by the wellknown ambiguity of such terms as "absolute" and "natural" rights. If by his use of these examples Pound intended to refer to rights *conferred by international law*—to legal rights— then the examples might not be open to the objections explained in the preceding paragraph. But, then, on this basis Pound's analogy between the "rights" of states under international law and the de facto claims of human beings within a municipal society is neither fruitful nor even acceptable. Modern international law still conceives such legal rights as held by states vis-à-vis other states and, with only minor exception, not by human beings at all. Legal rights no doubt are often legal advantages that support claims proceeding more or less from human beings as distinct from state entities. Yet to *assume* that those human claims coincide with, or even closely correspond to, legal rights of states under international law is to beg questions of the sociology of international law, on the answers to which orderly thought about international justice also depends.

If, on the other hand, the terms "absolute," "fundamental," or "natural" rights are understood in this context as referring not to rights under positive international law but to demands of so basic a nature that a "higher" ("natural") law requires positive law to support them by the conferment of legal rights, objections to Pound's position are different but not less serious. For whatever human claims are assumed to lie behind such "absolute," "fundamental," "natural," or "basic" rights of a state in this second sense, these cannot, whether we call them demands justified by higher "law" or, more simply, by justice, necessarily be coordinated with existing legal rights under the prevailing system of international law.

If, as I believe, these criticisms remain unanswered and unanswerable in terms of basic theory, they reinforce the obstacles that we have seen to be presented by the compartmentalized system of territorial states to the framing of a conception of justice on a humanitywide basis. For the aggregate of state entities cannot *as such* constitute a meaningful justice constituency; and their existence also blocks the ascertainment of the demands of men and women of all nations that is prerequired to bring them into a single justice constituency. A looser way of saying this is that the operation of that sense of common humanity that is presupposed by a humanitywide conception of justice seems to be gravely inhibited.[10]

Even among the learned, as I have already mentioned, contemporary discourse often overlooks the need for choice between the conception of international justice as justice between states (that is, within a justice constituency whose members, and therefore claimants and beneficiaries, are states) and that conception of it which is humanitywide justice (that is, within a justice constituency whose members, and therefore claimants and beneficiaries, are all the men and women of the world, regardless of the state to which they belong).[11] Diplomats and publicists seem to calculate in terms of state entitlement—but not entirely or consistently so. They also speak of justice to Asians, or Indians, or Africans, or Bantus, or oppressed or less-developed or under-privileged peoples, but they deal by and with governments of states. When aid to a developing country is under consideration, the number and poverty of its people and the responsibility to them of the state apparatus, its degree of honesty, and its efficiency as a channel to their welfare are often dominant factors. With "territorial" and "political" claims, on the other hand, like those concerning frontiers and unification of states, calculation rarely goes beyond state entity entitlement. Even when it seems to do so, it still usually stops at some hypothetical entity—for instance, at the claims to unity of the German or Chinese or Korean or Vietnamese "nation"—far short of the demands of the human beings finally involved.[12]

What is most troublesome concerning this ambivalence is not the duality of focus but the absence of sustained effort to draw some objective line between the occasions when one or the other is to be appealed to.[13] For the main point—that neither can serve as a *sole* basis of present thinking about international justice—does not exclude the possibility that each of them may, within ascertainable limits, provide at least some practical bases of judgment.

The following propositions might provide a starting point for thought in delimiting the respective influences of the justice constituencies of state entities, on the one hand, and of the men and women of the world, on the other.

1. Insofar as international justice requires transfer of goods, including (here and in the following paragraph) services and skills, from peoples better endowed to those less endowed, these goods must relate predominantly to the elementary means of *material* advancement, food, raw materials, machine tools, know-how, and the capital necessary for achievement and development of these. To these must be added, in the actual world, and despite the dangers of wasteful diversion to the concerns other than justice, the means of military security, whether in the form of arms, finance for securing arms, or military training.

The negative aspects of this proposition are less obvious but no less important. The proposition makes clear that international justice cannot at present be primarily concerned with the protection of the *ordinary interests of human personality*, but only with the material preconditions for these. This protection of personality interests still rests, and is likely to continue to do so, on adjustments *within the justice constituency of each state society*, for two reasons: (a) the crude, deplorable, but understandable general refusal of state entities to allow routine intrusion of other states or of international agencies, for the protection of the men and women from their own power;[14] and (b) the fact that even should this refusal soften, the wide variation of cultures and attendant values would still leave the authorities of each state as, prima facie, better qualified than any others for adjusting conflicting claims of personality among its citizenry.

2. Where (as is largely the case) justice requires transfers of such goods, services, and skills from one people to another for the purpose of accelerating the social and economic development of the receiving state, it is the latter that must be the final judge (after adequate counseling) of scale, pace, and direction of such development.[15] This by necessary (though less pleasant) implication also imports that the receiving state must be the judge of distribution among its own population of the burdens imposed and benefits conferred by such development.

3. The ideal of equal endowment of men and women throughout the world with the material goods cannot, in the foreseeable future, be a practical prescription of *international* justice. When this proposition is considered in conjunction with the earlier point that cultural diversity

among the world's peoples makes it rather impractical for international justice to prescribe directly the precise entitlements of rights of personality of all men and women, this may seem a grave renunciation of many noble hopes for world order and the impressive pretensions of declarations and covenants of human rights. Yet powers that are not within our reach can scarcely be said to be renounced, so that we face not a renunciation but only the as yet rather unalterable present facts of power over people jealously held by states. Moreover, even when the limits are thus recognized, *we are still left with other critical questions of minimum material endowment and the assurance of minimal rights of personality.* Questions of *minimum rights* of all mankind are one thing; those of *equality of rights* are another.

If we feel rebellious against this tempering of high aspirations, we should call to mind the stark realities that bid us to submit. The solid hostility with which most peoples confront South African apartheid policies, and the naked power which supports them, is not a function of failure to realize social, educational, political, economic, and legal equality of South African Bantus with other peoples throughout the world. They would appear in fact, in some of these respects, to compare more than favorably with some other African peoples whose governments denounce apartheid. The hostility is rather against legally enforced permanent inequality of Bantus *as compared with white men of the same state* and, in some respects, against failure to secure to them what can be regarded as an acceptable minimum. If we were to treat equality in these various aspects among all mankind as a present imperative of international justice, we would face vastly uncomfortable, if not impossible, duties with regard to a large and varied range of modern states. The arbiter of international justice (to offer some random instances) would have to meddle with tempo and method of fulfillment not only of the emancipation of the Bantus of South Africa but of the Indian commitment to abolish factually as well as legally the inequalities arising from the caste structure of Indian society. He would have to take sides in the chronic controversy concerning the million former Indians now in Ceylon, in the Malaysia-Singapore controversies concerning the Chinese in those countries, in the divisions within Indonesia, in Negro-white struggles in the United States, in Negro-Arab struggles in the Sudan, in colored-white conflicts in the United Kingdom and other countries, and in Chinese-Malay relations in Southeast Asia. He would have to wonder what can be made in terms of equality of all men and women of the forcible drafting of Katanga into the Congo, and Biafra into Nigeria, and to keep an eye on the treatment of their own tribal groupings, as well as their white inhabitants, by scores of new African and Asian states. Of such supervision these states (however zealous their desire to remold South African society) would surely be very intolerant indeed. As seen in chapters 3 and 7, especially in the text accompanying and following n. 12, the aspects of traditional international law that have the strongest support of Third World (as well as Soviet bloc) states are their own prerogatives of sovereignty. This is despite their own deliberate and indeed systematic intrusions on the sovereignty of selected target states in terms of liberation or related doctrines and economic demands.

4. It can be stated with some confidence that international justice has come in the present age to import a duty upon more affluent states to foster achievement of minimal subsistence for all the people of the world.[16] The precept importing such a duty may come to be unconditional, but it certainly still falls short of this. It is difficult to see, even when aid is not channeled through the receiving state's apparatus, how donor states can be asked not to show concerns as to who in fact benefits from the transfer. So far as this is so, donor states must also be entitled, consistently with justice, to weigh before they act the record and prospects of a recipient government for concern and efficiency in attending to the needs of its people. If it is true that after receiving six hundred million dollars in grant aid, a Tanzania formerly self-sufficient in food has ceased to be so, this fact is certainly relevant here. That this change may be related to the Tanzanian government's policies of compulsory collectivization of eleven million peasant farmers does not ease the perplexity. Even more troubling is the further indeterminate qualification on this duty, which must surely arise when a receiving government fails to take such measures as are feasible to discourage levels of procreation that cannot be sustained by any reasonably projected economic growth or availability of food.[17]

It may be indeed be argued that in certain relations arising from history, the duty imposed upon donor states is not subject even to such mild conditions. Between some peoples and others, it may be said, lie heavy duties of this kind, duties of restitution and reparation for great historic wrongs. The reaction of Tanzanian President Nyerere, at the Cancun meeting of October 1981, to U.S. criticism of his government's record in agricultural production rests implicitly on some such principle. The United States, he declared, was hypocritical in advocating free agricultural markets, since its own agrarian strength had been "built of slavery." In a similar mood, J. S. Bains argued that the Indian use of force for the liberation of Goa in 1961 was a legally and morally justified reaction to the Portuguese conquest of Goa in 1510, no Indian government having in the intervening four and a half centuries voluntarily accepted the legitimacy of the status quo subsisting during these centuries.[18] The gist of such a position cannot, of course, be as to rights under positive international law, for there it would confront rather settled doctrines of title by conquest and prescription, and the stale and endless juxtapositions of the legal contradictories of *ex iniuria non oritur ius* and *ex factis oritur ius*, not to speak of U.N. Charter obligations prohibiting use of force against the territorial integrity of other states. The gist of the argument must concern not law but justice. And on this level it provokes the important question as to whether the mission of delineating a future international legal order that is acceptably just to all peoples should be burdened at the outset with the impossible preliminary task of expunging all the black record of collective wrongs of the past. No generation of men could hold the gate of sanity against such a demand.

If we were to accept it as a part of the task of present international justice to right all historic wrongs between former generations of peoples, we would then confront further impossible questions: How, if at all, are we to assess and liquidate wrongs committed by former generations of some peoples against others? After how many generations, and on what terms, could collective moral indebtedness in justice be written off, and the past left to bury its dead?

Yet it has to be added that the attitudes here invoked in the name of feasibility still imply moral effort and responsibility of a very high level. For international justice thus envisaged still demands that some nations (largely but not only the ex-colonial Western powers) shall adopt a policy of sacrifice and helpfulness on a basis other than self-interest or reciprocal material benefits and to an extent measured only by their own capacity and the vast needs of states whose peoples lack subsistence. Conversely, this conception asks the present generations of many African and Asian nations to assume an attitude of uncalculating forgiveness towards wrongs of the past and to accept help for implementing their national tasks in a spirit of common aspiration towards a better human future. The irreversibility of most wrongs of past generations of nations joins their present aspirations for the common human future to bid us forward, with eyes ahead.

It must now be stressed, moreover, that it is not merely practical urgencies and mutual compassion but also the promise of technological advance in ways of peace that presses in the direction here indicated. For even if we were resolved to see the great and pervading wrongs of past generations righted by the making of present restitution and reparation, and even if it were feasible for the states concerned to make now the redistributions thus found due, would it not still be doubtful, to say the least, how far such amounts could be decisive or even very significant in the struggle of the new states for rapid development in pursuit of subsistence? No conceivable extension of the principle of unjust enrichment, now emerging in the sphere of international agreements, could reach these more general problems of the historical relations, of exploitation and the like, between developed states and developing states generally. That principle, moreover, is one in which equities on both sides have to be taken into account. In many cases the entitlement of the ex-colonial people would have to be adjusted to allow for benefits already received. The same relations that saw gross exploitation also often saw the transmission of substantial elements of educational, administrative, social, economic, and technological skills, as well as managerial and institutional resources, that later became part of the ex-colonial people's national inheritance and at least a first beginning of development.[19]

The very lapse of time usually involved, and the spectacular accompanying change in range and tempo of economic activity, has multiplied the scale of all the factors involved in the process of economic development, including gross national product, capital investment, technological base, and labor. The capital extracted by the exploiters since the eighteenth century, if restored according to the real values at the date of decolonization, would still almost always fall far short of what is essential for economic development of a now-independent state. Aid that may become available to developing states under a principle geared to the needs of their contemporary development seems likely far to exceed even generous estimates of reparations due for wrongs of past centuries before this multiplication of range and scale and of technological capacity to produce. Mutual compassion might march also with material success.[20]

Finally, in relation to these propositions relevant to delineating an international justice constituency, it must be said that the duty to make a sufficient transfer of goods and skills to permit general attainment of minimal subsistence is also pressed upon us by the harsh and otherwise intractable nature of the relations between the richer states and the poorer states by whom they are surrounded and to whom most of them are tied by this irreversible history.[21] Of course, the political and economic decisions leading to such changed use of resources would not come automatically from anticipation of the therapeutic effects of diversion from fear of war to constructive tasks of peace any more than from mere conscience, goodwill, and humane ideals.[22] But once we see the nature of the imperatives that lie behind the duty of aid, it is not at all naive to bring into the prognosis of the human future such likely accompanying changes.

It is appropriate to recall that one of the earliest modern statements of the demand that more affluent states assume responsibility for assisting in the attainment of humanitywide subsistence was that of a theologian rather than an economist, a political leader, the authors of the Atlantic Charter, or an international official. In 1943, Emil Brunner, interlocking prudential with ethical precepts, declared that many problems, such as the colonial problem, depended for their solution on somehow detaching economic life from its too-exclusive connection with national political life. With nations, as with individuals, the wealth of the rich is unjust *when it entails* the poverty of others, so that such nations, when they persist in regarding their special economic advantages as their unqualified "due" and in excluding others from preserves commanded by their power, are contributing to future wars. Economic imperialism, in this sense of the preservation or enhancement of economic advantages at the expense of others by superior political power, strains all peaceful ordering. And for this reason, Brunner argued, "the most far-reaching detachment of world economy from power politics is one of the most urgent postulates of international justice."[23] Whether and in what sense this demand has proved correct and feasible is a central point of the succeeding consideration of the "new international economic order" of the seventies and eighties.

10. Justice and the "New International Economic Order"

An approach to international justice in terms of contemporary urgencies leads rather inevitably to the area of international economic relations. Kenneth Boulding once explored, in a related context, whether it was possible to formulate with precision the meaning of "the world economic interest" as a final criterion by reference to which adjustment should be made.[1] The term "interest," as he there used it, obviously refers, not to a de facto demand conflicting with other de facto demands, but to a judgment as to where final community advantage lies in resolving such a conflict. In this sense, the notion of world economic interest may be understood as a criterion of economic justice for adjusting the conflicting economic claims of individual men and women constituting mankind as a whole. Can world economic interest in this sense of a world economic justice criterion be given a meaning sufficienty determinate for practical use?

Clearly, before we could use the notion of world economy in this context, we would have to define a base "condition" of the economy by reference to which improvement or setback, and therefore world economic interest, could be measured. For, in economic theory, before we can speak of such world economic interest, we have to formulate a condition, or a working model, of world economy by reference to which improvement and impairment in the realization of that interest can be measured. The prospect of evolving such a model or models is itself problematic. Closely related to the above preliminary difficulty is the identification, already stressed, of the relevant justice constituency of all mankind (here the *economic* sectors of it) in operationally useful terms. If we assume, however, that such a base line can be fixed, other major groups of problems still loom. What measures of quantity will reflect the level of satisfaction of human demands or needs throughout such economic, cultural, and developmental heterogeneity? How can we evaluate decrease of resources for some peoples as against aggregate increase for the rest? What weight should be given to reducing inequality, as distinct from increasing absolute levels?

One aim of "just" economic action should certainly be the reduction of economic inequalities between states as regards the production, exchange, distribution, and consumption of wealth. It would then be a material precept of international justice that economic relations should be so arranged that economic inequalities between nations are reduced. At one extreme, as I have already shown, economic *equality* among them is not attainable at present or in the foreseeable future; no precept of justice demanding it seems plausible. At the other extreme, it has not been too difficult to show that assistance by more developed to less developed states, so as to enable the peoples of the latter to reach an adequate level of subsistence, is a basic precept of international justice. In between these, we can perhaps venture, as I have just done, a precept of justice for *the reduction of inequalities.*[2] Even, however, if we do (and this is the main point here), such a precept can afford little guidance for action until it has been adjusted in the concrete world situation with the precept requiring the maximization of aggregate "world" economic welfare or resources. Thus Boulding himself, in terms of his own analysis, recognizes, as I have already observed, that his criterion for aggregate maximization by reference to per capita income would have to have built into it some kind of nonquantitative index of tolerable inequalities.[3] On one side of the line of tolerance we would treat equality as irrelevant; on the other side as decisive. On one side increase of world economic resources is decisive; on the other it is irrelevant.

What this means is that even if we look only at *economic* justice, nonmaterial values (or disvalues) intrude—here the disvalue attributed to inequality *that cannot be justified.* And it is this last emphasized qualification, of course, that throws the whole problem beyond the range of *merely* economic calculation.

It is, furthermore, not merely the disvalue of economic inequality that here complicates economic calculation.[4] The problems of social and cultural heterogeneity, as we have seen, already operate here. Similar quantities of material wealth, even in terms of "real" values, may have radically different meanings for different peoples, quite apart from variations between individuals. What will qualify as socioeconomic betterment, or reduction of inequality, is affected not only by economic quantities but also by the psychological facts of the need, receptiveness, and expectations found in the social inheritance of each particular people. The available ways of accumulating capital for "economic take-off" may also be severely limited by accepted ethico-political commitments. We must not think of this point merely in terms of sacred cows.[5] In past times abuses such as trade in slaves or narcotics or the exploitation of child labor have been important sources of capital accumulation. Moral constraints against such methods now operate severely in economic development, aggravating the tasks of developing countries and placing them under inequality as difficult to overcome as time is to recall.

The duty of the more developed states to help to assure a minimum human subsistence seems, as I have shown, virtually unconditional. This justice imperative is imposed by history and by the situations in which history has thrust the peoples concerned, as well as by ethical commitments that most of them and their governments have already assumed. I have now to add that, pace President Reagan's 1981 thesis (to be mentioned later), whatever the criteria, such duties cannot be implemented merely by ordinary processes of international trade. There is no escape in our age from Boulding's conclusion that if a world economic interest could be postulated, its pursuit would have to include processes not only of expansion of trade but also of a world "grants economy."[6] And I would here make explicit the vital rider that useful directives for the processes of a "grants economy" cannot be drawn from the notions of either world economic interest or interdependence unless we recognize the kind of justice imperative imposed by history on the relations of the more developed states to most of the newer states. If we are to refashion these relations into genuine interdependence, the measures must include a great international reallocation of resources as a matter of present international justice rather than of mere bargaining or mere bounty or even of enlightened long-term self-interest.

These problems of transfer for the sake of planetwide human subsistence are difficult enough even in a steady world economy. Despite some signs of impending recovery in the United States, this was far from the state of affairs in 1984. Whatever the other causes, the OPEC-inspired oil crisis following 1973 appears to have been a watershed. In terms, for example, of the developing countries, the massive escalation of national indebtedness, often at unprecedented levels of interest, transformed the economic picture. In the decade 1973–82, the indebtedness of most of the developing countries multiplied many times, and this included even developing countries with oil endowments. The debt of Brazil rose from $10 billion to 90 billion; that of Mexico from 7.2 billion to 80 billion; that of the Argentine from 3.5 billion to 38 billion; that of Peru from 2.4 billion to 8 billion; that of Chile from 3.4 billion to 22 billion; and that of Venezuela from 2.0 billion to 32 billion. In the same decade, oil prices peaked at twenty times the 1973 level, aggravating the in any case dramatic effects of inflation and abnormally high interest rates. From late 1977 to mid-1982, loans to non-OPEC Third World nations tripled from $94 billion to $270 billion, suggesting a substantial, if not generous, response to the oil needs of these nations. Debt crises of Poland and Yugoslavia preceded those in Latin America. Polish debts were renegotiated in 1981, but by mid-June 1983 there was pressure for them to be further renegotiated, no payment having been made on the 1982 principal ($900 million) of outstanding interest.

The Polish case displayed as illusory any expectation that the Soviet Union would rescue Communist bloc countries in case of need, and COMECON debts alone to Western banks in August 1982 stood at $80 billion. These developments, and above all the virtual insolvencies of Mexico, the Argentine, and Brazil from August 1982, seem to have preempted any major outcome of calls by the so-called Brandt Commission for general transfers and loans to less developed countries (LDCs) mentioned hereafter. In its fifth Annual Development Report, in August 1982, the Bank for International Settlements estimated that by 1985 the sum of all new credits to the developing nations would be less than total debt replacements. On 19 May 1983, Robert McNamara, president of the Overseas Development Council, pointed out that new loans to non-OPEC LDCs in 1981–92 had declined by 51 percent (from U.S. $40 billion to under $20 billion) and new loans to Latin America by 61 percent in 1981.

Between 13 August 1982, when the Mexican debt crisis broke, and the end of the year, it was estimated that a dozen debtor countries, 1,000 creditor banks, and $300 billion in loans were involved. The rescheduling and conversion of these loans pressed for and assisted by the International Monetary Fund and the World Bank were conditioned on further expansion of loans for bridging purposes by up to $55 billion up to February 1983. In these renegotiations the banks were rewarded for increased risks yet also somehow tacitly assured by the informal role of central banks of informal rescue through their own governments in case of trouble.[7] Questions of further rescheduling were raised by Brazil at an International Monetary Fund meeting of two hundred leading bankers from twenty-two countries in Brussels on 19 May 1983, leaving undecided creditors' demands for provision of further "bridging finance" through the Bank for International Settlements or the central banks. A further crisis, when these international bodies alleged that Brazil had not met the conditions (as to measures of austerity) entitling her to their assistance, was barely averted by new Brazilian undertakings on 14 July 1983. These involved a further currency devaluation (the eighteenth) since February 1983 and a restriction on the inflation-indexation of wages, rents, and mortgage payments to 80 percent of the consumer price index.

The Toronto meeting of the ten major industrialized nations and the International Monetary Fund of 1–5 September 1982 followed, by co-incidence, closely after Mexico's virtual declaration of bankruptcy in August 1982, with an external debt of $81 billion. Even before that, Congress had taken the step of stretching the United States' three-year contribution to the World Bank "soft window" of the International Development Agency over four years ("soft" loans to appropriate poor states accrue no interest for fifty years). And it was estimated that this would cause a 35–40 percent drop in funds available from that source. The United States, however, proposed a compensating global emergency reserve fund of $25,510 million, to be administered by the IMF to meet recession financial shocks; and it was agreed that this additional "crisis fund" should be contributed by the ten major industralized nations and operated through the IMF. About the same time, the Bank of America's William Bolin and former IMF official J. de Canto were proposing in *Foreign Affairs* for June 1983 an eight- to fifteen-year export development fund, to be backed by the United States Export-Import Bank, to finance increased exports from the heavily indebted developing states. This would obviously go far to convert informal governmental guarantees into formal ones.

The economic recession and the debt crisis in one sense supported the 1980 arguments about "mutual interests" in wealth transfers and trade assistance and preference for the less developed nations made by the Independent Commission of International Development, headed by former chancellor Willy Brandt and Prime Minister Olaf Palme of Sweden. The preoccupations, stringencies, budgetary constraints, and excuses of the recession; the debt crisis; and the politico-military concerns already referred to, however, left the longer-term issues of world poverty and the "new international economic order" rather unattended at Williamsburg in June 1983. And that U.S. Treasury Secretary Donald Regan had, on 19 May, asked Congress for an increase of $8 billion in the U.S. contribution to the IMF, of which $2.4 billion was to be made available for developing countries under the "General Agreement to Borrow," no doubt contributed to this quietus.

In human macrowelfare terms of unemployment, the 1973 decade began with 8 million unemployed in twenty-four Organization for Economic Cooperation and Development (OECD) countries. By 1980 the figure had risen to 25 million, and by 1982, to 30 million. According to official projections, this figure was expected to reach 32 million in 1983, though trade unions projections were closer to 37 million, including 10 percent of the work force in the United States, 10 percent in Italy, 12 percent in Canada, and 15 percent in the United Kingdom. The European Economic Community was said to have 22 million unemployed on 7 July 1983, and this figure was projected to rise to 30 million by 1990. The U.S. administration claimed a small decrease of the number of unemployed in mid-1983, but the AFL-CIO secretariat announced simultaneously that only about half the unemployed were receiving unemployment benefits. What all this amounted to in terms of individual suffering varied with the welfare systems of the various states, with very wide divergencies as to both the amount and the duration of weekly entitlement. For the worker with a dependent spouse and child, at the higher levels were West Germany, which paid $204 per week for 12 months (thereafter a means tested unemployment benefit); and Japan, which paid $210 per week for 90–300 days, according to seniority. At the other end, the United States paid about $112 per week for up to approximately 26 weeks.

In announcing on 19 May 1983 the increase in the U.S. contribution to the IMF for loan facilities to developing countries, Treasury Secretary Regan stressed that this was essential in America's own economic interests. It is a sad paradox that the very economic handicaps of developing countries that demand such other-regarding measures from democratic leaders of the developed states tend to become politically impracticable as democratic electorates perceive their own societies as also suffering deprivations. It is sad but inevitable, moreover, that the deprivations are felt only by reference to local expectations and may not even be thought to be severe by Third World standards of poverty. This is a matter to which I will have to return in chapter 12, but it must be faced even at this point.

It is not too difficult for experts or nonelected functionaries to hold verbally the balance between planetary subsistence for all mankind and the prosperity of the more developed states. The goals involved can be rationally and eloquently stated, as they were in Chairman McNamara's statement of 20 May 1983 for the Overseas Development Council. Global growth, said McNamara was sustainable only if industrial states, especially the United States, adopted fiscal and monetary policies leading to non-inflationary growth. Yet this was not enough. Not only growth in developed nations but also financial liquidity in middle-income nations, as well as a great increase in concessional financial aid in low-income countries, was essential. Simultaneously there had to be a reduction of economic protectionism and more adequate incorporation of the developing countries into the multilateral system of trade.

The first three years of President Reagan's administration, which witnessed pressure from many quarters for increased foreign aid, loans, and trade concessions, were also years of severe recession, 10 percent unemployment, and a political commitment to restraint in deficit financing. So-called razor gangs were mandated to cut (above all) welfare budgets and defense budgets. The PPSSCC Group (headed by J. Peter Grace) on 9 May 1983 was still recommending cuts in U.S. services of $25.8 billion, including hospital management, the Veterans Administration, and others. This was after severe cuts in food stamps and other welfare services of the previous years denounced as heartless by the administration's critics. The PPSSCC also projected ominously that if trends of Reagan's first three years continued, by 1990 the cost of annual social programs would exceed $1,000 billion, *without* the cost of nominal social security programs *stricto sensu*. Little more than a week later, on 19 May 1983, President Reagan was heard to observe as if by way of comment, that "the American people didn't send us to Washington to raise taxes. They sent us here to stop that." On a smaller scale, the incoming Australian Labour Government of 1983 found itself faced with hard choices between excessive deficits, the trimming of overseas budgetary commitments, severely unpopular measures for cutting back old-age pensions, and superannuation tax concessions. The outcome still has to be seen at this writing, as indeed is also the case in the conflict between commitments to freer trade within the original GATT framework and the impulse to protect employment and overseas reserves by more or less overt industrial and agricultural protectionism.

The electoral penalties that in democracies, may affect national leaders' pursuit of McNamara's international vision may be vastly increased when international commitments bring, as with the current overseas debt situation, serious hazards of undermining and collapse of the national banking and currency systems. When the remarkable recycling of petrodollars through operations of Western banks reaches the point where more than $300 billion has to be rescheduled, without servicing being assured, even then, disastrous dangers come into view.[8] For both the national and international spheres, collapse of the many banks involved would create national financial crises and would destroy the mainspring from which developing countries must draw most of their financial requirements. No doubt this indicates the desirability of concentrating the international tasks in multinational agencies such as the International Monetary Fund and the World Bank and winding down the functions of private banks. That, however, is scarcely a feasible remedy in the shorter term.[9]

When we face the magnitude of transfer problems involved, it is clear that this imperative of international justice bears major corollaries concerning other competing uses of the resources of states, especially the developed states. It is apparent that there may be the severest competition between the defense-security function and that of achieving minimal standards of life for all mankind.

It would be fatuous to conclude that progress towards minimal subsistence required by a humanitywide economic justice presupposes a world in which international security is attained without substantial arms expenditure; on the other hand, it is quite clear that such progress presupposes a world in which international security is attained despite a most drastic reduction in present arms expenditure. In the lead-up to the revived SALT talks on 30 November 1981, the projected Soviet defense budget for 1982 was 17.05 billion roubles; the projected U.S. budget was U.S. $196.5 billion. The U.S. defense budget for 1981 was U.S. $171.40 billion. For 1983 President Reagan proposed a defense budget of $198.5 billion. It is certainly not fatuous to say that it is an important corollary of the precepts of international justice that such expenditure on arms (and perhaps on other goals, such as space exploration) ought to be reduced as much and as quickly as possible. Only by wisely husbanding the world's resources can there emerge a genuine approach even to that degree of economic solidarity among nations implied in the common goal of minimum subsistence to all men.[10]

The melancholy of these observations is deepened by one new aspect of cold-war conflict thus revealed. As early as May 1983, the House Armed Services Committee approved a $188 billion defense bill, leaving $10.5 billion more demanded by the administration still to be fought over. While this astronomical level was not wholly attributable to new weaponry like the MX and the B-1 bomber *directly,* there is little doubt that it represents one aspect of what may be called 1983 "cold-war economics." This area of tension, of which one recent dramatic sign was the U.S.– Western European disagreement concerning the Siberia-to-Europe gas pipeline, is concerned finally with the relative economic capability of the two sides to sustain ever more expensive new weapon deployment. Though such statistics are always somewhat speculative, the Soviet trade deficit is said to have doubled in 1981 from the previous year, to $5.5 billion, requiring the sale of 300 metric tons of Soviet gold for $3.5 billion and $1 billion of credit from Japan and the West to meet this deficit. Even if we could be more confident of the outcome of this new kind of contest in capacity for conspicuous waste of global resources, it is tragic to contemplate at a time when hundreds of millions of human beings hover chronically on the brink of starvation and the projected world unemployment moves towards fifty million. (I will return to other aspects of armament control and reduction in chapter 12.)

The apparent harmony of the Williamsburg meeting of the ten major industrial nations in June 1983 was unexpected in view of a whole series of open conflicts of interest in the preceding period. These included European and U.S. grievances concerning Japanese export subsidies and import restrictions, especially regarding U.S. beef and oranges; prolonged altercation between the United States and Europe concerning deals of the European states with the Soviet Union linked to the pipeline project, as well as related problems of leakage of U.S. technology to the Soviet Union; sharp reverse reactions to the sudden end of the U.S. boycott of the Soviet Union, and the sale to the Soviet Union of six million tons of U.S. grain; and the growth of protectionism of both manufactures and agriculture as between the United States and the European members. All this is beside the intra-European issues, for instance, as to Danish access to mackerel fisheries claimed as exclusive by the United Kingdom, and issues of the United Kingdom with the rest of the European Economic Community touching agriculture and special areas and her financial contribution.

Despite these latent conflicts, the annex to the Williamsburg Declaration of 1 June 1983 set out a list of rather bland objectives: "achieving non-inflationary growth of income and employment and promoting exchange market stability through . . . convergence of economic performance"; reinforcing "multilateral cooperation" with IMF surveillance activities touching, *inter alia,* reduction of budgetary deficits and a disciplined monetary policy, allowing sustainable growth but not inflation; and stabilizing exchange markets pending study of exchange intervention (this last being, perhaps, as near as the conference came to a controversial issue—the French demand for international monetary reform).

That the Williamsburg Conference took place as the projected time approached for the emplacement of Pershing II and Cruise missiles in Europe at the end of 1983, while the vigorous campaign continued in Europe against this emplacement and in the United States itself for a nuclear weapon "freeze," and both the START (strategic) and the medium-range nuclear weapons talks continued, has been thought to explain this unexpected harmony among states who are also NATO partners. The first concern of these states at such a time, it was suggested, was both to strengthen the negotiating strength of the alliance and to ensure that if negotiation came to nothing, the deployment of medium-range nuclear missiles in Europe could proceed. While all this, if it were so, would be readily understandable, it is surely lamentable that an economic conference of countries whose unemployed had by 1983 reached well over 30 million was deterred from addressing not only problems of *aid* to the poorer states but even their own internal economic problems by the assumed need to deploy new arms costing many billions of dollars.

Even, indeed, if sanity in arms costs could be regained, so that required quantities of resources could be marshaled for human improvement, whether through trade or aid programs, the very division of them among the beneficiary states must become a matter of regular but manageable contention. So must the sharing between the more developed states of the burden of making aid available. We should take hope from the fact that these tasks seem far less formidable than they would have seemed thirty years ago, although this hope has lost some of its brightness amid the economic setbacks, and the surge in the costs of fuel, since the 1970s. Approaches to these problems have already been made in the allocation of burdens of such budgets as those of the United Nations, the International Monetary Fund, the World Bank, the International Development Association, and a score of other organizations, not to speak of the experience of quasi-public consortiums of private resources to meet particular emergencies.[11] Whether these are sufficient channels for the global decision making involved, symbolized now in the hortatory generalities of the program of the NIEO and the Charter of Economic Rights and Duties of States, was among the central issues at the Cancun summit meeting of leaders of twenty-two developed and Third World nations in October 1981 (and I shall shortly discuss it further in this chapter, as well as the next chapter). The eleventh special session of the General Assembly in August 1980 had pressed for a new round of "global negotiations" on trade, energy, finance, development, and raw materials. The double drive was here apparent—on the one hand, to extend the quasi-legislative role of the General Assembly and its organ UNCTAD; on the other, to supersede pro tanto the carefully shielded procedures of the International Monetary Fund and the World Bank.[12]

It is easy for lawyers to overlook the very revolutionary nature of the demands for international economic justice because of excessive concentration on the formulation of a legal agenda of tasks awaiting fulfillment for realizing the "new international economic order." Each article and, indeed, many subarticles of the Charter of Economic Rights and Duties of States cry out for major projects of legal research, whether these concern sovereignty over resources; foreign investment; transnational corporations; lawful nationalization of foreign property; international trade; transfer of technology; international financial and other institutions; or exploitation of the international seabed. In addition to the inherent difficulties of the substantive law areas involved, these tasks raise constituent problems as to who is the competent decisionmaker. Sometimes the action only of developing countries singly or in cooperation is involved, to be acquiesced in by others. Sometimes what may be involved is action by developed countries for the benefit of others; sometimes cooperation between developed and developing countries is required.

I have already pointed out that the central problem of this international economic area is a matter of international justice rather than of international law, of norms *de lege ferenda* rather than *de lege lata,* of desired rather than actual law. One of the virtues of the sober report of International Law Association Committee Chairman Kamal Hossain in 1980 is its recognition that the principles of the "new international economic order" may sometimes involve "established" legal precepts, as well as precepts or directive principles that are not yet law.[13] Some of the latter, for instance, as to "equity" may be so indeterminate as to leave matters largely to each decisionmaker; they are important instruments in "a strategy for the redistribution of wealth and power" (par. 34).

Even such balanced accounts, however, sometimes cover over this elementary truth by referring to principles such as equitableness as if they are not only law but also effective. Altercation often turns on a similar blurring of the line between existing law and desired law. When Chairman Hossain referred to "the right of all states to participate in decisionmaking with regard to not only existing but also evolving rules," Dutch discussant P. Peters wondered what he meant by "decision" about "existing" law and thought that "normally states would be bound by the existing rules" (par. 23 and p. 287). By contrast, a Bangladesh participant took it for granted that since developing countries constituted 70 percent of the world population, their share of the world's industry will have quadrupled by the year 2000 (287); and a Philippine speaker thought that the facts that we now had "a world community" and that more than 100 of the 160 U.N. members were developing nations made world redistribution of wealth imperative (290–91). An important intellectual device for rendering plausible the identification of precepts required by the claimants' criteria of justice is to introduce, sometimes rather concealedly, novel and debatable legislative notions.

One such notion is that insofar as the U.N. Charter is a "mandatory treaty," it is *ius cogens*, and therefore U.N. resolutions interpreting its principles "share . . . the mandatory nature of the mother norms which inspired them." It is also implicit in Chairman Hossain's point that any *emergent* principles of law would proceed on a basis of equality but "with the necessary exceptions by way of positive discrimination in favour of developing countries" (par. 39 [c] [ii] and p. 297).

The confrontation between demandant states and target states within the supposed global justice constituency was obvious at the adoption of the Charter of Economic Rights and Duties of States of 12 December 1974. The provision as to nationalization in Article 2 of the charter was adopted on a vote of 120 in favor, 6 of the more industrialized states against, and another 10 of the more industrialized states abstaining. The arguments were still reverberating in the late U.S. publicist Alwyn Freeman's remarks at the International Law Association's debates of 1980 (202–306).

Professor Ian Brownlie's claim, Freeman said, that Article 2 of the Charter of Economic Rights and Duties of States is *ius cogens* is "outrageous" and "sheer nonsense." "If there is *ius cogens* in this context, it is the sovereign right of every state . . . to protect its nationals abroad by diplomatic means, and not any putative right to deny justice to all." The claim that diplomatic protection was an artificial, nineteenth-century weapon of imperial interests was "a statement so far removed from fact and law that it falls outside the arena of scientific discourse" (303). From De Legnano in the fourteenth century through Gentile, Zouche, Suarez, and Grotius to the twentieth century, there was "an unbroken and unwavering line of authority" supporting the right of each state to protect its nationals. The right continued to be sanctified by scores of treaty provisions for arbitration of investment disputes, despite contrary suggestions in General Assembly resolutions concerning private foreign investments and their nationalization.

Behind disputes over Article 2 lie, of course, still wider claims that the new Third World countries are not bound, unless they so choose, by rules formed before they came into existence. Western publicists were still insisting in 1980 that the very 1962 General Assembly resolution on each state's permanent sovereignty over its resources gave no basis to the claim to be rid of the customary rule requiring "prompt, adequate and effective compensation" on nationalization. The opposed parties in 1962 had carefully reserved their positions on that matter (304–5). Of course, it does not follow that even if the existing law was at present equally applicable to Third World states, it ought to remain unchanged. It is a valuable aspect of the International Law Association's discussions in 1980 that they recognized the dependence of claims for a "new international economic order" on some analogy to "affirmative action" and "reverse discrimination" compensating historically disadvantaged groups within municipal societies (par. 33).

The analogy with "affirmative action" and "reverse discrimination" is, however, not perfect. For instance, these are usually adopted within municipal society by legislative measures constitutionally adopted by those who are to bear the burdens involved. Furthermore, they usually refer to justice to human beings, whereas there is no necessary correspondence between doing justice to an impoverished state and doing justice to its human members. Moreover, as Professor M. Reisman observed at the Belgrade Conference, the contents of the charter and other provisions about the NIEO are such a mixed bag of legal norms, merely emerging norms, and mere exhortations or *voeux* that it is futile to try to give the NIEO any single legal status. According to this view, insofar as legal change, and therefore consent by the states affected, is required, the causes of underdevelopment in Third World states must be recognized as many, including corrupt or inefficient indigenous government and the crippling impact of the twentyfold increase of oil prices after 1973. So that developed states cannot be held as sole scapegoats, to be stripped of their existing legal rights, without their consent. Reisman added that the choice of the doctrine of each state's permanent sovereignty over its resources as the foundation of demands for a new economic order was very incongruous with demands for transfers of resources from developed states based on interdependence and reciprocity. For such demands ignore this absolutism of each developed state's sovereignty over its resources.[14] And some incongruities of thinking are even found in Chairman Kamal Hossain's 1980 *Report.* The report suggests, for example, that implementation of new regimes for nationalization of foreign property, foreign investment, and primary commodities cartels would require action *only* by developing countries (par. 20), since developed states are enjoined *not to obstruct such action* (Charter Arts. 1, 5, 7, and 32). Burdens as to nonreciprocal tariff and other preferential benefits to developing countries are also treated as imposed by Articles 18–19, all this despite the refusal of the developed states to support the adoption of the charter in 1974. Recognition of the need for cooperation and reciprocation between developed and developing states seemed to have been limited by the chairman to the pursuit of indeterminate objectives such as "rational and equitable international economic relations," mentioned in Article 8, or the "social and economic progress" ("especially of developing countries"!), mentioned in Article 9.

The blurring of the basic distinction between existing legal entitlements and demands that changes in those entitlements be negotiated takes varied and subtle forms. Indian publicist S. Roy Chowdhury ostensibly recognized the above distinction, as well as that the introduction of reverse discrimination and preferential treatment of developing nations, rather than reciprocity and cooperation, is involved and that the Charter of Economic Rights and Duties of States is not legally binding in itself but rests on nonbinding General Assembly resolutions. Yet he still contrived to treat the "emerging" norms as having some kind of constitutive and legally revolutionary force, either because, he seemed to say, nonbinding General Assembly resolutions may become binding by repetition; or because legal change can be made by "consensus" of states generally as distinct from "consent" of the states prejudiced; or because moral or political commitments can produce "legal implications" (291–93). French Professor M. Flory posed similar issues, saying that the transforming of NIEO objectives into *droit positif* cannot be achieved by any merely *positivist* technique, adding that one possible technique is the use of new symbolic notions such as "charters," "guidelines," "programmes," "codes," and standard clauses (293–94).

These and other ingenious suggestions seem to beg a vital question. For example, when we focus on the controversial Article 2 of the Charter of Economic Rights and Duties of States, concerning a state's "full permanent sovereignty" over its resources, at least the following bitterly contested issues still have to be negotiated. What are the legal conditions of the host sovereign's competence to nationalize? What is the treatment legally required to be accorded to the "vested rights" of aliens? What is the extent of the host state's responsibility for unlawful acts against aliens? Has the test of "appropriate" compensation replaced the test of "adequate, prompt and effective" compensation? If it has, what matters are relevant to "appropriateness"? In particular, what is the relevance of the "unjust enrichment" principle to the test of "appropriateness," if that test is adopted? Behind these questions lie some even deeper ones. What weight is to be given to the subjective and self-serving opinions of the host state in legal reform? What terms, if any, of an apparently freely negotiated concession would be inconsistent with "permanent" sovereignty? Can a host state by a stabilizing clause limit its own right to claim such inconsistency? What degree of "inequality" of bargaining power impairs the validity of contracts? For it is important to observe, as to this last, that it is not and never has been true as to contracts in municipal law that any degree of inequality of bargaining power will impair validity. Only certain degrees and kinds of inequality, variable in different systems, have this effect, and this specification still has to be settled in international law. And overarching all these issues are those as to whether there is to be any compulsory jurisdiction (and if so, of whom) over investment disputes; and those as to the effect, if any, of the omission of a good faith principle from Article 2 of the Charter of Economic Rights and Duties of States.

The harsh fact is that beyond mood and rhetoric, the provisions of the charter are for the most part too fragmentary for implementation without major agreements still to be reached. Indeed, it is likely that the negative attitudes of developed states reflected crucial gaps in the charter, as well as objections to controversial articles, such as Articles 2 and 5. Such gaps, for example, concerned access for developed countries to natural resources, safeguards for private investments abroad; provisions for supplies of energy and food; and the standing and operational regimes under international law for transnational corporations and banks.

After discounting defensive reactions by Western states to what they see as self-serving claims of developing states to ride roughshod over international law, two basic points remain even when the claim of justice for some system of benign reverse discrimination has been granted: (1) that the active and unselfish cooperation of developed states is essential for any substantial movement in the NIEO; and (2) that important steps towards a better "order" may be achievable without the endless altercations about legal bindingness by seeking content for its principles and procedures for their implementation that are acceptable. This means, of course, that they have to emerge by dialogue and understanding, rather than be steam-rollered through by "automatic" majorities in the General Assembly or UNCTAD conferences. A similar point is to be made, *a fortiori*, as Oscar Schachter has observed, as to the interpretation of the requirements of standards such as "equity" (283–84). Other guidelines to acceptability lie, of course, in the contractual nature of investment, the mutuality of *pacta sunt servanda,* and trusted processes of third-party settlement of disputes, as with the International Committee for Settlement of Investment Disputes (ICBID). Bilateral arrangements may still open the way to generalization through most-favored-nation clauses or plain repetition.

It has, indeed, been suggested, even as to matters as controversial as guidelines for multinational enterprises (MNEs), that effectiveness may be achievable by voluntary adoption by the entities concerned. In support have been vouched the proceedings of a group of experts at the University of Bielefeld, *Legal Aspects of Codes of Conduct of International Enterprises,* in 1979; as well as a report of the OECD Committee for Investments and Multinational Enterprises in 1979 on the working of that organization's guidelines (310–11). "There are plenty of golden eggs left in the Western goose yet," Alwyn Freeman has said, "but you will not get them out faster by wringing its neck" (305). He should perhaps more correctly have said "get any more eggs," for in a trivial sense one could certainly get *some* eggs faster!

In terms of sovereignty, it has to be said that enjoyment of rights, powers, and immunities brings with it acceptance of related responsibilities and restraints and that it is part of the mission of international law, with all its imperfections, to attend to all of these.[15] No doubt, assertions of exclusive control of transnational matters by the host's domestic law seem an obvious way of protecting the interests of developing states. Yet insofar as acceptance by the developed states of other proposals for the "new international economic order" is still essential, it may also be misguided and vain. As R. K. Jain, of India, commented, "A way must be found to make sure of the cooperation of these countries because otherwise [the NIEO] would be an exercise in futility" (308–9). This may have to be seen as independent of whether the recession of the early 1980s continues or, as many thought as of mid-1983, a durable recovery led by a 6.6 percent growth in the United States' GNP is now in prospect. Yet, as the Belgrade UNCTAD Conference on Third World aid closed on 3 July 1983, no rapprochement was in sight as to either the dimensions or the directions of the transfers or loans required. For the first time since UNCTAD was founded, the "Group of 77" and the developed states could not agree on a final communiqué. The repair of this breakdown seems far more critical than the International Law Association's proposed "systematic study of comparative law principles, instruments, procedures and institutions of existing international economic organisations and their appraisal in view of the effective implementation" of the "new international economic order" (par. 39[b]).

11. International Justice and Responsibility of Rulers

 I have shown the cogent rational grounds for accepting a precept of international justice requiring richer states to afford means of ensuring a minimum level of subsistence for the men and women of all countries.[1] I have suggested that as an approach to righting wrongs of the past, such a precept would be more feasible and effective than any principle of restitution. I have also tried to show that acceptance of such a precept would provide valuable psychological incentives towards the further consolidation of an intelligible international justice constituency, towards the development of world resources to meet population pressure, and towards the reduction of wasteful expenditures such as those on armaments and space exploration. Can such a precept be regarded as accepted (or in the course of acceptance) among the peoples concerned and the national and international decisionmakers involved? In other words, assuming that we could delineate clearly the international justice constituency, could this precept be regarded as within enclaves of justice already won, or at least within such enclaves as are in the process of being won?

In this inquiry there is one sure starting point, namely, that the more developed states—those from whom the main sacrifices to fulfill such a precept would have to be expected—are mostly either Western capitalist democratic or Communist democratic states. No doubt other motives have often accompanied the sense of duty, such as redeeming past sins of exploitation and, less commendable, the search for political advantage. But, with equal certainty, the dominant factor has been a degree of diffusion onto the international scene from the comparatively well-held enclaves of municipal justice constituencies of precepts enjoining minimum subsistence for all inhabitants within each such constituency.

The authenticity of this diffusion is still obscured by the comparatively small proportion of aid resources channeled through U.N. and other multilateral operations and by the mixed motivations (just referred to)

117

that accompany bilateral aid arrangements. The thesis that multilateral channels are the more efficient channels for aiding developing countries towards subsistence is here confronted by the traditional power-political implications of bilateral aid, these implications being extraneous to the justice commitment. The most hopeful factor for neutralizing these extraneous drives of power politics is not, of course, the main justice precept itself concerning minimal subsistence; it may rather be a more general (and, as seen in chapter 8, a more richly ambiguous) precept of justice concerning equality. The relevant aspect of equality here appeals to the self-interest of the major developed states, for the "equal" sharing of the aid burdens, especially as against other developed states that have not yet assumed a proportionate burden.[2] This "equal" sharing by a common plan through a common channel manifests once again the fertile ambiguity of the principle of equality. In this context the equality principle presses, along with other factors, towards the multilateralization of aid already emergent as a contemporary trend.[3]

Yet, the important point for present purposes is that the questions that persist in debate are not whether aid is required from developed to developing countries, but how much aid, how transferred, how borne among the donors, how used by the donees, and whether the role of aid as distinct from trade in narrowing the North-South gap has not been exaggerated. The aspirations in Article 55 of the U.N. Charter for stability and well-being based on the equal rights of peoples, the securing of higher standards of living, full employment, and the conditions of economic and social progress and development and the pledge of members of the United Nations in Article 56 "to take joint and separate action in cooperation with the Organisation for the achievement of the purposes set forth in Article 55" are of course commonly invoked in General Assembly resolutions on technical and economic aid. The pioneering Marshall Plan for Europe, the Point Four and technical assistance programs, the resolution of the British Labour Party in 1957 to dedicate at least 1 percent of the gross national income for economic aid, a similar resolution passed by an overwhelming majority of the Council of Europe, and the target of 0.7 percent of GNP for official development assistance (ODA) set by the United Nations itself in the international development strategy for the second development decade for its developed members all add to the evidence of some kind of precept of international justice already emergent at the mid-twentieth century. An even more general movement towards the multilateral model would be an important step towards increasing the aid that can be marshaled, as well as the doing of justice among both contributors and recipients. And it would also make progressively clearer the requirements of justice that press imperatively for the available resources to be made more adequate.

How far can the union of full commitments of more developed states to minimal subsistence standards within their municipal domains, along with the beginnings of commitments in the world arena just discussed, be taken to prove that an enclave has also been won (or is in process of being won) *in some assumed world-justice constituency?*[4] Can we say that the duty to assure a universal minimum subsistence is about to be or has already been established as part of the movement of international life? It is tempting to assume (and certainly to hope) that since the domestic and foreign policies of these states are broadly controlled by the same leaders, the precepts of justice accepted by them in the domestic sphere can be regarded as equally established for the external relations of their state with other states.

So far as the ethical acceptability of the precepts are concerned, the problems that arise do not seem too difficult. The main one concerns the assurance with which the rulers of each state can ask their people to forego a modicum of their own material welfare in order to raise less fortunate people nearer to subsistence. The question is made sharper by the fact that not the donor governments and peoples but the governments of the receiving states will control the use of resources thus transferred and, above all, by doubts as to the compatibility of this transfer with democratic processes in the donor states. Can we see democratic leaders maintaining the support of electors at any point when the magnitude of the transfers to foreign nations for such purpose bites seriously into the level of welfare benefits and the personal affluence that domestic electors have grown to expect? These were grave questions before the advent of the world economic recession of the 1970s; they nag even more powerfully in the eighties. It is also a truism in the domestic politics of states that the long-term struggle for votes produces a steady rise in expected benefits and that only looming economic disaster (as in contemporary Britain) can arrest these processes, and then only with difficult and hazardous outcomes. The regular travails of American presidents in securing support for their foreign aid budgets are well known.

This danger that democratic leaders may lose electoral support, and with it political power, if they prefer the duties of international economic justice over claims of domestic justice that voters see as more urgent, is not limited to the greatest industrial states nor to the particular matter of grants by way of development assistance. Few doubted, even before the Melbourne Conference of Commonwealth Heads of Government in October 1981, the intense wish of Prime Minister Fraser's government to advance the so-called North-South negotiations. Both the Harries Committee report, *Australia's Relations with the Third World,* and the report of the Senate Standing Committee on Foreign Affairs and Defence, *The New International Economic Order: Implications for Australia* (1980), pressed for the restructuring of Australian industries by the phasing out of protectionist measures. Prime Minister Fraser himself, at UNCTAD V in Manila in May 1979, declared that protectionist measures must be resisted. "If they are not, they will put the growth of developing countries into jeopardy."[5] For the governing party to act on these convictions will still require considerable courage and incur serious federal risks. The automobile industry, which is regarded as a test case of the protection issue in Australia, was already the subject of serious division within Mr. Fraser's political party in November 1981.[6]

As the decade of the 1980s opened, it was possible to draw up an impressive list of international declarations and *Programschriften* that since 1960 have moved the issues of international economic justice towards the center of the stage, second only perhaps to the issues of peace and war. The aspirations and demands for economic change now symbolized with ambiguous simplicity by the title "new international economic order" (NIEO) represent a cumulation beginning with the generalities of the U.N. Charter already mentioned. They proceed, as I showed in chapter 10, through the General Assembly Resolution on Permanent Sovereignty of States over their Economic Resources (1962) through meetings of the U.N. Conference on Trade and Development (UNCTAD) beginning in 1966 but especially in 1976 and 1979, the Algiers meeting of "nonaligned" nations in 1973 and parallel special sessions of the General Assembly in May 1974 and September 1975, and the U.N. Conference on International Economic Cooperation of 1977. The aspirations and demands involved were described by the sixth special session in 1974 in a Declaration on the Establishment of a New International Economic Order (Resol. 3701 [S-VI], 1 May 1974) as based on "equity, sovereign equality, interdependence, common interest and cooperation among all States," aiming to reduce "the widening gap" between the developed and the developing countries,[7] and ensuring "steadily accelerating economic and social development." This declaration was immediately complemented, as already seen, by a program of action (Resol. 3202 [S-VI], 1 May 1974) and by the Charter of Economic Rights and Duties of States of 12 December 1974 (Resol. 3281 [XXIX]) at the seventh special session of the General Assembly in 1975.[8]

These aspirations and demands, whether in the context of UNCTAD or of the NIEO, are essentially demands of an aggregated majority, at first of 77 and now of about 120 less developed nations, pressing for major redistribution of world resources, at present vested in comparatively few "developed states." The establishment, after the oil crisis of 1973, of a smaller Conference on International Economic Cooperation (CIEC), in 1975, comprising 19 less developed and 8 developed nations, while less cumbrous as a forum for dialogue, has not changed the basic realities of the one-sided nature of the demands involved nor the truth that while redistribution can be negotiated, it cannot be imposed. Indeed, neither legal power nor actual power has proved to be available to impose these aspirations, whether in the continuing UNCTAD meetings at Manila in 1979, the eighth general session of the General Assembly in 1980, or the meeting of heads of state of 22 less developed and developed states at Cancun, Mexico, in October 1981. In the framework of the World Bank and the International Monetary Fund, moreover, the persuasive force of the aspirations is even less, since the decision-making structures and processes are carefully and firmly designed to protect the economic interests of the states making the greatest contributions to these mechanisms, which thus have the greatest stakes in these bodies. All this is not to deny the weight of these aspirations in terms of international justice; on the contrary, it is to focus attention precisely on those considerations. All this is no less clear in the recommendations of the Brandt Report, of 1980, where, however, the demands of justice are sought to be fortified by reference to the long-term economic, political, and security interests of the states against whom the demands are made.

The general state of the negotiations immediately before the Cancun meeting of 1981 may be briefly related.[9] As to terms of trade and commodity prices, agreement had been achieved at the 1977 CIEC Paris Conference on the general principle of a common fund to ensure improved stable conditions for the export and import trade of developing nations.[10] It was estimated that the financial provision required would be $3 billion immediately and $3 billion on call. One main divisive issue was how the burden of financing buffer stocks (window 1) was to be borne— whether by governments according to economic strength, when it would rest mainly on the developed states, or by the particular commodity associations, when the burden would be borne differently and more diffusely. Another issue was whether the fund should finance additional functions for the benefit of less developed states, such as export diversification and market research (window 2). Following further negotiating conferences, an agreement was finally reached on 28 June 1980. Under this agreement both windows would be established, by contributions of $1 million from each government (on the assumption that 150 governments would participate), the balance of $320 million for window 1 to be borne by Western industrialized states (68 percent), socialist states (17 percent), China (5 percent), and less developed states (10 percent). The less developed nations, although contributing only 10 percent, would have about one-half of the voting rights, though important decisions would require a three-fourths majority. For a variety of reasons, including difficulties of completing agreements as to the details of adjustments on additional commodities, no substantial advantage is yet in sight in the terms of trade of most developing countries.

As to debt renegotiation, cancellation, moratorium, rescheduling, or interest subsidisation, the position of the less developed countries has, of course, been grossly aggravated by extortionate oil prices. Eleven developed states in 1978 agreed to forgo debt payments from the poorest countries amounting to $6.2 billion.[11] As to other debtor nations, agreement was not reached on proposals of the Group of 77 at the fifth session of UNCTAD in 1977, and the main issue is whether relief should be accorded only as claimed by the developed states, on a case-by-case basis, or on the basis of some wider criterion. In 1975, due to the rise in oil and other prices, the deficits of less developed countries (other than those of OPEC) had risen to $38 billion.

From 1974 to 1978 the debts of non-oil producing developing countries rose from $142 billion to $315 billion, and by 1980 they were expected to exceed $420 billion. Anticipated debts for oil purchasers are a major problem per se. While demand for oil from developed states is estimated to decline by the year 2000 from 66 million barrels per day to 64 million, the demand from developing countries is estimated to rise from 11 million to 24 million. Proposals for a new World Bank affiliate were mooted at Cancun, increasing the presently projected U.S. $16 billion to finance the developing countries in this energy cost to U.S. $50 billion over the period 1981–86. Over the period 1980–90, U.N. projections raise the cost of oil to developing countries from its present $50 billion to $110 billion.

The claim of these countries to more influential participation and "more equitable" voting rights in international institutions such as the World Bank and the International Monetary Fund is very natural in view of the overwhelming influence that their great numbers give them in the General Assembly and in other U.N. organs. Although there have been some adjustments in their favor since 1972, developed countries still control about 61 percent of the voting rights, oil exporting countries about 9 percent, and other less developed countries about 29 percent.

Developmental aid and improved access to the markets of developed states are the other two principal targets of the bloc of states still misleadingly called the Group of 77. I have already adverted to the increasing shortfall from the target of 0.7 percent of GNP of a number of developed countries, including the United States, Western Germany, Japan, and Australia, though it is to be added that some of them, for example, the Netherlands, Norway, and Sweden, have exceeded that target.[12] Improvement of access to markets, depending as it does largely on the level of domestic protection, is also directly affected by domestic economic difficulties such as inflation and unemployment of the seventies, persisting into the eighties. Protectionist tendencies operate despite the standing framework for trade liberalization presented by GATT. Developing countries have been assisted by certain preferences within the GATT framework for some time; the benefit of such preferences flowed, however, in the nature of things, only to the more advanced developing countries. In the Tokyo round of GATT, in 1973, it was agreed that special consideration should be given to the needs of the developing countries. General reductions in tariffs in the various rounds of GATT, however, also decreased the value of preferences for less developed countries. This, together with safeguards projected against "cheap imports" from particular countries, still leaves in doubt what benefits to less developed states will emerge from this special consideration.

Movement in the bringing into effect of codes of conduct for transnational corporations and for the transfer of technology remained slight to 1981. The proposals had originated in the Commission on Transnational Corporations of the U.N. Economic and Social Council in 1975, and they were stalled mostly on the major issue of whether the codes should be on a voluntary or mandatory basis. On this issue the more developed states, including Australia, have (not surprisingly) favored the voluntary basis. The developing states, for their part, confronted the dilemma that they often wanted to attract transnational corporations, while an imposed code might drive them away.

The aspirations and the conflicts of interests surrounding what has come to be called too simply the North-South issue also became central to epochal tasks undertaken by the U.N. Conference on the Law of the Sea (UNCLOS), the hard core of unsettled matters concerning the resources of the deep ocean and the deep ocean beds declared by General Assembly resolution to be part of "the common heritage of mankind." The distribution of the resources involved between states whose technological capacity extracts them, and other states of the international community proposed to be represented by an "international seabed authority," is the core of this hard core.[13]

The difficulty of settling these matters, even as to resources not yet distributed, is now reflected in the disappointing failure of the new Law of the Sea Treaty, after eight years of negotiation, to bridge the gap between the most developed and the less developed states. On 9 March 1982, the eleventh and final negotiating session on the treaty opened in New York to deal with U.S. objections to deep-sea mining provisions, the text for which, like those for less controversial facets of the treaty, had been reached by "consensus." The Third World Group of 77 states (now numbering 120) argued that the United States had been a party to the negotiations concerning the seabed and that these were already adequate and did not need to be reopened. The United States, whose representative at the United Nations, Jean Kirkpatrick, was later (on 12 December 1982) to designate the Law of the Sea Treaty as part of a "redistributionist bonanza" prepared by U.N. bureaucrats, proposed amendments on five matters.

First, the United States asked for abandonment of the common "heritage of mankind" basis of the part of the treaty dealing with the seabed so that the control of mining would remain in national jurisdictions. Second, it sought to modify the parallel systems of exploitation by national private or government consortiums, on the one hand, and "the Enterprise" of the proposed international seabed authority, on the other. Third, it rejected the one-state, one-vote basis of the proposed thirty-six-member council of the new authority as not reflecting the realities of either technological capacities or consumption of resources and also as facilitating discrimination against the United States, for instance, as to strategic materials. Fourth, the United States resisted the demands that mandatory transfer of technology by private companies to "the Enterprise" be a condition of license to mine. Finally, the United States objected to amendment provisions allowing the treaty to be changed without its concurrence.

These requests not being met, President Reagan announced in July 1982 that the United States would not sign the treaty. A number of other states, including Australia, which shared some of the United States' anxieties, signified acceptance in order to have the benefits of treaty provisions as to navigation rights through straights and archipelagoes, territorial waters, two-hundred-mile economic zones, and exploitation rights in the continental shelf. France, West Germany, and the United Kingdom, however, like the United States, have indicated nonacceptance of the treaty; and Japan and Belgium were not among the thirty-four original signatories at Montego Bay in December 1982. The treaty is to come into force after ratification by sixty countries.

Provision was made for the preparatory commission for the seabed authority to begin work after ratification by merely 50 signatories. The United States, however, declared its intention at the end of December 1982 to withhold from its contribution to the United Nations the amount of $700,000, that being the amount of its contribution appropriated by the General Assembly for the preparatory commission. The confrontation thus remains unabated between the American view that the resources in question are vacant of any ownership *(res nullius)* and therefore open to national appropriation and the Third World claim that the resources are already owned in common by all mankind *(res communes)*, so that no single state may exploit them without leave, much less appropriate them. At the beginning of November 1983 only nine states had ratified. This means, in practical terms, that liberty of individual states and enterprises to exploit, under national supervision, competes with collective claims by less developed states to license or exclude, to supervise all operations, and to receive 35–70 percent of net mining profits. Outcomes do not, of course, depend on whether libertarian or communitarian ideologies are preferred so much as they do on technologies of exploitation and naval power.

The rift between industrialized nations, on the one hand, and most of the developing states, on the other, as to restraints necessary to check pollution in the global domain became dramatically evident at the 1969

U.N. conference on this question at Stockholm. Many less developed states resisted such restraints as unfairly hindering their economic growth, depriving them of the freedom of action that the now developed nations had enjoyed in the course of their own past development.

The aspirations emerging in these last two decades received a notable summation and endorsement in the Brandt Report of 1980, the report of a commission set up by World Bank President Robert McNamara in 1977 and including, notably, Willy Brandt, Edward Heath, Adam Malik, and Olaf Palme. It called for an immediate five-year program to marshal resources to be raised by aid grants; international taxes on seabed mining, trade, and arms expenditure; or by other means towards meeting the 0.7 percent target of development assistance, as well as for stabilization of energy prices and a global food program. This would be within a longer-term plan of international economic reform, including the creation of a world development fund to supplement other sources. The commission also stressed the importance of an approach through "global negotiations" to escape the obstacles affecting existing negotiatory channels, as well as a meeting of leaders of twenty-five developing and developed states to open this phase. (The outcomes of this last proposal at the Cancun meeting will be mentioned shortly.)

A central concern of this and other NIEO projects in the correction of the discrepancy in world prices between the primary products, which constitute 60 percent of all the exports of the poorer nations, and manufactured products, the prices of which are steadily inflated by operations of multinational corporations, as well as by trade union power and the higher living standards of industrialized nations. A key proposal would establish a common fund to support the prices of primary products in the world market, the cost of which would fall, of course, on the consumers of primary products in the developed countries. The model of the OPEC oil cartel in raising the price of crude oil obviously encouraged such proposals. Indeed, even the resentful demands stirred in Third World countries by the disastrous effect of this rise have been targeted on Western industrialized countries rather than on the affluent and often sparsely populated nations of the oil cartel states.[14] One demand endorsed at the Cancun North-South meeting of 24–25 October 1981 was for a "global energy policy," including a special World Bank affiliate for the promotion of energy development to assist with the emerging needs of developing states. Its fate will be mentioned in that context. Organically related to these proposals, in the vision of the Brandt Report, is the view that multinational corporations should be subjected to a regime and code of conduct, to ensure reinvestment of a major proportion of profits in the developing host country and a progressive transfer to that country of knowledge and techniques necessary for its indigenous development and economic growth. On the other hand, the Brandt proposals for major financing to forestall threatening bankruptcy of many developing countries and for related reforms of "international institutions" were not advanced at Cancun.

The Commonwealth Heads of Government Meeting in Melbourne in September–October 1981 ranged the forty-one governments concerned, claiming to represent a quarter of the world's entire population, behind the Brandt Report, though in general terms. The Melbourne Declaration there issued, in declaring the right "of all men and women . . . to live in ways that sustain . . . human dignity," the issues of life and death for "hundreds of millions," and the world tensions arising from "gross inequality of wealth and opportunity," marched with the stress in the present chapter on universal minimum subsistence of human beings and reduction of gross inequalities. Acknowledging the political commitment, clear vision, and intellectual realization required for forward movement, it saw the choices involved, not as "change or no change," but as "timely, adequate and managed change" or "disruptive, involuntary change imposed by breakdown and conflict." It invoked "humanitarian" and "moral" considerations but was concerned to correlate these with "self-interest itself" and with the larger "political and strategic dimensions of what is at stake."

The declaration eloquently proclaims the need for "political will and understanding of the needs of different countries" and for "personal commitment . . . of political leaders to advance the common cause of mankind" and "find a creative compromise." It avoids, however, any explicit reference to "international justice" and any reference at all to three critical problems explored in this chapter, namely, the tensions between justice to state entities and justice to human beings; the tensions between resource allocation in title of justice within each national community and such allocation among all mankind; and the problem in developed counties enjoying responsible government and high standards of living of maintaining electoral support where voters refuse a mandate for global reallocation.

As late, however, as the joint annual meeting of the International Monetary Fund and the World Bank in Washington at the end of September 1981, it was clear that the request of twenty-four developing states for issuance to them of an additional U.S. $13.8 billion of special drawing rights would be resisted by the ten controlling industrial powers. An assertion that no amount of aid would produce progress was the gist of President Reagan's speech to the fund on 29 September 1981. Nor, apparently, did his meetings with President Mitterrand (reputed to be a supporter of transfers towards a "welfare world") in October 1981, immediately before the Cancun Conference, change this position. In this light, it has proved to be too sanguine to believe that the North-South meeting at Cancun of 24–25 October 1981 did more than maintain some minimal continuity of dialogue between the various groups of states concerned. This in part was no doubt a marking of time, during "times of trouble," within the economies of major industrialized countries such as the United States, the United Kingdom, West Germany, and others. Third World demands for global negotiations, for price supports for their exports, and for a separate energy affiliate of the World Bank involving a virtual doubling of the bank's contribution to financing the rising oil needs of the Third World from their present $50 billion to $110 billion by 1990—and the bank's input from $16 billion to $30 billion—were strongly pressed but did not seriously advance.

They were already confronted, indeed, by a dispiriting performance even in terms of more conventional development aid. As against the 1 percent of GNP hopefully projected by the United Kingdom Labour Party and the Council of Europe in the 1950s and the 0.7 percent targeted by the United Nations, U.S. aid in 1981 amounted to 0.2 percent, and Australian aid to 0.45 percent. In the United States and elsewhere the value of grant aid was, moreover, being increasingly criticized as burdensome to donor economies afflicted by unemployment, inflation, and poverty among growing segments of the population. It was also being criticized as doing more harm than good to the donee states themselves.[15] Much of this aid allegedly never reached the needy of these countries but rather was diverted to enhance the pomp and splendor of capital cities and the military display of new nations, when it was not wasted by corruption. After receiving aid amounting to $600 million over fourteen years, Tanzania was charged as being less self-sufficient in food than she had been before the forcible collectivization of her 11 million peasants. Aid was proving harmful, the critics went on, even to the leadership of donee nations, since the search and competition for aid turned major energies away from the real tasks of government. Moreover, at best, aid could not much relieve the poverty of such nations so long as their populations continued to multiply at accustomed rates and so long as traditional patterns and attitudes blocking material improvement remained unchanged.[16]

While such criticisms were not limited to the United States, they were there elaborated the more abrasively, because the remarkable U.S. post–World War II initiatives in economic aid to foreign countries from the Marshall Plan and the Point Four Program onwards seemed to be rewarded by suspicion, dislike, and outright hostility from most of the Third World. Indignation by many Americans at what seemed to them a biting of the hand that fed received a predictably free-enterprise expression in President Reagan's address on foreign aid on 29 September 1981, immediately before the Cancun Conference. The President saw the real success of development aid, in those instances when it did succeed, as due to the operation of incentives through free enterprise. On the international plan it was to be sought both by nation-to-nation economic relations and by cooperation of states in the established international agencies such as the World Bank and the International Monetary Fund. By both these points, we clearly signaled a lack of interest in demands for new paths to be blazed through "global negotiations." As he saw it, progress depended rather on practical measures of cooperation between nations in trade, investment, agriculture, and foreign assistance.

The cross-section of industrialized and Third World states represented at Cancun at the invitation of Mexican President Lopez Portillo did not succeed in shifting this American approach.[17] It resisted arguments based on the fact that 35 percent of total U.S. exports and 39 percent of U.S. manufactured exports were to Third World markets and that U.S. multinational corporations had investments amounting to $42 billion in factories in those countries (being 25 percent of total U.S. direct investment abroad). The U.S. position was reinforced, rather than otherwise, by the fact that, oil apart, the United States takes more than half of the Third World's total exports. The foreign ministers had agreed in August 1981 that discussion should be informal and that no final communiqué should be issued; and the Canadian and Mexican cochairmen—Prime Minister Trudeau and President Portillo—issued only nonbinding final statements. These shed little light either on the trade-versus-aid issue or on the issue of global negotiations versus the international institutional status quo and bilateralism-as-we-go.

Reforms recommended by the Brandt Report and pressed at the Cancun North-South meeting in October 1981 would have tended to expand the functions of monetary and exchange management of the International Monetary Fund and the World Bank, for which President Mitterrand and other socialist governments in Europe continued later to press. But they made little progress at Cancun, and even Willy Brandt, in commenting on the outcome on 7 December 1981, declared that "not even developing countries would want to force through any reform on the basis of 'one nation, one vote.' " The standpat on the institutional status quo is scarcely surprising in view of the fact that decisions through such structures as the World Bank and the International Monetary Fund require the consent of the major donor nations. These operating rules do not include the one-state, one-vote principle, and proposals to move the rules in that direction involve structural reform in the ongoing economic system (as distinct, for example, from case-by-case debt cancellation) and thus face very adamant resistance. These institutions are therefore rather sheltered from the "moral" pressures of virtually automatic bloc votes, which characterize the proceedings of the U.N. General Assembly and UNCTAD. In those bodies, overwhelming majorities of states in the Third and Fourth worlds can readily be marshaled for demands against the numerically small minority of industrialized nations.[18] At Cancun,

President Reagan was not required to retreat from his rejection of demands for a transfer of resources from North to South, and he warned against views becoming "polarized" and against the "chances and agreement" becoming "needlessly sacrificed."

It is from time to time reported that some industrialized countries—for instance, Francois Mitterrand's France, Pierre Trudeau's Canada, Austria, and Sweden—are sympathetic to the demands of the South for the transfer of tens of billions of dollars of resources from the North. We may never be certain how seriously these reports are to be taken. Such evidence as is offered ususally refers to global projects in which, as with the United Nations and its specialized agencies, the lion's share of the budget would be provided by the United States. The Soviet Union does not join in such projects and will obviously not be much moved even by the criticism of the Mexican president at Cancun that it is "shirking its responsibility." In terms of world trade, Soviet bloc countries' involvement with developing states is small, and while such countries tend to support the South in voting, for instance, on the Common Fund, they have been reluctant to undertake commitments. So that potential donor nations other than the United States may win diplomatic grace by words that they are unlikely to be required, much less able, to match by deeds. Such nations do not at present (with the notable exception of Sweden, the Netherlands, and Norway) display a proportionate vision in exceeding the target of 0.7 percent of GNP at current market prices in official development assistance. Nor, for this very reason, are they likely to have to justify the budgetary priority of foreign needs over domestic needs to the electors on whom they depend for return to office. The critical issues for them (as for the American President and Congress) have still to arise as they move from the halls of rhetoric to the hustings of democratic elections.

12. World Order, Economic

Justice, and International Law

INTERNATIONAL LAW AS HOMOCENTRIC?

While I began this work with the recognition of the rather limited ambit and effectiveness of international law, my concern has been to explore its potential relevance and bearing for the prospects of orderly human life on this planet. The inquiry is provoked, on the one hand, by the grievous uncertainty of these prospects and the obvious lesions in planetary order manifest in daily sufferings and dangers to tens of millions of people and, on the other hand, by the currency in contemporary thought of a number of visions of world order. These visions are presented either as comporting with a reality already underlying the apparent chaos and conflict or as a program for moving out of this apparent chaos, conflict, and suffering into a functioning and self-reconciling planetary order.

Underlying the uncertain prospects, as well as the strivings to realize these visions, are the difficulties of access to knowledge of important parts of the phenomena to which they refer or of the possible contributions of international law to them. Most of the relevant phenomena—physical, biological, and economic—are comparatively accessible. Insofar, however, as these merge into elements of individual and group psychology, culture, and anthropology, affecting both the theory and the practice of international law, access presents problems. It became clear in chapter 1 that great obstacles affected the making of fruitful correlations between the content and process of international law and the psychological and cultural characteristics and demands of the men and women of the various states to which that law applies. These obstacles are not attributable merely to problems of the disciplines concerned. Even if all these were solved, and resources were available for constantly surveying and resurveying the endless data involved, insuperable difficulties would almost certainly remain.

The most obstinate of these arise from the distorting impact of value judgments on both human conduct and the observer's perceptions and interpretations of these. Even when actors and observers are from the same cultural milieu, they tend to be conditioned, and their observations colored, by stereotyped bodies of ideas that have gained widespread adherence. These arise from processes of cognitive irradiation and contamination in the form of ideologies, or isms, of various kinds, which control the interpretations of what is seen (and, indeed, often even control what is seen). The complex pluralism involved is further complicated, even when no deliberate manipulation or dissimulation in involved, by the diversity of cultural environments of different peoples. Human relations across frontiers are, however, also constantly subjected to blockages, distortions, and concealments arising from state policies and from the very existence of state sovereignties, and their exclusive control within and across their frontiers.

Efficient human communication in any case presupposes a certain community of ways of life, backgrounds of experience, and concepts and, of course, of the shared systems of symbolization that we know as language. An important thesis of chapter 1 is that the growth of the electronic media and other modern techniques of physical communication, far from deepening and widening the range of human communication, may have to be counted among factors gravely undermining it in the modern era. Insofar as the present study is focused on international law as a homocentric law rather than a mere law between state entities, defective human communication must raise basic questions as to the possibility of access to the relevant psychological, cultural, and anthropological phenomena. There may indeed be some awesome analogy between the paradox of planetwide physical communications that lead increasingly to blockage in human communication and the development of ever-increasing economic and physical interdependence of peoples accompanied by the threat of global destruction by the use of nuclear armaments.

This rather unpromising and indeed dispiriting context may give additional interest and importance to a number of modern attempts, despite all, to raise our hopes and expectations of international law. All of them invite us to view international law as somehow responsive to the ideas and principles that underlie the variety of human cultures, and of human demands, aspirations, and expectations, as well as creating or molding these ideas and principles and human demands, aspirations, and expectations.

A COMMON LAW OF MANKIND

One such framework, combining the mystique of the natural law tradition in which modern international law had its birth with that of the

Anglo-American common law, is that which presents international law as "the common law of mankind." It was dear to the heart of the late C. W. Jenks (see above, chapter 3). For him, the resources critical for controlling and ordering the vast and threatening struggles of political, social, and economic forces in the contemporary world were intellectual and cultural resources. Moreover, they were already available to us, since they were already embedded in the living cultures and legal orders of the principal national and religious groupings of mankind. Jenks saw nine principles as already established, or at least formative, in all legal cultures and thus available as "principles" of "the common law of mankind" (they are listed above in chapter 3). The main task, in Jenks's view, was to display by comparative "multi-cultural" and "multi-legal" methods the foundations of these principles which already existed in national legal orderings so that people all over the world could become conscious of "the common law" that all humanity shares.

To reduce national diversities and conflicts to mere superficial appearances beneath which intellectual effort can discover harmonious unity of ideas is certainly courageous. Unfortunately, many diversities and conflicts are simply not so reducible. They arise rather from demands by some against others for drastic changes in the distribution of material resources, power, or other values as at present sanctified in existing international law. Whether we think of access to the resources of the bed of the deep oceans, of the consequences for Western and non-OPEC Third World states of the oil cartel, of demands for the transfer of technology and other projects of the "new international economic order," the issues are a matter of reconciling *conflicting demands* rather than a mere pluralism of ideas. And even when we think of a struggle as "ideological" today, for instance, as between Moscow and Washington, the gist is concerned as much (if not more) with the struggle for dominating power and economic or strategic advantages as it is with ideologies. The controverted versions of international law are parts of the weaponry of political warfare to support adversary claims, not ideas engaged in a contest for truth. The adversaries, moreover, are state entities and their spokesmen. They do not necessarily (or even usually) consist of humankind in any planetary sense, except so far as state entities marshal them.

The failure of Wilfred Jenks's "multi-cultural, multi-legal" vision seems to be a rather inevitable result of its oversevere abstraction of intellectual elements from the complex of physical, normative, and material phenomena operative in the human situation, especially when we examine this situation in a planetary perspective. The redesign of international law into his common law of mankind is a task for elites—of intellectuals from among people, of lawyers from among intellectuals, and of jurists from among lawyers. Juristic elitism, unfortunately, is simply not enough.

POLICY-ORIENTED WORLD POWER PROCESS: WHOSE POLICY? WHOSE POWER?

The deficiencies of M. S. McDougal's vision of international law as a kind of "policy-oriented world power process" are of a rather opposite kind. Far from excessively abstracting the precepts of international law from the complexity of other phenomena relevant to them, the McDougal position seems to collapse (or inflate) international law into the conglomerate mass of all those phenomena, the whole laced, for good measure, into a comprehensive ethical (or at least pseudoethical) criticism of international law. In this view, international law is not distinguishable from the processes of intellectual, sociological, and ethical study, nor is the application of the law by international decisionmakers distinguishable from the study of this whole range of data. It is not so much that international law is to be evaluated by reference to community expectations; it is rather that norms become international law insofar as they express such community expectation.

McDougal, of course, seeks to transfer jurisprudential ideas first developed for municipal law and legal education into the international legal sphere. Even if the ideas involved were helpful for the municipal sphere, the question of their value for the international arena is a separate one. Whether, for example, McDougal's postulated goals of power, respect, enlightenment, wealth, well-being, skill, affection, rectitude, and sincerity, and the roles of decisionmakers in relation to them, are sufficiently similar in the two spheres is a question to be answered and not begged. Thus decisions of state decisionmakers under international law do not necessarily settle what they deal with. They usually merely raise questions about whether the extent of convergence among various decisionmakers meets the requirements of international law.

All this seems to require constant attention by international lawyers to the conduct, attitudes, aspirations, and expectations of ordinary human beings, members of all state communities, and of course of the whole planetary community. McDougal may indeed be found to assert roundly that from the perspective of scientific description "the individual human being is the ultimate actor in all arenas" and that the "world power process" is not only the heart of international law but the outcome of "the highly personal impact" of interaction and interdependence among human lives. This proposed intimate reference of international law to human beings is not, however, realized in this body of thought. McDougal points out that the complexity and range of the "world power process" (and of international law) must "dwarf, if not obliterate," the effectiveness of individuals. As seen in chapter 4, participation by individual citizens in the international law process is in one breath asserted to be fundamental and ultimate but is too often proved by the next breath to be rather illusory.

What is true of individuals as actors in this body of thought is also true of them as authors of demands or expectations and values. Its theorizing would seem to require constant checking by international decisionmakers about actual positions of actual human beings. The central notion of respect for each human being must mean at least this, if not, as some argue, that the demands and expectations of each individual are entitled to *equal* weight with those of every other. McDougal does not appear to offer to show how the required comprehensive empirical surveys of individuals throughout the world could ever really be made. Though decisionmakers are required to attend to the "general community interest," no way is demonstrated for drawing this from individual positions, nor is it clear how the decisionmaker is to make this judgment as an actor rather than an observer. The reality, as James Fawcett has recently observed in a related context, is that while we talk of international law as law of a human community in the sense of nations, a nation is really made up of "hundreds and thousands of cross-cutting human roles," and that the law can regard "only aggregate behaviour" of these nations, so that "the structural features chosen to classify national actors are quite gross."

There is indeed a much better reason than either McDougal or Fawcett gives why it is so difficult to take seriously their ostensible correlations between international law and the actions, demands, aspirations, and expectations of individual human beings and between these and those of the state entities on whom international law directly bears. This reason lies in the difficulties of human communication, especially across state frontiers, and the consequential difficulty of access by sociological observers, including any of McDougal's "decision-makers," to knowledge of an adequate range of individuals. The effect of advances in electronic communication has aggravated rather than eased this problem which is very critical for translating the claims and expectations, actions and interests, and rights and duties of states into those of the tens of hundreds of millions of human beings whom they represent. For the role of the state as a barrier, distorter, and diverter for human communications within and across frontiers is the gravest bar to making the kind of state-into-human and human-into-state translations that this kind of framework assumes to be essential. How could McDougal's (or any other) decision-makers overleap the coercive apparatus of 160-odd state entities, with their jealous control of communications, distributions, and stereotyping? Yet they would have to do this in order to make even a rough assessment of the demands, aspirations, and expectations of the thousands of millions of men and women of the planetary human community.

The truth, in brief, is that the collapse of international law into its sociology is an impossible way of doing sociology. And also, as Richard Falk in effect observes (see above, chapter 4, n. 3), it is also an impossible way of finding law. For the effect of this approach would be to intrude the relevance of the whole world context into each particular legal decision and, incidentally, to prevent an approach to uniform application.

The reason is that what McDougal presented as a kind of science obviously transcends empirical observation in a double sense. Insofar as it purports to base itself on facts of human psychology, culture, and environment to which observers-decisionmakers cannot get access, the hypotheses developed—for instance, as to what, in the particular context, is "the general community interest"—are neither verifiable nor falsifiable. Further, as this body of thought itself acknowledges, "basic public order goals must be explicitly postulated." Yet the empirical evidence to support these postulates can for the above reasons go no further than references to human rights documents and national constitutions. The bases of such postulated goals of the postulated international community finally have to be the "shared subjectivities" of theorists unchecked by reference to actual human beings, for indulging in which McDougal elsewhere despises the "historicalists." The final subjectivities of his own position cannot be concealed by the eloquence of his abstract invocations of "human dignity" for all people "everywhere," implying "a wide rather than narrow" shaping and sharing of values, including power.

The momentous nature of the issues both of human survival and of international economic justice is a reason why we should distrust our *individual* subjectivities. But this does not mean that we can necessarily trust our *shared* subjectivities. Yet even as careful a thinker as Richard Falk occasionally enters, perhaps unawares, on such hazardous ground. I say perhaps unawares because his entries are by way of attractive but rather circular slogans. In his *Studies,*[1] for example, he describes as ";system-diminishing globalism" activities that prejudice what in this work I have termed "the functional ordering of the planetary human community." He offers "overt militarism" as an example because, he says, it increases the reliance on military means, as well as the risks of war. Yet does this not beg questions, at any rate in today's major conflicts, as to when militarism must be regarded as culpable and when it may have to be exculpated or even advocated as necessary defense or even deterrence of a wickedly militarist adversary? Falk himself, as I showed in chapter 7, contemplated as of 1982 that military preparations—even nuclear weapon preparations— might be "required as a foundation for a more durable peace" or as "a precondition for denuclearisation" *(Demilitarisation,* 17).[2]

So, he insists, "waste" of resources is also "system-diminishing"—but when is use of resources waste? So, too, is eroding support for the United Nations. But can this be true without any inquiry as to what that organization is doing or failing to do at the particular time? We are offered, as a guide through such circularities, that "system-diminishing globalism" is "essentially imperial in conception" *(Studies,* 17). Yet this is not of much help to those many who at present see "essential imperialism" in both

Moscow and Washington or see it only in the adversary side and not in the side that they support.

Circularities equally affect the positive and the negative side of Falkian strategy, that is, the globalism that is "system-reforming" or "system-transforming" rather than "system diminishing." He offers nonaligned states, UNCTAD, the Group of 77, and demands for a "new international economic order" as examples of system-reforming globalism. He would sharply distinguish these from the OPEC cartel, which he sees as "system-maintaining." Mere "maintenance," as distinct from "reform," here refers, he thinks, to the failure to examine domestic values, adherence to a continuing statist *modus operandi,* and inaction in relation to armaments, nuclear weapons, and the like. For a crowning—but not surprising—circularity, however, Falk prefers his own position in the World Order Models Project. He characterizes it as "system-transforming" because the agendum of that project calls for "comprehensive restructuring" (including destructuring) and "a political program for imposing its vision on the historical process" *(Studies,* 18–19).

Perhaps, however, a certain verbal hesitation about such circularities is manifest in Falk's ringing peroration. He thinks that the function of utopian writing is "to suggest what life *could* or *should* be like if human potential or aspiration were to be fully realised" and that "to be Utopian is not necessarily to be unrealistic: on the contrary, it is to portray as realistically as possible what *could or may* come into being." For there is probably a certain comfort, and certainly some maneuvering space, in the leeways between *could* and *should* and between each of these and *may,* just as there is between what is "possible" and what is "plausible."

A PLANETARY HUMAN COMMUNITY: OVERLEAPING STATEHOOD!

I share most of the presuppositions indulged by Falk's view of international law as a potential functional ordering of the planetary human community. First, I share the judgment that international law as a legal ordering of coordinated sovereign states cannot assure the elementary contemporary needs of peaceable existence or, with any degree of certainty, even human survival. Second, I share the skepticism that any mere extension of the range of competence of decision-making elites of the type envisaged by McDougal can remedy this inadequacy. Third, I share the melancholy recognition that state entities by their very existence and function tend to prevent the spontaneous emergence, especially across frontiers, of the planetarywide consciousness necessary to support institutions performing essential functions for the planetary community. In pressing his World Order Models Project (WOMP), however, Falk seems to indulge two further assumptions which I have been unable to accept. One is that state entities will tolerate—or at any rate will not resist—the reduction and transfer of their functions and powers to alternative institutions for performing planetary functions, as these move into position. Another is that a sufficient number and range of state entities will be thus tolerant so as to allow the new alternative institutions to consolidate their positions and functions.

It is not easy to see an effective transfer of this kind, let alone a peaceable one, by the existing order of states. Whatever its other significance, the United Kingdom's Falklands expedition in 1982 warned us that even outside self-defense *strictu sensu,* force for the defense of rights was still in the international arena. The fact that this warning came from a supposedly "tired" Western democracy, not from a sovereignty-exalting Communist or Third World new state, is to be noted. It raises severe doubts as to whether most states, and especially the "new" states, will even permit the consciousness-raising dialogue and multilogue envisaged by Falk as a long-term approach to the transfer of functions. The mere reversal of the process of "nationalisation of truth" by states may itself be very difficult. What is involved in the proposed planetwide shift of functions is no mere change of form or style nor mere channel of transmission of set benefits and burdens. There is involved, for example, the jealous refusal of state entities—even in the midst of torrents of human-rights rhetoric—to allow any outside magisterial intrusion on their control of their own territory and population. There is involved each state's claim to be the final judge of development for its own people and the related claim to know what distribution of values among its people is warranted or required by the special historical or cultural context. On the statal side, therefore, I can see no multitude of abdicating sovereignties crowding the planetary horizon. On the other side, we are in an age of increasing mastery over natural forces and of escalating material expectations, even at the cost of severe pollution and depletion. In face of those facts, and of the responsiveness of rulers even in democratic countries, the prospects do not seem good for populist raising of planetary consciousness in most countries to a sufficient level of dynamic vigor to trigger many such abdications.

In his 1982 monographs *Demilitarisation* and *Studies,* Falk has schematicized his view of the transition period in terms of interaction between First-, Second-, and Third System actors. The First System he sees as the traditional order of states and their operations and the rules they set. The Second System is constituted by the United Nations and the specialized agencies, creatures of the states of the First System but operating under rules that may delegate some powers of initiative to Second System officials. The Third System is a more diffuse but also more pervasive system of power represented by nonofficial human beings acting as individuals or collectively through various associations, churches, trade unions, or other social movements or institutions, which he also refers to as "world order populism."

He is concerned to separate his positions in 1982 from both "wishful thinking" and "realism," and for this purpose he correctly admits that "a credible conception of system transformation" is critical. He accepts that "transition politics" is "the crucial link between the present world and a more humane and just one." Though he recognizes that there is "no master key," he does insist that the values to be realized affect means as well as ends, so as not to repeat the errors of past revolutions, which too often have "devoured their own followers and leaders" *(Studies,* 9, 11–12). He sees the mobilizing and consciousness-raising activity of Third System actors as a crucial trigger of transition, for the Second System, of the United Nations and specialized agencies, being creatures of the First System of sovereign states, can only be triggered into initiatives by effective activity of the Third System. This effective activity finally depends on populist resistance to oppression and dedication to world order values. Yet difficult problems of transition still arise, for, as Falk recognizes, Third System actors are within the territorial control of states, that is, of the First System, and it is these states which set "the rules of the game." So that those who lead or guide normative initiatives in the Third System must "take account of the political structure that exists in different regions and state polities" *(Studies,* 5) and work steadily to diminish the role of state power generally in society *(Studies,* 4 ff.).

With striking intellectual self-awareness, Falk sees the World Order Models Project, which he has pressed for many years, as reaching a critical point after 1978. This project, as he now sees it, broke from three earlier tendencies of thought about world order. One break was from the tendency to rely on enlightened self-interest of the privileged rather than on the values of oppressed people. Another was from the tendency, often unconscious, to associate world order with Pax Americana. Finally, there was a break from the wishful hope that somehow "world order" could come about without bitter and untidy political struggles for actualizing a new order. Yet he thought the alternative course set by WOMP for remedying these errors, by a kind of multicultural, multiregional exploration of "preferred worlds,"[3] was itself deficient, by dint of its elitism and lack of attention to grass-roots activity. So that he sees his 1982 positions as expressing a new stage (of "WOMP II"), which began in 1978 and is based on a "world order populism" extending the "actors" beyond the state system and its infrastructures and beyond international organizations to include "a third system consisting of people acting individually or collectively through voluntary social movements and associations" *(Studies,* 16).

When we take this movement of thought into account, however, Falk seems still to be indulging an undemonstrated assurance that because system change is "possible" it is also "plausible." He may well be correct in criticizing the assumption by "mainstream futures research" that there is "system continuity"; but even if this criticism were correct, this would not warrant the assemption that "system change is plausible." This is especially so if we mean by *change,* as he certainly does, a change in some desired direction. And the claim is not much assisted by referring to the ongoing dialectical process between the past, present, and future, nor by invoking the truism that "what we feel, believe, think, expect or wish shapes . . . the kind of future we transmit and posterity inherits" *(Studies,* 9, 11–12).

Nor, indeed, are the intractable problems of the transitional process removed by Falk's specification *(Studies,* 26–27) that efforts to change First System (state) operations must envisage the triple targets of *(a)* horizontal state blocs and rivalries; *(b)* vertical relations of stronger and weaker states, and *(c)* the dominance pattern of wealth, prestige, and knowledge by which power wielders in each state maintain their controls. He recognizes, in this very context, that prospects for demilitarization in the near future are not bright. In the meantime, he thinks, the struggle for security must still seek to displace "rulers' security" with "peoples' security," meaning by this latter the assurance in the least destructive manner of the general interests of people in autonomy and development.

"LAUNCH UNDER ATTACK" AND "BUILDING STOCKPILES DOWN"

In relation to the tactical use of nuclear weapons in Europe and issues of the deployment of intermediate nuclear weapons of the two sides, Desmond Ball, in his *Can Nuclear War Be Controlled?* (1981), concluded that "controlled nuclear war is a chimera" (see above, chapter 7). I should perhaps add here a no less fearsome conclusion in relation to the present phase of nuclear weapons technology and strategic planning. In part, the basis for pessimism is common to both tactical and strategic use—namely, the virtual certainty of breakdown of the communication system of nuclear command and its channels to the political level. Even, however, if this were not so, the chance of maintaining the balance of nuclear terror of the last three decades much further, without the actual use of such weapons, would appear to be fading.

The emergence of this truth has been obscured until recent years not only by a morass of controversies about the status of SALT II (especially with President Reagan's advent to office)[4] but also by the aftermath of much longer-term confusions in U.S. intelligence estimates of Soviet strategic nuclear strength following the supposed detente soon after the Cuban crisis after 1962. The conflict with later higher assessments long confounded U.S. negotiating positions in the resumption of strategic talks (START).[5] Indeed, before the reopening of the START talks in Geneva, the study by L. C. Carpenter prepared for and said to be endorsed by seven departments of the U.S. defense command, offered a picture disastrously clearer. Ostensibly secret, an unclassified version of its findings was nevertheless published at the very end of 1982.[6] The findings centered on the reality that the ability of the two sides to avoid nuclear war in the preceding three decades had turned on effective deterrence exerted on both sides by Mutual Assured Destruction (MAD). This meant that both sides focussed on ensuring the survival after a first strike of the weapons and means of delivery to inflict unacceptable retaliatory damage on the opponent. The targets envisaged for a first strike were sprawling, easy-to-hit urban concentrations, leaving the silos of missiles and warheads operational.

It is, of course, a notable fact that this balance of nuclear terror between Washington and Moscow has continued for more than three decades without the outbreak of major hostilities. Indeed, David Watt, writing in *The Australian*, 30 April–1 May 1983, offered the thesis that "in 40 years fear of nuclear weapons has done more to undermine war as an instrument of policy than anything else in the history of mankind." He concluded perversely: "Remove that fear and we are back where we started." Such removal, he thought, would still leave nations determined to use weapons to further or defend their interests, and even "conventional" weapons of the future would be ferocious. While this could conceivably be avoided by the creation of a new "world order," it was difficult to see either Moscow or Washington surrendering their liberty of self-defense and self-help in return for even the most legally binding paper assurances. While moral restraints might impose some checks on Western use of conventional weapons (as it prevented U.S. use of preemptive nuclear weapons against Moscow in the late 1940s), the probability was that Moscow would not be equally inhibited, so that, concluded Mr. Watt, nuclear deterrence—bad as it is—might still be better than any alternative available.

All this was by way of comment of President Reagan's strange (almost throwaway) expression of hope in March 1983 of finding an assured technology for blocking the physical approach of nuclear missiles and thus ending nuclear threats altogether. Such a comment—if it is more than merely making the best of a bad situation—seems desperately inadvertent to the realities of recent history, as well as the realities of recent technology. As to the former, in the last 40 years there have been well over 100 large-scale hostilities, in some of which powers that have nuclear weapons are involved, and even from 1980 to 1983, 6 new wars began, involving 4 million combatants. More than a quarter of the world's 164 states have been involved to a greater or lesser extent in these wars. And as James Reston pointed out in the *New York Times* on 1 April 1983, no less than 10 conflicts in the Middle East and Persian Gulf and 10 conflicts in Asia and Africa, not to speak of Latin America, were in the process of unfolding.

As to the realities of technology, the Carpenter Report centered on the finding that all proposals assuring that MX missiles when deployed would survive a first strike and be thus available for retaliatory action were erroneous. Soviet ICBMs, it was claimed, could now eliminate all U.S. strategic, military, industrial, and urban targets in less than one hour, and by all standard measures, the Soviet Union now has superiority in this respect until the 1990s. This situation had arisen not only from the growth of stockpiles of weapons but also from the new level of accuracy of nuclear missiles and warheads, even for pinpointing the enemy's missile silos. In 1983, the Soviet Union had available such accurate anti-silo missiles carrying no less than 4,600 warheads and possibly as many as 5,100 (600 were mounted on SS-17s, each with 4 warheads; 2,500 on SS-18s, each with 8, 10, or 14 warheads; and 1,500–2,000 on SS-19s, each with 6 warheads). With 5,000 such accurate warheads thus deployed, it is said, the Soviet Union could aim 2 at each U.S. target and still have 2,500 warheads left.

As U.S. Defense Secretary Caspar Weinberger, as well as Chairman of the Joint Chiefs of Staff General Vessey, informed a Senate Committee on 6 May 1983, if MX missiles were placed in existing silos, only one-quarter would survive a first strike, so that retaliation, if it were to take place at all, would have to take place before the first strike was actually sustained. The United States, for its part, commanded 2,100 warheads in 1983 (450 mounted on Minuteman IIs and 1,650 on Minuteman IIIs). The London Institute of Strategic Studies estimated the corresponding respective megatonnages as 3,995 for the Soviet Union and 1,178 for the United States. On the U.S. side, missiles based on Polaris and Poseidon submarines were not regarded as accurate enough for anti-silo targeting but only for use against cities under the MAD strategy. Yet, of course, submarine-based missiles, so long as the increased accuracy of warheads does not succeed in reaching them, may salvage for a time the deterrence of the MAD strategy.[7]

If the survivability of the means of retaliation is thus being correctly questioned, the entire strategy of deterrence by MAD would seem to be breaking down. Any replacement must take into account that the United States could not wait until after a first strike has actually taken place to retaliate against Soviet targets but would have to "launch under attack," that is, launch its retaliatory weapons as soon as it had warning of the impending first strike. On 11 November 1983, according to *Times* correspondent Richard Owen in Moscow, "Soviet military sources" were declaring a corresponding doctrine of "launch on warning" (or "automatic counter attack") as part of a possible response to deployment of Pershing IIs (said to be able to reach Soviet targets in eight to twelve minutes). Furthermore, to minimize the risk of retaliatory weapons being themselves knocked out before they could be used, there would have to be a shift on land away from silo-based missiles to small mobile missiles that would be moved constantly around the United States.

The U.S. Senate approved the financing of the first twenty-one MX missiles on 8 November 1983 by a vote of 56–37, the House having approved it by a smaller margin of 217–208 the week before. While the building of a number of MX missiles by 1987 and mounting them in silos in Wyoming and Nevada might serve transitionally as a bargaining counter, the Carpenter Report is said to have emphasized that the Soviet Union was turning out twenty high-accuracy warheads a week, each capable of destroying fixed MX targets. As to the targeting range commanded by Soviet missiles, a Brookings Institution report of December 1982 took the view that Soviet ICBM deployments could reach armed units in Turkey as well as in Guam, the Philippines, and Hawaii and of course in the continental United States and Canada, and their early warning systems; that mobile SS-20s in Central Russia could reach Europe, including southern Europe, the Near Eastern and Central Asian theaters, and even China; and that from the Soviet south missiles could reach Turkey, Israel, Iran, Greece, North Africa, South Africa, and Saudi Arabia.[8]

Of course, the primary function of the shift from MAD to Launch Under Attack would still be, if possible, to deter the enemy from any attempted first strike. How convincing a deterrent it could be would depend not only on the technology of the mobile weapons, for instance, as to accuracy, but also on the survival and efficiency of the communications and command system controlling these weapons. Besides the questions in relation to use of these weapons in tactical warfare, serious questions arise also from the special conditions of launch under attack and from the increasing use of computer technology for briefing military commanders and alerting personnel, both of which are factors that aggravate the danger of erroneous response. It was reported in *Newsweek*, on 10 January 1983, that the U.S. computer system had falsely signaled a Soviet missile launch in 1980. The error was then (presumably under MAD procedures) detected before any disaster could occur, but the question has properly to be asked whether this would be possible with launch under attack.

The 1980 error was attributed to a multiplicity of computer languages which the Department of Defense now plans to reduce to one language, named by the Pentagon ADA. The Pentagon has projected a budget of

$18 billion on a new communications systems between national leaders and officers operating the nuclear arsenal. But hazards from the very complexity of ADA are themselves likely to be momentous in implication.[9]

Insofar as erroneous initial launches and the breakdown of communications and command structures hinder the arrest of nuclear actions and reactions, the unthinkable question of whether a thermonuclear war could be fightable and even winnable has been forced, to the dismay of many, onto the attention of planners of both sides. Soviet Major-General A. S. Milovidov is reported to have denounced as "disorienting claim of bourgeois ideology" the idea that there can be no victor in a thermonuclear war; and V. D. Sololovsky, in his *Soviet Military Strategy* (1963), declared that "the waging of such a war must be regarded as the main task of . . . strategic leadership."[10] Some American theorists, such as Richard Pipes and Joseph Douglas, have regarded such earlier Soviet discussions of this matter as clues to Soviet first-strike strategy. It is clear at any rate that counterforce nuclear strategy refers to the design of destroying the other's nuclear forces rather than deterring by targeting on his cities. Implied are the aim of prevailing in nuclear war and reliance on increasingly accurate weapons or on defensive ABM or civil defense programs. Such tendencies have been criticized in both United States and Soviet policies. (See, recently, S. van Evera, *New York Times*, 28 January 1984.)

Former Defense Secretary McNamara, in the context of his recent advocacy of a "no first use" policy (discussed in the Introduction, above), was indeed constrained to admit that Soviet authorities thought right into the 1960s that nuclear wars could be fought and won, and into the late 1970s that though wars might begin by conventional means, they would almost inevitably escalate into nuclear war. Only as late as 27 May 1982, in an article in *Izvestia*, was the doctrine of "no first use" clearly espoused by Moscow, in Defense Minister Ustinov's declaration: "Only extraordinary circumstances—a direct nuclear aggression against the Soviet State or its allies—can compel us to resort to a retaliatory nuclear strike as a last means of self-defence." This was then endorsed by the late President Brezhnev at the U.N. Special Session on Disarmament in June 1982. Conversely, on 16 August 1982, there was reported to be a leakage in the United States of "a top secret Presidential directive" discussing the feasibility of winning a protracted nuclear war—lasting possibly 6 months—while selected targets (that is, political and command centers) were picked off. The report raised widespread protests, including that of former Secretary of State Cyrus Vance, who called the very notion "madness."

It is but a frill upon these broad bands of terror that the U.S. General Accounting Office (GAO) published an alarming report on 23 June 1983 to the effect that the Pentagon "is fielding weapons systems, without sufficient knowledge of their ability to survive or function in combat." Pentagon officials, the GAO declared, are "torn between committing funds for development of a weapon" and "development of a device for testing it." In relating to the new Phoenix and Patriot missiles and the Fleet Defense System, for example, the GAO claimed that the United States has no simulators that could "realistically duplicate" high-speed planes and missiles that fly at high altitudes or skim along the sea.

The equivocal signs at mid-1983 that both Moscow and Washington might be prepared to negotiate on the basis of parity in warheads rather than missiles, perhaps in combination with numbers of missiles and planes, were mentioned in chapter 7. In the first week of July 1983, as these conclusions began to be written, it was reported that Soviet nego-tiators at the Geneva strategic arms talks had proposed a limit of 1,200 for multiple-warhead land- and submarine-based missiles and a limit of 1,800 when bomber vehicles were included (down from 2,400 in the 1979 SALT II agreement). Of the above 1,200 non-bomber-delivered missiles, 1,080 were proposed as ICBMs (down from 1,320 under the 1979 agreement). The Soviet Union's proposals did not include any in terms of number of warheads, or single-warhead limits, though it had already endorsed the possibility of negotiation on that basis.[11]

How all this is to combine with other recent rhetoric about the two sides' "building down" their stockpiles by scrapping MIRVs and multiple warheads and substituting the small, mobile, single-warhead missile of the terrible age of launch under attack has not yet been clarified. These late proposals have no apparent relation, or only unintelligible ones, to the contrived resignation of Eugene Rostow as director of the U.S. Arms Control Agency negotiations in mid-January 1983, when both Paul Nitze, the U.S. negotiator, and Yuli A. Kivitsinsky, his Soviet counterpart, had moved the medium-range-missile negotiation away from the "zero op-tion" to a "walk in the woods" proposal that each side would have 50–100 missiles. This exploratory proposal had gone to the two governments and presumably had not been accepted; though Mr. Nitze stated on 18 Janu-ary 1983 that while the U.S. government saw the proposal as having inadequacies, it "was nevertheless seen to be a proper part of our ongoing negotiating process." On 19 July 1983, after a five-hour meeting, Chan-cellor Kohl (recently returned from Moscow) and President Mitterrand were reported still to have some optimism concerning the outcomes as to medium-range weapons.

Mystifying events of this kind, taken together with the rather sudden successful conclusion on 15 July 1983 of the lingering, three-year-old Madrid Conference on European Security and Cooperation, may per-haps signal a degree of forward movement. Among the less shadowy outcomes of the Madrid conference are a projected meeting on human rights in relation to family reunions and personal contacts in 1985 and one on further disarmament in Stockholm. At the ongoing European

Conventional Forces Reduction Negotiations, for which President Reagan, on 9 June 1982 in Berlin, had proposed Soviet-Nato parity at 700,000 ground troops and 200,000 air forces for each side, involving substantial reduction on both, there was still no outcome in July 1983.

Amid the anxious uncertainties about nuclear armaments, one certainly stands out. It is that no reliance can be placed on President Reagan's forecast of April 1983 that the United States (and presumably other nations) would, by the opening of the twenty-first century, have an impenetrable shield against incoming nuclear weapons, to be provided by advancements in science and technology. Scientist's objections were that it was dubious whether 100 percent interception could ever be assured; that the most plausible interception, from outer space, could not be effective against low-flying atmospheric missiles not against tactical uses of nuclear weapons; and that the defensive weapons themselves would be subject to attack. Moreover, insofar as only one side achieved such foolproof defense, and therefore could contemplate making a first strike with impunity, the whole system of deterrence would break down. These are sufficient reasons for certainty that humanity cannot be rescued in this manner from the risk of nuclear holocaust. Some critics have wanted to press ridicule even further. They have said that even if all the above problems were overcome, only when *both sides* came to have foolproof defenses, before either side made a first strike, could they then proceed to complete nuclear disarmament. Yet, observed a *New Yorker* comment in April 1983, this is a vastly long and expensive way of disarmament when the two sides have long had it within their power—if they only willed it—to dismantle and discard their nuclear armaments. This *New Yorker* argument itself, however, ignores the reality that in the world as it is, arms reduction is at least as fraught with risk as the arms race itself. We do not need to make such precious arguments to dispel any vain hopes stirred by this part of the President's deliverances.[12]

Even the weightiest recent proposal for rolling back nuclear arms— that of former Secretary of Defense Robert S. McNamara—does not venture to suggest that nuclear weapons can as yet be wholly dismantled and discarded. In one breath he concludes that "nuclear weapons serve no military purpose whatsoever. They are totally useless." Yet he proceeds in the very next breath (and in the very same sentence) to make the important exception "—*except only* to deter one's opponent from using them."[13] And he is careful to observe in the same context that the mere fact that Soviet thought has moved in the 1980s to the recognition that "there will be no victors in a nuclear war" certainly did not mean that the Soviet Union was no longer prepared for nuclear war in Europe. Nor, in McNamara's view, could this be confined to tactical weapons or the European theater. Yet, of course, the policy shifts proposed by Mr.

McNamara would have profound implications for the structure of NATO, scarcely explored by his proposals.[14] The proposals themselves have had some discussion earlier in this volume.

The death of President Andropov and the succession of President Chernenko, despite momentary flickers of hope, have scarcely changed the basic situation. The inertia indeed on the arms control front seems increased by Soviet resolve to yield no apparent advantage that might enhance President Reagan's prospects for re-election in November 1984, though Mr. Chernenko denied any such motivation on 8 April 1984. In his *Pravda* interview that day he turned back on the United States the charge of seeking nuclear domination, demanded "equality" and "equal security," and made a return to the status quo before the NATO deployment of medium-range missiles a condition of resumption of arms talks. The Geneva U.N. Disarmament Committee talks on chemical weapons continued, but Moscow in early April 1984 rejected out-of-hand suggestions from the President proposing a ban on such weapons. On the other hand, both there and at the Vienna talks on reduction of European forces, some measure of agreement toward on-site inspection seemed likely. Strategic and medium-range missile negotiations remained suspended. The chance, indeed, of concessions to Moscow by review of the status of the independent United Kingdom and French nuclear forces became more remote, as the Thatcher government's mandate was renewed and a 1983 *Guardian* opinion poll showed a rise of popular approval of the nuclear force from 72 percent to 77 percent. Assertion and reassertion by the United States of the confidence that the Soviet Union would return to arms control talks once the United States showed that "we can live without making concessions to them" (Paul Nitze, reported in *San Francisco Examiner*, 18 January 1984), or that deployment of Pershing II and Cruise missiles in Europe would lead the Soviet Union "to resume negotiations" (Defense Secretary Weinberger, closing the NATO ministerial conference in Turkey on 3 April 1984), have made little difference. The frustrating generality of such statements is perhaps matched by President Constantin Chernenko's on the dangers of the U.S. deployment, and the importance of "restoring international trust" (4 April 1984); not to speak of the Soviet assertion at the Stockholm security conference that a "non-use of force" declaration by the United States and NATO would be "a favorable element" toward resumption of arms control talks. What, after all, would such a new declaration add to the existing legal and political commitments under the U.N. Charter, the Helsinki Agreements, and other well-known agreements?

Meanwhile the hard facts following the Soviet walkout from nuclear arms control talks in November 1983 included Soviet deployment of SS-20s and SS-22s in East Germany and Czechoslovakia (reported on 18 January 1984 and confirmed by British Foreign Minister Heseltine at a

NATO ministerial meeting in London on 3 April 1984); NATO's initial deployment of Pershing II or cruise missiles in the United Kingdom and West Germany; and, most recently, of 112 Cruise missiles in Sicily in March 1984, despite substantial anti-nuclear demonstrations in Venice, Naples, and Rome. They also included continuing signs of intra-bloc discussion on both sides. It was reported from the above NATO ministerial meeting that the Netherlands had not yet decided whether it would accept the 44 missiles planned for deployment there in 1986. There had been earlier reports from the Soviet bloc of Roumanian and other satellite discontent with Soviet counterdeployments; and the suppression of anti-nuclear dissidents in Moscow and exiling of their leaders continued through the Andropov-Chernenko succession (*The Australian*, 31 December 1983–1 January 1984).

I concluded a series of radio lectures in January 1961 which were published later in that year by Harvard University Press as *Quest for Survival: The Role of Law and Foreign Policy*. There was no sanguine conclusion. I referred to the terrible choices that might face the Kremlin or the White House as to "whether to unleash the terrible deterrent or retaliatory power . . . held already against what each regards as even greater evils." I continued: "It would be the part of wisdom now, before such terrible choices are faced, to set up machinery, internationally guaranteed, to secure [the] continuity of personal communication under all circumstances, and up to the final moment. We are entitled to hope that the world will never reach such a final moment. But the minutes before such a moment should be made and kept available, beyond the faintest shadow of doubt, for this most solemn and fateful conference of all" (103).

The hot line between Washington and Moscow was, of course, established in 1963 after the Cuban missile crisis; and it has reportedly been used to good effect on several occasions, including the Six Day War of 1967 in the Middle East. It may be unromantic to recognize it as but a teletex channel between the Pentagon and the Kremlin. It remains a matter of comforting reassurance that mankind has already survived with it for more than two decades without the use of nuclear weapons. The thirty minutes available for deliberation in 1961 were only slightly more agonizing than the eight or twelve minutes prospectively available beneath the cloud of launch under attack. The constant and instant availability of the hot line remains more imperative for the decades to come. So does the establishment of a pattern of use that, without overdramatizing mere routine tensions, reflects the ever more momentous risks of mutual error, misunderstanding, or sheer miscalculation as to the use of nuclear weapons. The hope of guarding against those terrible risks in the decades to come is, at any rate, no more desperate than the corresponding hope seemed to most of us in 1961. Any time that can thus be gained increases the chances of rolling back the psychology, and perhaps even the technology, of nuclear weapons planning. There is a great deal to be said for the establishment at each end of the hot line of standing joint commissions of nuclear experts to monitor data relevant to nuclear alarms and advise both sides of their findings. Great paradoxes are, of course, involved in such proposals. Yet it remains a fact that the adversaries have in common a desperate will to survive, as well as a desperate fear of each other. Both share the most dire need to avoid error, confusion, and the collapse of communication.[15]

HUMAN DIGNITY AND UNILATERAL EROSION OF STATE POWER

R. St. John Macdonald has attempted to describe for the year 2000 the likelihood of a chaotic transition, rather than an orderly one, towards any of the international law utopias in earlier chapters. This is clearly related to Falk's depiction of a First System (of states) and the Second System (of international organizations), contrasted with the Third System, which Falk describes as "world order populism." Both of these formulations, however, neglect to work out the significance for the international legal order of a cardinal fact, which indeed they note. This is the fact that while Western developed states are, generally speaking, open societies, most Third World states, as well as Communist states, are not.

We must no doubt applaud the outcomes of the comparative "liberalism" and "pluralism" of Western societies as the product of movements enhancing the values of dignity and respect of human beings. It is tempting also to state these (using McDougal's terms) as a stage in the realization of "human dignity" in the "world power process." Yet the empirical evidence, still sadly growing as we move into the eighties, is that the vast majority of men and women of the world, governed by the vast majority of states, are not in the process of vindicating any comparable sphere of human dignity or autonomy *as against their governments*. And this immediately brings into question any supposed correlation between realization of basic human values and either "the world power process" or the maturation of a "common law of mankind," or of a humanitywide law based on planetary multilogue.

Nor, by the same token, can we confidently assume that the erosion of state authority in Western countries, whether in the sphere of war and peace after Vietnam, in internal security after Watergate, in the flowering of educational and civil liberties after the Warren Court and the assassination of President Kennedy, or in the exciting liberation movements of racial or sexual or similar insurgent groups, correlates with any growing prospects of basic international accommodation. For the fact is that major groupings of the world's states and state decisionmakers, controlling the vast majority of human beings, resist and often reverse the retraction of state power. And they do so not only vis-à-vis their own peoples but vis-à-vis other states and decisionmakers as well.

So far are such states from steadily enhancing values like human dignity and autonomy that arbitrary edicts, arrests and imprisonments, torture, exile, spurious commitments to lunatic asylums or "reeducation" procedures, and daily censorship and "nationalization of truth" are routinely used to repress them. And many of these states—including the Soviet Union and the People's Republic of China—remain still notable for their exaltation of national sovereignty and the absolute power of the state above all other doctrines of traditional international law.[16] I pointed out in chapter 7 that so long as the Soviet Union succeeds in resisting the assurance of claims to human dignity and autonomy and freedom of expression and criticism and thus avoids the erosions of state power manifest in Western states as such claims are increasingly assured, the Soviet Union gains important strategic advantages in the East-West confrontation.[17] This is very apparent in Western popular movements of the eighties for a nuclear "freeze," especially in the area of intermediate-range missiles in Europe, a matter already discussed.[18]

President Mitterrand's quip that "the Soviet Union produces weapons while the West produces pacifists" may, of course, be exaggerated. Yet it has a critical point underlying the core argument of Eugene Rostow as a founding member of the influential Committee on the Present Danger, and Director of the Reagan Administration's Arms Control and Disarmament Agency until January 1983. This is that the Soviet Union's goal is to institutionalize her claim to nuclear superiority, especially by promoting the anti-nuclear campaign in Europe, the United States, and Japan. The effect would be to change the world balance of power, undermine the United States' capacity to conduct foreign policy, and generally to impose a Pax Sovietica without the need to go to war (*San Francisco Examiner,* 10 February 1984). Professor Rostow prescribed "effective Western policies of deterrence, containment, and collective security." Yet this, too, leaves us with but a generality: that we are faced as regards nuclear weapons with "an insanity from which mankind can be delivered only by Soviet-American agreement." The effects of unilateral erosion of state powers in democratic polities remain a hard fact in this context.

This sociological truth should not be concealed by our devotion to civil liberties, liberation movements, or even the full gamut of postulated goals of a planetary world order. To overlook it may, as already suggested, play into the hands of Soviet political warfare. We have pointed out that even if we assume, contrary to Pentagon assessments, that the Soviet Union neither has nor seeks nuclear superiority, fears of long-term Western strategic vulnerability seem to have multiple foundations. Western strategic interests seem to be direly exposed in the current situation. First, Western powers remain deeply vulnerable, despite the build-up of reserves and the glut for the time being, to interruption of oil supply, deliberate or (as in the Iran-Iraq War) incidental. This vulnerability increases as the Soviet Union moves (for example, in Afghanistan) nearer to the channels of supply and as the completion of the impressive Soviet-Western project for the gas line from Siberia changes patterns of Western fuel consumption.[19] Second, Western Europe remains exposed to Soviet conventional military superiority whenever nuclear weapons are out of the picture. Third, the Western powers suffer serious moral, diplomatic, and strategic disadvantages from the so-called nonalignment of Third World states, even though this springs not so much from merit as from the historical accident that Imperial Russia was a comparatively unsuccessful colonizer. Fourth, in view of a recent report of the U.S. General Accounting Office (*New York Times,* 15 March 1984), vulnerability also arises from the substantial dependence of weapons maintenance (including the F-15 jet fighter) and of military communications systems, on 4,500 civilian technicians, whose obligations to continue service after wartime mobilization or undeclared war are not legally and often not even morally binding.

Thus, even if we regarded Soviet manipulation through the "peace and disarmament" symbols of the fifties as excusable or even morally correct Soviet defensive maneuvers, the present situation may require reassessment. For present Soviet strategies, now remarkably and diffusely supported by long-term and usually admirable erosions of state power in the West, begin from assumptions of military parity that render bipolar "competition" basically offensive.

Values implied in erosions of state power are very precious to liberal minds, within their national communities. We have pointed out that recognition of the *international* effects of progressive limitation on the arbitrary powers of their own state for the vindication of human values raises for them a true moral dilemma. Such vindications against their own state are a matter for pride and rejoicing by Western democratic peoples. These same vindications may, however, have the effect *internationally* of subjecting all peoples, Western and other, to the comparatively uninhibited naked power of states antagonistic to their own. Pride and rejoicing in the progressive realization of human values may, then, for a future generation become a matter for wistful (and even then secret) nostalgia.

In chapter 7, I quoted with strong agreement Falk's observation that compliance by a state with international law is only a stabilizing factor "if there is a minimum of mutuality." It is understandable that an observer who believes that he represents forces of rightness and survival may easily lose sight of this truth; but it is still dangerous to lose sight of it.

The truth that Falk formerly found almost self-evident between the adversary standpoints of Washington and Moscow seems recently to have faded from his view as between the Third System and First System actors in the campaign to displace First System statal actors. His latest works, *Demilitarisation* and *Studies,* present mostly a posture consistent with the foregoing. They seem to proceed, in other words, on a Ghandian nonviolence model, lest the "revolution eat up" its children and its leaders in the struggle to take over the global functions of traditional state sovereignties.

Yet the concluding paragraphs of *Demilitarisation* (17–18) reopen this whole program to the anarchy of political warfare and indeed of conventional and even nuclear warfare. Of course, they begin from the reformative strategy of restricting the military structures and doctrines of states to defensive concepts. It has already been pointed out that this neglects the difficulties of the "defensive-offensive" distinction, of which Falk is certainly aware. Despite this, he is ready to endorse the use of the threat of the Nuremberg aggressive war count to restrain use of force by states (16–17), ignoring the related difficulties there of defining and applying the notions involved. Despite these difficulties, he seems to be saying, "Third System activists . . . can act *as if* the Nuremberg Principles are binding" and thereby raise questions of accountability of the leaders of states. This advice suggests a readiness to inhibit use of force by the states of one side, with the effect, of course, of strengthening (whether intentionally or not) the military position of the adversary. Falk is here ready to diversify what he calls "demilitarising priorities," even to the point of heightening militarization, "from setting to setting." Thus, those in the "front line" of opposition to states may, he believes, have to augment their war-fighting capacities in the short run (17). In "anti-imperial contexts," he observes, "belligerence may be required as a foundation for a more durable peace," and, indeed, "additional proliferation of nuclear capabilities may be a precondition for denuclearization" (17).

In such terms, Falk seems to be denying his important earlier insight that unless the erosion of state power can be given effect also with the adversary state or states, it may operate in the present world context as an invitation for the imposition internationally of a Pax Sovietica, and internally of despotic government by an alien dominator. Certainly, there was in 1982 no comparable felt (and certainly no expressed) urgency about eroding the will or ability of the Soviet bloc to use force. And this is all the more striking since *Demilitarisation* confesses an earlier error of failing to recognize the danger of a Pax Americana (12–15).

A related neglect of his own wise counsel is found in Falk's insistence in 1982 on Third System (that is, populist) pressure for civil liberties on First System actors (states) as a means of "opening up space" for pressing citizens' normative concerns. But he at least admitted (instancing the case of Sakharov) that this would be more effective in pressing "demilitarising themes" on the West than on the Communist states. Yet, finally, apparently the only inference Falk drew in 1982 was that Western claims to favor demilitarization but to be hindered by Soviet attitudes should be exposed as spurious (12–13). One may hope that so radical a change of perception may have to be attributed to that writer's reaction merely to changes in the presidency of the United States rather than to the principles involved.

ECONOMIC JUSTICE: THE DUTIES OF DEVELOPED STATES TO DEVELOPING STATES

Demands for the redistribution of planetary resources are, as already observed, claims in title of justice rather than of existing legal obligations. As such, they are subject to serious contentions as to the criteria of justice and their application. (Their application itself, of course, is further complicated by different perceptions of the facts, of the way in which the economic system works, of who benefits, of how it can or should be improved, and of the likely success of suggested changes.)[20] It is precisely some of these criteria that are central concerns of earlier chapters, in particular chapters 8 and 10.

The outcomes of negotiations must, however, also inevitably be influenced by the various kinds of bargaining power available to the economically weaker parties. These include, for example, the cartel model offered by OPEC so far as this might be applicable to commodities that are staple exports of the less developed states, as well as the rather limited use of the oil weapon by OPEC states to support the claims of less developed states.[21] They include the threat of danger of default of less developed states on their debts, including the considerable debts to Western banks;[22] and the market opportunities for developed countries that economic progress of the developing states would present. They also include the "moral" pressure generated by the less developed nations in fora such as the General Assembly and UNCTAD, where their votes dominate, or in political or economic groupings or movements favoring Third World states within the various developed states. Such grouping may obviously include creditors of the developing countries: American private bankers, for example, had no less than hundreds of billions of dollars of debt in non-oil-producing developing countries, well exceeding their total equity-capital and loan-loss reserves. They include, finally, the danger of the spread of Communist economic, political, or ideological influence in the Third World, in default of Western concessions; and the divisions of outlook on these matters among the developed nations, among whom some, such as the Netherlands, Norway, and Sweden, tend, for instance as to the Common Fund, to be more receptive to Third World claims. Indeed the direct involvement of developing states with demands for economic changes tends to align them with ideologies of central-state planning as opposed to "free enterprise" and "free markets" (adversely in this respect, as in demands for radical changes in the status quo, to the prevailing ideologies of Western industrialized countries).[23]

These and such other bargaining counters as developing states can marshal may sway the richer nations to diminish or renounce in their favor vested entitlements under the legal status quo, but only *on particular matters*.[24] It is melodramatic to say, as U.N. Secretary-General Waldheim once did, that this measure of power makes "NIEO the price of peace"; but it is also cynical to be confident that "confrontation between developed and developing countries is likely to be limited to a 'war of words.'"[25] We may also argue whether NIEO objectives or effects are to give developing states a bigger share of a static cake or to enlarge the cake by expanding the cake trade for wider benefit. The balance of such arguments still remains inconclusive, and it probably always will.

In the last resort, I believe, significant *overall* movement towards the global goals of the NIEO will still finally depend on the degree of perception and acceptance of the duties of international justice, even if these duties have to be presented to the constituencies to which the donor governments are responsible, as required by their own long-term interests. It involves questions of international law *de lege ferenda*, not *de lege lata*—as it ought to be, not as it is.[26] Of course, even if the developed nations fully embraced these duties and were able in terms of their domestic politics to implement them, one critical problem of this chapter would remain. This is whether international justice requires merely that the benefit of these renunciations be channeled to the state entities of the less developed peoples and the elites that control these or whether justice also requires some assurance of the substantial flow-through of benefits to individual men and women of the peoples concerned. I concluded in chapter 9 that there may be no present means of assuring such a flow-through, any more than there is any present means of assuring economic equality between all the human beings of the globe. I have also suggested, however, that these conclusions still leave as imperative duties of international justice the assurance of minimum subsistence to all human beings and the reduction, at a feasible pace, of the grosser material inequalities that at present afflict them.[27]

These imperatives remain, even as we acknowledge that Third World countries vary widely in the degree of oppressions and deprivation suffered by their peoples and that some, for instance, South Korea and Taiwan, show a trend towards improvement of per capita income of the poorest 50 percent of their population towards levels found in the developed states.[28] The duties of the developed states in this context do not require them to do the impossible; rather, they require them to do at least what is feasible in the existing situation to move mankind forward towards the goals of universal subsistence and removal of the grosser inequalities. I agree with R. J. Wickes that there is neither an intellectual nor an ethical basis for withholding feasible concessions on the ground that these will not at present assure the subsistence of the poorest groups.[29] I also think, however, that the imperative duties of justice require all actors concerned to sustain, even as they perform these duties, a steady resolve that benefits shall flow increasingly to the men, women, and children of the globe *through* state organs, not just *to* state organs.

RESPONSIBILITY OF DEMOCRATIC RULERS AND INTERNATIONAL AID

These precepts address themselves to national leaders of developed states as well as to their peoples. It is most appropriate that national leaders should be summoned, as the Melbourne Declaration in 1981 again summoned them, to recognize "the essential interdependence of peoples and states" and the congruence of "humanitarian considerations" with the long-term "self-interest" of states and to show the "political will and . . . understanding" essential for "creative compromise." Yet, as I have been concerned to point out, even the deepest personal commitments of enlightened national leaders may still not be enough. So far as concerns electoral support, the issues presented by dedication of national resources *to other nations* do not appear in the same light as transfers for the maintenance of subsistence from one group to another within each national community. Within that *national* community, or "national justice constituency," enclaves are already controlled that afford a psychological basis for the sacrifices entailed by obeying the precepts. The precepts have not only been articulated to rationalize actual developments; they have also been internalized by the members of the community, as grounding a recognized duty in the above sense.

On the other hand, while the corresponding precepts for transfers from nation to nation have perhaps already been articulated, in the hope of future developments, it is doubtful whether the citizenries of many states have as yet internalized them sufficiently to ensure steady acceptance of the sacrifices involved in their fulfillment. And insofar as even the wealthiest societies, such as the United States, still contain substantial population elements living (by local standards) at below subsistence level, the precept enjoining subsistence *for all of the nation* may be felt (and, indeed, obviously *is* felt) positively to conflict with the enjoining subsistence for *all mankind.* Emil Brunner wisely observed in 1943, in precisely this context of international justice in the economic sphere, that it is "the tragic lot of really good statesmen that they are often forced by their people to act otherwise than their own insight dictates." For, as that writer adds, "it is a part of every man's natural disposition that he wishes to be *justly dealt with,* but it is by no means a part of man's nature to deal *justly with others* and to intend justice even when it runs counter to his own advantage."[30]

These discouraging factors are, of course, intensified by the arrival of rather intractable economic problems of industrialized countries in the seventies and eighties.[31] Even as a general U.S.-led recovery was being predicted in 1983, the Organization for Economic Cooperation and Development saw unemployment in Europe as rising to 20 million, or nearly 12 percent of the work force. At about the same time, the stability of 1,000 creditor banks of the developed countries was under chronic threat of default from a dozen and more debtor countries, involving loans of about U.S. $300 billion, though some bankers, for example, Vice-Chairman Taylor of Manufacturers Hanover Trust, gave a sanguine account of the banks' position as late as 10 November 1983. COMECON debts alone to Western banks in August 1982 amounted to U.S. $80 billion.

Two of the most impressive achievements of twentieth-century political democracies underlie the tension between the precept enjoining subsistence for all members of the nation and the precept enjoining subsistence for all mankind. One is the widespread and often generous welfare systems provided by each state concerned; the other is the prevalence of widespread, if not universal, suffrage within each state, which subjects the exercise of political power by national leaders to a frequent test of popular support by general elections. The two achievements, operating together in times of economic stringency, may be disastrous for the ideals of economic justice between nations, even when national leaders try sincerely to pursue them. Recent surveys, for example, show many troubled sectors of welfare systems throughout Europe as well as in Japan. These sometimes arise from economic and demographic changes, including mounting costs of health care and pensions as life expectancies extend and the related shrinking of the work force which has to bear the cost, as well as economic recessional factors in many states.[32] This obviously presents electoral problems for democratic governments inclined to increase foreign aid not to speak of defense budgets.[33]

In all these circumstances, it seems surprising that theorists extremely sensitive to economic justice so consistently neglect the problems that Brunner, from his own theological standpoint, stated so well so long ago. Richard Falk, for example, in his latest statement, is concerned to designate important areas of what he calls "world order research" (*Studies,* 23–25). He wants us to study the theory of social change in terms broader than Marxist class terms, identifying and raising consciousness of other kinds of oppression; including structural oppression. He wants research into the conceptual and normative relations between political economy and world order, asking whose hands guide various "international regimes" and what norms compete to govern a particular regime. He calls for monitoring of the role of international organizations in applying norms in these regimes, as well as to how actual foreign policies of particular states mesh with the requirements of world order and the formulations of foreign policy by national leaders. In the context of so much acute controversy concerning the "new international economic order" and national leadership in foreign policy, the difficulties for world order arising from conflicts between the principle of responsibility of rulers in political democracy and the supposed requirements of a new world order assuredly deserve more attention. It is but a straw in the wind that the increase of $9.3 billion in U.S. support for funding the less developed countries by the International Monetary Fund, itself a part of the eighty-three-nation increase of available funds by $40 billion, had so tremulous a passage through the Congress. This increase was only finally approved by the House of Representatives on 18 November 1983 by a vote of 226–186, in which the majority for the Republican President's proposal depended on his persuading 157 Democrats to support the measure, which a majority of Republicans actually opposed. Even then, this support by the Democratic members was only achieved by a kind of package deal, tying this support to the President's acceptance of a $15.6 billion authorization for housing and community development within the United States.

The underlying tensions between tasks of doing justice between peoples externally and those of doing justice within the national community are certainly not sufficiently indicated by references to the "evolving character of the state system," as if there were no pertinent distinctions to be made between states in this regard.

INTERNALIZATION OF PRINCIPLES OF INTERNATIONAL ECONOMIC JUSTICE

This conclusion again returns us to basic presuppositions of any careful inquiry concerning *international* justice. How far can we get with such an enterprise before we succeed in delineating the membership of an international justice constituency? And what constituency can we delineate here that will simultaneously embrace the human claims involved and the rather inescapable interposing authority of *state* decisionmakers—both donor and donee? The victory itself has to be won on its own ground, by men's acceptance of the obligations transcending their national communities that international justice implies.

We are returned here to rather ultimate questions of the capacity of men and women generally to widen their consciousness to embrace all their fellow creatures and to act out that consciousness to the limits at least of the brotherhood of man. Whether or not we recognize for individuals the transcending capacity of human consciousness, moreover, we still have to translate the spiritual capacities of individual persons into the temporal capacities of nations, acting through such orderly processes of self-governance as each has achieved.

We should not despair before this task. We are, indeed, entitled to note some clear signs that the establishment of precepts as to the right of minimal subsistence at home, in the domestic lives of the developed states, is already extending itself towards embracing all mankind.[34] Some internalization of this concern for all mankind is already manifest in a degree of sacrifice of national affluence which responsible governments have been able to bring their peoples to accept. The future task is to extend these bridgeheads. In part it is the task of time, and the change that time brings. Even now, the demographic and other scientific realities are infiltrating the minds of most citizens of the advanced countries. So is the relation of gross economic inequalities between nations to tensions and the danger of war. So is the monstrous dissipation of resources in the search for military security.[35]

From all this, and the promise of plenty from advancing technology and the "green revolution," as yet only dimly seen, great developments are possible, both as to sacrifices needed and as to people's readiness for them. These are features of the longer perspective that the tribulations of the present world recession should not cause us to forget. Institutionalization of performance of the precept through regular conscientious governmental action, even on a modest scale, sensitizes citizens to the international responsibilities that affluence brings and the sacrifices that affluence makes bearable. It also internalizes the related precepts. Escalation in the scale of trade and aid, which is at the heart of the future task, is itself a cumulative process. Each people's will to sustain the sacrifices involved may well, by a beneficent paradox, increase with the regularity with which the sacrifices are shown by national leaders to be imperative for the dignified sustenance of the whole human family.

Appendixes

1. DEFINITION OF AGGRESSION, RESOLUTION ADOPTED BY THE GENERAL ASSEMBLY ON THE REPORT OF THE SIXTH COMMITTEE, 14 DECEMBER 1974 (A/9890) A/Res/3314 [XXIX]

The General Assembly,

Having considered the report of the Special Committee on the Question of Defining Aggression, established pursuant to its resolution 2330 (XXII) of 18 December 1967, covering the work of its seventh session held from 11 March to 12 April 1974, including the draft Definition of Aggression adopted by the Special Committee by consensus and recommended for adoption by the General Assembly.[1]

Deeply convinced that the adoption of the Definition of Aggression would contribute to the strengthening of international peace and security,

1. *Approves* the Definition of Aggression, the text of which is annexed to the present resolution;

2. *Expresses its appreciation* to the Special Committee on the Question of Defining Aggression for its work which resulted in the elaboration of the Definition of Aggression;

3. *Calls upon* all States to refrain from all acts of aggression and other uses of force contrary to the Charter of the United Nations and the Declaration on Principles of International Law concerning Friendly Relations and Co-operation among States in accordance with the Charter of the United Nations;[2]

4. *Calls the attention* of the Security Council to the Definition of Aggression, as set out below, and recommends that it should, as appropriate, take account of that Definition as guidance in determining, in accordance with the Charter, the existence of an act of aggression.

DEFINITION OF AGGRESSION

The General Assembly,

Basing itself on the fact that one of the fundamental purposes of the United Nations is to maintain international peace and security and to take effective collective measures for the prevention and removal of threats to the peace, and for the suppression of acts of aggression or other breaches of the peace,

Recalling that the Security Council, in accordance with Article 39 of the Charter of the United Nations, shall determine the existence of any threat to the peace, breach of the peace or act of aggression and shall make recommendations, or decide what measures shall be taken in accordance with Articles 41 and 42, to maintain or restore international peace and security,

Recalling also the duty of States under the Charter to settle their international disputes by peaceful means in order not to endanger international peace, security and justice,

Bearing in mind that nothing in this Definition shall be interpreted as in any way affecting the scope of the provisions of the Charter with respect to the functions and powers of the organs of the United Nations,

[1]*Official Records of the General Assembly, Twenty-ninth Session, Supplement No. 19* (A/9619 and Corr. 1).

[2]General Assembly resolution 2625 (XXV), annex.

Considering also that, since aggression is the most serious and dangerous form of the illegal use of force, being fraught, in the conditions created by the existence of all types of weapons of mass destruction, with the possible threat of a world conflict and all its catastrophic consequences, aggression should be defined at the present stage,

Reaffirming the duty of States not to use armed force to deprive peoples of their right to self-determination, freedom and independence, or to disrupt territorial integrity,

Reaffirming also that the territory of a State shall not be violated by being the object, even temporarily, of military occupation or of other measures of force taken by another State in contravention of the Charter, and that it shall not be the object of acquisition by another State resulting from such measures or the threat thereof,

Reaffirming also the provisions of the Declaration on Principles of International Law concerning Friendly Relations and Co-operation among States in accordance with the Charter of the United Nations,

Convinced that the adoption of a definition of aggression ought to have the effect of deterring a potential aggressor, would simplify the determination of acts of aggression and the implementation of measures to suppress them and would also facilitate the protection of the rights and lawful interests of, and the rendering of assistance to, the victim,

Believing that, although the question whether an act of aggression has been committed must be considered in the light of all the circumstances of each particular case, it is nevertheless desirable to formulate basic principles as guidance for such determination,

Adopts the following Definition of Aggression:*

* Explanatory notes on articles 3 and 5 are to be found in paragraph 20 of the report of the Special Committee on the Question of Defining Aggression *(Official Records of the General Assembly, Twenty-ninth Session, Supplement No. 19* [A/9619 and Corr. 1]). Statements on the Definition are contained in paragraphs 9 and 10 of the report of the Sixth Committee (A/9890).

Article 1

Aggression is the use of armed force by a State against the sovereignty, territorial integrity or political independence of another State, or in any other manner inconsistent with the Charter of the United Nations, as set out in this Definition.

Explanatory note: In this Definition the term "State":

(a) Is used without prejudice to questions of recognition or to whether a State is a Member of the United Nations;

(b) Includes the concept of a "group of States" where appropriate.

Article 2

The first use of armed force by a State in contravention of the Charter shall constitute *prima facie* evidence of an act of aggression although the Security Council may, in conformity with the Charter, conclude that a determination that an act of aggression has been committed would not be justified in the light of other relevant circumstances, including the fact that the acts concerned or their consequences are not of sufficient gravity.

Article 3

Any of the following acts, regardless of a declaration of war, shall, subject to and in accordance with the provisions of article 2, qualify as an act of aggression:

(*a*) The invasion or attack by the armed forces of a State of the territory of another State, or any military occupation, however temporary, resulting from such invasion or attack, or any annexation by the use of force of the territory of another State or part thereof;

(*b*) Bombardment by the armed forces of a State against the territory of another State or the use of any weapons by a State against the territory of another State;

(*c*) The blockade of the ports or coasts of a State by the armed forces of another State;

(*d*) An attack by the armed forces of a State on the land, sea or air forces, or marine and air fleets of another State;

(*e*) The use of armed forces of one State which are within the territory of another State with the agreement of the receiving State, in contravention of the conditions provided for in the agreement or any extension of their presence in such territory beyond the termination of the agreement;

(*f*) The action of a State in allowing its territory, which it has placed at the disposal of another State, to be used by that other State for perpetrating an act of aggression against a third State;

(*g*) The sending by or on behalf of a State of armed bands, groups, irregulars or mercenaries, which carry out acts of armed force against another State of such gravity as to amount to the acts listed above, or its substantial involvement therein.

Article 4

The acts enumerated above are not exhaustive and the Security Council may determine that other acts constitute aggression under the provisions of the Charter.

Article 5

1. No consideration of whatever nature, whether political, economic, military or otherwise, may serve as a justification for aggression.

2. A war of aggression is a crime against international peace. Aggression gives rise to international responsibility.

3. No territorial acquisition or special advantage resulting from aggression is or shall be recognized as lawful.

Article 6

Nothing in this Definition shall be construed as in any way enlarging or diminishing the scope of the Charter, including its provisions concerning cases in which the use of force is lawful.

Article 7

Nothing in this Definition, and in particular article 3, could in any way prejudice the right to self-determination, freedom and independence, as derived from the Charter, of peoples forcibly deprived of that right and referred to in the Declaration on Principles of International Law concerning Friendly Relations and Co-operation among States in accordance with the Charter of the United Nations, particularly peoples under colonial and racist régimes or other forms of alien domination; nor the right of these peoples to struggle to that end and to seek and receive support, in accordance with the principles of the Charter and in conformity with the above-mentioned Declaration.

Article 8

In their interpretation and application the above provisions are interrelated and each provision should be construed in the context of the other provisions.

2. TREATY BANNING NUCLEAR WEAPON TESTS IN THE ATMOSPHERE, IN OUTER SPACE, AND UNDER WATER, 5 AUGUST 1963 (UNITED NATIONS TREATY SERIES 480:45)

The Government of the United States of America, the United Kingdom of Great Britain and Northern Ireland, and the Union of Soviet Socialist Republics, hereinafter referred to as the "Original Parties,"

Proclaiming as their principal aim the speediest possible achievement of an agreement on general and complete disarmament under strict international control in accordance with the objectives of the United Nations which would put an end to the armaments race and eliminate the incentive to the production and testing of all kinds of weapons, including nuclear weapons,

Seeking to achieve the discontinuance of all test explosions of nuclear weapons for all time, determined to continue negotiations to this end, and desiring to put an end to the contamination of man's environment by radioactive substances,

Have agreed as follows:

Article I

1. Each of the Parties to this Treaty undertakes to prohibit, to prevent, and not to carry out any nuclear weapon test explosion, or any other nuclear explosion, at any place under its jurisdiction or control:

(a) in the atmosphere; beyond its limits, including outer space; or underwater, including territorial waters or high seas; or

(b) in any other environment if such explosion causes radioactive debris to be present outside the territorial limits of the State under whose jurisdiction or control such explosion is conducted. It is understood in this connection that the provisions of this subparagraph are without prejudice to the conclusion of a treaty resulting in the permanent banning of all nuclear test explosions, including all such explosions underground, the conclusion of which, as the Parties have stated in the Preamble to this Treaty, they seek to achieve.

2. Each of the Parties to this Treaty undertakes furthermore to refrain from causing, encouraging, or in any way participating in, the carrying out of any nuclear weapon test explosion, or any other nuclear explosion, anywhere which would take place in any of the environments described, or have the effect referred to, in paragraph 1 of this Article.

Article II

1. Any Party may propose amendments to this Treaty. The text of any proposed amendment shall be submitted to the Depositary Governments which shall circulate it to all Parties to this Treaty. Thereafter, if requested to do so by one-third or more of the Parties, the Depositary Governments shall convene a conference, to which they shall invite all the Parties, to consider such amendment.

2. Any amendment to this Treaty must be approved by a majority of the votes of all the Parties to this Treaty, including the votes of all of the Original Parties. The amendment shall enter into force for all Parties upon the deposit of instruments of ratification by a majority of all the Parties, including the instruments of ratification of all of the Original Parties.

Article III

1. This Treaty shall be open to all States for signature. Any State which does not sign this Treaty before its entry into force in accordance with paragraph 3 of this Article may accede to it at any time.

2. This Treaty shall be subject to ratification by signatory States. Instruments of ratification and instruments of accession shall be deposited with the Governments of the Original Parties—the United States of America, the United Kingdom of Great Britain and Northern Ireland, and the Union of Soviet Socialist Republics—which are hereby designated the Depositary Governments.

3. This Treaty shall enter into force after its ratification by all the Original Parties and the deposit of their instruments of ratification.

4. For States whose instruments of ratification or accession are deposited subsequent to the entry into force of this Treaty, it shall enter into force on the date of the deposit of their instruments of ratification or accession.

5. The Depositary Governments shall promptly inform all signatory and acceding States of the date of each signature, the date of deposit of each instrument of ratification of and accession to this Treaty, the date of its entry into force, and the date of receipt of any requests for conferences or other notices.

6. This Treaty shall be registered by the Depositary Governments pursuant to Article 102 of the Charter of the United Nations.

Article IV

This Treaty shall be of unlimited duration.

Each Party shall in exercising its national sovereignty have the right to withdraw from the Treaty if it decides that extraordinary events, related to the subject matter of this Treaty, have jeopardized the supreme interests of its country. It shall give notice of such withdrawal to all other Parties to the Treaty three months in advance. . . .

3. TREATY ON THE PROHIBITION OF THE EMPLACEMENT OF NUCLEAR WEAPONS AND OTHER WEAPONS OF MASS DESTRUCTION ON THE SEABED AND THE OCEAN FLOOR AND IN THE SUBSOIL THEREOF, 11 FEBRUARY 1971 (UNITED STATES TREATY SERIES, 1972, PT. 1, 703–9)*

The States Parties to this Treaty,
Recognizing the common interest of mankind in the progress of the exploration and use of the seabed and the ocean floor for peaceful purposes,
Considering that the prevention of a nuclear arms race on the seabed and the ocean floor serves the interests of maintaining world peace, reduces international tensions and strengthens friendly relations among States,

*Ratified 18 May 1972.

Convinced that this Treaty constitutes a step towards the exclusion of the seabed, the ocean floor and the subsoil thereof from the arms race,

Convinced that this Treaty constitutes a step towards a treaty on general and complete disarmament under strict and effective international control, and determined to continue negotiations to this end,

Convinced that this Treaty will further the purposes and principles of the Charter of the United Nations, in a manner consistent with the principles of international law and without infringing the freedoms of the high seas,

Have agreed as follows:

Article I

1. The States Parties to this Treaty undertake not to emplant or emplace on the seabed and the ocean floor and in the subsoil thereof beyond the outer limit of a seabed zone, as defined in article II, any nuclear weapons or any other types of weapons of mass destruction as well as structures, launching installations or any other facilities specifically designed for storing, testing or using such weapons.

2. The undertakings of paragraph 1 of this article shall also apply to the seabed zone referred to in the same paragraph, except that within such seabed zone, they shall not apply either to the coastal State or to the seabed beneath its territorial waters.

3. The States Parties to this Treaty undertake not to assist, encourage or induce any State to carry out activities referred to in paragraph 1 of this article and not to participate in any other way in such actions. . . .†

Article III

1. In order to promote the objectives of and insure compliance with the provisions of this Treaty, each State Party to the Treaty shall have the right to verify through observation the activities of other States Parties to the Treaty on the seabed and the ocean floor and in the subsoil thereof beyond the zone referred to in article I, provided that observation does not interfere with such activities. . . .‡

Article V

The Parties to this Treaty undertake to continue negotiations in good faith concerning further measures in the field of disarmament for the prevention of an arms race on the seabed, the ocean floor and the subsoil thereof.

Article VI

Any State Party may propose amendments to this Treaty. Amendments shall enter into force for each State Party accepting the amendments upon their acceptance by a majority of the States Parties to the Treaty and, thereafter, for each remaining State Party on the date of acceptance by it.

Article VII

Five years after the entry into force of this Treaty, a conference of Parties to the Treaty shall be held at Geneva, Switzerland, in order to review the operation of this Treaty with a view to assuring that the purposes of the preamble and the provisions of the Treaty are being realized. Such review shall take into account

†Article II delimits "the seabed zone."

‡Subparagraphs 2–6 lay down rules for verifying observation by any state party and consequential procedure.

any relevant technological developments. The review conference shall determine, in accordance with the views of a majority of those Parties attending, whether and when an additional review conference shall be convened.

Article VIII

Each State Party to this Treaty shall in exercising its national sovereignty have the right to withdraw from this Treaty if it decides that extraordinary events related to the subject matter of this Treaty have jeopardized the supreme interests of its country. It shall give notice of such withdrawal to all other States Parties to the Treaty and to the United Nations Security Council three months in advance. Such notice shall include a statement of the extraordinary events it considers to have jeopardized its supreme interests.

Article IX

The provisions of this Treaty shall in no way affect the obligations assumed by States Parties to the Treaty under international instruments establishing zones free from nuclear weapons.

Article X

1. This Treaty shall be open for signature to all States. Any state which does not sign the Treaty before its entry into force in accordance with paragraph 3 of this article may accede to it at any time. . . .

4. TREATY ON PRINCIPLES GOVERNING THE ACTIVITIES OF STATES IN THE EXPLORATION AND USE OF OUTER SPACE, INCLUDING THE MOON AND OTHER CELESTIAL BODIES, 1974

The States Parties to this Treaty,

Inspired by the great prospects opening up before mankind as a result of man's entry into outer space,

Recognizing the common interest of all mankind in the progress of the exploration and use of outer space for peaceful purposes,

Believing that the exploration and use of outer space should be carried on for the benefit of all peoples irrespective of the degree of their economic or scientific development,

Desiring to contribute to broad international co-operation in the scientific as well as the legal aspects of the exploration and use of outer space for peaceful purposes,

Believing that such co-operation will contribute to the development of mutual understanding and to the strengthening of friendly relations between States and peoples,

Recalling resolution 1962 (XVIII), entitled 'Declaration of Legal Principles Governing the Activities of States in the Exploration and Use of Outer Space,' which was adopted unanimously by the United Nations General Assembly on 13 December 1963,

Recalling resolution 1884 (XVIII), calling upon States to refrain from placing in orbit around the Earth any objects carrying nuclear weapons or any other kinds of weapons of mass destruction or from installing such weapons on celestial bodies, which was adopted unanimously by the United Nations General Assembly on 17 October 1963, . . .

Convinced that a Treaty on Principles Governing the Activities of States in the Exploration and Use of Outer Space, including the Moon and Other Celestial Bodies, will further the purposes and principles of the Charter of the United Nations,

Have agreed on the following:

Article 1

The exploration and use of outer space, including the Moon and other celestial bodies, shall be carried out for the benefit and in the interests of all countries, irrespective of their degree of economic or scientific development, and shall be the province of all mankind.

Outer space, including the Moon and other celestial bodies, shall be free for exploration and use by all States without discrimination of any kind, on a basis of equality and in accordance with international law, and there shall be free access to all areas of celestial bodies.

There shall be freedom of scientific investigation in outer space, including the Moon and other celestial bodies, and States shall facilitate and encourage international co-operation in such investigation.

Article 2

Outer space, including the Moon and other celestial bodies, is not subject to national appropriation by claim of sovereignty, by means of use or occupation, or by any other means. . . .

Article 4

States Parties to the Treaty undertake not to place in orbit around the Earth any objects carrying nuclear weapons or any other kinds of weapons of mass destruction, install such weapons on celestial bodies, or station such weapons in outer space in any other manner.

The Moon and other celestial bodies shall be used by all States Parties to the Treaty exclusively for peaceful purposes. The establishment of military bases, installations and fortifications, the testing of any type of weapons and the conduct of military manoeuvres on celestial bodies shall be forbidden. The use of military personnel for scientific research or for any other peaceful purposes shall not be prohibited. The use of any equipment or facility necessary for peaceful exploration of the Moon and other celestial bodies shall also not be prohibited. . . .*

Article 6

States Parties to the Treaty shall bear international responsibility for national activities in outer space. . . .†

---

*Article 5 deals with the duties of assistance to astronauts.

†Article 7 concerns the launching state's responsibility for damage; Article 8, ownership of objects in space; Article 9, mutual due regard for others' activities in space; Article 10, foreign observers on space flights; Article 11, notification of activities in outer space; Articles 12–17, reciprocal access to space facilities, and so on; joint activities; activities by international organizations; and final clauses.

5. EXTRACT FROM U.N. DOC. A/RES./35/156 ON STRATEGIC ARMS LIMITATION TALKS, 12 DECEMBER 1980

The General Assembly,

Recalling its resolutions 2602 A (XXIV) of 16 December 1969, 2932 B (XXVII) of 29 November 1972, 3184 A and C (XXVIII) of 18 December 1973, 3261 C (XXIX) of 9 December 1974, 3484 C (XXX) of 12 December 1975, 31/189 A of 21 December 1976 and 32/87 G of 12 December 1977,

Reaffirming once again its resolution 33/91 C of 16 December 1978, in which it, *inter alia:*

(a) Reiterated its satisfaction for the solemn declarations made in 1977 by the heads of State of the Union of Soviet Socialist Republics and the United States of America, in which they stated that they were ready to endeavour to reach agreements which would permit starting the gradual reduction of existing stockpiles of nuclear weapons and moving towards their complete, total destruction, with a view to a world truly free of nuclear weapons,

(b) Recalled that one of the disarmament measures deserving the highest priority, included in the Programme of Action set forth in section III of the Final Document of the Tenth Special Session of the General Assembly, was the conclusion of the bilateral agreement known as SALT II, which should be followed promptly by further strategic arms limitation negotiations between the two parties, leading to agreed significant reductions of and qualitative limitations on strategic arms,

(c) Stressed that in the Programme of Action it was established that, in the task of achieving the goals of nuclear disarmament, all nuclear-weapon States, in particular those among them which possess the most important nuclear arsenals, bear a special responsibility.

Recalling that the SALT II agreement—which bears the official title of "Treaty between the United States of America and the Union of Soviet Socialist Republics on the Limitation of Strategic Offensive Arms"—was finally signed on 18 June 1979, after six years of bilateral negotiations, and that its text, together with the texts of the Protocol to the Treaty and a joint statement, both signed on the same date as the Treaty, and a joint communiqué issued also on 18 June 1979, was issued as a document of the Committee on Disarmament,

Reaffirming that, as stated in its resolution 34/87 F of 11 December 1979, it shares the conviction expressed by the Union of Soviet Socialist Republics and the United States of America in the joint statement of principles and basic guidelines for subsequent negotiations on the limitation of strategic arms that early agreement on the further limitation and further reduction of strategic arms would serve to strengthen international peace and security and to reduce the risk of outbreak of nuclear war,

Bearing in mind that in the same resolution it expressed its trust that the SALT II Treaty would enter into force at an early date, inasmuch as it constituted a vital element for the continuation and progress of the negotiations between the two States possessing the most important arsenals of nuclear weapons;

Recalling that, at its first special session devoted to disarmament, it proclaimed that existing arsenals of nuclear weapons alone were more than sufficient to destroy all life on earth, that the increase in weapons, especially nuclear weapons, far from helping to strengthen international security, on the contrary weakened it, and that the existence of nuclear weapons and the continuing arms race posed a threat to the very survival of mankind, for which reasons the General Assembly declared that all the peoples of the world had a vital interest in the sphere of disarmament, . . .

Convinced that the signature in good faith of a treaty, especially if it is the culmination of prolonged and conscientious negotiations, carries with it the presumption that its ratification will not be unduly delayed,

1. *Deplores* that the Treaty between the United States of America and the Union of Soviet Socialist Republics on the Limitation of Strategic Offensive Arms (SALT II) has not yet been ratified, notwithstanding that it was signed on 18 June 1979 and in spite of the many other reasons existing for such ratification as illustrated by those summarized in the preamble of the present resolution;

2. *Urges* the two signatory States not to delay any further the implementation of the procedure provided for in article XIX of the Treaty for its entry into force, taking particularly into account that not only their national interests but also the vital interests of all the peoples are at stake in this question;

3. *Trusts* that, pending the entry into force of the Treaty, the signatory States, in conformity with the provisions of the Vienna Convention on the Law of Treaties, will refrain from any act which would defeat the object and purpose of the Treaty;

4. *Reiterates its satisfaction,* already expressed in its resolution 34/87 F, at the agreement reached by both parties in the joint statement of principles and basic guidelines for subsequent negotiations on the limitation of strategic arms, signed the same day as the Treaty, to the effect of continuing to pursue negotiations, in accordance with the principle of equality and equal security, on measures for the further limitation and reduction in the number of strategic arms, as well as for their further qualitative limitation which should culminate in the SALT III treaty, and to the effect also of endeavouring in such negotiations to achieve, *inter alia,* the following objectives:

(a) Significant and substantial reductions in the numbers of strategic arms;

(b) Qualitative limitations on strategic offensive arms, including restrictions on the development, testing and deployment of new types of strategic offensive arms and on the modernization of existing strategic offensive arms; . . .

6. INTERNATIONAL COVENANT ON CIVIL AND POLITICAL RIGHTS, 1966 (ENTERED INTO FORCE 23 MARCH 1976), ANNEX TO U.N.G.A. RES. 2200 (XXI), 16 DECEMBER 1966

PREAMBLE

The States Parties to the Present Covenant,

Considering that, in accordance with the principles proclaimed in the Charter of the United Nations, recognition of the inherent dignity and of the equal and inalienable rights of all members of the human family is the foundation of freedom, justice and peace in the world, . . .

Agree upon the following articles:

PART I
Article 1

1. All peoples have the right of self-determination. By virtue of that right they freely determine their political status and freely pursue their economic, social and cultural development.
2. All peoples may, for their own ends, freely dispose of their natural wealth and resources without prejudice to any obligations arising out of international economic co-operation, based upon the principle of mutual benefit, and international law. In no case may a people be deprived of its own means of subsistence.
3. The States Parties to the present Covenant, including those having responsibility for the administration of Non-Self-Governing and Trust Territories, shall promote the realization of the right of self-determination, and shall respect that right, in conformity with the provisions of the Charter of the United Nations.

PART II
Article 2

1. Each State Party to the present Covenant undertakes to respect and to ensure to all individuals within its territory and subject to its jurisdiction the rights recognized in the present Covenant, without distinction of any kind, such as race, colour, sex, language, religion, political or other opinion, national or social origin, property, birth or other status.
2. Where not already provided for by existing legislative or other measures, each State Party to the present Covenant undertakes to take the necessary steps, in accordance with its constitutional processes and with the provisions of the present Covenant, to adopt such legislative or other measures as may be necessary to give effect to the rights recognized in the present Covenant.
3. Each State Party to the present Covenant undertakes:
   (*a*) To ensure that any person whose rights or freedoms as herein recognized are violated shall have an effective remedy, notwithstanding that the violation has been committed by persons acting in an official capacity;
   (*b*) To ensure that any person claiming such a remedy shall have his right thereto determined by competent judicial, administrative or legislative authorities, or by any other competent authority provided for by the legal system of the State, and to develop the possibilities of judicial remedy;
   (*c*) To ensure that the competent authorities shall enforce such remedies when granted.

Article 3

The States Parties to the present Covenant undertake to ensure the equal right of men and women to the enjoyment of all civil and political rights set forth in the present Covenant.

Article 4

1. In time of public emergency which threatens the life of the nation and the existence of which is officially proclaimed, the State Parties to the present Covenant may take measures derogating from their obligations under the present Covenant to the extent strictly required by the exigencies of the situation, provided that such measures are not inconsistent with their other obligations under international law and do not involve discrimination solely on the ground of race, colour, sex, language, religion or social origin.

2. No derogation from Articles 6, 7, 8 (paragraphs 1 and 2), 11, 15, 16 and 18 may be made under this provision.

3. Any State Party to the present Covenant availing itself of the right of derogation shall immediately inform the other States Parties to the present Covenant, through the intermediary of the Secretary-General of the United Nations of the provisions from which it has derogated and of the reasons by which it was actuated. A further communication shall be made, through the same intermediary on the date on which it terminates such derogation.

Article 5

1. Nothing in the present Covenant may be interpreted as implying for any State, group or person any right to engage in any activity or perform any act aimed at the destruction of any of the rights and freedoms recognized herein or at their limitation to a greater extent than is provided for in the present Covenant.

2. There shall be no restriction upon or derogation from any of the fundamental human rights recognized or existing in any State Party to the present Covenant pursuant to law, conventions, regulations or custom on the pretext that the present Covenant does not recognize such rights or that it recognizes them to a lesser extent.

PART III
Article 6

1. Every human being has the inherent right to life. This right shall be protected by law. No one shall be arbitrarily deprived of his life.

2. In countries which have not abolished the death penalty, sentence of death may be imposed only for the most serious crimes in accordance with the law in force at the time of the commission of the crime and not contrary to the provisions of the present Covenant and to the Convention on the Prevention and Punishment of the Crime of Genocide. This penalty can only be carried out pursuant to a final judgement rendered by a competent court.

3. When deprivation of life constitutes the crime of genocide, it is understood that nothing in this article shall authorize any State Party to the present Covenant to derogate in any way from any obligation assumed under the provisions of the Convention on the Prevention and Punishment of the Crime of Genocide.

4. Anyone sentenced to death shall have the right to seek pardon or commutation of the sentence. Amnesty, pardon or commutation of the sentence of death may be granted in all cases.

5. Sentence of death shall not be imposed for crimes committed by persons below eighteen years of age and shall not be carried out on pregnant women.

6. Nothing in this article shall be invoked to delay or to prevent the abolition of capital punishment by any State Party to the present Covenant.

Article 7

No one shall be subjected to torture or to cruel, inhuman or degrading treatment or punishment. In particular, no one shall be subjected without his free consent to medical or scientific experimentation.

Article 8

1. No one shall be held in slavery; slavery and the slave-trade in all their forms shall be prohibited.

2. No one shall be held in servitude.

3. (*a*) No one shall be required to perform forced or compulsory labour;

(*b*) Paragraph 3 (*a*) shall not be held to preclude, in countries where imprisonment with hard labour may be imposed as a punishment for a crime, the performance of hard labour in pursuance of a sentence to such punishment by a competent court;

(*c*) For the purpose of this paragraph the term 'forced or compulsory labour' shall not include:

    i) Any work or service, not referred to in sub-paragraph (*b*), normally required of a person who is under detention in consequence of a lawful order of a court, or of a person during conditional release from such detention;

    ii) Any service of a military character and, in countries where conscientious objection is recognized, any national service required by law of conscientious objectors;

    iii) Any service exacted in cases of emergency or calamity threatening the life or well-being of the community;

    iv) Any work or service which forms part of normal civil obligations.

Article 9

1. Everyone has the right to liberty and security of person. No one shall be subjected to arbitrary arrest or detention. No one shall be deprived of his liberty except on such grounds and in accordance with such procedure as are established by law.

2. Anyone who is arrested shall be informed, at the time of arrest, of the reasons for his arrest and shall be promptly informed of any charges against him.

3. Anyone arrested or detained on a criminal charge shall be brought promptly before a judge or other officer authorized by law to exercise judicial power and shall be entitled to trial within a reasonable time or to release. It shall not be the general rule that persons awaiting trial shall be detained in custody, but release may be subject to guarantees to appear for trial, at any other stage of the judicial proceedings, and, should occasion arise, for execution of the judgement.

4. Anyone who is deprived of his liberty by arrest or detention shall be entitled to take proceedings before a court, in order that that court may decide without delay on the lawfulness of his detention and order his release if the detention is not lawful.

5. Anyone who has been the victim of unlawful arrest or detention shall have an enforceable right to compensation.

Article 10

1. All persons deprived of their liberty shall be treated with humanity and with respect for the inherent dignity of the human person.

2. (*a*) Accused persons shall, save in exceptional circumstances, be segregated from convicted persons and shall be subject to separate treatment appropriate to their status as unconvicted persons;

(*b*) Accused juvenile persons shall be separated from adults and brought as speedily as possible for adjudication.

3. The penitentiary system shall comprise treatment of prisoners the essential aim of which shall be their reformation and social rehabilitation. Juvenile offenders

shall be segregated from adults and be accorded treatment appropriate to their age and legal status.

Article 11

No one shall be imprisoned merely on the ground of inability to fulfil a contractual obligation.

Article 12

1. Everyone lawfully within the territory of a State shall, within that territory, have the right to liberty of movement and freedom to choose his residence.
2. Everyone shall be free to leave any country, including his own.
3. The above-mentioned rights shall not be subject to any restrictions except those which are provided by law, are necessary to protect national security, public order (*ordre public*), public health or morals or the rights and freedoms of others, and are consistent with the other rights recognized in the present Covenant.
4. No one shall be arbitrarily deprived of the right to enter his own country.

Article 13

An alien lawfully in the territory of a State Party to the present Convenant may be expelled therefrom only in pursuance of a decision reached in accordance with law and shall, except where compelling reasons of national security otherwise require, be allowed to submit the reasons against his expulsion and to have his case reviewed by, and be represented for the purpose before, the competent authority or a person or persons especially designated by the competent authority. . . .*

Article 16

Everyone shall have the right to recognition everywhere as a person before the law.

Article 17

1. No one shall be subjected to arbitrary or unlawful interference with his privacy, family, home or correspondence, nor to lawful attacks on his honour and reputation.
2. Everyone has the right to the protection of the law against such interference or attacks. . . .†

Article 20

1. Any propaganda for war shall be prohibited by law.
2. Any advocacy of national, racial or religious hatred that constitutes incitement to discrimination, hostility or violence shall be prohibited by law. . . .‡

*Article 14 concerns procedures and minimum guarantee in criminal cases; Article 15, retroactive punishment.

†Article 18 concerns freedom of thought, conscience, and religion; Article 19, free opinions and expression.

‡Article 21 concerns peaceful assembly; Article 22, freedom of association; Article 23, freedom of marriage and in marriage; Article 24, minor children; Article 25, voting and public activities; Article 26, equal protection of the law; Article 27, ethnic, religious, or linguistic minorities.

In Part IV, Articles 28–39 concern the constitution and procedure of the Human Rights Committee; Article 40, reports by parties to the committee; Articles 41–44, optional acceptance by parties of committee competence to receive complaints of breach or to refer to an ad hoc conciliation commission.

In Part VI, Articles 48–53 concern final clauses.

OPTIONAL PROTOCOL TO THE INTERNATIONAL COVENANT ON CIVIL AND POLITICAL
RIGHTS, 1966

The States Parties to the present Protocol,

Considering that in order further to achieve the purposes of the Covenant on
Civil and Political Rights (hereinafter referred to as the Covenant) and the
implementation of its provisions it would be appropriate to enable the Human
Rights Committee to set up in Part IV of the Covenant (hereinafter referred to as
the Committee) to receive and consider, as provided in the present Protocol,
communications from individuals claiming to be victims of violations of any of the
rights set forth in the Covenant,

Have agreed as follows:

...§

7. CONFERENCE ON SECURITY AND CO-OPERATION IN EUROPE: FINAL ACT ("HELSINKI AGREEMENT") (1 AUGUST 1975)

(INTERNATIONAL LEGAL MATERIALS 14: 1292–1325)

(This document has been reproduced from an official text provided by the
U.S. Department of State. The conference formally opened in July 1973; the
working session began in September 1973 and ended in July 1975, after the
preparation of this final document. The document, signed by the thirty-five
nations participating in the conference, has no legally binding effect.)

The Conference on Security and Co-operation in Europe, which opened at
Helsinki on 3 July 1973 and continued at Geneva from 18 September 1973 to 21
July 1975, was concluded at Helsinki on 1 August 1975 by the High Representa-
tives of Austria, Belgium, Bulgaria, Canada, Cyprus, Czechoslovakia, Denmark,
Finland, France, the German Democratic Republic, the Federal Republic of
Germany, Greece, the Holy See, Hungary, Iceland, Ireland, Italy, Liechtenstein,
Luxembourg, Malta, Monaco, the Netherlands, Norway, Poland, Portugal,
Romania, San Marino, Spain, Sweden, Switzerland, Turkey, the Union of Soviet
Socialist Republics, the United Kingdom, the United States of America and
Yugoslavia. . . .

Motivated by the political will, in the interest of peoples, to improve and
intensify their relations and to contribute in Europe to peace, security, justice and
co-operation as well as to rapprochement among themselves and with the other
States of the world.

Determined, in consequence, to give full effect to the results of the Conference
and to assure, among their States and throughout Europe, the benefits deriving
from those results and thus to broaden, deepen and make continuing and lasting
the process of détente,

The High Representatives of the participating States have solemnly adopted
the following:

§Articles 1–6 concern procedure for receiving and handling individual complaints;
Articles 8–12, provisions as to signature, ratification, coming into force, amendments,
denunciations, and federal states; Article 13, final clauses.

QUESTIONS RELATING TO SECURITY IN EUROPE

The States participating in the Conference on Security and Co-operation in Europe,

Reaffirming their objective of promoting better relations among themselves and ensuring conditions in which their people can live in true and lasting peace free from any threat to or attempt against their security;

Convinced of the need to exert efforts to make detente both a continuing and an increasingly viable and comprehensive process, universal in scope, and that the implementation of the results of the Conference on Security and Co-operation in Europe will be a major contribution to this process;

Considering that solidarity among peoples, as well as the common purpose of the participating States in achieving the aims as set forth by the Conference on Security and Co-operation in Europe, should lead to the development of better and closer relations among them in all fields and thus to overcoming the confrontation stemming from the character of their past relations, and to better mutual understanding; . . .

Recognizing the indivisibility of security in Europe as well as their common interest in the development of co-operation throughout Europe and among themselves and expressing their intention to pursue efforts accordingly;

Recognizing the close link between peace and security in Europe and in the world as a whole and conscious of the need for each of them to make its contribution to the strengthening of world peace and security and to the promotion of fundamental rights, economic and social progress and well-being for all peoples;

Have adopted the following:

(a) DECLARATION OF PRINCIPLES GUIDING RELATIONS BETWEEN PARTICIPATING STATES

The participating States,

Reaffirming their commitment to peace, security and justice and the continuing development of friendly relations and co-operation; . . .

Expressing their common adherence to the principles which are set forth below and are in conformity with the Charter of the United Nations, as well as their common will to act, in the application of these principles, in conformity with the purposes and principles of the Charter of the United Nations;

Declare their determination to respect and put into practice, each of them in its relations with all other participating States, irrespective of their political, economic or social systems as well as of their size, geographical location or level of economic development, the following principles, which all are of primary significance, guiding their mutual relations:

I. *Sovereign equality, respect for the rights inherent in sovereignty.* The participating States will respect each other's sovereign equality and individuality as well as all the rights inherent in and encompassed by its sovereignty, including in particular the right of every State to juridical equality, to territorial integrity and to freedom and political independence. They will also respect each other's right freely to choose and develop its political, social, economic and cultural systems as well as its right to determine its laws and regulations.

Within the framework of international law, all the participating States have equal rights and duties. They will respect each other's right to define and conduct as it wishes its relations with other States in accordance with international law and in the spirit of the present Declaration. They consider that their frontiers can be changed, in accordance with international law, by peaceful means and by agreement. They also have the right to belong or not to belong to international organizations, to be or not to be a party to bilateral or multilateral treaties including the right to be or not to be a party to treaties of alliance; they also have the right to neutrality.

II. *Refraining from the threat or use of force.* The participating States will refrain in their mutual relations, as well as in their international relations in general, from the threat or use of force against the territorial integrity or political independence of any State, or in any other manner inconsistent with the purposes of the United Nations and with the present Declaration. No consideration may be invoked to serve to warrant resort to the threat or use of force in contravention of this principle.

Accordingly, the participating States will refrain from any acts constituting a threat of force or direct or indirect use of force against another participating State. Likewise they will refrain from any manifestation of force for the purpose of inducing another participating State to renounce the full exercise of its sovereign rights. Likewise they will also refrain in their mutual relations from any act of reprisal by force.

No such threat or use of force will be employed as a means of settling disputes, or questions likely to give rise to disputes, between them.

III. *Inviolability of frontiers.* The participating States regard as inviolable all one another's frontiers as well as the frontiers of all States in Europe and therefore they will refrain now and in the future from assaulting these frontiers.

Accordingly, they will also refrain from any demand for, or act of, seizure and usurpation of part or all of the territory of any participating State.

IV. *Territorial Integrity of States.* The participating States will respect the territorial integrity of each of the participating States.

Accordingly, they will refrain from any action inconsistent with the purposes and principles of the Charter of the United Nations against the territorial integrity, political independence or the unity of any participating State, and in particular from any such action constituting a threat or use of force.

The participating States will likewise refrain from making each other's territory the object of military occupation or other direct or indirect measures of force in contravention of international law, or the object of acquisition by means of such measures or the threat of them. No such occupation or acquisition will be recognized as legal.

V. *Peaceful settlement of disputes.* The participating States will settle disputes among them by peaceful means in such a manner as not to endanger international peace and security, and justice. . . .

In the event of failure to reach a solution by any of the above peaceful means, the parties to a dispute will continue to seek a mutually agreed way to settle the dispute peacefully.

Participating States, parties to a dispute among them, as well as other participating States, will refrain from any action which might aggravate the situation to such a degree as to endanger the maintenance of international peace and security and thereby make a peaceful settlement of the dispute more difficult.

VI. *Non-intervention in internal affairs.* The participating States will refrain from any intervention, direct or indirect, individual or collective, in the internal or external affairs falling within the domestic jurisdiction of another participating State, regardless of their mutual relations. . . .

Accordingly, they will, inter alia, refrain from direct or indirect assistance to terrorist activities, or to subversive or other activities directed towards the violent overthrow of the regime of another participating State.

VII. *Respect for human rights and fundamental freedoms, including the freedom of thought, conscience, religion or belief.* The participating States will respect human rights and fundamental freedoms, including the freedom of thought, conscience, religion or belief, for all without distinction as to race, sex, language or religion.

They will promote and encourage the effective exercise of civil, political, economic, social, cultural and other rights and freedoms all of which derive from the inherent dignity of the human person and are essential for his free and full development.

Within this framework the participating States will recognize and respect the freedom of the individual to profess and practise, alone or in community with others, religion or belief acting in accordance with the dictates of his own conscience.

The participating States on whose territory national minorities exist will respect the right of persons belonging to such minorities to equality before the law, will afford them the full opportunity for the actual enjoyment of human rights and fundamental freedoms and will, in this manner, protect their legitimate interests in this sphere. . . .

They confirm the right of the individual to know and act upon his rights and duties in this field.

In the field of human rights and fundamental freedoms, the participating States will act in conformity with the purposes and principles of the Charter of the United Nations and with the Universal Declaration of Human Rights. They will also fulfil their obligations as set forth in the international declarations and agreements in this field, including inter alia the International Covenants on Human Rights, by which they may be bound.

VIII. *Equal rights and self-determination of peoples.* The participating States will respect the equal rights of peoples and their right to self-determination, acting at all times in conformity with the purposes and principles of the Charter of the United Nations and with the relevant norms of international law, including those relating to territorial integrity of States.

By virtue of the principle of equal rights and self-determination of peoples, all peoples always have the right, in full freedom, to determine, when and as they wish, their internal and external political status, without external interference, and to pursue as they wish their political, economic, social and cultural development.

The participating States reaffirm the universal significance of respect for and effective exercise of equal rights and self-determination of peoples for the development of friendly relations among themselves as among all States; they also recall the importance of the elimination of any form of violation of this principle.

IX. *Co-operation among States.* The participating States will develop their co-operation with one another and with all States in all fields in accordance with the purposes and principles of the Charter of the United Nations. In developing their co-operation the participating States will place special emphasis on the fields as set forth within the framework of the Conference on Security and Co-operation in Europe, with each of them making its contribution in conditions of full equality.

They will endeavour, in developing their co-operation as equals, to promote mutual understanding and confidence, friendly and good-neighbourly relations among themselves, international peace, security and justice. They will equally endeavour, in developing their co-operation, to improve the well-being of peoples and contribute to the fulfilment of their aspirations through, inter alia, the benefits resulting from increased mutual knowledge and from progress and achievement in the economic, scientific, technological, social, cultural and humanitarian fields. . . . To take effective measures which by their scope and by their nature constitute steps towards the ultimate achievement of general and complete disarmament under strict and effective international control. . . .

X. *Fulfilment in good faith of obligations under international law.* The participating States will fulfil in good faith their obligations under international law, both those obligations arising from the generally recognized principles and rules of international law and those obligations arising from treaties or other agreements, in conformity with international law, to which they are parties.

In exercising their sovereign rights, including the right to determine their laws and regulations, they will conform with their legal obligations under international law; they will furthermore pay due regard to and implement the provisions in the Final Act of the Conference on Security and Co-operation in Europe.

The participating States confirm that in the event of a conflict between the obligations of the members of the United Nations under the Charter of the United Nations and their obligations under any treaty or other international agreement, their obligations under the Charter will prevail, in accordance with Article 103 of the Charter of the United Nations. . . .

The participating States, paying due regard to the principles above and, in particular, to the first sentence of the tenth principle; "Fulfilment in good faith of obligations under international law," note that the present Declaration does not affect their rights and obligations, nor the corresponding treaties and other agreements and arrangements. . . .

The participating States declare their intention to conduct their relations with all other States in the spirit of the principles contained in the present Declaration.

(b) MATTERS RELATED TO GIVING EFFECT TO CERTAIN OF THE ABOVE PRINCIPLES
(i) The participating States,
Reaffirming that they will respect and give effect to refraining from the threat or use of force and convinced of the necessity to make it an effective norm of international life,
Declare that they are resolved to respect and carry out, in their relations with one another, inter alia, the following provisions which are in conformity with the

Declaration on Principles Guiding Relations between Participating States: . . .
—To refrain from any manifestation of force for the purpose of inducing another participating State to renounce the full exercise of its sovereign rights.
—To refrain from any act of economic coercion designed to subordinate to their own interest the exercise by another participating State of the rights inherent in its sovereignty and thus to secure advantages of any kind. . . .

DOCUMENT ON CONFIDENCE-BUILDING MEASURES AND CERTAIN ASPECTS OF SECURITY
AND DISARMAMENT

The participating States,
Recognizing that the exchange of observers by invitation at military manoeuvres will help to promote contacts and mutual understanding;
Having studied the question of prior notification of major military movements in the context of confidence-building;
Recognizing that there are other ways in which individual States can contribute further to their common objectives;
Convinced of the political importance of prior notification of major military manoeuvres for the promotion of mutual understanding and the strengthening of confidence, stability and security;
Accepting the responsibility of each of them to promote these objectives and to implement this measure, in accordance with the accepted criteria and modalities, as essentials for the realization of these objectives;
Recognizing that this measure deriving from political decision rests upon a voluntary basis;
Have adopted the following:

I

Prior notification of major military manoeuvres. They will notify their major military manoeuvres to all other participating States through usual diplomatic channels in accordance with the following provisions: . . .
Notification will be given 21 days or more in advance of the start of the manoeuvre or in the case of a manoeuvre arranged at shorter notice at the earliest possible opportunity prior to its starting date.
Notification will contain information of the designation, if any, the general purpose of and the States involved in the manoeuvre, the type or types and numerical strength of the forces engaged, the area and estimated time-frame of its conduct. The participating States will also, if possible, provide additional relevant information, particularly that related to the components of the forces engaged and the period of involvement of these forces.
Prior notification of other military manoeuvres. . . .
To the same end, the participating States also recognize that they may notify other military manoeuvres conducted by them.
Exchange of observers. The participating States will invite other participating States, voluntarily and on a bilateral basis, in a spirit of reciprocity and goodwill towards all participating States, to send observers to attend military manoeuvres.
The inviting State will determine in each case the number of observers, the procedures and conditions of their participation, and give other information which it may consider useful. It will provide appropriate facilities and hospitality. . . .

Prior notification of major military movements. In accordance with the Final Recommendations of the Helsinki Consultations the participating States studied the question of prior notification of major military movements as a measure to strengthen confidence.

Accordingly, the participating States recognize that they may, at their own discretion and with a view to contributing to confidence-building, notify their major military movements. . . .

II

Questions relating to disarmament. The participating States recognize the interest of all of them in efforts aimed at lessening military confrontation and promoting disarmament which are designed to complement political dètente in Europe and to strengthen their security. They are convinced of the necessity to take effective measures in these fields which by their scope and by their nature constitute steps towards the ultimate achievement of general and complete disarmament under strict and effective international control, and which should result in strengthening peace and security throughout the world. . . .

CO-OPERATION IN THE FIELD OF ECONOMICS, OF SCIENCE AND TECHNOLOGY AND OF THE ENVIRONMENT

The participating States, . . .

Aware of the diversity of their economic and social systems,

Reaffirming their will to intensify such co-operation between one another, irrespective of their systems,

Recognizing that such co-operation, with due regard for the different levels of economic development, can be developed, on the basis of equality and mutual satisfaction of the partners, and of reciprocity permitting, as a whole, an equitable distribution of advantages and obligations of comparable scale, with respect for bilateral and multilateral agreements.

Taking into account the interests of the developing countries throughout the world, including those among the participating countries as long as they are developing from the economic point of view; reaffirming their will to co-operate for the achievement of the aims and objectives established by the appropriate bodies of the United Nations in the pertinent documents concerning development, it being understood that each participating State maintains the positions it has taken on them; giving special attention to the least developed countries, . . .

will endeavour to reduce or progressively eliminate all kinds of obstacles to the development of trade;

will foster a steady growth of trade while avoiding as far as possible abrupt fluctuations in their trade;

consider that their trade in various products should be conducted in such a way as not to cause or threaten to cause serious injury—and should the situation arise, market disruption—in domestic markets for these products and in particular to the detriment of domestic producers of like or directly competitive products; as regards the concept of market disruption, it is understood that it should not be invoked in a way inconsistent with the relevant provisions of their international agreements; if they resort to safeguard measures, they will do so in conformity with their commitments in this field arising from international agreements to which they are parties and will take account of the interests of the parties directly concerned; . . .

Have adopted the following:

1. COMMERCIAL EXCHANGES

General provisions

The participating States,

Conscious of the growing role of international trade as one of the most important factors in economic growth and social progress, . . .

The participating States,

Conscious of the importance of the contribution which an improvement of business contacts, and the accompanying growth of confidence in business relationships, could make to the development of commercial and economic relations,

will take measures further to improve conditions for the expansion of contacts between representatives of official bodies, of the different organizations, enterprises, firms and banks concerned with foreign trade, in particular, where useful, between sellers and users of products and services, for the purpose of studying commercial possibilities, concluding contracts, ensuring their implementation and providing after-sales services; . . .

Economic and commercial information:

The participating States,

Conscious of the growing role of economic and commercial information in the development of international trade,

Considering that economic information should be of such a nature as to allow adequate market analysis and to permit the preparation of medium and long term forecasts, thus contributing to the establishment of a continuing flow of trade and a better utilization of commercial possibilities,

Expressing their readiness to improve the quality and increase the quantity and supply of economic and relevant administrative information,

Considering that the value of statistical information on the international level depends to a considerable extent on the possibility of its comparability,

will promote the publication and dissemination of economic and commercial information at regular intervals and as quickly as possible.

Marketing

The participating States,

Recognizing the importance of adapting production to the requirements of foreign markets in order to ensure the expansion of international trade. . . .

2. INDUSTRIAL CO-OPERATION AND PROJECTS OF COMMON INTEREST

Industrial co-operation

The participating States, . . . propose to encourage the development of industrial co-operation between competent organizations, enterprises and firms of their countries; . . . recognize further that, if it is in their mutual interest, concrete forms such as the following may be useful for the development of industrial co-operation: joint production and sale, specialization in production and sale, construction, adaptation and modernization of industrial plants, co-operation for the setting up of complete industrial installations with a view to thus obtaining part of the resultant products, mixed companies, exchange of "know-how," of technical information, of patents and of licences, and joint industrial research within the framework of specific co-operation projects; . . .

Consider it desirable:

—to improve the quality and the quantity of information relevant to industrial co-operation, in particular the laws and regulations, including those relating to foreign exchange, general orientation of national economic plans and programmes as well as programme priorities and economic conditions of the market; and

—to disseminate as quickly as possible published documentation thereon; . . .

consider it desirable to further improve conditions for the implementation of industrial co-operation projects, in particular with respect to:

—the protection of the interests of the partners in industrial co-operation projects, including the legal protection of the various kinds of property involved;

—the consideration, in ways that are compatible with their economic systems, of the needs and possibilities of industrial co-operation within the framework of economic policy and particularly in national economic plans and programmes; . . .

recognize the usefulness of an increased participation of small and medium sized firms in industrial co-operation projects.

Projects of common interest

The participating States,

Considering that their economic potential and their natural resources permit, through common efforts, long-term co-operation in the implementation, including at the regional or sub-regional level, of major projects of common interest, and that these may contribute to the speeding-up of the economic development of the countries participating therein, . . .

consider that the fields of energy resources, in particular, petroleum, natural gas and coal, and the extraction and processing of mineral raw materials, in particular, iron ore and bauxite, are suitable ones for strengthening long-term economic co-operation and for the development of trade which could result;

consider that possibilities for projects of common interest with a view to long-term economic co-operation also exist in the following fields:

—exchanges of electrical energy within Europe with a view to utilizing the capacity of the electrical power stations as rationally as possible; [research for nuclear energy; etc.]. . . .

3. PROVISIONS CONCERNING TRADE AND INDUSTRIAL CO-OPERATION

. . .

Harmonization of standards. . . .
Arbitration. . . .
Specific bilateral arrangements. . . .

4. SCIENCE AND TECHNOLOGY

The participating States,

Convinced that scientific and technological co-operation constitutes an important contribution to the strengthening of security and co-operation among them, in that it assists the effective solution of problems of common interest and the improvement of the conditions of human life, . . .

Affirming that such co-operation can be developed and implemented bilaterally and multilaterally at the governmental and non-governmental levels, for example, through intergovernmental and other agreements, international programmes, co-operative projects and commercial channels, while utilizing also various forms of contacts, including direct and individual contacts, . . .
Possibilities for improving co-operation. . . .
Fields of co-operation
   Consider that possibilities to expand co-operation exist within the areas given below as examples, noting that it is for potential partners in the participating countries to identify and develop projects and arrangements of mutual interest and benefit: [agriculture, energy, new technologies, transport, physics, chemistry, meteorology, hydrology, oceanography, seismology, glaciology, computers, space research, medicine, environment].
Forms and methods of co-operation
   Express their view that scientific and technological co-operation should, in particular, employ the following forms and methods: [books and literature exchanges and visits, use of international organizations, etc.]. . . .

5. ENVIRONMENT

Aims of co-operation
   Agree to the following aims of co-operation, in particular: [study, effectiveness of protection of environment, harmonization of policies, promotion, etc.]. . . .
Fields of co-operation
   To attain these aims, the participating States will make use of every suitable opportunity to co-operate in the field of environment and, in particular, within the areas described belows as examples:
Control of air pollution. . . .
Water pollution control and fresh water utilization. . . .
Protection of the marine environment. . . .
Land utilization and soils. . . .
Nature conservation and nature reserves. . . .
Improvement of environmental conditions in areas of human settlement. . . .
Fundamental research, monitoring, forecasting and assessment of environmental changes. . . .
Legal and administrative measures. . . .
Forms and methods of co-operation
   The participating States declare that problems relating to the protection and improvement of the environment will be solved on both a bilateral and a multilateral, including regional and subregional, basis, making full use of existing patterns and forms of co-operation. They will develop co-operation in the field of the environment in particular by taking into consideration the Stockholm Declaration on the Human Environment, relevant resolutions of the United Nations General Assembly and the United Nations Economic Commission for Europe Prague symposium on environmental problems.
   The participating States are resolved that co-operation in the field of the environment will be implemented in particular through [information exchanges, conferences, personnel exchanges, joint programs, etc.]. . . .
   The participating States agree on the following recommendations on specific measures:

—to develop through international co-operation an extensive programme for the monitoring and evaluation of the long-range transport of air pollutants, starting with sulphur dioxide and with possible extension to other pollutants, and to this end to take into account basic elements of a co-operation programme which were identified by the experts who met in Oslo in December 1974 at the invitation of the Norwegian Institute of Air Research;

—to advocate that within the framework of the United Nations Economic Commission for Europe a study be carried out of procedures and relevant experience relating to the activities of Governments in developing the capabilities of their countries to predict adequately environmental consequences of economic activities and technological development.

6. CO-OPERATION IN OTHER AREAS

Development of transport
. . .

Promotion of tourism. . . .
Economic and social aspects of migrant labour. . . .
Training of personnel. . . .

QUESTIONS RELATING TO SECURITY AND COOPERATION IN THE MEDITERRANEAN

The participating States,

Conscious of the geographical, historical, cultural, economic and political aspects of their relationship with the non-participating Mediterranean States,

Convinced that security in Europe is to be considered in the broader context of world security and is closely linked with security in the Mediterranean area as a whole, and that accordingly the process of improving security should not be confined to Europe but should extend to other parts of the world, and in particular to the Mediterranean area, . . .

Noting with appreciation the interest expressed by the non-participating Mediterranean States in the Conference since its inception, and having duly taken their contributions into account,

Declare their intention:

—to promote the development of good-neighbourly relations with the non-participating Mediterranean States in conformity with the purposes and principles of the Charter of the United Nations, on which their relations are based, and with the United Nations Declaration on Principles of International Law concerning Friendly Relations and Co-operation among States and accordingly, in this context, to conduct their relations with the non-participating Mediterranean States in the spirit of the principles set forth in the Declaration on Principles Guiding Relations between Participating States;

—to seek, by further improving their relations with the non-participating Mediterranean States, to increase mutual confidence, so as to promote security and stability in the Mediterranean as a whole;

—to encourage with the non-participating Mediterranean States the development of mutually beneficial co-operation in the various fields of economic activity, especially by expanding commercial exchanges, on the basis of a common awareness of the necessity for stability and progress in trade relations, of their mutual economic interests, and of differences in the levels of economic development, thereby promoting their economic advancement and well-being; . . .

CO-OPERATION IN HUMANITARIAN AND OTHER FIELDS

The participating States,

Desiring to contribute to the strengthening of peace and understanding among peoples and to the spiritual enrichment of the human personality without distinction as to race, sex, language or religion, . . .

Have adopted the following:

1. Human Contacts

The participating States,

Considering the development of contacts to be an important element in the strengthening of friendly relations and trust among peoples, . . .

Express their intention now to proceed to the implementation of the following:

(a) Contacts and Regular Meetings on the Basis of Family Ties. In order to promote further development of contacts on the basis of family ties the participating States will favourably consider applications for travel with the purpose of allowing persons to enter or leave their territory temporarily, and on a regular basis if desired, in order to visit members of their families.

Applications for temporary visits to meet members of their families will be dealt with without distinction as to the country of origin or destination; existing requirements for travel documents and visas will be applied in this spirit. . . .

They confirm that the presentation of an application concerning contacts on the basis of family ties will not modify the rights and obligations of the applicant or of members of his family.

(b) Reunification of Families. The participating States will deal in a positive and humanitarian spirit with the applications of persons who wish to be reunited with members of their family, with special attention being given to requests of an urgent character—such as requests submitted by persons who are ill or old. . . .

Until members of the same family are reunited meetings and contacts between them may take place in accordance with the modalities for contacts on the basis of family ties.

The participating States will support the efforts of Red Cross and Red Crescent Societies concerned with the problems of family reunification.

They confirm that the presentation of an application concerning family reunification will not modify the rights and obligations of the applicant or of members of his family. . . .

(c) Marriage between Citizens of Different States. The participating States will examine favourably and on the basis of humanitarian considerations requests for exit or entry permits from persons who have decided to marry a citizen from another participating State.

The processing and issuing of the documents required for the above purposes and for the marriage will be in accordance with the provisions accepted for family reunification. . . .

(d) Travel for Personal or Professional Reasons. The participating States intend to facilitate wider travel by their citizens for personal or professional reason. . . .

They confirm that religious faiths, institutions and organizations, practising within the constitutional framework of the participating States, and their representatives can, in the field of their activities, have contacts and meetings among themselves and exchange information.

(e) Improvement of Conditions for Tourism on an Individual or Collective Basis. . . .

(f) Meetings among Young People. The participating States intend to further the development of contacts and exchanges among young people by encouraging [exchanges, contacts, programs, etc.]. . . .

(g) Sport. . . .

2. Information

The participating States, . . .

Express their intention in particular:

(a) Improvement of the Circulation of, Access to, and Exchange of Information

(i) *Oral Information*—To facilitate the dissemination of oral information through the encouragement of lectures and lecture tours by personalities and specialists from the other participating States, as well as exchanges of opinions at round table meetings, seminars, symposia, summer schools, congresses and other bilateral and multilateral meetings.

(ii) *Printed Information*—To facilitate the improvement of the dissemination, on their territory, of newspapers and printed publications, periodical and non-periodical, from the other participating States. . . .

(iii) *Filmed and Broadcast Information*—To promote the improvement of the dissemination of filmed and broadcast information. . . .

(b) Co-operation in the Field of Information—To encourage co-operation in the field of information on the basis of short or long term agreements or arrangements. . . .

(c) Improvement of Working Conditions for Journalists. The participating States, desiring to improve the conditions under which journalists from one participating State exercise their profession in another participating State, intend in particular to [improve conditions concerning journalists' visa, stay, movements, etc.]. . . .

The participating States reaffirm that the legitimate pursuit of their professional activity will neither render journalists liable to expulsion nor otherwise penalize them. If an accredited journalist is expelled, he will be informed of the reasons for this act and may submit an application for re-examination of his case.

3. Co-operation and Exchanges in the Field of Culture

The participating States,

Considering that cultural exchanges and co-operation contribute to a better comprehension among people and among peoples, and thus promote a lasting understanding among States, . . .

Express their intention now to proceed to the implementation of the following:

Extension of Relations. To expand, and improve at the various levels co-operation and links in the field of culture, in particular by:

—concluding, where appropriate, agreements on a bilateral or multilateral basis, providing for the extension of relations among competent State institutions and non-governmental organizations in the field of culture, as well as among people engaged in cultural activities, taking into account the need both for flexibility and the fullest possible use of existing agreements, and bearing in mind that agreements and also other arrangements constitute important means of developing cultural cooperation and exchanges;

—contributing to the development of direct communication and co-operation among relevant State institutions and non-governmental organizations, including, where necessary, such communication and co-operation carried out on the basis of special agreements and arrangements;

—encouraging direct contacts and communications among persons engaged in cultural activities, including, where necessary, such contacts and communications carried out on the basis of special agreements and arrangements.

Mutual Knowledge. Within their competence to adopt, on a bilateral and multilateral level, appropriate measures which would give their peoples a more comprehensive and complete mutual knowledge of their achievements in the various fields of culture. . . .

Exchanges and Dissemination. To contribute to the improvement of facilities for exchanges and the dissemination of cultural property, by appropriate means, in particular by [facilities for cheap and secure movements of books and works of art, customs facilities, film loans, etc.].

Access. To promote fuller mutual access by all to the achievements—works, experiences and performing arts—in the various fields of culture of their countries, and to that end to make the best possible efforts, in accordance with their competence, . . .

Contacts and Co-operation. To contribute, by appropriate means, to the development of contacts and co-operation in the various fields of culture, especially among creative artists and people engaged in cultural activities. . . .

Fields and Forms of Co-operation. To encourage the search for new fields and forms of cultural co-operation, to these ends contributing to the conclusion among interested parties, where necessary, of appropriate agreements and arrangements. . . .

* * *

National minorities or regional cultures. The participating States, recognizing the contribution that national minorities or regional cultures can make to co-operation among them in various fields of culture, intend, when such minorities or cultures exist within their territory, to facilitate this contribution, taking into account the legitimate interests of their members.

4. Co-operation and Exchanges in the Field of Education
The participating States,

Conscious that the development of relations of an international character in the fields of education and science contributes to a better mutual understanding and is to the advantage of all peoples as well as to the benefit of future generations, . . .

Express to these ends their intention in particular:

(a) Extension of Relations. To expand and improve at the various levels co-operation and links in the fields of education and science. . . .

(b) Access and Exchanges. To improve access, under mutually acceptable conditions, for students, teachers and scholars of the participating States to each other's educational, cultural and scientific institutions, and to intensify exchanges among these institutions in all areas of common interest, . . .

(c) Science. Within their competence to broaden and improve co-operation and exchanges in the field of science. . . .

To develop in the field of scientific research, on a bilateral or multilateral basis, the co-ordination of programmes carried out in the participating States and the organization of joint programmes, especially in the areas mentioned below, which may involve the combined efforts of scientists and in certain cases the use of costly or unique equipment. [Exact and natural sciences, medicine, humanities, and social sciences are listed.]

(d) Foreign Languages and Civilizations. To encourage the study of foreign languages and civilizations as an important means of expanding communication among peoples for their better acquaintance with the culture of each country, as well as for the strengthening of international co-operation; to this end to stimulate, within their competence, the further development and improvement of foreign language teaching and the diversification of choice of languages taught at various levels, paying due attention to less widely-spread or studied languages, and in particular [various activities are listed].

(e) Teaching Methods. To promote the exchange of experience, on a bilateral or multilateral basis in teaching methods at all levels of education, including those used in permanent and adult education, as well as the exchange of teaching materials. . . .

* * *

FOLLOW-UP TO THE CONFERENCE

The participating States, . . .

1. *Declare their resolve,* in the period following the Conference, to pay due regard to and implement the provisions of the Final Act of the Conference. . . .

2. *Declare furthermore their resolve* to continue the multilateral process initiated by the Conference. . . .

3. The first of the meetings indicated above will be held at Belgrade in 1977. A preparatory meeting to organize this meeting will be held at Belgrade on 15 June 1977. The preparatory meeting will decide on the date, duration, agenda and other modalities of the meeting of representatives appointed by the Ministers of Foreign Affairs; . . .

The original of this Final Act, drawn up in English, French, German, Italian, Russian and Spanish, will be transmitted to the Government of the Republic of Finland, which will retain it in its archives. Each of the participating States will receive from the Government of the Republic of Finland a true copy of this Final Act.

The text of this Final Act will be published in each participating State, which will disseminate it and make it known as widely as possible. . . .

Wherefore, the undersigned High Representatives of the Participating States, mindful of the high political significance which they attach to the results of the Conference, and declaring their determination to act in accordance with the provisions contained in the above texts, have subscribed their signatures below:

Done at Helsinki,
on 1st August
1975

8. U.N. GENERAL ASSEMBLY RESOLUTIONS ON WORLD
ECONOMIC PROBLEMS, 1084TH PLENARY MEETING,
19 DECEMBER 1961

1706 (XVI). Establishment of a United Nations capital development fund (19 December 1961) (item 28 [*b*])

9. CHARTER OF ECONOMIC RIGHTS AND DUTIES OF STATES, 12 DECEMBER 1974 (U.N.G.A. RES. 3281 (XXIX) (*U.N. MONTHLY CHRONICLE*, FEBRUARY 1975, 2ᴺ12)

On 12 December 1974, the General Assembly adopted the Charter of Economic Rights and Duties of States, contained in resolution 3281 (XXIX). It was adopted by a roll-call vote of 120 in favour to 6 against, with 10 abstentions. In the preamble of the resolution, the Assembly stressed the fact that "the Charter shall constitute an effective instrument towards the establishment of a new system of international economic relations based on equity, sovereign equality, and interdependence of the interests of developed and developing countries".

PREAMBLE

The General Assembly,
   Reaffirming the fundamental purposes of the United Nations, in particular, the maintenance of international peace and security, the development of friendly relations among nations and the achievement of international co-operation in solving international problems in the economic and social fields,
   Affirming the need for strengthening international co-operation in these fields,

Reaffirming further the need for strengthening international co-operation for development,

Declaring that it is a fundamental purpose of this Charter to promote the establishment of the new international economic order, based on equity, sovereign equality, interdependence, common interest and co-operation among all States, irrespective of their economic and social systems,

Desirous of contributing to the creation of conditions for:

(a) The attainment of wider prosperity among all countries and of higher standards of living for all peoples,

(b) The promotion by the entire international community of economic and social progress of all countries, especially developing countries,

(c) The encouragement of co-operation, on the basis of mutual advantage and equitable benefits for all peace-loving States which are willing to carry out the provisions of this Charter, in the economic, trade, scientific and technical fields, regardless of political, economic or social systems,

(d) The overcoming of main obstacles in the way of the economic development of the developing countries,

(e) The acceleration of the economic growth of developing countries with a view to bridging the economic gap between developing and developed countries,

(f) The protection, preservation and enhancement of the environment,

Mindful of the need to establish and maintain a just and equitable economic and social order through:

(a) The achievement of more rational and equitable international economic relations and the encouragement of structural changes in the world economy,

(b) The creation of conditions which permit the further expansion of trade and intensification of economic co-operation among all nations,

(c) The strengthening of the economic independence of developing countries,

(d) The establishment and promotion of international economic relations, taking into account the agreed differences in development of the developing countries and their specific needs,

Determined to promote collective economic security for development, in particular of the developing countries, with strict respect for the sovereign equality of each State and through the co-operation of the entire international community,

Considering that genuine co-operation among States, based on joint consideration of and concerted action regarding international economic problems, is essential for fulfilling the international community's common desire to achieve a just and rational development of all parts of the world,

Stressing the importance of ensuring appropriate conditions for the conduct of normal economic relations among all States, irrespective of differences in social and economic systems, and for the full respect for the rights of all peoples, as well as the strengthening of instruments of international economic co-operation as means for the consolidation of peace for the benefit of all,

Convinced of the need to develop a system of international economic relations on the basis of sovereign equality, mutual and equitable benefit and the close interrelationship of the interests of all States,

Reiterating that the responsibility for the development of every country rests primarily upon itself but that concomitant and effective international co-operation is an essential factor for the full achievement of its own development goals,

Firmly convinced of the urgent need to evolve a substantially improved system of international economic relations,

Solemnly adopts the present Charter of Economic Rights and Duties of States.

CHAPTER 1. FUNDAMENTALS OF INTERNATIONAL ECONOMIC RELATIONS

Economic as well as political and other relations among States shall be governed, *inter alia,* by the following principles:

(a) Sovereignty, territorial integrity and political independence of States;

(b) Sovereign equality of all States;

(c) Non-aggression;

(d) Non-intervention;

(e) Mutual and equitable benefit;

(f) Peaceful coexistence;

(g) Equal rights and self-determination of peoples;

(h) Peaceful settlement of disputes;

(i) Remedying of injustices which have been brought about by force and which deprive a nation of the natural means necessary for its normal development;

(j) Fulfilment in good faith of international obligations;

(k) Respect for human rights and fundamental freedoms;

(l) No attempt to seek hegemony and spheres of influence;

(m) Promotion of international social justice;

(n) International co-operation for development;

(o) Free access to and from the sea by land-locked countries within the framework of the above principles.

CHAPTER II. ECONOMIC RIGHTS AND DUTIES OF STATES

Article 1

Every State has the sovereign and inalienable right to choose its economic system as well as its political, social and cultural systems in accordance with the will of its people, without outside interference, coercion or threat in any form whatsoever.

Article 2

1. Every State has and shall freely exercise full permanent sovereignty, including possession, use and disposal, over all its wealth, natural resources and economic activities.

2. Each State has the right:

(a) To regulate and exercise authority over foreign investment within its national jurisdiction in accordance with its laws and regulations and in conformity with its national objectives and priorities. No State shall be compelled to grant preferential treatment to foreign investment;

(b) To regulate and supervise the activities of transnational corporations within its national jurisdiction and take measures to ensure that such activities comply with its laws, rules and regulations and conform with its economic and social policies. Transnational corporations shall not intervene in the internal affairs of a host State. Every State should, with full regard for its sovereign rights, co-operate with other States in the exercise of the right set forth in this subparagraph;

(c) To nationalize, expropriate or transfer ownership of foreign property, in which case appropriate compensation should be paid by the State adopting such measures, taking into account its relevant laws and regulations and all circumstances that the State considers pertinent. In any case where the question of compensation gives rise to a controversy, it shall be settled under the domestic law of the nationalizing State and by its tribunals, unless it is freely and mutually agreed by all States concerned that other peaceful means be sought on the basis of the sovereign equality of States and in accordance with the principle of free choice of means.

Article 3
In the exploitation of natural resources shared by two or more countries, each State must co-operate on the basis of a system of information and prior consultations in order to achieve optimum use of such resources without causing damage to the legitimate interest of others.

Article 4
Every State has the right to engage in international trade and other forms of economic co-operation irrespective of any differences in political, economic and social systems. No State shall be subjected to discrimination of any kind based solely on such differences. In the pursuit of international trade and other forms of economic co-operation, every State is free to choose the forms of organization of its foreign economic relations and to enter into bilateral and multilateral arrangements consistent with its international obligations and with the needs of international economic co-operation.

Article 5
All States have the right to associate in organizations of primary commodity producers in order to develop their national economies to achieve stable financing for their development, and in pursuance of their aims, to assist in the promotion of sustained growth of the world economy, in particular accelerating the development of developing countries. Correspondingly all States have the duty to respect that right by refraining from applying economic and political measures that would limit it.

Article 6
It is the duty of States to contribute to the development of international trade of goods, particularly by means of arrangements and by the conclusion of long-term multilateral commodity agreements, where appropriate, and taking into account the interests of producers and consumers. All States share the responsibility to promote the regular flow and access of all commercial goods traded at stable, remunerative and equitable prices, thus contributing to the equitable development of the world economy, taking into account, in particular, the interests of developing countries.

Article 7
Every State has the primary responsibility to promote the economic, social and cultural development of its people. To this end, each State has the right and the responsibility to choose its means and goals of development, fully to mobilize and use its resources, to implement progressive economic and social reforms and to ensure the full participation of its people in the process and benefits of development. All States have the duty, individually and collectively, to co-operate in order to eliminate obstacles that hinder such mobilization and use.

Article 8

States should co-operate in facilitating more rational and equitable international economic relations and in encouraging structural changes in the context of a balanced world economy in harmony with the needs and interests of all countries, especially developing countries, and should take appropriate measures to this end.

Article 9

All States have the responsibility to co-operate in the economic, social, cultural, scientific and technological fields for the promotion of economic and social progress throughout the world, especially that of the developing countries.

Article 10

All States are juridically equal and, as equal members of the international community, have the right to participate fully and effectively in the international decision-making process in the solution of world economic, financial and monetary problems, *inter alia,* through the appropriate international organizations in accordance with their existing and evolving rules, and to share equitably in the benefits resulting therefrom.

Article 11

All States should co-operate to strengthen and continuously improve the efficiency of international organizations in implementing measures to stimulate the general economic progress of all countries, particularly of developing countries, and therefore should co-operate to adapt them, when appropriate, to the changing needs of international economic co-operation.

Article 12

1. States have the right, in agreement with the parties concerned, to participate in subregional, regional and interregional co-operation in the pursuit of their economic and social development. All States engaged in such co-operation have the duty to ensure that the policies of those groupings to which they belong correspond to the provisions of the Charter and are outward-looking, consistent with their international obligations and with the needs of international economic co-operation and have full regard for the legitimate interests of third countries, especially developing countries.

2. In the case of groupings to which the States concerned have transferred or may transfer certain competences as regards matters that come within the scope of the present Charter, its provisions shall also apply to those groupings, in regard to such matters, consistent with the responsibilities of such States as members of such groupings. Those States shall co-operate in the observance by the groupings of the provisions of this Charter.

Article 13

1. Every State has the right to benefit from the advances and developments in science and technology for the acceleration of its economic and social development.

2. All States should promote international scientific and technological cooperation and the transfer of technology, with proper regard for all legitimate interests including, *inter alia,* the rights and duties of holders, suppliers and recipients of technology. In particular, all States should facilitate the access of developing countries to the achievements of modern science and technology, the transfer of technology and the creation of indigenous technology for the benefit

of the developing countries in forms and in accordance with procedures which are suited to their economies and their needs.

3. Accordingly, developed countries should co-operate with the developing countries in the establishment, strengthening and development of their scientific and technological infrastructures and their scientific research and technological activities so as to help to expand and transform the economies of developing countries.

4. All States should co-operate in exploring with a view to evolving further internationally accepted guidelines or regulations for the transfer of technology, taking fully into account the interests of developing countries.

Article 14

Every State has the duty to co-operate in promoting a steady and increasing expansion and liberalization of world trade and an improvement in the welfare and living standards of all peoples, in particular those of developing countries. Accordingly, all States should co-operate, *inter alia*, towards the progressive dismantling of obstacles to trade and the improvement of the international framework for the conduct of world trade and, to these ends, co-ordinated efforts shall be made to solve in an equitable way the trade problems of all countries, taking into account the specific trade problems of the developing countries. In this connexion, States shall take measures aimed at securing additional benefits for the international trade of developing countries so as to achieve a substantial increase in their foreign exchange earnings, the diversification of their exports, the acceleration of the rate of growth of their trade, taking into account their development needs, an improvement in the possibilities for these countries to participate in the expansion of world trade and a balance more favourable to developing countries in the sharing of the advantages resulting from this expansion, through, in the largest possible measure, substantial improvement in the conditions of access for the products of interest to the developing countries and, wherever appropriate, measures designed to attain stable, equitable and re-munerative prices for primary products.

Article 15

All States have the duty to promote the achievement of general and complete disarmament under effective international control and to utilize the resources freed by effective disarmament measures for the economic and social develop-ment of countries, allocating a substantial portion of such resources as additional means for the development needs of developing countries.

Article 16

1. It is the right and duty of all States, individually and collectively, to eliminate colonialism, *apartheid,* racial discrimination, neo-colonialism and all forms of foreign aggression, occupation and domination, and the economic and social consequences thereof, as a prerequisite for development. States which practise such coercive policies are economically responsible to the countries, territories and peoples affected for the restitution and full compensation for the exploitation and depletion of, and damages to, the natural and all other resources of those countries, territories and peoples. It is the duty of all States to extend assistance to them.

2. No State has the right to promote or encourage investments that may constitute an obstacle to the liberation of a territory occupied by force.

Article 17

International co-operation for development is the shared goal and common duty of all States. Every State should co-operate with the efforts of developing countries to accelerate their economic and social development by providing favourable external conditions and by extending active assistance to them, consistent with their development needs and objectives, with strict respect for the sovereign equality of States and free of any conditions derogating from their sovereignty.

Article 18

Developed countries should extend, improve and enlarge the system of generalized non-reciprocal and non-discriminatory tariff preferences to the developing countries consistent with the relevant agreed conclusions and relevant decisions as adopted on this subject, in the framework of the competent international organizations. Developed countries should also give serious consideration to the adoption of other differential measures, in areas where this is feasible and appropriate and in ways which will provide special and more favourable treatment, in order to meet the trade and development needs of the developing countries. In the conduct of international economic relations the developed countries should endeavour to avoid measures having a negative effect on the development of the national economies of the developing countries, as promoted by generalized tariff preferences and other generally agreed differential measures in their favour.

Article 19

With a view to accelerating the economic growth of developing countries and bridging the economic gap between developed and developing countries, developed countries should grant generalized preferential, non-reciprocal and non-discriminatory treatment to developing countries in those fields of international economic co-operation where it may be feasible.

Article 20

Developing countries should, in their efforts to increase their over-all trade, give due attention to the possibility of expanding their trade with socialist countries, by granting to these countries conditions for trade not inferior to those granted normally to the developed market economy countries.

Article 21

Developing countries should endeavour to promote the expansion of their mutual trade and to this end may, in accordance with the existing and evolving provisions and procedures of international agreements where applicable, grant trade preferences to other developing countries without being obliged to extend such preferences to developed countries, provided these arrangements do not constitute an impediment to general trade liberalization and expansion.

Article 22

1. All States should respond to the generally recognized or mutually agreed development needs and objectives of developing countries by promoting increased net flows of real resources to the developing countries from all sources, taking into account any obligations and commitments undertaken by the States concerned, in order to reinforce the efforts of developing countries to accelerate their economic and social development.

2. In this context, consistent with the aims and objectives mentioned above and taking into account any obligations and commitments undertaken in this regard,

it should be their endeavour to increase the net amount of financial flows from official sources to developing countries and to improve the terms and conditions thereof.

3. The flow of development assistance resources should include economic and technical assistance.

Article 23

To enhance the effective mobilization of their own resources, the developing countries should strengthen their economic co-operation and expand their mutual trade so as to accelerate their economic and social development. All countries, especially developed countries, individually as well as through the competent international organizations of which they are members, should provide appropriate and effective support and co-operation.

Article 24

All States have the duty to conduct their mutual economic relations in a manner which takes into account the interests of other countries. In particular, all States should avoid prejudicing the interests of developing countries.

Article 25

In furtherance of world economic development, the international community, especially its developed members, shall pay special attention to the particular needs and problems of the least developed among the developing countries, of land-locked developing countries and also island developing countries, with a view to helping them to overcome their particular difficulties and thus contribute to their economic and social development.

Article 26

All States have the duty to coexist in tolerance and live together in peace, irrespective of differences in political, economic, social and cultural systems, and to facilitate trade between States having different economic and social systems. International trade should be conducted without prejudice to generalized non-discriminatory and non-reciprocal preferences in favour of developing countries, on the basis of mutual advantage, equitable benefits and the exchange of most-favoured-nation treatment.

Article 27

1. Every State has the right to enjoy fully the benefits of world invisible trade and to engage in the expansion of such trade.

2. World invisible trade, based on efficiency and mutual and equitable benefit, furthering the expansion of the world economy, is the common goal of all States. The role of developing countries in world invisible trade should be enhanced and strengthened consistent with the above objectives, particular attention being paid to the special needs of developing countries.

3. All States should co-operate with developing countries in their endeavours to increase their capacity to earn foreign exchange from invisible transactions, in accordance with the potential and needs of each developing country and consistent with the objectives mentioned above.

Article 28

All States have the duty to co-operate in achieving adjustments in the prices of exports of developing countries in relation to prices of their imports so as to promote just and equitable terms of trade for them, in a manner which is remunerative for producers and equitable for producers and consumers.

CHAPTER III. COMMON RESPONSIBILITIES TOWARDS THE INTERNATIONAL COMMUNITY

Article 29

The sea-bed and ocean floor and the subsoil thereof, beyond the limits of national jurisdiction, as well as the resources of the area, are the common heritage of mankind. On the basis of the principles adopted by the General Assembly in resolution 2749 (XXV) of 17 December 1970, all States shall ensure that the exploration of the area and exploitation of its resources are carried out exclusively for peaceful purposes and that the benefits derived therefrom are shared equitably by all States, taking into account the particular interests and needs of developing countries; an international régime applying to the area and its resources and including appropriate international machinery to give effect to its provisions shall be established by an international treaty of a universal character, generally agreed upon.

Article 30

The protection, preservation and the enhancement of the environment for the present and future generations is the responsibility of all States. All States shall endeavour to establish their own environmental and developmental policies in conformity with such responsibility. The environmental policies of all States should enhance and not adversely affect the present and future development potential of developing countries. All States have the responsibility to ensure that activities within their jurisdiction or control do not cause damage to the environment of other States or of areas beyond the limits of national jurisdiction. All States should co-operate in evolving international norms and regulations in the field of the environment.

CHAPTER IV. FINAL PROVISIONS

Article 31

All States have the duty to contribute to the balanced expansion of the world economy, taking duly into account the close interrelationship between the well-being of the developed countries and the growth and development of the developing countries, and the fact that the prosperity of the international community as a whole depends upon the prosperity of its constituent parts.

Article 32

No State may use or encourage the use of economic, political or any other type of measures to coerce another State in order to obtain from it the subordination of the exercise of its sovereign rights.

Article 33

1. Nothing in the present Charter shall be construed as impairing or derogating from the provisions of the Charter of the United Nations or actions taken in pursuance thereof.

2. In their interpretation and application, the provisions of the present Charter are interrelated and each provision should be construed in the context of the other provisions.

Article 34

An item on the Charter of Economic Rights and Duties of States shall be inscribed in the agenda of the General Assembly at its thirtieth session, and thereafter on the agenda of every fifth session. In this way a systematic and comprehensive consideration of the implementation of the Charter, covering both progress achieved and any improvements and additions which might become necessary, would be carried out and appropriate measures recommended. Such consideration should take into account the evolution of all the economic, social, legal and other factors related to the principles upon which the present Charter is based and on its purpose.

10. U.S. RESERVATIONS TO THE CHARTER OF ECONOMIC RIGHTS AND DUTIES OF STATES, 1 MAY 1973 (U.N. DOC. A/PV. 2229, *INTERNATIONAL LEGAL MATERIALS* 13: 744–46)

Mr. SCALI (United States of America): . . . We seriously question what value there is in adopting statements on difficult and controversial questions that represent the views of only one faction.

Some have referred to the procedure by which these documents have been formulated as that of "consensus." My delegation believes that the word "consensus" cannot be applied in this case. The document which will be printed as the written product of this special General Assembly does not in fact, whatever it is called, represent a consensus in the accepted meaning of that term. My delegation did not choose to voice objection to the resolution presented to us this evening even though, at the last moment, it was presented without mention of the word "consensus."

The intent, however, was clear. This was intended as a consensus procedure, but our objecting at the last second would only have served to exacerbate commitments that we did not intend to fulfil. Thus, as Secretary of State Kissinger recently told the Foreign Ministers of Latin America and the Caribbean, the United States will promise only what it can deliver. And we will make what we can deliver count. . . .

It is easy to agree to yet another set of principles, to another programme of action, to more steps that other nations should take. But each nation must ask itself what it can do, what contribution it can make. The needs of the poor will not be met by empty promises; the needs of an expanding global economy will not be met by new restrictions on supply and demand; the growing interdependence of all nations cannot be managed on the basis of confrontation.

There are provisions in the Declaration and the Special Program to which the United States Government cannot lend its support. I will deal here only with our most important reservations.

Perhaps the most difficult subject which the Declaration of Principles addresses is that of permanent sovereignty over natural resources. It will be recalled that this problem was successfully dealt with by the General Assembly in 1962, when, in a meeting of minds of developing and developed countries, widespread agreement was achieved on the terms of resolution 1803 (XVII). The United States delegation regrets that the compromise solution which resolution 1803 (XVII) embodies was not reproduced in this Declaration. If it were, on this count the United States would gladly lend its support. Resolution 1803 (XVII) provides, among other things, that, where foreign property is nationalized, appropriate compensation shall be paid in accordance with national and international law; it also provides that foreign investment agreements by and between States shall be observed in good faith. By way of contrast, the present Declaration does not couple the assertion of the right to nationalize with the duty to pay compensation in accordance with international law. For this reason, we do not find this formulation complete or acceptable. . . .

11. U.N. CONVENTION ON THE LAW OF THE SEA, 1982

The States Parties to this Convention,
Prompted by the desire to settle, in a spirit of mutual understanding and co-operation, all issues relating to the law of the sea and aware of the historic significance of this Convention as an important contribution to the maintenance of peace, justice and progress for all peoples of the world, . . .
Believing that the codification and progressive development of the law of the sea achieved in this Convention will contribute to the strengthening of peace, security, co-operation and friendly relations among all nations in conformity with the principles of justice and equal rights and will promote the economic and social advancement of all peoples of the world, in accordance with the Purposes and Principles of the United Nations as set forth in the Charter,
Affirming that matters not regulated by this Convention continue to be governed by the rules and principles of general international law,
Have agreed as follows: . . .

PART V. EXCLUSIVE ECONOMIC ZONE
Article 55. Specific Legal Régime of the Exclusive Economic Zone
The exclusive economic zone is an area beyond and adjacent to the territorial sea, subject to the specific legal régime established in this Part, under which the rights and jurisdiction of the coastal State and the rights and freedoms of other States are governed by the relevant provisions of this Convention.
Article 56. Rights, Jurisdiction and Duties of the Coastal State in the Exclusive Economic Zone
1. In the exclusive economic zone, the coastal State has:
(a) sovereign rights for the purpose of exploring and exploiting, conserving and managing the natural resources, whether living or non-living, of the waters superjacent to the sea-bed and of the sea-bed and its subsoil, and with regard to other activities for the economic exploitation and exploration of the zone, such as the production of energy from the water, currents and winds;
(b) jurisdiction as provided for in the relevant provisions of this Convention with regard to:
   (i) the establishment and use of artificial islands, installations and structures;
   (ii) marine scientific research;

(iii) the protection and preservation of the marine environment;
(c) other rights and duties provided for in this Convention.

In exercising its rights and performing its duties under this Convention in the exclusive economic zone, the coastal State shall have due regard to the rights and duties of other States and shall act in a manner compatible with the provisions of this Convention.

3. The rights set out in this article with respect to the sea-bed and subsoil shall be exercised in accordance with Part VI.

Article 57. Breadth of the Exclusive Economic Zone

The exclusive economic zone shall not extend beyond 200 nautical miles from the baselines from which the breadth of the territorial sea is measured. . . .*

Article 59. Basis for the Resolution of Conflicts regarding the Attribution of Rights and Jurisdiction in the Exclusive Economic Zone

In cases where this Convention does not attribute rights or jurisdiction to the coastal State or to other States within the exclusive economic zone, and a conflict arises between the interests of the coastal State and any other State or States, the conflict should be resolved on the basis of equity and in the light of all the relevant circumstances, taking into account the respective importance of the interests involved to the parties as well as to the international community as a whole. . . .†

Article 61. Conservation of the Living Resources

1. The coastal State shall determine the allowable catch of the living resources in its exclusive economic zone.

2. The coastal State, taking into account the best scientific evidence available to it, shall ensure through proper conservation and management measures that the maintenance of the living resources in the exclusive economic zone is not endangered by over-exploitation. As appropriate, the coastal State and competent international organizations, whether subregional, regional or global, shall cooperate to this end. . . .‡

Article 62. Utilization of the Living Resources

1. The coastal State shall promote the objective of optimum utilization of the living resources in the exclusive economic zone without prejudice to article 61.

2. The coastal State shall determine its capacity to harvest the living resources of the exclusive economic zone. Where the coastal State does not have the capacity to harvest the entire allowable catch, it shall, through agreements or other arrangements and pursuant to the terms, conditions, laws and regulations referred to in paragraph 4, give other States access to the surplus of the allowable catch, having particular regard to the provisions of articles 69 and 70, especially in relation to the developing States mentioned therein. . . .§

---

*Article 58 concerns the rights of non-coastal states in the zone.

†Article 60 concerns artificial islands, installations, and structures in the exclusive economic zone.

‡Paragraphs 3–6 set certain conservation norms and procedures.

§Paragraphs 3–5 set certain utilization norms and procedures. Article 63 concerns stocks occurring within the exclusive economic zones of two or more coastal states or both within the exclusive economic zone and in an area beyond and adjacent to it. Article 64 concerns highly migratory species.

Article 65. Marine Mammals

Nothing in this Part restricts the right of a coastal State or the competence of an international organization, as appropriate, to prohibit, limit or regulate the exploitation of marine mammals more strictly than provided for in this Part. States shall co-operate with a view to the conservation of marine mammals and in the case of cetaceans shall in particular work through the appropriate international organizations for their conservation, management and study.

Article 66. Anadromous Stocks

1. States in whose rivers anadromous stocks originate shall have the primary interest in and responsibility for such stocks.

2. The State of origin of anadromous stocks shall ensure their conservation by the establishment of appropriate regulatory measures for fishing in all waters landward of the outer limits of its exclusive economic zone and for fishing provided for in paragraph 3(b). The State of origin may, after consultations with the other States referred to in paragraphs 3 and 4 fishing these stocks, establish total allowable catches for stocks originating in its rivers. . . .‖

Article 67. Catadromous Species

1. A coastal State in whose waters catadromous species spend the greater part of their life cycle shall have responsibility for the management of these species and shall ensure the ingress and egress of migrating fish. . . .#

Article 68. Sedentary Species

This Part does not apply to sedentary species as defined in article 77, paragraph 4.

Article 69. Right of Land-locked States

1. Land-locked States shall have the right to participate, on an equitable basis, in the exploitation of an appropriate part of the surplus of the living resources of the exclusive economic zones of coastal States of the same subregion or region, taking into account the relevant economic and geographical circumstances of all the States concerned and in conformity with the provisions of this article and of articles 61 and 62. . . .**

Article 70. Right of Geographically Disadvantaged States

1. Geographically disadvantaged States shall have the right to participate, on an equitable basis, in the exploitation of an appropriate part of the surplus of the living resources of the exclusive economic zones of coastal States of the same subregion or region, taking into account the relevant economic and geographical circumstances of all the States concerned and in conformity with the provisions of this article and of articles 61 and 62.

2. For the purposes of this Part, "geographically disadvantaged States" means coastal States, including States bordering enclosed or semi-enclosed seas, whose geographical situation makes them dependent upon the exploitation of the living resources of the exclusive economic zones of other States in the subregion or region for adequate supplies of fish for the nutritional purposes of their popu-

‖Paragraphs 3–5 set certain norms and procedures as to these stocks.
#Paragraphs 2 and 3 concern allocation of other responsibilities.
**Paragraphs 2–5 concern norms and procedures for settling participations.

lations or parts thereof, and coastal States which can claim no exclusive economic zones of their own. . . .††
Article 73. Enforcement of Laws and Regulations of the Coastal State
1. The coastal State may, in the exercise of its sovereign rights to explore, exploit, conserve and manage the living resources in the exclusive economic zone, take such measures, including boarding, inspection, arrest and judicial proceedings, as may be necessary to ensure compliance with the laws and regulations adopted by it in conformity with this Convention. . . .‡‡

PART VI. CONTINENTAL SHELF
Article 76. Definition of the Continental Shelf
. . .

Article 82. Payments and Contributions with respect to the Exploitation of the Continental Shelf beyond 200 Nautical Miles
1. The coastal State shall make payments or contributions in kind in respect of the exploitation of the non-living resources of the continental shelf beyond 200 nautical miles from the baselines from which the breadth of the territorial sea is measured.
2. The payments and contributions shall be made annually with respect to all production at a site after the first five years of production at that site. For the sixth year, the rate of payment or contribution shall be 1 per cent of the value or volume of production at the site. The rate shall increase by 1 per cent for each subsequent year until the twelfth year and shall remain at 7 per cent thereafter. Production does not include resources used in connection with exploitation.
3. A developing State which is a net importer of a mineral resource produced from its continental shelf is exempt from making such payments or contributions in respect of that mineral resource.
4. The payments or contributions shall be made through the Authority, which shall distribute them to States Parties to this Convention, on the basis of equitable sharing criteria, taking into account the interests and needs of developing States, particularly the least developed and the land-locked among them. . . .§§
Section 2. Conservation and Management of the Living Resources of the High Seas
Article 116. Right to Fish on the High Seas
All States have the right for their nationals to engage in fishing on the high seas subject to:
   (a) their treaty obligations;
   (b) the rights and duties as well as the interests of coastal States provided for, *inter alia,* in article 63, paragraph 2, and articles 64 to 67; and
   (c) the provisions of this section.

---

††Paragraphs 3–6 set norms and procedures for participation. Article 72 concerns restrictions on the transfer of rights.
‡‡Paragraphs 2–4 describe related procedures. Article 74 concerns delimitation of the exclusive economic zone between states with opposite or adjacent coasts. Article 75 concerns charts and lists of geographical coordinates.
§§Article 83 delimits the shelf between states with opposite or adjacent coasts. Articles 86–120 are in Part VII, on the high seas.

Article 117. Duty of States to Adopt with Respect to Their Nationals Measures for the Conservation of the Living Resources of the High Seas
All States have the duty to take, or to co-operate with other States in taking, such measures for their respective nationals as may be necessary for the conservation of the living resources of the high seas. . . .||||

Article 120. Marine Mammals
Article 65 also applies to the conservation and management of marine mammals in the high seas.

PART XI. THE AREA
Section 1. General Provisions
Article 133. Use of Terms
For the purposes of this Part:
(a) "resources" means solid, liquid or gaseous mineral resources *in situ* in the Area at or beneath the sea-bed, including polymetallic modules;
(b) resources, when recovered from the Area, are referred to as "minerals". . . .##

Section 2. Principles Governing the Area
Article 136. Common Heritage of Mankind
The Area and its resources are the common heritage of mankind.

Article 137. Legal Status of the Area and Its Resources
1. No State shall claim or exercise sovereignty or sovereign rights over any part of the Area or its resources, nor shall any State or natural or juridical person appropriate any part thereof. No such claim or exercise of sovereignty or sovereign rights nor such appropriation shall be recognized.

2. All rights in the resources of the Area are vested in mankind as a whole, on whose behalf the Authority shall act. These resources are not subject to alienation. The minerals recovered from the Area, however, may only be alienated in accordance with this Part and the rules, regulations and procedures of the Authority.

3. No State or natural or juridical person shall claim, acquire or exercise rights with respect to the minerals recovered from the Area except in accordance with this Part. Otherwise, no such claim, acquisition or exercise of such rights shall be recognized.

Article 138. General Conduct of States in Relation to the Area
The general conduct of States in relation to the Area shall be in accordance with the provisions of this Part, the principles embodied in the Charter of the United Nations and other rules of international law in the interests of maintaining peace and security and promoting international co-operation and mutual understanding.

Article 139. Responsibility to Ensure Compliance and Liability for Damage
1. States Parties shall have the responsibility to ensure that activities in the Area, whether carried out by States Parties, or state enterprises or natural or juridical persons which possess the nationality of States Parties or are effectively

||||Articles 118 and 119 deal with conservation of living resources of the high seas.
##Articles 134 and 135 deal with the scope of provisions as to "the Area" declared to be "the common heritage of mankind."

controlled by them or their nationals, shall be carried out in conformity with this Part. The same responsibility applies to international organizations for activities in the Area carried out by such organizations.

2. Without prejudice to the rules of international law and Annex III, article 22, damage caused by the failure of a State Party or international organization to carry out its responsibilities under this Part shall entail liability; States Parties or international organizations acting together shall bear joint and several liability. A State Party shall not however be liable for damage caused by any failure to comply with this Part by a person whom it has sponsored under article 153, paragraph 2(b), if the State Party has taken all necessary and appropriate measures to secure effective compliance under article 153, paragraph 4, and Annex III, article 4, paragraph 4.

3. States Parties that are members of international organizations shall take appropriate measures to ensure the implementation of this article with respect to such organizations.

Article 140. Benefit of Mankind

1. Activities in the Area shall, as specifically provided for in this Part, be carried out for the benefit of mankind as a whole, irrespective of the geographical location of States, whether coastal or land-locked, and taking into particular consideration the interests and needs of developing States and of peoples who have not attained full independence or other self-governing status recognized by the United Nations in accordance with General Assembly resolution 1514 (XV) and other relevant General Assembly resolutions.

2. The Authority shall provide for the equitable sharing of financial and other economic benefits derived from activities in the Area through any appropriate mechanism, on a non-discriminatory basis, in accordance with article 160, paragraph 2(f)(i).

Article 141. Use of the Area Exclusively for Peaceful Purposes

The Area shall be open to use exclusively for peaceful purposes by all States, whether coastal or land-locked, without discrimination and without prejudice to the other provisions of this Part. . . .***

Article 144. Transfer of Technology

1. The Authority shall take measures in accordance with this Convention:
(a)   to acquire technology and scientific knowledge relating to activities in the Area; and
(b)   to promote and encourage the transfer to developing States of such technology and scientific knowledge so that all States Parties benefit therefrom.

2. To this end the Authority and States Parties shall co-operate in promoting the transfer of technology and scientific knowledge relating to activities in the Area so that the Enterprise and all States Parties may benefit therefrom. In particular they shall initiate and promote:
(a)   programmes for the transfer of technology to the Enterprise and to developing States with regard to activities in the Area, including, *inter alia*, facilitating the access of the Enterprise and of developing States to the relevant technology, under fair and reasonable terms and conditions;

***Articles 142 and 143 deal with rights of coastal states and marine research facilities.

(b) measures directed towards the advancement of the technology of the Enterprise and the domestic technology of developing States, particularly by providing opportunities to personnel from the Enterprise and from developing States for training in marine science and technology and for their full participation in activities in the Area. . . .†††

Article 189. Limitation on Jurisdiction with regard to Decisions of the Authority

The Sea-Bed Disputes Chamber shall have no jurisdiction with regard to the exercise by the Authority of its discretionary powers in accordance with this Part; in no case shall it substitute its discretion for that of the Authority. Without prejudice to article 191, in exercising its jurisdiction pursuant to article 187, the Sea-Bed Disputes Chamber shall not pronounce itself on the question of whether any rules, regulations and procedures of the Authority are in conformity with this Convention, nor declare invalid any such rules, regulations and procedures. Its jurisdiction in this regard shall be confined to deciding claims that the application of any rules, regulations and procedures of the Authority in individual cases would be in conflict with the contractual obligations of the parties to the dispute or their obligations under this Convention, claims concerning excess of jurisdiction or misuse of power, and to claims for damages to be paid or other remedy to be given to the party concerned for the failure of the other party to comply with its contractual obligations or its obligations under this Convention.

Article 190. Participation and Appearance of Sponsoring States Parties in Proceedings

1. If a natural or juridical person is a party to a dispute referred to in article 187, the sponsoring State shall be given notice thereof and shall have the right to participate in the proceedings by submitting written or oral statements.

2. If an action is brought against a State Party by a natural or juridical person sponsored by another State Party in a dispute referred to in article 187, sub-paragraph (c), the respondent State may request the State sponsoring that person to appear in the proceedings on behalf of that person. Failing such appearance, the respondent State may arrange to be represented by a juridical person of its nationality.

Article 191. Advisory Opinions

The Sea-Bed Disputes Chamber shall give advisory opinions at the request of the Assembly or the Council on legal questions arising within the scope of their activities. Such opinions shall be given as a matter of urgency.

PART XII. PROTECTION AND PRESERVATION OF THE MARINE ENVIRONMENT

Section 1. General Provisions

Article 192. General Obligation

States have the obligation to protect and preserve the marine environment.

Article 193. Sovereign Right of States to Exploit Their Natural Resources

States have the sovereign right to exploit their natural resources pursuant to their environmental policies and in accordance with their duty to protect and preserve the marine environment. . . .‡‡‡

---

†††Article 145 protects "the marine environment." Article 188 provides recourses for settlement of disputes.

‡‡‡Article 194 concerns measures against pollution.

Article 195. Duty Not to Transfer Damage or Hazards or Transform One Type of Pollution into Another

In taking measures to prevent, reduce and control pollution of the marine environment, States shall act so as not to transfer, directly or indirectly, damage or hazards from one area to another or transform one type of pollution into another.

Article 196. Use of Technologies or Introduction of Alien or New Species

1. States shall take all measures necessary to prevent, reduce and control pollution of the marine environment resulting from the use of technologies under their jurisdiction or control, or the intentional or accidental introduction of species, alien or new, to a particular part of the marine environment, which may cause significant and harmful changes thereto.

2. This article does not affect the application of this Convention regarding the prevention, reduction and control of pollution of the marine environment. . . .

Article 198. Notification of Imminent or Actual Damage

When a State becomes aware of cases in which the marine environment is in imminent danger of being damaged or has been damaged by pollution, it shall immediately notify other States it deems likely to be affected by such damage, as well as the competent international organizations.

12. U.S. STATEMENT OF OBJECTIONS TO THE U.N. CONVENTION ON THE LAW OF THE SEA, 3 JUNE 1982 (EXTRACTED FROM U.N. DOC. A/CONF. 62/SR. 182, THIRD CONFERENCE ON THE LAW OF THE SEA)

This convention was signed by 118 states at Montego Bay in December 1982. To November 1983 only nine countries had ratified, not including the United States, the United Kingdom, West Germany, and the Soviet Union. Sixty ratifications are required for it to come into force.

Mr. MALONE (United States of America): . . . His delegation had come to the current session willing to work and negotiate with other delegations to find mutually acceptable solutions and had proposed a set of amendments that would have satisfied its objectives yet provided a fair and balanced system to promote the development of deep sea-bed resources. In a spirit of conciliation, it had later revised its proposed amendments to take into account views expressed by other delegations.

Three misconceptions had arisen about United States motivations. The first misconception had been that the United States was seeking essentially to nullify the basic bargain reflected in the draft Convention. In fact, even if all the changes proposed by the United States had been accepted, there would still have been an international regulatory system for the deep sea-bed and an international mining entity. There had been no desire to destroy that system at all; rather the intention had been to structure it in a way that would best serve the interests of all nations by enhancing sea-bed resource development.

The second misconception had been that the primary interest of the United States in the deep sea-bed régime related to protecting a few United States business interests. That was a drastic misjudgement of the United States motivation and its commitment to certain principles. Finally, a widespread view which was also false was that the United States would in the end accept an unsatisfactory deep sea-bed régime because of the navigation provisions that served other national interests. On the contrary, the United States had consistently maintained that every part of the Convention must be satisfactory. . . .

It was important to make clear how far the Conference had fallen short of the objectives of the United States. First, the sea-bed mining provisions would deter the development of deep sea-bed mineral resources; such development was in the interest of all countries and especially of the developing countries. By denying the play of basic economic forces in the market place, the Convention would create yet another barrier to rational economic development. Second, while there had been improvements to ensure access to deep sea-bed minerals for existing miners, the United States did not believe that the access necessary in the future to promote the economic development of those resources had been assured. At the same time, a system of privileges would be established for the Enterprise that would discriminate against private and national miners. Third, the decision-making process established in the deep sea-bed régime did not give a proportionate voice to the countries most affected by the decisions and would thus not fairly reflect and effectively protect their interests. Fourth, the Convention would allow amendments to come into force for a State without its consent, which was clearly incompatible with United States processes for incurring treaty obligations. Moreover, after having made substantial investments in deep sea-bed mining, the choice of either accepting an amendment at some future time or being forced to withdraw from the Convention entirely was not acceptable. Lastly, the deep sea-bed régime continued to pose serious problems for the United States by creating precedents that were inappropriate; the provisions on mandatory transfer of technology, potential distribution of benefits to national liberation movements and production limitations posed key problems for the United States Congress. . . .

Many delegations had come to the negotiations with different perspectives and diverse interests, and there were even differences of opinion on the meaning of the concept of the common heritage of mankind and the consequences flowing therefrom. Despite those differences, his delegation had held to the conviction that negotiation and compromise could produce a convention serving the interests of all States. Unfortunately, the Convention in its current form did not meet those standards. It would not bring more orderly and productive uses of the deep sea-bed to reality and it would not serve the broader goal of bringing the developed and developing countries closer together. . . .

13. DECLARATION ON THE HUMAN ENVIRONMENT: STOCKHOLM DECLARATION, 1972

The United Nations Conference on the Human Environment having met at Stockholm from 5 to 16 June 1972, and having considered the need for a common outlook and for common principles to inspire and guide the peoples of the world in the preservation and enhancement of the human environment, proclaims: . . .

6. A point has been reached in history when we must shape our actions throughout the world with a more prudent care for their environmental consequences. Through ignorance or indifference we can do massive and irreversible harm to the earthly environment on which our life and well being depend. Conversely, through fuller knowledge and wiser action, we can achieve for ourselves and our posterity a better life in an environment more in keeping with human needs and hopes. There are broad vistas for the enhancement of environmental quality and the creation of a good life. What is needed is an enthusiastic but calm state of mind and intense but orderly work. For the purposes of attaining freedom in the world of nature, man must use knowledge to build in collaboration with nature a better environment. To defend and improve the human environment for present and future generations has become an imperative goal for mankind—a goal to be pursued together with, and in harmony with, the established and fundamental goals of peace and of worldwide economic and social development.

7. To achieve this environmental goal will demand the acceptance of responsibility by citizens and communities and by enterprises and institutions at every level, all sharing equitably in common efforts. Individuals in all walks of life as well as organizations in many fields, by their values and the sum of their actions, will shape the world environment of the future. Local and national governments will bear the greatest burden for large scale environmental policy and action within their jurisdictions. International cooperation is also needed in order to raise resources to support the developing countries in carrying out their responsibilities in this field. A growing class of environmental problems, because they are regional or global in extent or because they affect the common international realm, will require extensive cooperation among nations and action by international organizations in the common interest. The conference calls upon the governments and peoples to exert common efforts for the preservation and improvement of the human environment, for the benefit of all the people and for their posterity.

Principles

States the common conviction that—

1. Man has the fundamental right to freedom, equality and adequate conditions of life, in an environment of a quality which permits a life of dignity and well being, and bears a solemn responsibility to protect and improve the environment for present and future generations. (In this respect, policies promoting or perpetuating apartheid, racial segregation, discrimination, colonial and other forms of oppression and foreign domination stand condemned and must be eliminated.)

2. The natural resources of the earth including the air, water, land, flora and fauna and especially representative samples of natural ecosystems must be safeguarded for the benefit of present and future generations through careful planning or management as appropriate.

3. The capacity of the earth to produce vital renewable resources must be maintained and wherever practicable restored or improved.

4. Man has a special responsibility to safeguard and wisely manage the heritage of wildlife and its habitat which are now gravely imperilled by a combination of

adverse factors. Nature conservation including wildlife must therefore receive importance in planning for economic development.

5. The non-renewable resources of the earth must be employed in such a way as to guard against the danger of their future exhaustion and to ensure that benefits from such employment are shared by all mankind.

6. The discharge of toxic substances or of other substances and the release of heat, in such quantities or concentrations as to exceed the capacity of the environment to render them harmless, must be halted in order to ensure that serious or irreversible damage is not inflicted upon ecosystems. (The just struggle of the peoples of all countries against pollution should be supported.)

POLLUTION CONTROL

7. States shall take all possible steps to prevent pollution of the seas by substances that are liable to create hazards to human health, to harm living resources and marine life, to damage amenities or to interfere with other legitimate uses of the sea.

8. Economic and social development is essential for ensuring a favorable living and working environment for man and for conditions on earth that are necessary for the improvement of the quality of life.

9. Environmental deficiencies generated by the conditions of underdevelopment and natural disasters pose grave problems and can best be remedied by accelerated development through the transfer of substantial quantities of financial and technological assistance, as a supplement to the domestic effort of the developing countries and such timely assistance as may be required.

10. For the developing countries, stability of prices and adequate earnings for primary commodities and raw material are essential to environmental management since economic factors as well as ecological processes must be taken into account.

11. The environmental policies of all states should enhance and not adversely affect the present or future development potential of developing countries, nor should they hamper the attainment of better living conditions for all, and appropriate steps should be taken by states and international organizations with a view to reaching agreement on meeting the possible national and international economic consequences resulting from the application of enviromental measures.

12. Resources should be made available to preserve and improve the environment, taking into account the circumstances and particular requirements of developing countries and any costs which may emanate from their incorporating environmental safeguards into their development planning and the need for making available to them, upon their request, additional international technical and financial assistance for this purpose.

13. In order to achieve a more rational management of resources and thus to improve the environment, states should adopt an integrated and coordinated approach to their development planning so as to ensure that development is compatible with the need to protect and improve the human environment for the benefit of their population.

14. Rational planning constitutes an essential tool for reconciling any conflict

between the needs of development and the need to protect and improve the environment. . . .*

16. Demographic policies which are without prejudice to basic human rights and which are deemed appropriate by governments concerned, should be applied in those regions where the rate of population growth or excessive population concentrations are likely to have adverse effects on the environment or development, or where low population density may prevent improvement of the human environment and impede development.

17. Appropriate national institutions must be entrusted with the task of planning, managing or controlling the environmental resources of states with the view to enhancing environmental quality. . . .†

21. States have, in accordance with the Charter of the United Nations and the principles of international law, the sovereign right to exploit their own resources pursuant to their own environmental policies, and the responsibility to ensure that activities within their jurisdiction or control do not cause damage to the environment of other states or of areas beyond the limits of national jurisdiction. . . .‡

23. Without prejudice to such general principles as may be agreed upon by the international community, or to the criteria and minimum levels which will have to be determined nationally, it will be essential in all cases to consider the systems of values prevailing in each country, and the extent of the applicability of standards which are valid for the most advanced countries but which may be inappropriate and of unwarranted social cost for the developing countries. . . .§

*Paragraph 15 concerns planning for human settlements and urbanization.

†Paragraphs 18–20 concern the roles of education and science and technology in environmental protection.

‡Paragraph 22 concerns liability for environmental damage.

§Paragraphs 24–26 concern international cooperation, the role of international organizations and nuclear weapons.

Notes

1. THE SOCIOLOGICAL SUBSTRATUM OF INTERNATIONAL LAW

1. Among the pioneering statements see M. Huber, "Beiträge zu Kenntnis des soziologischen Grundlagen der Völkerrechts und der Staatengesellschaft," *Jahrbuch des öffentlichen Rechts der Gegenwart* 4 (1910): 57, 62; and D. Schindler, "Contributions à l'étude des facteurs sociologiques et psychologiques du droit international," *Hague Recueil* 46 (1933): 233–326, esp. 237–38, 241–57.

2. Many books on international law may read as if the meaning and effect of propositions of law that they discuss are independent of any extralegal substratum. Abstraction from the concrete situation adapted to the object of study is, of course, a legitimate procedure. Beyond the limits of that object, the abstraction should not be mistaken for the reality.

3. These matters may be treated too lightly even by distinguished exponents. See, for example, M. S. McDougal, "International Law, Power, and Policy: A Contemporary Conception," *Hague Recueil* 82 (1953): 137–252, esp. 187. McDougal writes "What we are attempting to do is, almost literally, slowly to turn a globe or sphere (the context of world social and power processes) for the purpose of spotlighting, investigating and relating to total context now one set of decisions, with all their goals and conditioning variables, and then another set." But how do we come to adequate *cognition* of "their goals and conditioning variables?" (164).

4. There is usually a rather intractable *hiatus irrationalis* between the facts of different strata of reality. While beginning and end are known, the process of becoming and the mediating components usually are not knowable with assurance.

5. K. Singer, *The Idea of Conflict* (Melbourne: Melbourne University Press, 1949), 20, observed: "Interests, even those of the most crude and obvious kind, can become motives only if conceived in terms of thought: neither hunger nor oppression produce revolutions. . . ." And on p. 22: " . . . man's life cannot be added up from external conditions providing stimuli to which he has to respond by a quasi-mechanical reaction." See also C. G. Jung, "Psychological Factors Determining Human Behaviour," *Factors Determining Human Behaviour*, Harvard Tercentenary Publications (Cambridge, Mass., 1937), 48–63.

6. It is surprising to find such facts so often neglected, especially in work concerned with the cultural and ethical conditions of world organization. N. Maim, *Weltwissenschaft* (Stuttgart, 1946), 8–9, argues that world needs cannot be satisfied through states and nations as single entities but only through a world organization. He then says: "It is obvious that the leading spiritis of the world organisation should have a mentality (*Gesinnung*) which is distinct (*unterschiedlich*) from the national mentality of the statesmen." How is this "men+~¹

211

ity" to be placed and kept commanding the world organization in which the nationalization of truth remains rampant and human communication across frontiers is increasingly fettered?

7. J. L. Kunz thought that the contemporary crisis of international law was "only a function, a part, a facet of the total crisis in which the Western man finds himself in the middle in the XXth century." Whatever the ambit of the crisis, it seems clear that the breakdown of human communication is a central manifestation of it (see J. L. Kunz, *Del derecho internacional clasico al derecho internacional nuevo* [Mexico City, 1953], 55). Among many works on this "total" crisis see K. Mannheim, *Man and Society in an Age of Reconstruction* [London: Routledge, 1942]; idem, *Diagnosis of Our Time* [1941]; G. Orwell, *Nineteen Eighty-Four* [London: Secker and Warburg, 1949]; L. Paul, *The Annihilation of Man: A Study of the Crisis in the West* [New York, 1945]; and H. Kohn, *The Twentieth Century: A Midway Account of the Western World* [London: Gollancz, 1950]). The existence of crisis seems inescapable, even if we reject Proudhon's terrible advance projections of it (*Oeuvres complètes*, vol. 10 [1929], 205 ff.). Doomsaysings, of course, continued and even multiplied as we moved into the nuclear and computer eras (see, for example, Jonathan Schell, *The Fate of the Earth* [1982]; and the declaration of the Stockholm U.N. conference on the environment, below, app. 14).

8. Thus, "the rights of man" held more in common for Frenchmen and Americans in 1789 than it probably does in 1984. The same may be said of the values implied in the terms "civilized nation" and "liberty" and in many other basic verbal symbols (see Kunz, *Del derecho internacional clasico*, 373; see also G. Schwarzenberger's bitter observation ["The Standard of Civilisation in International Law," *Current Legal Problems* 8 (1955): 234]: "The international lawyer must be content to point out the ominous character of a movement which has first led to a coalescence of international law and civilisation, but, on a global level, appears now to point towards the evanescence of the standard of civilisation from international law." And see K. Jaspers, *Origin and Goal of History*, trans. M. Bullock [London: Routledge, 1953], 134: "In this process intellectual concepts become banners and badges. Words are used like counterfeit coins, with their meaning reversed but with the emotions formerly attached to them preserved [liberty, fatherland, State, nation, empire, etc.]." See also J. Stone (*Legal Controls of International Conflict* [Sydney, London, and New York, 1954; supp., Sydney and New York, 1959], 318–23 [discourse 15]).

9. J. Fawcett, *Law and Power in International Relations* (1982), 13–14.

10. The condemnation by F. Honig ("The Cold War as an Instrument of National Policy," *Yearbook of World Affairs*, 1953, 45, 53) of state-sponsored propaganda designed to injure foreign states in times of peace stood ill even at that time with the apparent endorsement of the work of the United States Psychological Strategy Board (54–55). By 1984 it seems naive.

11. We cannot explore here the deeper ground hypothesized by J. Burckhardt (*Welt-geschichtliche Betrachtungen*, 7th ed. [Berne, 1949], 37), namely, that the state is not primarily an embodiment of morality. "The ethical has an essentially different *forum* than the state; it is already a great deal (*enorm viel*) that the latter sustains (*aufrecht halt*) the conventional law." Inadvertence to the point in the text is perhaps a main lack of the pioneering work of D. Schindler ("Contribution à l'étude des facteurs sociologiques et psychologiques du droit international," esp. 286 ff., 297–313). Schindler assumes that the state entity is, sociologically speaking, something given; in my view the clarification of the relations between state entities and the interests, attitudes, and behavior of human beings within and between the state domains is a basic problem for the sociology of international law. Nonjuristic approaches have been open to similar comment. Thus, any construction such as F. del Vecchio's "La société des nations au point de vue de la philosophie du droit international," ibid., 38 (1931): 545–645, postulating a unity of mankind "en un certain sens" and ignoring the role of state entities in human communication, is defective.

12. See C. J. Olmstead's proposal that the International Law Association promote such a convention (*International Law Association Report* [London, 1980], 293). See also J. Stone and

R. Woetzel, *On the Feasibility of an International Criminal Court* (Geneva: World Peace through Law Centres, 1970), esp. 315–41.

13. There is an illuminating metaphor in W. Reich, *Character Analysis* (London: Vision Press, 1950), 145, 323: "The character consists in a *chronic* alteration of the ego which one might describe as rigidity . . . . Its meaning is the protection of the ego against external and internal dangers. As a protective mechanism which has become chronic it can rightly be called an *armour*. This armour inevitably means a reduction of the total psychic mobility" (145).

14. See the intimidating summation in McDougal, "International Law, Power, and Policy," 137–41: " . . . a movement towards 'garrison-police' States . . . with increasing militarisation, governmentalisation, centralisation, concentration, and regimentation, and in which all values other than power are 'politicised,' in such practices as . . . the 'requisitioning of talent and skill,' the 'administration of hate' and 'withdrawal of affection,' the 'requisitioning of loyalty,' the 'dogmatisation and ritualisation' of rectitude, and so on." Cf. generally H. D. Lasswell, *The World Revolution of Our Time* (Stanford, 1951). For the bearing of these matters on McDougal's own approach see below, chap. 4.

15. This position is related to though different from that of Charles de Visscher (*Théories et réalités en droit international public* [1953], trans. P. E. Corbett [1957], 92) that "the State by its mere existence conduces to the intransigent assertion of sovereignty. It is therefore pure illusion to expect from the mere arrangement of inter-state relations the establishment of a community order: this can find a solid foundation only in the development of the international spirit in men." De Visscher was denying the correspondence of international law to any "community" discoverable in its substratum. I am questioning the accessibility to reliable inquiries of this part of the substratum.

2. INTERNATIONAL LAW AS HUMANITY BASED

1. H. D. Lasswell and M. Kaplan, *Power and Society* (New Haven: Yale University Press, 1952), xxiv, 131.

2. See M. S. McDougal, H. D. Lasswell, and W. M. Reisman, "Theories about International Law: Prologue to a Configurative Jurisprudence," *Virginia Journal of International Law* 8 (1967–68): 188–299, esp. 197–98.

3. G. Schwarzenberger, "Civitas Maxima," *Yearbook of World Affairs* (London, 1975), 336.

4. See R. A. Falk, *Statecraft in an Era of World Order, Delay, and Renewal*, Arthur F. Yencken Memorial Lectures, Australian National University (1974), 31–52, esp. 49–52.

5. Schwarzenberger, "Civitas Maxima," 351.

3. "THE COMMON LAW OF MANKIND"

1. The attractive eloquence of this "common law of mankind" theme invites endorsement, even from thinkers who cannot endorse its substance. See, for example, W. G. Friedmann, "The Relevance of International Law to the Processes of Economic and Social Development," in *The Future of the International Legal Order*, ed. R. A. Falk and C. E. Black, 4 vols. (Princeton: Princeton University Press, 1969–72), 2:3–35, esp. 16. Friedmann's position turns on invocation of the rather different doctrine of "general principles of law" to fill gaps in the traditional international law (see esp. 24 ff.). For a more detailed critique of this book see J. Stone, *Of Law and Nations* (Buffalo, N.Y.: Wm. S. Hein, 1974), 41–70.

2. C. W. Jenks, *The Common Law of Mankind* (New York: Praeger, 1958), 174, 4, and 175–76, respectively. If he had been writing in 1984, Jenks would perhaps have added that since 1945 no less than eighteen thousand international treaties have been registered with the United Nations, as many as were concluded in the preceding two thousand years, and

that the number of volumes of the U.N. Treaty Series since 1945 (nine hundred) is more than double the number of volumes of treaties from the Treaty of Westphalia in 1648 to the demise of the League of Nations in 1945 (see the remarks of L. B. Sohn in "Reflections on Order, Freedom, Justice, Power: The Challenges for International Law," *Proceedings of the 75th Annual Meeting of the American Society of International Law*, (1981), 194. On the "mirages" involved, see the introductory address of Leo Gross, ibid., 186–92).

3. Majid Khadurri and H. J. Liebesny, *Law in the Middle East* (Washington, D.C.: Middle East Institute, 1955), 249–50, quoted in Jenks, *The Common Law of Mankind*, 76.

4. Jenks, *The Common Law of Mankind*, 76. On the capital importance of this consensus for establishing "the common law of mankind" see ibid., 106, where Jenks speaks of "deducing" from the consensus "the basic foundations of a universal system of law." Whatever its prospects for transforming international law, such a program would at least promote valuable scholarly activity. Even if, after a few decades of work of all available scholars, state attitudes were unchanged, the program would still stand unimpeached, since its commitments are too vast and indeterminate in relation to its objectives ever to be falsifiable.

5. See the fuller critique in Stone, *Of Law and Nations*, 41–70, esp. 59–64.

6. I agree in this skepticism with A. A. Fatouros, "Participation of the 'New States' in the International Law of the Future," in Falk and Black, *Future of the International Legal Order*, 1:317–71. Fatouros observes that only with "a positive intense conviction" (scarcely now in sight) shared by developed and new states "will it be possible for the developed countries to make the short-run sacrifices demanded of them, and for the developing states to wait for future benefits without violently rejecting or undermining the present legal order" (370–71). Yet the assumptions indulged by Jenks are also often indulged, even if only implicitly, by many leading thinkers, as when Richard Falk and S. S. Kim pointed in 1982 to the "basis for globalist identity that lies buried in every major cultural tradition" (*World Order Studies and the World System* [New York, 1982], 28).

4. POLICY-ORIENTED WORLD POWER PROCESS

1. Cf. M. S. McDougal, "International Law, Power, and Policy: A Contemporary Conception," *Hague Recueil* 82 (1953): 137–252, esp. 143–60, 190–91. McDougal enumerates five tasks of "policy-relevance" (197), namely: (1) clarification of goals of decision; (2) description of trends as to goals; (3) description of conditions affecting past decisions; (4) projection of future movements given no intervention; and (5) recommendation of the jurisprudence as to strategies, etc., to realize "preferred goals." Insofar as, for that matter, the inquirer himself "postulates" the goals, both tasks (1) and (5) pertain in the present view to the field of justice within the field of jurisprudence. But, of course, McDougal wishes his observer not only to discover and describe facts, etc., but also to be free to postulate goals and prefer one to another (see below, n. 9 and text preceding n. 38). The effects of this takeover will appear below. On my general positions see J. Stone, *Legal Controls of International Conflict* (Sydney, London, and New York, 1954; supp., Sydney and New York, 1959), esp. xxxi–lv, 1–25; idem, "Problems Confronting Sociological Enquiries concerning International Law," *Hague Recueil* 89 (1956): 63–180, hereinafter cited as Stone, "Sociological Enquiries"; and idem, "International Law and International Society," *Canadian Bar Review* 30 (1952): 164–74, esp. 166–67, 174.

2. M. S. McDougal, H. D. Lasswell, and W. M. Reisman, "Theories about International Law: Prologue to a Configurative Jurisprudence," *Virginia Journal of International Law* 8 (1967–68): 188–299, esp. 194–98, 260–61, 270–75 hereinafter cited as McDougal, Lasswell, and Reisman, "Theories," is concerned to insist that what McDougal calls his "configurative jurisprudence" of international law covers not only what are here called sociological inquiries but also inquiries as to justice in the international community. His jurisprudence studies "the interrelations of law and community process," involving contextual and prob-

lem-oriented work, by whatever methods are appropriate to this aspect of the subject (195–97). It must also, however, be policy-oriented, and he is critical, for example, of R. A. Falk, P. E. Corbett, and myself for not dealing with ends or goals (260–61, 270–75, 288). On the uncertainties of these McDougal positions see O. R. Young, "International Law and Social Science: The Contributions of Myres S. McDougal," *American Journal of International Law* 66 (1972): 62.

Denial that criteria of justice for evaluating policies can be separately considered ignores longstanding work. See, for example, J. Stone, *The Province and Function of Law* (Sydney and London, 1946), passim, esp. chap. 1; idem, *Human Law and Human Justice* (Sydney, London, and Stanford, 1965; reprint, 1968); idem, "Approaches to the Notion of International Justice," in *The Future of the International Legal Order*, ed. R. A. Falk and C. E. Black, 4 vols. (Princeton: Princeton University Press, 1969–72), 1:372–460. Topics relevant here that are dealt with there include: the role of natural law and conscience (380–403), equivocations of equality of nations (403–24), state and human beings as claimants to justice (430–37), the blocking and distorting role of the state (437–52), and obstacles to redistribution (452–60) (see below, chaps. 6, 8, and 9).

3. R. A. Falk, who is far from being a traditional international lawyer, repeatedly returns to the point in "The Relevance of Political Context to the Nature and Function of International Law: An Intermediate View," in *The Relevance of International Law: Essays in Honor of Leo Gross*, ed. K. Deutsch and S. Hoffman (Cambridge, Mass.: Schenkman, 1968), 140–41, 150, 151. He states pithily that we should "conjoin law to politics without collapsing one into the other" (144). Social scientists have indeed charged that McDougal's definition of law in terms of effective authoritative decisions on the distribution of values in society covers all aspects of society, so that by definition law's relation to society cannot be studied, since it is already settled by definition (see Young, "International Law and Social Science," 65 ff. Cf., for example, the conception of political science in D. Easton, *The Political System* [New York: Knopf, 1953], chap. 5).

Of course, the fault of collapsing law into politics and sociology is indulged also by others. It is virtually a keynote of J. Fawcett's *Law and Power in International Relations* (1982). See esp. pp. 37–39, where he finds it unnecessary to invoke either the basic norm or any other criterion for recognizing international law. Rather, "international legal order is a matter of fact, not of theory or principle" (37). It exists because "the formation and observance of certain rules or standards, both nationally and in international relations, meet in fact certain political, social or economic needs of nation-states." But this simply ignores that predictability which requires the practitioner (whom Fawcett has earlier distinguished from the political or juristic observer) to find rules without examining the whole range of contemporary, political, social, and economic phenomena bearing on international relations. With Fawcett, too, though the McDougal frame is not explicitly invoked, this collapse is covered by presenting "law as process," of which the purposes may range from consultation to management, with structures ranging from ad hoc conference to standing organizations; by methods ranging from negotiation to mandatory decision; and by recommendations, decisions, and regimes.

4. The "process" notion thus straddling international law and "the world power process" is a veritable ambush against adversaries. See, for example, the thesis in M. S. McDougal and W. M. Reisman, "The Changing Structure of International Law: Unchanging Theory for Enquiry," *Columbia Law Review* 65 (1965): 810–18, hereinafter cited as McDougal and Reisman, "Unchanging Theory," purporting to dispose in one sweep of some of the lamented W. G. Friedmann's work by pointing out that the law is "process," not "rules." Therefore, for example, the *non liquet* problem does not exist! Cf. the later version by the same authors with H. D. Lasswell, "The World Constitutive Process of Authoritative Decision," in Falk and Black, *Future of the International Legal Order*, 1:73–154.

5. See J. J. Paust, "The Concept of Norm: Towards a Better Understanding," *Temple Law Quarterly* 53 (1980): 226–90.

6. See M. S. McDougal, "Jurisprudence for a Free Society," *Georgia Law Review* 1 (1966):

5; H. D. Lasswell and M. S. McDougal, "Trends in Theories about Law: Comprehensiveness in Conception of Constitutive Process," *George Washington Law Review* 4 (1972): 7.

7. See M. S. McDougal and F. P. Feliciano, *Studies in World Public Order* (New Haven: Yale University Press, 1960), 295 and passim; M. S. McDougal et al., *The Interpretation of Agreements and World Public Order* (New Haven: Yale University Press, 1967), of which see the critique in R. A. Falk, "On Treaty Interpretation and the New Haven Approach," *Virginia Journal of International Law* 8 (1968): 322–55.

8. McDougal, "International, Law, Power, and Policy."

9. Young makes the interesting point that this formulation of the 1940s, when social science still aspired to be "value free," made this "policy orientation" important at the time (Young, "International Law and Social Science," 74–75, commenting on M. S. McDougal and H. D. Lasswell, "Legal Education and Public Policy: Professional Training in the Public Interest," *Yale Law Journal* 52 [1943], esp. 217–33). Yet it was out of step in the 1940s, as ironically it also seemed to be in the 1970s.

10. The clarity is too often obscured by such circularities as that international law is "a comprehensive process of decision, *sustained by dispositions of effective power,* which identifies certain decision-makers as authoritative for the whole community, prescribes the criteria by which decisions are to be taken . . . *allocates important bases of power among the established decision-makers* . . . and finally produces a flow of particular decisions . . . about the shaping and sharing of the different values sought in the world power process" (McDougal and Reisman, "Unchanging Theory," 819–20, emphasis added). It is to be observed that the two italicized phrases cannot *both* mean what they say and imply. (There is a rather similar circularity in Fawcett's *Law and Power in International Relations,* 18, where he wishes with Hans Kelsen to identify a legal order by its overall effectiveness, while also saying that "confrontations between law and power bear on the effectiveness" of a legal order. Power must surely bear both on the "lawness" of law *and* on its "effectiveness.")

Cf. McDougal and Reisman, "Unchanging Theory," 820: "the continuous flow of decisions about various value processes which come out of the most comprehensive process may conveniently be called 'public order.' " Obscurity is further deepened by the multiple references elaborately stipulated for the term "decision." See McDougal, Lasswell, and Reisman, "Theories," 192, citing M. S. McDougal et al., "The World Constitutive Process of Authoritative Decisonmaking," *Journal of Legal Education* 19 (1967): 253, 415. These stipulated references embrace (1) access to intelligence data; (2) promotion, or advocacy; (3) prescription; (4) invocation, that is, characterization, of the issue; (5) application of the prescription; (6) termination; (7) appraisal of effectuation of public policies.

11. See on this special arena the valuable survey in L. B. Sohn, "The Growth of the Science of International Organisations," in Deutsch and Hoffman, *Relevance of International Law,* 251–69.

12. See Young, "International Law and Social Science," 63–64, on McDougal's use of social science notions of municipal origin, such as elites, leadership, power, social change, etc., in relation to current learning in social science.

13. As Young points out (ibid., 65–66), it does not meet the problem in the text to refer to decisionmakers in subsystems or subcommunities. Even if McDougal precisely delimited all these, he would still have to find the "law" in some other group of unspecified decisionmakers. For an enterprising inventory see G. A. Sumida, "Transnational Movements and Economic Structure," in Falk and Black, *Future of the International Legal Order,* 4:524–68. See also P. Allott, "Language, Method, and the Nature of International Law," *British Yearbook of International Law* 45 (1971): 129–31.

14. Strangely, since in McDougal, Lasswell, and Reisman, "Theories," 266 n. 270, McDougal does refer to my substantial thesis on this point.

15. Ibid., 269. McDougal does not advert to this main thesis of my Hague lectures of 1956 (Stone, "Sociological Enquiries," passim), which also inquired into the difficulties of acting on it.

16. See above, chap. 1, and Stone, *Legal Controls*, xli–xliv, 321–22, 327–29.

17. See McDougal and Reisman, "Unchanging Theory," 810, 813–15. See also below, n. 35.

18. McDougal and Reisman, "Unchanging Theory," 823–28, esp. 826, 835.

19. McDougal, "International Law, Power, and Policy," 138–39, citing Lasswell, *The World Revolution of Our Time.*

20. There is a similar inadvertence in McDougal, Reisman, and Lasswell, "The World Constitutive Process of Authoritative Decision," and in H. D. Lasswell, "Future Systems of Identity in the World Community," in Falk and Black, *Future of the International Legal Order,* 4:1–31. This matter of sociological inaccessibility is, of course, different from the much canvassed questions about individuals as bearers of rights and duties under international law. See, for example, H. Baade, "Individual Responsibility," in ibid., 291–327.

21. McDougal, Reisman, and Lasswell, "The World Constitutive Process of Authoritative Decision," 73–154, esp. 74, n. 1.

22. R. A. Falk, "The Adequacy of Contemporary Theories of International Law: Gaps in Legal Thinking," *Virginia Law Review* 50 (1964): 231–65, esp. 234–35, hereinafter cited as Falk, "Contemporary Theories."

23. Young, "International Law and Social Science," 70–72.

24. Fawcett, *Law and Power in International Relations,* 47 and 41, respectively.

25. Ibid., 48–70, 80–90, 117–19.

26. See M. S. McDougal, H. D. Lasswell, and I. A. Vlasic, *Law and Public Order in Space* (New Haven: Yale University Press, 1963); M. S. McDougal and F. P. Feliciano, *Law and Minimum World Public Order: The Legal Regulation and International Coercion* (New Haven: Yale University Press, 1961); M. S. McDougal and W. T. Burke, *The Public Order of the Oceans: A Contemporary International Law of the Sea* (New Haven: Yale University Press, 1962); M. S. McDougal, H. D. Lasswell, and J. C. Miller, *The Interpretation of Agreements and World Public Order* (New Haven: Yale University Press, 1967); M. S. McDougal, H. D. Lasswell, and L.-C. Chen, "Human Rights and World Public Order: Human Rights in Comprehensive Context," *Northwestern University Law Review* 72 (1977–78): 227.

27. Compare the vast indeterminacies from McDougal's rebuke to the late W. G. Friedmann for lack of understanding of "an unorganised process of decision" (McDougal and Reisman, "Unchanging Theory," 820) and from his distinction between a "lower" and "higher" degree of a perceived common interest (ibid., 829). Indeed, if the effect of the impenetrable indeterminacies, circularities, and empirical unfalsifiabilities of the approach here noted is taken into account, the uncharitable might say that the words used by McDougal against Friedmann's *Changing Structure of International Law* (New York: Columbia University Press, 1964), that its results are *"post hoc* and anecdotal," could apply to McDougal's own exposition (McDougal and Reisman, "Unchanging Theory," 832). The anecdote is obviously, however, writ very large, indeed in complicated epic. I entirely agree with R. A. Falk, "Contemporary Theories," 239–41, on "the false issue of complementarity of legal norms" that allows the theorist to have it all ways.

28. Young, "International Law and Social Science," 69–70, 73.

29. There is a formidable attempt to apply the goals in a specific area in B. H. Weston, "International Law and the Deprivation of Foreign Wealth," in Falk and Black, *Future of the International Legal Order,* 4:36–182. Weston has to add, even then, that the decisionmaker does not escape from final "creative choice," though the method "illuminates the choices" that are "open," assuming "commitment to truly genuine community policies" (182). The extraordinary phrase "truly genuine community policies" is eloquent of the uncertainty of criteria for such policies.

30. The late W. G. Friedmann observed in 1971 that "instead of any trend towards a gradual transfer of national prerogatives to worldwide international authority, the national state remains not only the major focus of national allegiance, but the basic unit of international law and the power center of international society" ("The Reality of International

Law: A Reappraisal," *Columbia Journal of Transnational Law* 10 (1971): 55 ff.). Cf. Friedmann, "U.S. Policy and the Crisis of International Law," *American Journal of International Law* 59 (1965): 856–71, esp. 870–71; and the no less sober views on various areas in T. J. Farer, "Law and War," in Falk and Black, *Future of the International Legal Order*, 3:15–78, esp. 76–78. See also D. Wilkes, "Territorial Stability and Conflict," in ibid., 165–209; W. B. Bader, "The Proliferation of Conventional Weapons," ibid., 210–23; A. Kramish, "The Proliferation of Nuclear Weapons," ibid., 224–51; H. Feiveson, "Arms Control and Disarmament," ibid., 336–69, esp. 337–56, 368–69; R. J. Barnet, "Towards the Control of International Violence: The Limits and Possibilities of Law," ibid., 370–91, esp. 386–91; and G. Schwarzenberger, *The Dynamics of International Law* (Abingdon: Professional Books, 1976), 77–90, esp. 90, and 110–29. Schwarzenberger perhaps overstates the matter in declaring that the United Nations, like the old League of Nations, is an "inter-war" order rather than an "order of peace" and that even a real "international law of coordination" only operates in fleeting moments of natural catastrophe *other than war* (116). But the point of E. B. Haas ("Collective Security and the Future International System," in Falk and Black, *Future of the International Legal Order*, 1:226–316, esp. 227–38) seems quite unanswerable: "The U.N. . . . will be a reconciliation system unable to carry out the collective security task as well as does the current [1969] U.N. . . . If the Security Council harbours the danger of big power dominance, the General Assembly hides the peril of flabby majorities without the collective will to act" (316).

31. See McDougal and Feliciano, *Law and Minimum World Public Order.*

32. See generally R. A. Falk, "Beyond International Relations," the second of the Arthur F. Yencken Memorial Lectures, in *Statecraft in an Era of World Order, Delay and Renewal;* Australian National University (1974), 39.

33. McDougal and Burke, *Public Order of the Oceans.*

34. For balanced overviews see L.F.E. Goldie, "The Management of Ocean Resources: Regimes for Structuring the Maritime Environment," in Falk and Black, *Future of the International Legal Order*, 4:154–247; and in McDougalian terms, W. T. Burke, "Ocean Sciences, Technology, and the Future International Law of the Sea," in ibid., 2:182–264. Cf. Falk, "Beyond International Relations," 31. But see now P. Allott, "Power Sharing in the Law of the Sea," *American Journal of International Law* 77 (1983):1–30, for a somewhat sanguine effort to present the outcome of the mountainous labor of the Third U.N. Conference on the Law of the Sea as an example of how states "are appointed as representatives of the international community as a whole by the international legislator who confers powers on them and thereby recognises the world's self government" (27). See below in this same chapter and n. 44. For the final act of the conference see *International Legal Materials* 21 (1982): 1245, and on the Convention on the Law of the Sea see ibid., 1261. See also below, chap. 11.

35. See McDougal, Lasswell, and Chen, "Human Rights and World Public Order."

36. See, for example, McDougal and Reisman, "Unchanging Theory," 818–19.

37. So L. C. Green speaks of law as "intended to facilitate the living together of individuals within a group" but rather quickly makes clear that the relevant group in international law is a group of states rather than of human beings (see L. C. Green, "The Nature of International Law," *University of Toronto Law Journal* 14 [1961–62]:176–93; for discussion of "modernist" trends then emerging, see ibid., 179–89). On the de facto subjectivity of McDougal's international decisionmakers' operations with the "goals," cf. Falk, "Contemporary Theories," 234–35; S. Hoffmann, "The Study of International Law and the Theory of International Relations," *Proceedings of the American Society of International Law* [1963], 26, 33. Of course, McDougal does not intend this subjectivity (see idem, "Some Basic Theoretical Concepts . . . ," *Journal of Conflict Resolution* 4 [1964]: 331).

38. See, for example, Paust, "The Concept of Norm," esp. 286 ff.: for examples there offered of McDougal's ambivalence on this crucial matter see ibid., 287 and n. 233.

39. As called for in M. S. McDougal, *The Application of Constitutive Prescriptions: An Addendum to Justice Cardozo*, Benjamin Cardozo Lecture, Association of the Bar of the City of New York, New York, 1978.

40. McDougal, Lasswell, and Reisman, "Theories," 206–7, 232–33, 298.

41. Allott, "Language, Method, and the Nature of International Law," 116–17, 121–31.

42. "The Identity of International Law," in Bin Cheng, ed., *International Law: Teaching and Practice* (1982), 38–42.

43. That paper was also the basis for an article with a similar title (see above, n. 34).

44. Ibid., 27. Other examples in the article are too numerous to mention. I select only one on a matter of which I, as well as Allott in 1971, was very critical of the "policy science" position. Allott now finds as "a novel and fruitful idea" the International Court majority's words in the *North Sea Continental Shelf Cases* (*International Court of Justice Reports*, 1969, 46), that the laissez-faire treatment of the living resources of the high seas is now replaced by "a duty to have regard to the rights of other States and needs of conservation for the benefit of all." So that, says Allott, "the Rule of Law" of which the essence is "the actualisation of the general interest" (26–27), and the limitation of all "law" and "powers under law" to the function of "serving the interests of society" (27), now applies to international law both customary and treaty. Without clarifying (any more than does "policy science") the reliable methods of finding "benefit to *all*" or "*the* interest of society" and of reconciling the conflict within and between values constantly involved, he is able to proclaim that this "true significance of much of the LOS Convention" will assist us in meeting such grave legal problems as those quoted in the text!

45. McDougal, Lasswell, and Reisman, "Theories," 192, 201, 283, 253.

46. See Young, "International Law and Social Science," 67–68. For Lasswell's late summation of the elements of his methodology see Lasswell, "Future Systems of Identity in the World Community," in Falk and Black, *Future of the International Legal Order*, 4:1–31.

5. LAW AS FUNCTIONAL ORDERING OF THE PLANETARY HUMAN COMMUNITY

1. R. A. Falk, *Statecraft in an Era of World Order, Decay, and Renewal*. Arthur F. Yencken Memorial Lectures, Australian National University (1974), 31–54, esp. 32–37, 43–45. For Falk's elaboration of central guidance involved in various models of world order see R. A. Falk, *A Study of Future Worlds* (New York: Free Press, 1975). The general introduction to this last book, by S. H. Mendlovitz, describes the World Order Models Project to which Falk tells us he has devoted most of his time in recent years. See Falk, *Statecraft in an Era of World Order*, 49–54, where he sketches a transition path from the present territorial, state-based inter-national order to an order that has "non-territorial central guidance systems" and permits a "drastic redistribution of power, wealth and influence."

2. Falk, *Statecraft in an Era of World Order*, 31 and passim.

3. See his development of "theory" in R. A. Falk, "The Adequacy of Contemporary Theories of International Law: Gaps in Legal Thinking," *Virginia Law Review* 50 (1964): 231–65, especially on the "global" and "revolutionary" phase of international law (242–43), on the shifting bases of obligation (243–47), on the antinomy of force and consensus on "fundamental issues" and the need of functional "central management" (247–48), here-inafter cited as Falk, "Contemporary Theories." So cf. R. A. Falk, "The Relevance of Political Context to the Nature and Function of International Law: An Intermediate View," in *The Relevance of International Law: Essays in Honor of Leo Gross*, ed. K. W. Deutsch and S. Hoffman, (Cambridge, Mass.: Schenkman, 1968), hereinafter cited as Falk, "Political Context," 133–52, which seems to be essentially a statement of Falk's reservations and riders on the McDougal positions, as his own "world order model" approach developed. For his systematic analysis of existing international law and its levels of existence see idem, "The Interplay of the

Westphalia and Charter: International Conceptions of International Legal Order," in *The Future of the International Legal Order*, ed. R. A. Falk and C. E. Black, 4 vols. (Princeton: Princeton University Press, 1969–72), 1:33–70, esp. 43 ff.

4. Falk, *Statecraft in an Era of World Order*, 32, 34.

5. Falk, "Contemporary Theories," 248–49. On the central transition problem see Falk, "Interplay." One senses that his focus in the quotation is different from that which underlay his coeditorship of *Future of the International Legal Order*, which is stated in volume 1 to be concerned with next steps—"practical problems confronting the international legal order a generation at a time," as opposed to "constructing an ideal world in theory" (see C. E. Black, ibid., 1:31, as well as 1:ix). The basic soundness of Falk's position described in the text contrasts with the too common assumption that because the system of territorial sovereign states is "obsolete," it must necessarily disappear (see, for example, H. Sprout and M. Sprout, "The Ecological Viewpoint and Others," in ibid., 4:569–605).

6. I am here perhaps adding somewhat to reasons given by Falk (*Statecraft in an Era of World Order*, 43–44, 47–48) for rejecting Hedley Bull's optimism on this matter.

7. For a fuller development of this point see J. Stone, "Approaches to the Notion of International Justice," in Falk and Black, *Future of the International Legal Order*, 1:372–460, esp. 452 ff.; and below, chaps. 11 and 12.

8. In Falk, "Political Context," 143, in 1968, after outlining his divergence from some McDougal positions, especially as to the need for distinguishing the "intellectual discipline" of the study of world order from the impartial assessment of international legality (140–41, 151), be claims for himself a "realistic bias." By this he means one "that avoids both unwarranted despair and wishful thinking . . . so often responsible for distorting the reception of international law in the direction either of cynicism or despair." We must respect "the limits of legal ordering as an independent variable in the existence of a social system" (143).

9. Falk, "Political Context," 143.

10. See Falk, *Statecraft in an Era of World Order*, 33–41.

11. On the U.N. World Population Conference at Budapest in 1974, see ibid., 33–37.

12. It can no doubt be argued that in terms of paper declarations and programs, the establishment of standards of human welfare as an area of "central guidance" has well begun (see, for example, L. Gordenker, "Livelihood and Welfare," in Falk and Black, *Future of the International Legal Order*, 4:248–67; and R. St. J. Macdonald, D. M. Johnston, and G. L. Morris, eds., *The International Law of Human Welfare* [Leyden: Sijthoff, 1978]. See also the discussions of "internationalisation" of "population policy" on grounds analogous to attempts to control genocide, in R. A. Falk, "World Population and International Law," *American Journal of International Law* 63 [1969]: 517; M. E. Caldwell, "Population," in Falk and Black, *Future of the International Legal Order*, 4:32–67, esp. 64–67; and J. Carey, "The International Legal Order of Human Rights," ibid., 4:268–90, esp. 284–87).

13. And this point produces a strange paradox with Falk, *Statecraft in an Era of World Order*, 38, where Falk points out that the attempt to control multinationals produces an enhancement of the statist economic role, citing, *inter alia*, R. J. Barnet and R. Mueller, *The Global Reach: The Power of Multinationals* (Beaverton, Oreg.: Touchstone Books, 1975).

6. INTERNATIONAL LAW AND THE LIMITS OF KNOWLEDGE

1. Cf. J. L. Kunz, "Observaciones teóricas sobre el status del derecho internacional y su porvenir," *Revistas de la escuela national de jurisprudencia* (Mexico) 8 (1946):74–79.

2. This, I suppose, was partly why Judge Alvarez's admirable pioneering in this area made so little headway. See, for example, his proposals for "two new and closely interrelated sciences, the 'science of international life' and the 'science of national psychologies in

international affairs' " (A. Alvarez, "The Reconstruction and Codification of International Law," *International Law Quarterly* 1 [1947]:469–81).

3. M. Huber, "Beiträge zu Kenntnis des soziologischen Grundlagen der Völkerrechts und der Staatengesellschaft," *Jahrbuch des öffentlichen Rechts der Gegenwart* 4 (1910): 133.

4. Cf. Falk, "The Adequacy of Contemporary Theories of International Law: Gaps in Legal Thinking," *Virginia Law Review* 50 (1964): 231.

5. Cf. in many respects the agendum in ibid., 249–60. Important additional items include study of legitimation of "civil disobedience on an international level" (255–57); the overlapping of persistent breach and creation of new rules (253); the line between "crisis decisionmaking" and "bureaucratic decisionmaking" and the typologies of crises and bureaucracies (258–60); the range of international actors (260–61); and the role of "tacit and informal norms," typified, for example, by U.S.–U.S.S.R. nuclear coexistence modus vivendi (262–63), on which see E. McWhinney, "Soviet and Western International Law and the Cold War in Era of Bipolarity: Inter-Bloc Law in a Nuclear Age," *Canadian Yearbook of International Law* 1 (1963): 63–81; and idem, *Peaceful Coexistence and the Soviet-Western International Law* (Leyden: Sijthoff, 1964).

6. Alongside the Corbetts, the de Visschers, and others, McDougal has turned many international lawyers out of the grooves of formal analysis, of which there is a notable example at the beginning of the traumatic 1960s in M. S. Korowicz, "Present Aspects of Sovereignty," *Hague Recueil* 1 (1961):5–113. So cf. the view of P. Allott, "Language, Method, and the Nature of International Law," *British Yearbook of International Law* 45 (1971): 133, as to its value in sensitizing lawyers to "an exceptionally complex and confusing world" and a contribution to international politics in the sense of "value-based dialogue about international matters" rather than as a method of "finding international law." Its value and limits as a contribution to the sociology of international law are, of course, the subject of the text above.

7. For some further elaborations, with illustrations of early work, now greatly expanded, see J. Stone, "Problems Confronting Sociological Enquiries concerning International Law," *Hague Recueil* 89 (1956):63–180, esp. 138–57.

8. A. N. Whitehead, *Science and the Modern World* (Cambridge, 1943), 23, 232.

9. This pressure may tempt even the ablest scholars to catalog all the accumulating wrongs and evils of the times, including, for example, the urban conditions of Calcutta, and demand that they be remedied by improvements of international law, as the late W. G. Friedmann ("The Reality of International Law: A Reappraisal," *Columbia Journal of Transnational Law* 10 [1971]:46–60) seemed to do.

10. R. St. J. Mcdonald, G. L. Morris, and D. M. Johnston, "International Law and Society in the Year 2000," *Canadian Bar Review* 51 (1973):316–32. Cf. the interpretation of W. G. Friedmann's *Changing Structure of International Law* (New York: Columbia University Press, 1964) in A. S. Miller, "Transitional Transnational Law," *Columbia Law Review* 65 (1965):844–46.

11. Cf. on the disorderly coexistence of national state, regional, and international actors and between universal and regional "strategies of world order" E. Frey-Wouters, "The Prospects for Regionalism in World Affairs," in *The Future of the International Legal Order,* ed. R. A. Falk and C. E. Black, 4 vols. (Princeton: Princeton University Press, 1969–72), 1:463–555, esp. 543–55; and on this as "an intermediate level of political integration," L. H. Miller, "The Prospects for Order through Regional Security," in ibid., 1:591. Cf. in relation to promotion of "human values" ibid., 594.

12. On inter-bureaucracy conflicts in more traditional areas see R. J. Barnet, "Toward the Control of International Violence: The Limits and Possibilities of Law," in ibid., 3:370–91, esp. 384–91.

13. Cf. the more speculative projection for "world parties" catering for disagreements within a "world order" after transition from mere international law in G. Modelski, "World Parties and World Order," in ibid., 1:182–225, esp. 219–25.

14. Macdonald, Morris, and Johnston, "International Law and Society in the Year 2000," 316, 332. For a projection somewhere between Falk's functional central guidance and the functional fertile chaos of Macdonald, Morris, and Johnston see G. Gottlieb, "The Nature of International Law: Toward a Second Concept of Law," in Falk and Black, *Future of the International Legal Order* 4:331–83, esp. 367–83.

7. HUMAN VALUES AND THE DISPARATE EROSION OF STATE POWER

1. This, and not the "artificial reason" of law, even when it is used as an instrument of policy, is the deeper reason for agreement with S. Hoffman, *The State of War* (New York: Praeger, 1965), 131, that "not every legal norm can be traced back to political and social realities: this fact should, in turn, give to political sociologists of law a sense of perspective and modesty."

2. J. W. Burton, *Peace Theory* (New York: Knopf, 1962), 198.

3. The "nationalisation of truth," as I described it in my *Legal Controls of International Conflict* (Sydney, London, and New York, 1954; supp., Sydney and New York, 1959), xli–xliii, 327–29; and in my "Problems Confronting Sociological Enquiries concerning International Law," *Hague Recueil* 89 (1956):63–180, esp. 104–14. Cf. R. A. Falk, "The Interplay of the Westphalia and Charter: International Conceptions of International Legal Order," in *The Future of the International Legal Order*, ed. R. A. Falk and C. E. Black, 4 vols. (Princeton: Princeton University Press, 1969–72), 1:63–64.

4. See S. Ogden, "Sovereignty and International Law: The Perspective of the P.R.C.," *New York Journal of International Law and Politics* 7 (1974):1–32, esp. 11–13, 30 (including Chinese attacks on Jenks's "common law of mankind" and Jessup's "transnational" ideas); 13–15 (Chinese defense of traditional international law against Western publicist criticism); 22–24, 32 (Chinese rejection of personality claims for international governmental organizations and individuals); 24–25 (Chinese rejection of Lauterpacht's "rights of man" doctrine); 27 (the Chinese view that human rights cannot be violated in a Communist state); and 24–26 (Chinese selective support of terrorism).

5. See R. A. Falk, "The Relevance of Political Context to the Nature and Function of International Law: An Intermediate View," in *The Relevance of International Law: Essays in Honor of Leo Gross*, ed. K. Deutsch and S. Hoffman (Cambridge, Mass.: Schenkman, 1968), 137, hereinafter cited as Falk, "Political Context."

6. Ibid., 140. Cf. P. Allott, "Language, Method, and the Nature of International Law," *British Yearbook of International Law* 45 (1971): 126, where Allott makes the related observation as to McDougal's positions that "whatever the high ideals of those who believe in it or practice it, the danger is that it will be a more apt weapon for those who they would least wish to assist—the dialectical materialism and the cynical practitioner of *Realpolitik*."

7. Falk, "Political Context," 140.

8. McDougal strangely observed in 1968 (in M. S. McDougal, H. D. Lasswell, and W. M. Reisman, "Theories about International Law: Prologue to a Configurative Jurisprudence," *Virginia Journal of International Law* 8 [1967–68]:188–299, 294) that "it serves no clarifying purpose to assume that the world will suffer either annihilation or coerced subordination to the totalitarian system of public order imposed by one huge imperial power." One must observe per contra that it may certainly "clarify" the purpose of survival of his entire gamut of postulated goals—and much else.

9. Falk, "Political Context," 150.

10. See N. Podhoretz, *The Present Danger* (New York: Simon & Schuster, 1980). The Committee on the Present Danger, with many distinguished members, provided important support in President Reagan's election campaign.

11. *London Times*, 15 July 1983. An opinion survey of one thousand respondents in April 1984, commissioned by the conservative Committee on the Present Danger, was based on twenty arms-related issues. It showed inter alia that (1) of the eighty-one percent favoring a bilaterial "freeze," seventy percent made "verifiability" a condition of this; (2) seventy-one

percent would not trust the U.S.S.R. to honor a "freeze"; and (3) sixty-six percent favored use of nuclear weapons as a deterrent against Soviet attacks on U.S. allies (*USA Today*, 20 April 1984).

12. Modernist terms such as "new international economic order" or "world legal order" should also not conceal the rather old-fashioned, self-serving, and materialist nature of the underlying demands. Such abstractions can, however, be an attractive cover, as seen in J. R. Friedman, "The Confrontation of Equality and Equalitarianism: Institution-Building through International Law," in Deutsch and Hoffmann, *Relevance of International Law*, 175–218, esp. 213–18. For further discussion see below, chap. 10–12.

13. See on this aspect D. Livingston, "Science, Technology and International Law," in Falk and Black, *Future of the International Legal Order*, 4:68–123; and H. J. Taubenfeld and R. F. Taubenfeld, "Modification of the Human Environment," ibid., 124–54, esp. 150–51.

14. On these selective attitudes of new states see also L. C. Green, "The Impact of New States on International Law," *Israel Law Review* 4 (1969): 26. See esp. as to human rights and related manipulations of the General Assembly 41–43, 59–60; on the coalition of political interests manipulating international law, treaty law, and the Charter, 43–48, 50; and on anarchic implications generally, 31, 46–47, 58, 60.

15. For an overall view nearer my own see the courageous and elegant statement of J.H.E. Fried, "How Efficient is International Law?" in Deutsch and Hoffmann, *Relevance of International Law*, 92–132, esp. 96–97, 129–32. It deals systematically with four main supposed terminal symptoms, namely, that (1) this law is inherently weak and not viable ("orphan theory"); (2) it is too vague and manipulable ("harlot theory"); (3) it is nonenforceable ("jailer theory," or better, "jailbreaker theory"); (4) that it is still, after centuries, in its infancy ("never-never theory"). I may perhaps add as real contemporary threats to the traditional law a good deal of modern "theoretical" writing and (more seriously) the ever more frequent travesties of this law in the U.N. General Assembly. In emulation of Fried, I dub this last the "when-we-holler, it's law" theory (see J. Stone, *Israel and Palestine: Assault on the Law of Nations* [Baltimore: Johns Hopkins University Press, 1981], esp. 4–8, 56–58, 125–31).

8. JUSTICE AND EQUALITY AMONG NATIONS

1. See the development of this theme in J. Stone, *The Province and Function of Law* (Sydney and London, 1946), esp. 782–85.

2. See, generally, J. Stone, *Human Law and Human Justice* (Sydney, London, and Stanford, 1965; reprint, 1968).

3. For an elaboration of the preceding paragraphs on equality as the criterion of justice see J. Stone, "Justice Not Equality," in *Justice*, ed. E. Kamenka and A. Tay (London: Edward Arnold, 1979), 96–115; idem, "Equal Protection and the Search for Justice," *Arizona Law Review* 22 (1980):1–17. On equality between states see in a vast literature E. D. Dickinson, *The Equality of States in International Law* (Cambridge, Mass.: Harvard University Press, 1920); J. Goebel, Jr., "The Equality of States," pts. 1–3, *Columbia Law Review* 23 (1923): 113, 247; and P. H. Kooijmans, *The Doctrine of the Legal Equality of States* (Leyden: Nijhoff, 1964). For the latest general study of equality in terms of political theory see A. Gutman, *Liberal Equality* (Cambridge and New York, 1981), 170–72, unsatisfyingly brief on international justice and equality.

4. On which see Stone, *Human Law and Human Justice*, esp. 325–35, and works cited above, in n. 3.

5. The interesting work of I. Detter, "The Problem of Unequal Treaties," *International and Comparative Law Quarterly* 15 (1966): 1069, seems insensitive to these equivocations. It identified equality with an "inference" from "the idea of sovereignty" (1070; and see below, text following n. 25) and for the rest distinguishes only "forensic equality" and equality in "exercise" of rights, relying on A. D. McNair, "Equality in International Law," *Michigan Law Review* 26 (1927): 136.

6. See C. H. Alexandrowicz, "New and Original States: The Issue of Reversion to Sovereignty," *International Affairs* 45 (1969):465–80.

7. For example, in the Declaration on the Granting of Independence to Colonial Countries and Peoples, in General Assembly Resolution 1514 (XV). Cf. other related U.N. and other declarations during and after World War II, collected in Detter, "Unequal Treaties," 1069, 1071–72.

8. This tension between the principle of equality and the idea of justice is not resolved by metaphors such as "the nation's subjective right, as already a juridical person, to pass from the larval to the more perfect State" (A. Bonnichon, "The Principle of Nationalities and Implied Ethical Requirements," *World Justice* 7 [1965–66]:22–23. Cf. on the indeterminacy of the self-determination principle and its abuse in political warfare F. Peters, "The Right of Nations to Auto-Determination," ibid., 2 [1960–61]:147–62).

9. Since it tends to force the birth of nonviable state entities, impairing the prospects of later viability, and adding meanwhile to the instabilities of international politics. Cf. Bowett's point that self-determination has "wider ramifications" than "decolonization" and Emerson's identification of the various "incarnations" of the self-determination principle (D. W. Bowett, "Self-Determination and Political Rights in the Developing Countries," *Proceedings of the American Society of International Law*, 1966, 129–31; and R. Emerson, "Self-Determination," ibid., 131–41. See also on the "mini-States" M. Broderick, "Associated Statehood: A New Form of Decolonization," *International and Comparative Law Quarterly* 17 [1968]:368–403; and P. M. Allan, "Self-Determination in the Western Indian Ocean," *International Conciliation*, no. 560 [1966]).

10. See Stone, *Human Law and Human Justice*, 341–44; and idem, *Social Dimensions of Law and Justice* (Sydney and Stanford, 1966; reprint, Holmes Beach, Fla., 1977), 496–98. See also below, chaps. 11–12.

11. Demands are, of course, in fact made on behalf of state entities, which can be analogized, in some sense, to those made by individuals and groups within the national legal orders. The question is what value the analogy has (see below, chaps. 11–12; see also W. G. Friedmann, "The Relevance of International Law to the Processes of Economic and Social Development," in *The Future of the International Legal Order*, ed. R. A. Falk and C. E. Black, 4 vols. [Princeton: Princeton University Press, 1969–72], 2:3–35).

12. On the antecedents of the equality principle as a "fundament" of the feudal system see Goebel, "The Equality of States," esp. 113–16., 140–141. And see Goebel's salutary attack on the tendency to identify the emergence of the equality principle with the advent of Grotius and the other founders of international law (the "delusion that both science and law itself were born *anno* 1625"). Cf. J. Stone, *Legal Controls of International Conflict* (Sydney, London, and New York, 1954; supp., Sydney and New York, 1959), 11.

13. C. H. Alexandrowicz, *Introduction to the Theory of the Law of Nations in the East Indies in the 16th, 17th, and 18th Centuries* (Oxford: Clarendon Press, 1967); and the brief historical account, with useful documentation, in Detter, "Unequal Treaties," 1067, 1073–81.

14. Cf. the echoing polemics in P. J. Baker, "The Doctrine of Legal Equality of States," *British Yearbook of International Law* 4 (1923–24), 1–20.

15. It affords little guidance to say (e.g., with Detter, "Unequal Treaties," 1069, 1070) that "voting rights" should be the same "unless there is explicit agreement to another effect." On voting differentiations see H. Weinschell, "The Doctrine of Equality of States and Its Recent Modifications," *American Journal of International Law* 45 (1951): 417; and B. Broms, *The Doctrine of Equality of States As Applied in International Organisations* (Helsinki, 1959). And cf. contemporary problems as to the International Monetary Fund and the World Bank, not only in this chapter but also in chaps. 10–12.

16. For the relevance of Aquinas's thought to jurisprudential endeavors *provided* the directives there specified are observed, see Stone, *Human Law and Human Justice*, esp. 214–18. M. Wilks, *The Problem of Sovereignty in the Later Middle Ages: The Papal Monarchy with Augustinus Triumphus and the Publicists* (Cambridge: Cambridge University Press, 1963), has

surveyed the strife of scholastic ideas of the hierocrats and anti-hierocrats, the floundering of these and other contending schools of thought in the *via media* of Thomism. He sees an "intellectual schizophrenia" (characterized as "the endemic disease of the scholastics") as arising from fascination with the Thomist synthesis.

17. E. de Vattel, *Law of Nations*, 7th American ed. (Philadelphia: T. & J. V. Johnson, 1849), 7–8.

18. Cf. E. Reibstein, "Die Dialektik der soveränen Gleichheit bei Vattel," *Zeitschrift für ausländisches öffentliches Recht und Völkerrecht* 19 (1958): 607–36. See also, Stone, *Legal Controls*, 15–17, and the discussion in Kooijmans, *Doctrine*, 85–86.

19. Vattel, *Law of Nations*, 7.

20. Ibid., 113–20. Vattel admits that "those astute leaders of Nations will turn into ridicule the doctrines in this Chapter." But at the end, he answers the doubt whether men in power will follow "the Laws of Nature" by ruminating that "to lose all hope of making an impression upon any of them would be to despair of human nature." We still perhaps are maneuvering between these rocks of self-deception and despair.

21. Cf. Stone, *Legal Controls*, 15–17.

22. Cf. the contemporary debates as to the nature of the duties of the developed states towards the less developed states, and the "new international economic order," below, in chaps. 10–12. The notion of conscience is central to Vattel's crucial distinction between perfect and imperfect rights. "Obligations," he wrote, "are internal insofar as they bind the conscience and are deduced from the rules of our duty; they are external when considered relatively to other men as producing some right on their part. Internal obligations are always the same in nature, though they may vary in degree; external obligations, however, are divided into *perfect* and *imperfect*, and the rights they give rise to are likewise *perfect* and *imperfect*. So that 'external' obligations are '*imperfect*' when 'the corresponding obligation depends upon the judgment of him who owes it.'" For, otherwise, "he would cease to have the right of deciding what are his obligations according to the law of conscience," when he "ought to be free" to decide such matters (Vattel, *Law of Nations*, 7 and passim).

23. See U. Kirdar, *The Structure of United Nations Economic Aid to Underdeveloped Countries* (The Hague: Nijhoff, 1966), 231–32; and R. Higgins, *Conflict of Interests: International Law in a Divided World* (Chester Springs, Pa.: Dufour, 1965), 47–98, esp. 51–54. See also below, chap. 10.

24. See chaps. 9–12.

25. See, generally, Stone, *Legal Controls*, 30–32, and literature there cited; and Kooijmans, *Doctrine*, 131–39.

26. See A. Larson and C. W. Jenks, eds., *Sovereignty within the Law* (New York: Oceana Publications, 1965); and F. H. Hinsley, *Sovereignty* (New York: Basic Books, 1966).

27. For general expositions see Dickinson, *Equality of States*, 100–148, esp. 131–144; and Kooijmans, *Doctrine*, 106–25.

28. Dickinson, *Equality of States*, 334–36; see also Goebel's criticisms in n. 12 above.

29. Baker, "Doctrine of Legal Equality."

30. He distinguished (1) great powers; (2) small independent states; (3) dependent states; and (4) the semi-civilized states, equality being meaningful for the first two.

31. M. Ginsberg, *Justice in Society* (London: Heinemann, 1965), 196–97, asserted as "the axiom of justice" for states as for individuals the Kantian principle that justice for our own state is justice also for other states. In this he based the duties of states to transcend their own interests and work towards displacement of war by "a rule of law" (196–97). He recognized that practical implementation of these generalities is "complicated" (208). One purpose here is, of course, to explore these and other "complications." Philosophers have generally not focused on the problems raised by these competing references. See, for example, H. Sidgwick, *Elements of Politics* (London and New York, 1919), 285–97, passim. For an anti-rational utilitarian position see B. Bosanquet, "Patriotism in the Perfect State," *The International Crisis in Its Ethical and Psychological Aspects*, by Eleanor M. Sidgwick et al.

(London and New York: M. Milford, 1915), 138; and idem, "The Function of the State in Promoting the Unity of Mankind," *Proceedings of the Aristotelian Society*, 1917, 43–44.

32. See on the *Ecclesia* as "a universal mode of right living rather than the actually existing community of mortals which endeavours to follow it" Wilks, *Sovereignty in the Later Middle Ages*. Wilks's discussion of the concept bears out its multiplicity of meanings in medieval theological literature. Cf. J. V. Schall, "Ethics and International Affairs," *World Justice* 6 (1964): 462–75; A. Dondeyne, "Cultural Encounters: True and False Universalisms," ibid., 3, no. 1 (1961–62): 35–49. And on "the right of individuals demanding their own city" as a basis of national self-determination see Bonnichon, "The Principle of Nationalities and Implied Ethical Requirements."

33. See, generally, Wilks, *Sovereignty in the Later Middle Ages.*

34. See Vitoria, *De Indis et de iure belli relectiones,* trans. J. P. Bate, in *Classics of International Law,* 22 vols. (New York: Oxford University Press for the Carnegie Endowment for International Peace, 1911–50; reprint, Dobbs Ferry, N.Y.: Oceana Publications, 1963–66), 163–87, and the introduction by E. Nys, 9–53. See also J. B. Scott, *Law, the State, and International Community,* vol. 1 (New York: Columbia University Press, 1939), 310–23; A. Nussbaum, *A Concise History of the Law of Nations,* rev. ed. (New York: Macmillan, 1954), 79–84; and in relation to equality, Kooijmans, *Doctrine,* 57–62.

35. For a balanced and stimulating critique of the classical and modern literature see W. Schiffer, *The Legal Community of Mankind* (New York: Columbia University Press, 1954).

36. See, generally, R. St. J. Macdonald, D. M. Johnston, and G. L. Morris, eds., *The International Law of Human Welfare* (Leyden: Sijthoff, 1978); and E. B. Haas, *Beyond the Nation State: Functionalism and International Organisation* (Stanford: Stanford University Press, 1964).

37. See above, chap. 3. Haas (*Beyond the Nation State,* 453–57) has properly cautioned against overestimating the role of experts, e.g., the Eurocrats of the European community, in producing a community of mankind.

38. See chaps. 6 and 9. And cf. Haas, *Beyond the Nation State,* 429–58, on the limited potentialities (pace David Mitrany) of functionalism as a decisive factor towards world integration.

39. It does show clearly, however, that the equality hitherto at all entrenched in international law is equality "before the law," that is, under uniform rules. Voting equality as in the General Assembly and its suborgans is still exceptional; but see this chapter and chap. 10 on the pressure for its extension in the economic sphere (see R. McKeon, "Equality and Justice," in VI *Nomos, Justice,* 44–61, esp. 58–60; and idem, "The Concept of Mankind and Mental Health," *Ethics* 77 [1966–67]: 29–37). As discussion of the "new international economic order" (NIEO) elsewhere in this book and esp. in chap. 10 will show, the hard core of that problem lies, not in equality, but in finding the precepts, or rather criteria, of justice and guide the necessary discriminations. See above, following n. 3, for the contradictory references of equality here in play.

40. To say that "the principles of equality" among states are preeminent, that the only equality required by justice is of "entitlement to consideration," and that "differences in treatment require justification in terms of relevant differences, and . . . shall be proportionate to the differences" and also to deny both that states are equal and that "states ought to be treated in the same way" does not much advance the matter (see Ginsberg, *Justice in Society,* passim).

41. See the contribution to the symposium in *Florida Law Review* 19 (1966–67), esp. M. S. McDougal and H. D. Lasswell, "Jurisprudence in Policy-oriented Perspective," 486–513.

42. R. Tucker, *Just War and Vatican Council II: A Critique* (New York: Council on Religion and International Affairs, 1966), 19–20.

43. See S. Hoffmann, "International Systems and International Law," in *Strategy of World Order,* ed. R. A. Falk and S. H. Mendlovitz, vol. 2, *International Law* (New York, 1966), 134–66, esp. 164–66.

9. STATES, HUMAN BEINGS, AND INTERNATIONAL JUSTICE

1. On the "enclave" metaphor see J. Stone, *Human Law and Human Justice* (Sydney, London, and Stanford, 1965; reprint 1968), 322–55; and idem, *Social Dimensions of Law and Justice* (Sydney and Stanford, 1966; reprint, Holmes Beach, Fla., 1977) 775–76, 797–98.

2. Yet, as E. Brunner has reminded us, "Isaiah's lovely picture of the future is not contained in history: *it is the end of history*," and biblical prophecies of world peace and world justice presuppose that "the conditions of life in the reality of earthly history will entirely pass away." So that the last ages of earthly history . . . are not looked to as times of perfect peace but as times of unprecedented world tumult" (E. Brunner, *Justice and the Social Order*, trans. M. Hottinger [(New York and London: Harper and Brothers, 1956], 199–201, emphasis added). But contrast the view of Jewish religious doctrine in S. Greenberg, "Judaism and World Justice," *World Justice* 5 (1963–64): 314–21. And see, generally, N. Bentwich, *The Religious Foundations of Internationalism*, 2d ed. (London: Allen and Unwin, 1959), passim.

3. Cf. F. J. Kutten, "Inter-Human Relations . . . ," *World Justice* 2 (1960–61): 43–68, esp. 57–61; W. H. Roberts, "The International Political Common Good," ibid., 178–98; J. Stone, "Problems Confronting Sociological Enquiries concerning International Law," *Hague Recueil* 89 (1956): 65–180; and idem, *Legal Controls of International Conflict* (Sydney, London, and New York, 1954; supp., Sydney and New York, 1959), xli–xliv.

4. Stone, *Legal Controls*, xli–xliv, 321–22, 327–29.

5. On this see also ibid., 318–23, 335–48.

6. See K. E. Boulding, "The Concept of World Interest," in *Strategy of World Order*, ed. R. A. Falk and S. Mendlovitz, vol. 4, *Disarmament and Economic Development* (1966), 507–8 (originally printed in *Economics and the Idea of Mankind*, ed. B. F. Hoselitz [New York: Columbia University Press, 1965]; and for parallel conclusions from a functionalist standpoint, E. B. Haas, *Beyond the Nation State: Functionalism and International Organisation* [Stanford: Stanford University Press, 1964]).

7. See J. Stone, *The Province and Function of Law* (Sydney and London, 1946), 595–99, 773–74.

8. Transformations in the cultural and social systems in the world as a whole are thus implied in hopes for arresting, and even more for reducing, economic inequalities (see B. F. Hoselitz, "Unity and Diversity in Economic Structure," in his *Economics and the Idea of Mankind*, 63–96, esp. 93–96). Cf. Haas's observation that "national and regional pluralism in the European case have been congruent; but the opposite seems to have been true in the West Indies," pointing to a related correlation of political change with sociocultural transformation (Haas, *Beyond the Nation State*, 450–53).

9. See J. Stone, *Social Dimensions of Law and Justice* (Sydney and Stanford, 1966; reprint, Holmes Beach, Fla., 1977), 171–75; idem, *Human Law and Human Justice*, 273 and n. 37.

10. It is sadly easy to gloss over this hard fact, as when G. Del Vecchio, "Natural Law as the Foundation of a Society of the Human Race," *World Justice* 4 (1962–63): 307–14, asserts that the state's duty to assure justice to the individual is "a first and unchallengeable condition of its very existence . . . the limit and essential condition of its lawful authority over individuals (313). It does not correct this to complain that so many states are clearly in default by such criteria. Nor does it help, as with R. J. Th. Rutten, "Inter-Human Relations—How Do They Stand Today," ibid., 2 (1960–61): 43–68, esp. 56–58, to lose sight of the state entity problem altogether by talking only of "peoples" and "nations." Cf. with the position in the text W. H. Roberts, "The International Political Common Good."

11. See for succinct statements on the related problem of the standing of individuals in international law Stone, *Legal Controls*, 118–19; and W. G. Friedmann, *Changing Structure of International Law* (New York: Columbia University Press, 1964), 40–44, and the voluminous literature there mentioned. Since the more technical legal aspects of this and related

questions of the status of individuals in international law already enjoy a very substantial literature, they will not here be further considered.

12. The quotation marks within which the words "act of free choice" (e.g., in relation to the future of West Irian) are usually enclosed in current discussions, speak eloquently on this point.

13. Some of the tough underlying questions concern (1) the accessibility to knowledge of mankind seen as a single humanity; (2) the acceptability of the individual as the unit at the base of social and economic construction, if the laws of interaction are to be understood; and (3) the nation as a competing base for such understanding. For these and related questions as they affect economic aspects see the penetrating study by E. McKinley, "Mankind in the History of Economic Thought," in Hoselitz, *Economics and the Idea of Mankind*, 1–40, esp. 18 ff. and 36–40.

14. On special attitudes of the Soviet Union relevant to this matter see L. Friendl, "The Soviet Conception of International Law," *World Justice* 2 (1960–61): 198–227, esp. 212–14, 226–27. And see, generally H. A. Rommen, "Towards the Internationalisation of Human Rights," ibid., 1 (1959–60): 147, 173; M. Hickey, "The Philosophical Argument for World Government," ibid., 6 (1964): 185–210, esp. 202–10; K. N. Waltz, *Man, the State, and War* (New York: Columbia University Press, 1959); and P. T. de Chardin, "Sauvons l'humanité," in *P. T. de Chardin et la politique africaine*, ed. L. S. Senghor (Paris, 1962).

15. I need scarcely add that in my view, jealous cleaving to "absolute sovereignty" does not justify the rejection by states receiving aid of counsel and even stipulations offered in good faith by aiding organizations or states.

16. The U.N. Experts Report of 1954, indeed, formulated noneconomic criteria of underdevelopment in terms of individual human beings rather than states, and notably: (1) expectation of life at birth; (2) infant mortality rate; (3) per capita nutrition rate; (4) five- to fourteen-year-old school population; (5) percentage of illiteracy by age and sex groups; (6) percentage unemployment; (7) distribution among economic groupings; and (8) individual consumption as percentage of national revenue. See, generally, A. Shonfeld, *The Attack on World Poverty* (London: Chatto and Windus, 1961): and the general theme of U. Kirdar, *The Structure of United Nations Economic Aid to Underdeveloped Countries* (The Hague: Nijhoff, 1966), centered around U.N. aid projects. Cf. A. Farran, "The Changing Economic Order and International Law," *Australian Outlook* 34 (1980): 179–87, esp. 185, and Symposium, "Basic Human Needs—The International Law Connection," *Proceedings of the American Society of International Law*, 1978, 227 ff., on "basic human needs" as an irreducible standard for all people implicitly required by the International Covenant on Economic Social and Cultural Rights and the Universal Declaration of Human Rights.

17. There are, of course, major controversies. See, for example, C. Clark, "The Earth Can Feed Its People," *World Justice* 1 (1959–60): 35–55; and idem, "Demographic Problems on a World Scale," ibid., 6 (1964–65): 435–40. See also the approach of John XXIII's Encyclical Letter *Mater et Magistra* under the rubric "Population Increase and Economic Development," on which see A. McCormack, "International Social Justice in Mater et Magistra," *World Justice* 4 (1962–63): 52, 70–73, which ends on the note: "Why do you offer us contraceptives instead of bread?"; and see the modified view in P. Anciaux, "Ethical Aspects of Demographic Policy," ibid., 5 (1963–64): 520. Much, of course, turns on the chronological relation of population growth and economic take-off (see A. Shonfeld, "The Attack on World Poverty," ibid., 2 [1960–61]: 445–65, esp. 464–65; A. Nevett, "Population and Resources in India," ibid., 466–88, esp. 488; and P. V. Sukhatme, "The Phenomenon of Hunger as F.A.O. Sees It," ibid., 5 [1963–64]: 147–68).

18. *India's International Disputes* (London: Asian Publishing House, 1966), 195–208.

19. See Friedmann, *Changing Structure of International Law*, 206–10, for further discussion in the context of an emergent principle of "unjust enrichment." Cf. on this point P. T. Bauer, *Equality, the Third World, and Economic Delusion* (Cambridge, Mass.: Harvard University Press; London: Weidenfeld & Nicholson, 1981).

20. What this present discussion adds, however, is that the main warrant of success here is a function of the absence of practical alternatives, rather than of abstract ideals alone, or of orientation of "thought" and "passion" on both sides, as R. McKeon well observes in "The Concept of Mankind and Mental Health," *Ethics* 77 (1966): 29 and esp. 33–37. Nor should the intellect be other than content to be brought thus close to religious and spiritual preoccupations. See, for example, C. Santamaria, "In Search of a Concept of Peace," *World Justice* 2 (1960–61): 5 and esp. 23; Greenberg, "Judaism and World Justice," 314–21, esp. the reminder (314) of the Old Testament doctrine that a world judged by the standards of justice untempered by mercy could not continue to exist. See J. F. Cronin, "Our International Obligations: Thoughts on the International Common Good," *World Justice* 1 (1959–60): 298–317, esp. on the difference between the mood here invoked and "charity." Cf. the call to Asian intellectuals to transcend their reactions to historical injustices in P.K.T. Sih, "The Mind of Asia in the Modern World," ibid., 3 (1961–62): 18–34. And see the statement of the dedicated economist Barbara Ward, "The U.N. and the Decade of Development," ibid., 7 (1965–66): 308–35, esp. 333–35, precisely in terms of the Hebrew prophets, and her numerous later pronouncements. Lingering recessions of the 1970s and 1980s have for the moment weakened impulses of compassion and stirred negative assessments of aid transfers. See, for example, Bauer, *Equality, the Third World, and Economic Delusion,* and many official U.S pronouncements, especially since 1981. These should not be allowed to obscure the enduring moral imperatives involved.

21. See the attempt to restate traditional—especially ethical-philosophical—discussions of "individual and society" within the frame of a "concept of mankind" in McKeon, "The Concept of Mankind and Mental Health," 29–37. He considers the bearing of this concept on action in relation to (1) aspiration; (2) thought; (3) passions; (4) morality. And see O. Klineberg, *The Human Dimension of International Relations* (New York: Holt, Rinehart & Holt, 1963), 145–50.

22. See H. Kahn, *On Thermo-Nuclear War* (Princeton, 1960); idem, *On Escalation: Metaphors and Scenarios* (New York: Praeger, 1965); T. Schelling, *Arms and Influence* (New Haven: Yale University Press, 1966); B. Brodie, *Escalation and the Nuclear Option* (Princeton, 1966); and C. D. Blacker and G. Duffy, *International Arms Control,* 2d ed. (1983). And see, generally, the illuminating survey of styles and dimensions of contemporary strategic thinking in J. Chapman, "American Strategic Thinking," *Air University Review—Canadian Confederation Centennial Number,* 1967, 25–33. Cf. with the point in the text on the pernicious consequences for world ordering of the psychological insecurity and uncertainty involved in the "balance" of nuclear terror, Klineberg, *The Human Dimension of International Relations,* passim.

23. Brunner, *Justice and the Social Order,* 216; and see below for Brunner's statement on the justice thus attainable in an earthly sense. We are aware, of course, in making this claim for Brunner, of the vigor of the attack on "economic imperialism" from the side of communism and socialism, but Brunner's message is directed to richer states in both camps. There were also, of course, significant bodies of wartime opinion that demanded action to give reality to "freedom from want" as a plank of the "five freedoms" of the Atlantic Charter (see, for example, J. Stone, *The Atlantic Charter* [Sydney: Angus & Robertson, 1942], esp. chaps. 3, 7, and 8). But this was focused on just ordering *within* states rather than transfers between them.

10. JUSTICE AND THE "NEW INTERNATIONAL ECONOMIC ORDER"

1. See K. E. Boulding, "The Concept of World Interest," in *Strategy of World Order,* ed. R. A. Falk and S. Mendlovitz, vol. 4 (1966; originally printed in *Economics and the Idea of Mankind,* ed. B. F. Hoselitz [New York: Columbia University Press, 1965]).

2. On the ways in which developed countries have fostered inequality, and possible countermeasures, see B. Semnel, "On the Economics of Imperialism," in Hoselitz, *Economics and the Idea of Mankind,* 193–232, esp. 229–32. And on the cultural and social changes required, especially in the poorer states, for correcting the tendency to greater inequality, see B. F. Hoselitz, "Unity and Diversity in Economic Structure," ibid., 62–97, esp. 93–97.

3. See Boulding, "The Concept of World Interest," 497–99.

4. Thus Boulding acknowledges that "any concept of world economic interest implies an ethical system of some sort" (ibid., 511) and that "technical economics alone cannot provide an unequivocal definition of world interest, although it can help in relating whatever definition is arrived at to the ethical system that is implied by it" (513). See, generally, ibid., 513–15.

5. See on cultural pressure for large families in relation to population problems J. Delcourt, "The Birth Rate . . . Social and Cultural Aspects," *World Justice* 2 (1960–61): 169–96; and in relation to rural development, M. L. Meyer, "Community Development and Developing Nations," ibid., 5 (1963–64): 208–9; generally, W. Banning, "Meeting of Cultures," ibid., 3 (1961–62): 5–18; and Hoselitz, "Unity and Diversity in Economic Structure," 62–97, esp. 97.

6. Boulding, "The Concept of World Interest," 505–8.

7. The IMF and the World Bank were themselves activated by U.S. Treasury Secretary Regan and Secretary of State Shultz. These bodies, by the terms they stipulated for "bridging money," have forced austerity on the debtors as to the level of service on loans, and also forced contributions of new money by private banks. The rewards included increased interest margins and fees, amounting, for example, in the case of Mexico to $800 million in 1983, besides the implicit government guarantee for the new loans and relaxation of U.S. federal banking regulations.

8. See R. S. Weinert, "International Finance: Banks and Bankruptcy," *Foreign Policy* 50 (1983): 138.

9. The long-term function is, of course, not to be confused with current emergency "bridging" operations to fend off defaults. See, on the one hand, K. W. Dam, *The Rules of the Game: Reform and Evolution in the International Monetary System* (Chicago: University of Chicago Press, 1982); J. Gold, *Legal and Institutional Aspects of the International Monetary System* (Washington, D.C.: I.M.F., 1979); and idem, *Special Drawing Rights,* IMF Pamphlet Series, 13 (Washington, D.C. 1969); and on the other hand, T. Killick, ed., *Adjustment and Financing in the Developing World: The Role of the I.M.F.* (Washington, D.C., 1982). And see, generally, M.A.G. Van Meerhaeghe, *A Handbook of International Economic Institutions* (The Hague and Boston: Martinus Nijhoff, 1982).

10. Such wastage of resources is found in developing as well as developed countries, as the enormous current purchases of arms by, for example, Saudi Arabia, Libya, and Iraq remind us. Pre-Khomeini Iran bought $483 million worth of arms through the U.S. Foreign Military Sales Program in 1979, and $150 million worth in 1980. Saudi arms purchases in 1973–79 cost $26 billion, and her projected 1981–84 purchases add another $8.5 billion. The Thai military budget is one-fifth of the total budget.

11. U. Kirdar, *The Structure of United Nations Economic Aid to Underdeveloped Countries* (The Hague: Nijhoff, 1966), has statistics on the distribution of the burden of aid as between Communist bloc and Western nations as well as a breakdown of Western aid in terms of each donor's gross national production (see 281–96, 311–512). On aid by Arab oil-producing states see below, chap. 11, n. 13.

12. Cf. on these drives A. Farran, "The Changing Economic Order and International Law," *Australian Outlook* 34 (1980), esp. 182–84; and S. Zamora, "Voting in International Economic Operations," *American Journal of International Law* 74 (1980): 566.

13. *International Law Association Report,* 1980, pars. 34–37.

14. Ibid., 298–99.

15. See "State Responsibility, Self-Help, and International Law," *Proceedings of the American Society of International Law*, 1979, 242.

11. INTERNATIONAL JUSTICE AND THE RESPONSIBILITY OF RULERS

1. On the pre-NIEO thinking generally see W. W. Rostow, "The Take-Off into Self-sustained Growth," *Economic Journal* 66 (1956): 25–48; G. M. Meier and R. E. Baldwin, *Economic Development* (New York: Wiley, 1957); A. O. Hirschman, *The Strategy of Economic Development* (New Haven, 1958); B. Higgins, *Economic Development* (London: Constable, 1959); B. F. Hoselitz, ed., *Theories of Economic Growth* (Glencoe, Ill.: Free Press, 1960); W. W. Rostow, *Stages of Economic Growth* (Cambridge: Cambridge University Press, 1960); A. Shonfeld, *The Attack on World Poverty* (London: Chatto and Windus, 1961); I. Adelman, *Theories of Economic Growth* (Stanford: Stanford University Press, 1961); H. W. Singer, "Trends in Economic Thought in Underdevelopment," *Social Research*, Winter 1961, 387–414; N. A. Khan, *Problems of Growth of an Undeveloped Economy: India* (Bombay: Asia Publishing House, 1961); J. Tinbergen, *Shaping the World Economy* (New York, 1962); E. E. Hagen, *On the Theory of Social Change* (Homewood, Ill., 1964); and Barbara Ward, "The U.N. and the Decade of Development." *World Justice* 7 (1965–66): 308–35. See above, chap. 8; this chapter, and below, chap. 12. On the U.N. Conference on Trade and Development (UNCTAD) see now the massive K. P. Sauvant, ed., *Collected Papers of the Group of 77*, 6 vols. (1981); and idem, *The Group of 77: Evolution, Structure, and Organisation* (New York: Oceana, 1981). On various commodity agreements see E. Ernst, *International Commodity Agreements* (The Hague, 1982). On the NIEO see below, n. 7.

2. Among which Mexican President Portillo at the Cancun meeting in October 1981 singled out the Soviet Union as "shirking its responsibility" for development aid. And see G. Myrdal, *Beyond the Welfare State* (London: Duckworth, 1960), 188–89.

3. Wastage in Western-Communist competition in allotting aid is aggravated by effects of the cold war on the distribution and use of aid. Thus recipient nations often have not been selected according to needs; and aid received has been excessively diverted to military purposes ancillary to cold-war tensions. See also, on the vast armaments expenditures by Arab oil-producing states, above, chap. 10, n. 1.

4. I have used the enclave metaphor as yielding historical insight rather than as an instrument of rigorous thought, and I agree with my colleague A. R. Blackshield's outline of its limitations if pressed beyond this (see "The Enclave of Justice: The Meaning of a Jurisprudential Metaphor," *Maine Law Review* 19 [1967]: 131–80, esp. 136–38). His discussion of the processes of "internalisation" of precepts of justice in relation to it is a promising line for further development.

5. See the critical comments as to the textile, footwear, and other industries which follow this quotation in Australian Senate Standing Committee on Foreign Affairs and Defence, *The New International Economic Order: Implications for Australia* (Canberra, 1980), 28–29; on the phasing out of protectionism see ibid., 5–6, 15–16. Cf. Minister of Foreign Affairs Peacock's observations in the House of Representatives, 18 September 1980, reprinted in *Australian Foreign Affairs Record*, September 1980, 338, 341.

6. *The Australian*, 21–22 November 1981.

7. On comparative developed-country and developing-country growth rates see the analysis and tables in Australian Senate Standing Committee, *The New International Economic Order*, 23–25, noting the wide variations between developing countries inter se. Per capita income varied even more widely—from U.S. $110 in Bangladesh, to U.S. $610 in the Ivory Coast, to U.S. $3,700 in Singapore and U.S. $15,500 in Kuwait (ibid., 24). Except in resource-rich countries like Kuwait, it is well pointed out, high growth is correlated (as in Singapore and Taiwan) with dynamic trade, not aid.

8. Other official proposals related more or less closely to NIEO include General

Assembly Resolutions, which respectively requested both the U.N. Institute for Training and Research (UNITAR) and the U.N. Committee on International Trade Law (UNCITRAL) to report on international economic law, especially the legal implications of NIEO. An agendum of the UNCITRAL Working Group drawn up in New York in January 1980 concerned legal aspects of (*a*) commodity agreements; (*b*) foreign investments; (*c*) bilateral industrial cooperation; (*d*) common clauses in various international contracts; (*e*) transnational corporations; and (*f*) concessions and other national resource agreements. They also include projects for codes of conduct on transnational corporations and on transfer of technology, for rules on international restrictive business practices, and for amendment of GATT (see the list of means of implementing a code for transnational corporations in ECOSOC, Doc. E/C 10/AC 219, 22 December 1978). Obviously such legal tasks must reqire coordination not only with those of international bodies such as GATT and UNCTAD already mentioned but also with many others, such as those on industrial property (WIPO), maritime law (IMCO), aviation (ICAO), labor (ILO), transnational corporations (Commission on Transnational Corporations), and of course the International Law Commission.

On the NIEO see B. Rivero, *New Economic Order and International Development* (Oxford and New York: Pergamon, 1980); R. C. Amacher, "The New International Economic Order," *Journal of Social and Political Studies* 5 (1980) 107–18; A. Farran, "The Changing Economic Order and International Law," *Australian Outlook* 34 (1980). 179–87; R. J. Wickes, "The New International Economic Order: Progress and Prospects," *Australian Outlook* 34 (1980): 41–63; Australian Senate Standing Committee, *The New International Economic Order;* K. Hossain, ed., *Legal Aspects of the N.I.E.O.* (London: Pinter; New York: Nichols Publications, 1980). In relation to energy see D. P. Hann, "Perspective on the World Economy: The Energy Situation and the NIEO," *Economic Forum* 11 (1980–81): 101–8, and J. R. Hanson and O. R. Morgan, "Encouraging Future Opecs," *Policy Review,* 1980, 123–32; in relation to arms expenditure see P. Lock, "The NIEO and Armaments," *Economics* 22 (1980): 56–85; in relation to the Soviet Union and the Eastern bloc see E. Laszlo and J. Kurtzman, eds., *Eastern Europe and the NIEO: Representative Samples of Socialist Perspectives* (New York: Pergamon Press, 1980), and T. T. Gati, "The Soviet Union and the North-South Dialogue," *Orbit* 24 (1980): 241–70; in relation to wealth transfer see B. Steinbach, "Automatic Transfer Payments to the Developing Countries . . . ," *Intereconomics* 15 (1980): 34–38; in relation to income distribution see W. R. Clyne, "International Economic Reform and Income Distribution," *CEPA Review,* April 1980, 103–12; and in relation to technology transfer see W. Tikentscher, *The Draft International Code on Transfer of Technology* (Munich: Max Planck Institute, 1980). For an admirable classified bibliography to 1980 see T. Nawaz, *The New International Economic Order* (London: Pinter, 1980). And in relation to U.S. foreign policy see R. K. Olson, *U.S. Foreign Policy and the NIEO: Negotiating Global Problems, 1974–1981* (Boulder, Colo.: Westview Press, 1981), with bibliography.

9. See Wickes, "The New International Economic Order," 41–63 (with well-selected documentation); Australian Senate Standing Committee, *The New International Economic Order,* esp. 11–49; and other literature cited above in n. 8.

10. Countries that are in some respects developed may share this concern with developing countries. Thus 85 percent of Australian export income is derived from agriculture and minerals (see the valuable discussion of the Integrated Programme for Commodities [IPC], proposed at UNCTAD IV in Nairobi in 1976, and the Common Fund in Australian Senate Standing Committee, *The New International Economic Order,* 29–34). Australian support for the Common Fund is also based, however, on wider, long-term grounds (see ibid., 5–6, 51. And see ibid., 17–19, for the history of the common fund idea before NIEO, and, generally, 11–15 for a brief account of the movement after World War II, through GATT and UNCTAD phases, into the NIEO period). As to the unclarity of the basic distinction between the "developed" and "developing" countries, see the Australian Treasury evidence in connection with Australian Senate Standing Committee, *The New International Economic*

Order, in the transcript of evidence to the Standing Committee, *Official Hansard Report* (1980), 858.

11. For a brief account of other measures favoring the least developed countries see Australian Senate Standing Committee, *The New International Economic Order*, 38–39.

12. The Australian development aid in 1978 was 0.32 percent and had not increased in real terms since 1967, though at the 1977 Commonwealth Heads of Government Conference, Australia reaffirmed its commitment to the 0.7 percent target. The increase in 1981 was from 0.43 percent to 0.45 percent (see Australian Senate Standing Committee, *The New International Economic Order*, 36–37, where other aspects, including the "untying" of grant aid, are canvassed). The so-called Harries Report is the official Australian government paper *Australia and the Third World* (Canberra, 1979).

13. On other matters the main issues between developing (often also the coastal) states and developed states have been adequately compromised. The developed states, mainly concerned with freedom of movement on the high seas and with exploiting the seabed, have won a two-hundred-mile navigation zone and a wide zone for exploitation. Developing states have successfully claimed a two-hundred-mile exclusive economic and fishing zone.

14. OPEC countries were substantial contributors to the International Fund for Agricultural Development in 1975, but they have not increased this commitment by much since that time. In 1979, a higher percentage of aid came from Saudi Arabia, Iraq, and Kuwait than from the developed states, but for the most part, this aid was channeled to selected fellow Islamic countries. It was not accompanied by substantial investment even in these developing countries (see the note "Global Negotiations: The General Background," in *Australian Foreign Affairs Record*, September 1980, 334, 337).

15. See the controversial thesis of P. T. Bauer, *Equality, The Third World and Economic Delusion* (Cambridge, Mass.: Harvard University Press; London: Weidenfeld & Nicholson, 1981). Up to the present, these doubts have not spread to Australia. See Australian Senate Standing Committee, *The New International Economic Order*, 7, on grants for development assistance; and cf. ibid., 38–39, on special consideration for needs of the least developed countries.

16. Insofar as it is true that it is the lower-income, lower-growth countries that usually have the fastest population growth, there is of course a rather blatant vicious circle in this criticism.

17. The fourteen Third World nations were Algeria, Bangladesh, Brazil, China, Guyana, India, Ivory Coast, Mexico, Nigeria, Philippines, Saudi Arabia, Tanzania, Venezuela, and Yugoslavia. The industrialized nations included Britain, Canada, France, Japan, Sweden, and West Germany.

18. Peter Day reported quizzically even from the smaller Cancun meeting (*The Australian*, 24–25 October 1981) that the statistic of 8 billion hungry people in the present world was left uncorrected despite the fact that total world population would not (on the assumed projections) reach 5.6 billion until the year 2000.

12. WORLD ORDER, ECONOMIC JUSTICE, AND INTERNATIONAL LAW

1. R. A. Falk and S. S. Kim, *World Order Studies and the World System* (New York, 1982), 17 ff.

2. R. A. Falk, *Normative Initiatives and Demilitarisation: A Third System Approach* (New York: World Law Fund, 1982), hereinafter cited as *Demilitarisation*.

3. See R. A. Falk, *A Study of Future Worlds* (New York: Free Press, 1975).

4. SALT II, not ratified by the United States, has nevertheless been thought to set limits that both sides de facto generally respect. On 28 March 1984, the Secretary of State told a Senate Committee that the Soviet Union might "break out" of Salt II after its nominal date of

expiration in 1985, and that the United States might also not observe it. The launch of the new Trident submarine in late 1984 would push the number of U.S. sea- and land-based missiles with multiple warheads to 24 in excess of the SALT II limit.

5. The highlighting and correction of the post-Cuban missile crisis underestimates are widely credited to John T. Hughes, special assistant to the director of the Defense Intelligence Agency (DIA) from 1962–71 and deputy director since 1971. Interpreting U-2 photography and the like, Hughes claimed that the Soviet build-up of heavy weapons, MIRVs, and new weapons was unabated during the whole period of detente, though he did not actually assert Soviet superiority nor did he assert any particular Soviet motivations. Cf. F. Kaplan, *The Wizards of Armageddon* (New York: Simon & Schuster, 1983).

6. *The Australian,* 1–2 January 1983.

7. For a late non-official account see Milton Hoenig, *Nuclear Weapons Databook* (Natural Resources Defense Council, 1983). The "overkill" capacities are apparent, even allowing for mutual neutralizing efforts of the adversaries and the role of weapons redundancy in meeting surprise breakthroughs.

8. On 7 February 1984, according to Japanese Foreign Minister Abe, the Soviet Union had deployed no fewer than 144 SS-20 missiles against various Asian states.

9. These hazards are additional to those arising from other novelties, for example, from the impossibility of surveillance of weapons like the "sea-launched Cruise missile," which is said to be 6 meters long, launchable from a truck, undetectable in preparation, and versatile and accurate in operation.

10. V. D. Sololovsky, *Soviet Military Strategy* (Englewood Cliffs, N.J.: Prentice-Hall, 1963). A thesis similar to that of Sololovsky appears in M. P. Skirdo, *The People, the Army, the Commander,* trans. D.G.I.S. Multilingual Section, Ottawa (Ottawa: Dept. of the Air Force, 1978).

11. Former National Security Adviser Brzezinski has proposed (in a closed lecture at the National Defense University and in a television interview on 22 January 1984 with David Brinkley) control limits that translate the terms of SALT II and later proposals of Moscow and Washington into an agreed ceiling of warheads a modest 12 percent below present levels. Other exchanges concern Soviet and U.S. allegations of breaches of the ABM treaty of 1972 and of SALT II following the November 1983 initial deployment of Pershing II and Cruise missiles. They continued through the meeting of Foreign Minister Gromyko and Secretary of State Schultz at the Stockholm Security Conference on 17 January 1984, which both characterized in terms of frost.

12. Nevertheless, long-term plans for anti-satellite research (ASAT) (*N.Y.T.,* 20 January 1984), and a head of the project were announced in March 1984. An account of early activity for construction of a new beam-line at Stanford's Synchroton Radiation Laboratory, under guidance of a consortium of institutions, including the Lawrence Livermore National Laboratory, has been given by the president of Stanford University, Donald Kennedy (*San Francisco Chronicle, This World,* Sunday, 25 March 1984). Defense Secretary Weinberger assured the NATO Ministeral Meeting at Izmir, Turkey that ASAT (which he called a "Strategic Defense Initiative" [S.D.I.]) was for European as well as U.S. defense and would not replace nuclear and conventional forces (April 1984). Reactions included concern for the weapon's effect on arms control, and for the arms race between offensive and defensive weapons. The American move was also supported as a response to alleged Soviet work contrary to the Anti-Ballistic Missile Treaty of 1972. A heat-seeking prototype miniature air-launched system (PMALS) of about one-ton weight has already been reported to have been successfully launched into space from an F-15 fighter. The event was greeted with dismay by the Washington-based Arms Control Association headed by Ambassador Gerard Smith and Paul Warnke. On 5 May 1984, Mr. Weinberger declared the U.S. intention to share with the Soviet Union research knowledge on defensive space weapons.

13. "The Military Role of Nuclear Weapons: Perception and Misperception," *Foreign*

Affairs 62, no. 1 (1983): 59–80, esp. 75. Cf. an earlier cogent proposal in R. C. Tucker, "No First Use of Nuclear Weapons: A Proposal," in *Strategy of World Order*, ed. R. A. Falk and S. Mendlovitz, vol. 4, *Disarmament and Economic Development* (New York: World Law Fund, 1966).

14. See on this aspect Henry Kissinger, "A Plan to Reshape NATO," *Time*, 5 March 1984, pp. 20–24; Ronald Steel, "Poor Little Europe," *Ambassador Magazine*, February 1984, pp. 44–47; and the March 1984 Report of the British Atlantic Committee headed by Royal Air Force Marshall Lord Cameron, entitled "Diminishing the Nuclear Threat: NATO's Defense and New Technology" (*N.Y.T.*, 11 March 1984).

15. The declaration of Defense Secretary Weinberger (on 5 May 1984) of the U.S. administration's intention to share with the Soviet Union its research knowledge on defensive space weapons could surely be part of the agendum of such standing joint commissions. After the rather impotent pessimism of Jonathan's Schell's *The Fate of the Earth* (1982), we need perhaps to seize some of the mood and resolve of themes of Freeman Dyson's *Weapons and Hope* (Harper & Row, 1984). One is that defensive weapons do have advantages, including moral superiority; another is that the live and let live principle, while offering no utopia, does offer negotiability, and at least the possibility of reducing the risk of holocaust. See Dyson, work cited, especially 65–97, 181–214, 239–90.

16. See S. Ogden, "Sovereignty and International Law: The Perspective of the P.R.C.," as cited above, in chap. 7, n. 4.

17. As observed in chap. 7, n. 8, I disagree profoundly with the view of M. S. McDougal, H. D. Lasswell, and W. M. Reisman, "Theories about International Law: Prologue to a Configurative Jurisprudence," *Virginia Journal of International Law* 8 (1967–68), 294, to the effect that it "serves no clarifying purpose to assume that the world will suffer either annihilation or coerced subordination to the totalitarian system of public order imposed by one huge imperial power."

18. There are reports of weakened anti-nuclear activity in the West since Soviet suspension of arms control talks, not only among the West German "Greens" but also among the protestors at Greenham Common and the 86,000 dues-paying members of the Nuclear Disarmament Movement in the United Kingdom (James M. Markham, *N.Y.T.*, 11 March 1984). The causes seem various including, perhaps, the exodus of East Germans to West Germany permitted by the East German government of 7,000 per month in February and March 1984—greater than in any prior whole year; and, certainly, friction among "Greens" as to the role played by communist members.

19. The *Wall Street Journal* reported on 12 January 1984 that West European parties to Soviet pipeline contracts were already bound to buy a minimum of 80 percent of stipulated volume at a contract price of $34 a barrel (as against the present market price of $29).

20. Australian Senate Standing Committee on Foreign Affairs and Defence, *The NIEO: Implications for Australia*, (Canberra, 1980), 5.

21. Cf. R. J. Wickes, "The New International Economic Order: Progress and Prospects," *Australian Outlook* 34 (1980):53–54.

22. As of 29 March 1984 loans of thirteen leading American private banks to Argentina, Brazil, Chile, Mexico, Venezuela, and the Philippines alone were estimated to amount to almost $60 billion. In most of the countries concerned, the total external debt was four or five times greater than export earnings; and annual debt repayments equalled or exceeded more than half the export earnings. It required extraordinary measures, including loans from other Latin American debtor nations (bridged by United States agencies) to ensure that the Argentinian government of Mr. Alfonsin did not default on interest and service payments due on 31 March 1984 (*Washington Post*, 28 March 1984).

Speculation was rife (and pertinent) before the agreement emerged on these measures as to the likely effects of a chain reaction from an Argentinian default on the then-total world debt of $600 billion, not to speak of its effect on the Eurodollar market estimated at $1.5

trillion (*N.Y.T.*, 13 February 1984). The need for multi-year, as distinct from year-to-year, adjustments was already being canvassed (see, e.g., *Wall Street Journal*, 12 March 1984, pp. 1, 25).

23. The continuance of this alignment is, of course, a major assumption of the Brandt Report. Yet, as of 1984, no fewer than twenty of the fastest growing nations have been of the Third World. Rapid technological movements throughout the industrial world from "chimney-stack" to "high-tech" industries suggest likely expansion of these trends.

24. For sober assessments of some of the strengths and weaknesses of NIEO claimants and related statistics see ibid., 52–63; and Farran, "The Changing Economic Order and International Law," ibid., 179–87, esp. 185. It is perhaps a ground for faith in long-term accommodation that questions of compensation for expropriation of property of foreign nationals have faded in political and economic importance since World War II. U.N. General Assembly resolution 1803 (XVII), of 14 December 1962, on Permanent Sovereignty over Natural Resources maintained (though in somewhat hazy terms) the duty of "appropriate compensation," *inter alia,* "in accordance with international law." This remains incorporated in the declaration contained in Resolution 3201 (S–VI), of 1 May 1974, though that declaration also refers without mention of compensation under international law to a "right of nationalisation and transfer of ownership to nationals" (see texts in *International Legal Materials* 14 [1975]: 251 ff.). Curiously, also, the Charter of Economic Rights and Duties of States, Resolution 3281 (XXIX), of 12 December 1974, still requires "appropriate compensation," though this is to be settled by the expropriating state's domestic law and tribunals unless freely agreed between the states concerned. In this continuing uncertainty, it is clear that neither side stands adamantly on its positions—the developed states because of the more momentous issues raised by NIEO demands, the less developed states because, after all, NIEO demands still have to be negotiated, and confiscatory expropriation is not a way of attracting needed investments. See R. B. Lillich, ed., *Economic Coercions and the NIEO* (Charlottesville, 1976); idem, ed., *International Law of Responsibility for Injury to Aliens* (Charlottesville: University Press of Virginia, 1983); and generally on natural resources I. Brownlie, "Legal Status of Natural Resources in International Law," *Hague Recueil* 162 (1979): 255.

25. Cf. recent assessments of bargaining factors in Australian Senate Standing Committee, *The New International Economic Order*, 51–53; Wickes, "The New International Economic Order," 52–63; and A. Farran, "Resources, Political Pressures, and the International Legal Order," *Australian Outlook* 35 (1981): 119–25.

26. Cf. D.H.N. Johnson, evidence before the Australian Senate Standing Committee on Foreign Affairs and Defence (Australian Senate Standing Committee, *The New International Economic Order*, 20). And see the balanced and stimulating discussion in Farran, "The Changing Economic Order and International Law," 179–87. As to the possible transformation of NIEO demands into customary international law, Farran seems oversanguine. He rather neglects the effect of the adverseness of the groupings of states involved as an obstacle to finding the necessary acquiescence "by sufficient numbers [of states], with sufficient frequency," to satisfy the constitutive requirements of customary law.

27. Even though these two goals may not proceed in harness, as R. J. Wickes suggests ("The New International Economic Order," 62–63).

28. See the illustrative tables drawn from various sources in ibid., 59–60.

29. Ibid., 60–61.

30. See E. Brunner, *Justice and the Social Order*, trans. M. Hottinger (New York and London: Harper and Brothers, 1956), 219, 228.

31. On the less favorable position for non-oil-producing developing countries in 1980 than in 1973 and related problems see the valuable note "Global Negotiations: The General Background," *Australian Foreign Affairs Record*, September 1980, 335–38, esp. on the OPEC countries' unwillingness to invest in other developing countries. See also above, chap. 11, n.

14. Of course, there may be grave domestic restraints on international cooperation, even where there is no responsible government in the Western sense. The weekly *Peking Review* has recently estimated that only 300 million of China's 800 million peasants are actively involved in production under the ideologically and constitutionally enjoined commune system. The surplus peasant population will have to be restrained for other functions as modernization and privatization proceeds (*Agence France Press,* 23 October 1981).

32. Jill Smolowe and M. E. Lerner, "The Welfare State in Crisis," *Newsweek,* 25 July 1983; Jacob Young et al., "Japan's Welfare Woes," ibid.

33. Related problems have been raised concerning the maneuvering space of the Soviet government (Peter Samuel, "Can the Soviet Arms Build-up Last?" *The Australian,* 11–12 September 1983).

34. On the quite long process already in train see the historical study of the Charter of Economic Rights and Duties of States in R. F. Meagher, *The Quest for International Power and Welfare . . .* (1977).

35. Among late figures are those of the U.S. Congressional Budget Office (*N.Y.T.,* 27 March 1984) as follows: (1) the existing Reagan "build-down" proposal would save about $30 billion by the year 2000; (2) canceling further MX ICBMS could save $14 billion in five years, and merely not increasing MX production from twenty-one to forty missiles would save $4.4 billion; (3) the "build-down" would reduce the number of U.S. strategic warheads by thirty percent, to a total of 1995, and would reduce by fifty-five percent the Soviet Union's missile payload (including a thirty-four percent reduction in her payload of ICBMS in silos).

The same report estimated a total of $1,700 billion in military expenditure over the next five years, of which (apart from "build-down") $290 billion would be for strategic forces, involving a rise of the number of U.S. warheads *of all kinds* from the present 14,300 to 17,500.

Yet, at this same time, the representatives of thirty-five western and communist bloc states, under auspices of the Conference on Security and Cooperation in Europe, were concluding at Athens that no method of peaceful dispute settlement could be found (*N.Y.T.,* 30 April 1984).

Index

JULIUS STONE is Distinguished Professor at the University of California Hastings College of the Law and a professor at the University of New South Wales. He received the award of the American Society of International Law for his major work, *Legal Controls of International Conflict.* He is the author of thirty-two books, among which are *Human Law and Human Justice, Of Law and Nations, Conflict through Consensus,* and *Israel and Palestine* (the last two also published by Johns Hopkins).

The Johns Hopkins University Press

VISIONS OF WORLD ORDER

This book was composed in Baskerville type by Brushwood Graphics Studio from a design by Susan P. Fillion. It was printed on 50-lb. Booktext paper and bound in Holliston Sturde-tan by BookCrafters.